Families in Later Life

Connections and Transitions

ALEXIS J. WALKER

MARGARET MANOOGIAN-O'DELL

LORI A. MCGRAW

DIANA L. G. WHITE

PINE FORGE PRESS

Thousand Oaks, California

London   New Delhi

For information, address:

Pine Forge Press
A Sage Publications Company
2455 Teller Road
Thousand Oaks, California 91320
E-mail: sales@pfp.sagepub.com

Sage Publications Ltd.
6 Bonhill Street
London EC2A 4PU
United Kingdom

Sage Publications India Pvt. Ltd.
M-32 Market
Greater Kailash I
New Delhi 110 048 India

Publisher: Stephen D. Rutter
Assistant to the Publisher: Ann Makarias
Production Editor: Diana E. Axelsen
Editorial Assistant: Cindy Bear
Copy Editor: Alison Binder
Typesetter: Lynn Miyata
Indexer: Rachel Rice
Cover Designer: Michelle Lee

Printed in the United States of America

01 02 03 04 05 06 07 7 6 5 4 3 2 1

Library of Congress Cataloging-in-Publication Data

Main entry under title:
   Families in later life: Connections and transitions /
by Alexis J. Walker . . . [et al.].
       p.   cm.—
   Includes bibliographical references and index.
   ISBN 0-7619-8702-9 (pbk.: alk. paper)
   1. Aged—United States—Family relationships.   2. Aged—United
States—Social conditions.   I. Walker, Alexis Joan, 1952–
HQ1064.U5 F288   2000
305.26'0973—dc21   00-009551

About the Authors

Alexis J. Walker holds the Jo Anne Leonard Petersen Chair in Gerontology and Family Studies and is Professor of Human Development and Family Sciences at Oregon State University, where she directs the undergraduate certificate program in gerontology. Her research on mother-daughter relationships and family caregiving has been funded by the National Institute on Aging.

Margaret Manoogian-O'Dell is a doctoral student focusing her academic work on family gerontology and women's studies. She has spent the last 15 years working directly with undergraduate and graduate students in cocurricular and advising functions and has taught family studies and adult development and aging courses to undergraduates. Her current research concerns older women and intergenerational relationships.

Lori A. McGraw is a doctoral candidate in human development and family studies at Oregon State University, where she teaches undergraduate courses that focus on individual and family development and the connections among social hierarchies. Her research highlights women's unpaid family labor and their family ties.

Diana L. G. White is a human development and family studies doctoral student at Oregon State University. Her research interests involve bereavement and intergenerational responses to family crises. She is Deputy Director of the Oregon Geriatric Education Center at Oregon Health Sciences University, a program that provides professional development opportunities for health care professionals throughout Oregon.

About the Publisher

Pine Forge Press is a new educational publisher, dedicated to publishing innovative books and software throughout the social sciences. On this and any other of our publications, we welcome your comments, ideas, and suggestions.

Please call or write to:
Pine Forge Press
A Sage Publications Company
31 St. James Ave., Suite 510
Boston, MA 02116
617-753-7512
E-mail: info@pfp.sagepub.com

Visit our World Wide Web site, your direct link to a multitude of online resources:

www.pineforge.com

Contents

PART II

Connections Across the Generations in Midlife
**Caregiving, grandparenthood, and work are
intergenerational themes in middle age.**

PART V

Challenges and Possibilities in Later Life
**Amid a web of multigenerational family connections,
oldest old adults focus their energies and attentions
on their most significant social ties.**

Preface

Several years ago, a publisher suggested to Alexis that a reader for undergraduate students on families in middle and later life would be an important addition to the field. She agreed completely. Too often, gerontological research focuses on individuals without attention to their close connections to others, especially family members. When family issues emerge in the literature, researchers generally focus on dependent older people or on spouses as overburdened caregivers. The depth and richness of their relationships and other aspects of family life are often neglected. Thus, the idea of developing a reader was intriguing—and there was certainly a need for one—but it simmered on a back burner as other tasks took priority.

In the meantime, Alexis invited Diana, Lori, and Margaret, who share her interest in exploring intergenerational relationships, to join her in studying these ties. Avid readers all, we formed a weekly study group, reading and discussing both academic writing and fiction devoted to intergenerational relationships in middle and later life. We read many pieces and learned a great deal. We also shared family stories and the importance of our own connections to older family members. Through discussions of the readings and our experiences, we concluded that much about older adult family life is not in the academic literature. This was particularly true for issues facing older women and people of color.

We decided to put our new knowledge to work by taking on the development of this reader. Conceptualized as a companion to more traditional textbooks, the reader is aimed at helping students understand that older people are developing human beings with close connections to others. Furthermore, the reader illustrates how older adults and their family members experience transitions: not always in predictable ways or at predictable times.

We knew that there was no resource like the reader we envisioned. We also knew that such a resource would be increasingly important as the U.S. population ages and becomes more diverse. Most of all, we wanted to share some of the compelling work we had discovered and the energy and excitement we feel in exploring the family connections and transitions of older adults.

We began by developing a framework for selecting readings and identifying types of connections and transitions that are key to understanding family life. We included both same-generation connections, such as partners and siblings, and cross-generation connections, such as the relationships between parents and adult children and between grandparents and grandchildren. We sought readings that reflected families as sources of both support and strain. We wanted to give attention to transitions and roles such as adult children's leaving home, grandparenthood, retirement, bereavement, caregiving, and the formation of new partnerships.

Our reader includes middle- and later-life families who vary in their racial and ethnic identities, class backgrounds, and sexual orientations. We pay particular attention to how gender shapes family ties. Although we show how family life varies for people in different social positions, we also illustrate similarities in experience. We looked for readings that reflect the life course idea of on-time and off-time family experiences, as well as events that happen to most people and those that are more rare. To provide compelling illustrations of central concepts, we selected a mix of academic writing, fiction, essays, and poetry.

Having developed our framework, we read widely during the next year, and we each brought our favorite readings to the group. In some of our targeted areas, we were disappointed to find little material. In others, we discovered many fine pieces. Because we all loved work that could not be included, the process of making final selections was a painful one. Our framework helped us by highlighting important family issues and experiences and the social context in which they occur. As we agonizingly discarded one piece or another, we consoled ourselves by saying, "We'll address that issue in the framing essay."

We edited the academic articles and many of the essays to meet page limits, always attempting to maintain the integrity of the authors' work. In the end, we are pleased with the breadth and quality of materials included, although we have enough work for another volume!

One of the many challenges we faced was how to organize the readings. We had before us a variety of options: by type of transition, for example, or by type of relationship or connection. Every attempt was messy, however. The lives of individuals and their families occur neither in neat categories nor according to specific timelines. Life experiences are not always efficiently confined to one period of the life span. For example, new love can occur in late life, bereavement can occur at any time within any type of relationship, and grandparenthood extends for decades. In the end, we arranged our volume by age of the person given a central voice in the work. We began with readings focused on parents with young adult children, followed by those focused on early midlife, and continuing on through old age. This developmental structure parallels individual life yet it allows us to demonstrate that change through time and variability with age are key.

Finally, it was time for the framing essays. Although the writing process can be challenging, we were surprised to discover that despite extensive notes and discussion, the hard part in editing this book was not nearly over. Our framing essays had to convey our main concern that people change and grow through time and in a variety of ways.

Throughout all its phases, however, this project has been enormously satisfying. During a two-year period, we have enjoyed great literature, provocative research, engaging conversation, terrific food, and good humor. We came to know each other well as we shared stories of our own family transitions and connections. Although other projects such as articles and dissertations were put on hold for a while, we are grateful for the opportunity to have worked together on this book. We hope that readers share our pleasure and joy in reading and learning about the social lives of older adults.

From beginning to end, our work was collaborative. Alexis was the team leader and took major responsibility for editing. Lori, Diana, and Margaret contributed equally and chose to be listed alphabetically. We are grateful to Sandra Frye, who helped in the preparation of the final manuscript. We also acknowledge our own intergenerational family connections and those who have inspired us through the years: our parents, Emily and Bob Guion, Janice and Jeffrey McGraw, Rita and Haig Manoogian, and Lois and Bernard Walker; and our grandparents, Carrie and Roy Guion, Cleora and O. S. Firestone, Mafra Lykins Marini and Finley Lykins, Lorraine and Eugene McGraw, Maria and Ludwig Helmprecht, Satenig and Garabed Manoogian, Lillian and Alex Guadagno, and Lilly and Wilfred Walker.

Introduction:
Understanding the Family Lives
of Older Adults

Family gerontologists focus on understanding the social ties of older adults, particularly their family relationships. In contrast to the common belief that older people are isolated from family members and friends, family gerontologists have shown that older persons have rich and varied social lives. Maturity in adulthood is often described as determined by one's capacity for love and for work. Middle- and later-life adults exhibit tremendous capacity for both. Family gerontologists have illustrated how work—both paid and unpaid—remains pivotal for shaping aging adults' identities and ties with others. Older persons' participation in social relations and their engagement in productive work create a context that enhances their visions of themselves and their world. In this reader, we explore ways in which older persons construct a sense of identity, build positive family relationships, and pursue purposeful work—just as younger people do.

Any discussion about families in later life must include an explanation of what we mean by *family*. As we explore the everyday family lives of aging people, we demonstrate that narrow definitions of family do not capture the diverse ways that people relate as family members. Traditionally, families have been conceived of as persons related by blood or marriage living in the same household. As you will see in Part I, our definition is more broadly conceptualized. We highlight the interdependence of older people. By *interdependence*, we mean the way their thoughts, feelings, and behaviors are intricately connected with those of others. We accept as family those persons who are bound by ties of marriage, blood, or commitment, legal or otherwise, who consider themselves a family.

Although we pay particular attention to family relationships, we do so with sensitivity to the broader contexts within which older people live. Family gerontology is an interdisciplinary field that encompasses anthropology, demography, family studies, history, psychology, sociology, and other areas. Each of these disciplines provides an important lens through which to view the broader context of aging people and their family ties. For example, an older woman's retirement experience is shaped not only by her individual talents (an emphasis in psychology) but also by the quality of her marital relationship (family studies), her participation in unpaid family work (sociology), job market constraints and opportunities (history and economics), and cultural beliefs about the proper work for women (anthropology). The content of our reader reflects this interdisciplinary nature of family gerontology. We integrate information from many perspectives, including the personal experiences of writers and poets, to provide a broad view of individuals and families in middle and later life.

Our worldview, as well, is interdisciplinary or eclectic. The life course perspective described by Vern Bengtson and Katherine Allen (1993) provides a framework that best conveys our theoretical approach or worldview. The life course perspective is a way "to examine the unfolding history of intimate connections in families and the social context of such long-term relationships in terms of social structure and historical location" (p. 469). The perspective also provides a way to understand changes or transitions that middle- and later-life families experience and the meanings that older people give to these transitions.

In our introduction, we explore issues from a life course perspective. For example, we discuss some of the demographic characteristics of today's aging population and how historical changes in technology and health sciences have altered the experiences of middle- and later-life families. We also discuss the importance of social processes that create different experiences for families, depending on their location in the social hierarchy. Finally, we discuss developmental change as it pertains to issues of identity, family ties, and work.

Who Are Today's Older Adults?

Today's older people constitute the largest group of aging adults ever to live in the United States. In 1997, persons 65 years or older numbered 34.1 million and represented 12.7% of the U.S. population (AARP, 1998). One reason for the size of this group is that today more than three fourths of all persons live until their 65th birthday. This unprecedented change in the average length of life is a recent phenomenon. In fact, two thirds of the total increase in human longevity took place during the 1900s (Skolnick, 1991). The older population will continue to grow significantly in the future as well. By 2030, there will be about 70 million older adults, representing 20% of the U.S. population (AARP, 1998).

As more people are living increasingly longer lives, family gerontologists have sought to discover how these changes influence middle- and later-life families. For example, elder care previously was not a major, long-term task for most families because fewer persons lived to be old (Coontz, 1992). Today, caregiving for dependent older people is a substantial challenge for many families. Family members provide 80% of the in-home care to older people with chronic illness even when formal services are used (U.S. Senate Special Committee on

Aging, 1992). Family gerontologists are interested in assisting caregiving families and informing health care providers and policymakers.

Older persons not only constitute a larger group than in the past but also are more diverse in race and ethnicity. In 1997, people of color represented 15.3% of older Americans (AARP, 1998). Today's aging population is varied and complex, and it will become increasingly so in the future. Ethnic and racial minorities are projected to represent 25% of older adults in 2030, an increase of nearly two thirds from 1997 (AARP, 1998). People of color are becoming more predominant in the United States and also are becoming more diverse. For example, the term *Hispanic* encompasses Americans of Mexican, Puerto Rican, Central and South American, and Cuban descent, among others. Similarly, Asian Americans officially are composed of at least 11 nations of origin including China, India, Japan, Korea, Vietnam, and the Philippines. The category of American Indian represents many tribes with distinctive languages, spiritual belief systems, and histories. As much variability exists, then, within any racial-ethnic group as between people of color and the dominant White culture.

Older persons have also become progressively wealthier compared with their counterparts in the early 1900s. Living standards in general have risen since World War II, and the rise has been sharpest for older adults (Cherlin & Furstenberg, 1986). This increase in the standard of living, however, is an average that masks tremendous variability in economic well-being. For example, people of color are disproportionately poor relative to Whites. About 3.4 million elderly persons were below the poverty level in 1997. Of this group, approximately 9% were White, 24% were Hispanics, and 26% were African American (AARP, 1998). These numbers are striking because Whites constitute a majority of the older population. They are the least likely group, however, to be poor.

How Has Family Life for Older People Changed During the 20th Century?

Today's older people have experienced many of the social and technological changes that took place in the 1900s. These changes brought about transformations in the terrain of family life. For example, technological advances in reproductive health gave women now in their 60s more control over the number and spacing of their children. Because of this greater control, many parents decided to have fewer children and to space them at closer intervals. This childbearing pattern has resulted in fewer years spent raising children than were spent even 50 years ago.

Technological advances in other areas of medical and public health served to increase longevity for most Americans. This longevity has changed experiences of family life as well. Around the turn of the 20th century, for example, most women lived an average of 10 to 15 years after their last child matured to adulthood. Today, women can expect to live an additional 40 years after their children gain independence. Older married couples often live more than a third of a century with no children in their household (Coontz, 1992). Instead of raising children, as was common in the past, middle- and later-life couples are tending to relationships with their adult children and, perhaps, cultivating new relationships with their grandchildren. Historically, people simply did not live long enough to become active grandparents. In 1900, only one in four grandchildren had four living grandparents at birth. Today, most adults live long enough to know most of their grandchildren (Cherlin & Furstenberg, 1986).

Because people are living longer, marriages that endure are lasting for increasingly longer periods. In 1900, one or both partners in a marriage were likely to have died before their children reached adulthood. Today, it is common for couples to remain married for 50 years (Riley, 1983). More diversity exists in the ways that couples arrange their relationships, too. Today, some older people choose to live together without a marriage certificate, something they rarely did in the past. Divorce rates are much higher today as well, so it is not unusual for older adults to have divorced and remarried sometime in their lives. Finally, because younger people are even more likely to divorce, older people today are interacting with new and complex stepfamily systems.

Although it is important to acknowledge the changes that have taken place during the lifetimes of today's older adults, it is equally important to recognize that much about aging and family life has remained the same. Americans continue to value marriages and families and consistently provide family members with emotional and practical support (Rossi & Rossi, 1990). Women remain primary caregivers for dependent family members, including those who are aging. Finally, women and men have always shared the pursuit of financial resources for their families, although the nature of this pursuit continues to vary, depending on circumstances such as race and social class. For example, working-class women have always combined the unpaid work of child care and housework with low-wage jobs to help support their families. In recent years, middle-class women have followed this same pattern, pursuing employment when their children are young in addition to after their children leave home.

Finally, the changes that occurred during the 20th century have not had a unified impact on today's older people. Within this group exists significant variation in life experiences from one cohort to the next. The term *cohort* is used by social scientists to describe a group of people born within a narrow band of years who share certain social and historical experiences. People in a particular cohort not only have lived through a specific historical event but have done so at the same time in their lives.

Glen Elder's (1974) research on the Great Depression provides an interesting account of how cohort membership and larger social forces influenced the lives of today's older adults. Elder found that those people who were teenagers when the Great Depression began showed fewer ill effects than those who were in early elementary school. The younger cohort spent a longer period under economic hardship, which altered the trajectory of their lives. For example, many of these children received few resources for education and vocational training—a disadvantage that limited their prosperity in later life. Those who were teenagers when the Great Depression hit, however, seemed to benefit from the experience. The teenage cohort played a large role in helping their families survive, and this early experience encouraged a belief in hard work. This belief, combined with legislation that financed the college educations of those who served in World War II, allowed many persons in the teenage cohort to increase their wealth later in life. Elder's study shows that different cohorts experience sociohistorical events in different ways and that these differences produce varied experiences in later years.

How Does the Social Context Shape Family Life?

Although older people and their families have many shared experiences by virtue of being alive at similar times in history, their experiences vary with their social position. Although we, as individuals, experience our lives as unique, shaped by the particular people and circumstances we meet during our lifetimes, we also are part of a larger social pattern that reflects social hierarchies. Hierarchies based on race, class, gender, age, sexual orientation, and ability create systems of disadvantage and of privilege. These systems are embedded in the fabric of our social lives and are not easily changed. For example, social class is not an identity held by an individual but a series of relations that pervade our entire society and shape our social institutions and relationships with others (Andersen & Collins, 1995). For substantive change to occur, all levels of social life must be affected, from individual experiences to economic structures—a daunting challenge indeed. In the United States, Whites are privileged relative to people of color, wealthy people are privileged relative to less wealthy people, and men are privileged relative to women.

At times, people are consciously aware of our system of inequity; sometimes they are not. Peggy McIntosh (1998) writes of her awakening recognition of White privilege after noticing that men acknowledged women's disadvantages but denied men's advantages. She writes, "As a white person, I realized I had been taught about racism as something that puts others at a disadvantage, but had been taught not to see one of its corollary aspects, White privilege, which puts me at an advantage"

(p. 76). She describes many ways that she receives unearned advantages over people of color, a few of which follow:

> I can, if I wish, arrange to be in the company of people of my race most of the time. Whether I use checks, credit cards, or cash, I can count on my skin color not to work against the appearance that I am financially reliable. I can easily find academic courses and institutions that give attention only to people of my race. (p. 79)

Those who are advantaged receive disproportionate access to resources, opportunities, and rewards. Experiences of privilege and disadvantage have a cumulative effect that results in diverse and unequal life circumstances in old age. For example, older people of color are disproportionately likely to experience poverty, have less access to health care, and receive poorer treatment for health problems—circumstances with which proportionately fewer older Whites contend.

The way that social hierarchies play out in the lives of all people, including those who are aging, is complicated because an individual can occupy a position of disadvantage and advantage simultaneously. For example, a White wealthy woman has lower social value relative to her wealthy husband but is privileged by virtue of her access to financial resources. Should she become divorced, however, her vulnerability becomes more apparent. In turn, the partners in an African American working-class couple share the experiences of living in a racist, classist society but differ in the value of their gender. For example, African American women, relative to African American men, receive lower pay and are more responsible for providing the unpaid labor of child care and housework.

These couples illustrate how one family can be set apart from another family on the basis of social position. The White wealthy couple has advantages over the African American working-class couple that result from and contribute to unfair life circumstances, particularly in old age. For example, older people of color have far less accumulated wealth than do Whites, including such resources as savings or property. It is important to recognize, however, that many White persons live in poverty as well. More White persons are in poverty than the combined numbers of African Americans, Asians, Native Indians, and Hispanics in poverty. In 1992, 19,012,000 persons of color, compared with 24,523,000 White persons, lived in poverty (Andersen & Collins, 1995). This class system interacts with racism, however, leading to greater rates of poverty for ethnic and racial minorities.

The couples described above also show that individuals *within* families can be positioned differently in the social hierarchy—a process that creates inequality. Gender, like race and class, is an experience that is influenced more from social practices than from biological differences between women and men. Relations between women and men are structured at every level of social life—individual, relational, familial, legal, and economic—to create complex systems of inequality that favor men (Ferree, 1991).

Barrie Thorne (1992) explains how inequality among family members creates a "tangle of love and domination" in families (p. 20). For example, older married couples can draw happiness from memories of their long lives together. These loving memories, however, may be mixed with a history of the husband's being advantaged by the lesser amount of unpaid labor he does, the greater level of leisure activities he pursues, and the greater frequency that decisions were made to privilege his paid work. Of course, this within-family inequality varies, depending on the racial and class position of each partner. Still, a general pattern of unfairness, favoring men, pervades U.S. heterosexual partnerships.

How Are Identity, Connections With Others, and Pursuit of Work Central in the Lives of Older People?

Three developmental themes are addressed throughout our reader: identity, relationships, and work. These three themes provide the foundation from which people build the entirety of their lives. Steven Marks (1986) describes marriage as a process in which partners attempt to combine their values concerning identity, relationships, and work to create a shared vision of what is important. For example, some couples choose to emphasize their relationship, while others place greater emphasis on their separate work lives. As long as the partners agree, the relationship remains satisfying. Here in this section, we provide a general introduction to the themes and how they pertain to middle- and later-life families.

Identity

For many, turning 40 is an important social marker signaling the beginning of middle age. Around this age, people may begin to realize that their time to live is limited relative to the time they had when they were younger (Neugarten, 1972). With this subtle change in perspective, many persons reassess their lives to determine their future course. Some think this process is problematic, and popular media seem to portray middle-aged people as in crisis. The overwhelming majority of persons do not experience a painful crisis, however, but adjust to midlife changes through a gradual, long-term process. Most midlife people operate from a position of psychological strength, and this pattern continues into old age.

A challenge of identity in middle age and later life is to continue to experience mastery and productivity through work that enhances one's own well-being and that of others. Individuals also must continue to address their needs for agency and for communion with others (Bakan, 1966; McAdams, Ruetzel, & Foley, 1986). In middle and later life, then, individuals must combine a strong sense of self with a sense of commitment to others. In other words, psychosocial growth continues throughout adulthood into old age. In this volume, we emphasize the developmental and social nature of identity in middle and later life, particularly as it is shaped by family relationships.

Social Relationships

Individuals travel through life in the company of others, in what Kahn and Antonucci (1980) call a "social convoy." With increasing life spans, these journeys are lasting longer. For example, parent-adult child relationships used to last for 20 or 30 years. Today, these relationships exist for 50 years or more. To extend the convoy metaphor further, families, compared with families in the early 1900s, are traveling together in increasingly diverse groupings via a variety of family forms. As noted earlier, divorce and remarriage patterns have resulted in more complex family structures. Also, the ability to choose whether to have children, when to have them, and how many to have has given couples enormous flexibility in the types of families they will or will not have. These family arrangements affect one's social environment in middle and later life. For example, couples are more likely now than in the past to remain childless or to have one or two children, reducing the number of adult children with whom they will relate.

Although more diversity exists in family arrangements, family solidarity—affection, assistance and support, and time spent together—remains strong (Bengtson, Rosenthal, & Burton, 1990; Rossi & Rossi, 1990). We focus on two broad types of family relationships: cross-generation (vertical) and same-generation (horizontal) ties. We examine parent-child and grandparent-grandchild ties through middle and later life. We also explore marriage, including divorce, remarriage, and widowhood. We address lifelong singlehood, cohabiting relationships, and long-term lesbian and gay relationships as well. Finally, we discuss the importance of sibling relationships during the course of adulthood.

Through our study of family relations in later life, we discredit the idea that the American family is in decline. Instead, we show that families continue to maintain strong ties while creating new family structures that are adaptive to present-day social changes. For example, when adult children divorce, they rely on parents for emotional and financial support. An understanding of intergenerational relations illustrates that although one family tie ends, another tie may be strengthened.

Work

As we stated earlier, we define work broadly to include all activities that are useful, both to ourselves and to others. A majority of persons in today's labor force are either underpaid or unpaid, a condition that has dire financial consequences for these workers in later life. Being a woman or a person of color makes it much more likely that work will be unpaid or underpaid.

Older people, as well, are likely to be participants in the unpaid labor force. For example, people aged 65 and older are just as likely as younger people are to participate in volunteer organizations, provide informal help to family and friends, and maintain and clean their homes (Herzog, Kahn, Morgan, Jackson, & Antonucci, 1989). We highlight the ways that our economic structure, with its demarcation between valued, paid work and less valued, unpaid work, creates a system of over-privilege for some and underprivilege for others.

We are also concerned with the connection between work and family life and explore how experiences in one domain influence experiences in the other. For example, studies have shown that stressful experiences at work can result in more negative family interactions later in the day. In later life, retirement provides the context for important work-family negotiations. As you will see in Part IV, however, most couples navigate the retirement transition with little change in their marital relationship.

Conclusion

The life course perspective highlights how older people and their families change or develop through time. We conceptualize development as a lifelong process of change in how individuals relate to themselves and others and how they pursue purposeful activity. We focus not only on change but also on stability. These periods of change and stability are roughly associated with age, although we do not argue for a universal trajectory of age-related stages and transitions. Instead, we acknowledge that within a particular sociohistorical context, most adults encounter similar age-related challenges. We have organized our chapters according to broad age categories common in family gerontology. The first three sections address midlife (roughly from 35 to 65 years of age). The last two sections address old age, from young-old through oldest old (roughly from age 55 through the end of life). We also recognize differences in the timing of these experiences. For example, first-time grandparenthood can occur early in middle age or in old age, although the median age for becoming a grandparent is in the mid to late 40s.

Within these age categories, we focus on important developmental transitions, such as a teenager's leaving home or the end of a close relationship because of a death. Transitions are important periods of change for individuals and their families that can result in both positive and negative outcomes. These outcomes depend on the skills and resources available to those experiencing the transitions and the circumstances surrounding them. Researchers have shown, for example, that unexpected transitions are more difficult to negotiate than ones that are planned. Imagine how the experience of retirement would be different for someone retiring according to a self-determined, 10-year plan compared with someone who is forced to retire by an employer. Both of these transitions, however, require skill and resources to navigate through them successfully.

The life course perspective also draws attention to how social hierarchies create different experiences both *within* families and *between* families. Our emphasis is on how social constructs or classifications shape individual development and family life. We explore how older persons' lives and relationships are influenced by inequities that generate different views and experiences of social reality. We provide an opportunity for you to listen to diverse voices as older adults talk about their family experiences. Older people may be constrained by social circumstances, but they also have agency or are purposeful in creating meaningful lives despite the challenges they encounter. Examples of both agency and constraint in the lives of older people are provided throughout our reader.

In Part I, we explore how middle-aged parents negotiate ties with their children as these children move into adulthood. We also lay the foundation for understanding relationships between parents and their adult children through the life course. In Part II, we continue our discussion of parent-child relationships, including the process of coping with the death of a child. We also discuss grandparenting and issues surrounding caregiving. In Part III, we focus on the intimate relationships of middle-aged and older adults and the importance of sibling relationships through the life course. We also cover the diversity of kin ties, including grandparenthood, and the importance of kinkeeping. Finally, we talk about how the death of a parent affects one's life and marital relationships. In Part IV, our main focus is on work commitments and coping with relationship loss. We also address the experiences of providing care for spouses and dependent adult children. Finally, in Part V, we describe how oldest old adults focus their energies and attentions on their most significant social ties. In addition, we address challenges that older people may face, such as elder abuse and neglect, and explore how the quality of later life is influenced by health and economic circumstances.

First, however, we begin our reader with a poem by Lois Tschetter Hjelmstad that depicts a multigenerational family coming together to share a meal in later life. Family meals and holidays provide important opportunities for building and maintaining connections, as this poem illustrates. The poem is particularly significant because it acknowledges the many years of happiness and heartbreak experienced by this extended family.

1

The Gathering

Lois Tschetter Hjelmstad

We sit around a table
in an unfamiliar restaurant—
my brother, my sister, and I
our mates smiling at us
from across the table
our parents (who are eighty-six)
completing the circle

The tinkle of ice in other glasses
the murmur of other conversations
are background to our communion

It has taken a long time
to come to this place
    past the early rivalry
    past the fierce competition
    past the wary friendliness
    past the hurts, both small and large

But somehow
we finally
cut to the chase

We lucked out—
it wasn't too late

I revel in the peaceful knowledge
I sigh for the lost years
I weep for the short tomorrow

PART I

Negotiating Ties With Young Adults

People do not always mean the same thing by the word *family*. When adult children move away, for example, their parents still think of them as "the children," and they welcome their visits back home as a chance for "the family" to be together again. Similarly, adult children often say that they are going to visit their family on a return trip to see their parents. These same children, however, will describe themselves and their own children as a family. Older parents, their adult children, and their grandchildren will speak of the last time their family got together when describing a reunion that featured all relatives on the grandfather's side.

This same word is used to describe even more unusual variations. Grandparents consider their son's children to be part of their family although the son neither lives with nor has custody of his children following divorce. The child born to the partner of a lesbian daughter, and the child's mother, are welcomed into the family by the daughter's parents. An older couple, married for 70 years, who never had children, think of themselves as a family. A stepdaughter who lives separately from but is taking care of her widowed stepmother is a family member to the stepmother. Finally, a longtime friend, the only surviving social contact for an older man, is family to the widower.

The families described in the first paragraph fit a relatively conventional definition. Those in the second paragraph, however, are more consistent with the ways in which families have been changing during the past 30 years. We all need to be clear on what we mean by families because there are so many variations and so many ways of thinking of them. Our beliefs about families have implications for the behavior we expect of family members, the relationships we envision for family members, and the programs and policies we establish to support families. Because changes in families that have occurred during the last three decades disproportionately involved younger members of society, these changes have implications for the ties between young adult children and their middle-aged parents. These relationships are the focus of Part I.

Key Issues

This discussion and the readings in Part I illustrate the following:

1. There is a mismatch between what people believe about family and the reality of families as they exist today. Although families share a number of characteristics, they are far more variable in practice than is evident in typical thinking about them. Few families today conform to the traditional picture of a wife, her husband, and their biological children who are younger than 18 years of age.

2. One major way in which families differ is through their race, their ethnicity, and their social class. People of different racial, ethnic, cultural, and class backgrounds have varying expectations about family life and the behavior of family members.

3. Family relationships are influenced by changing demographic patterns. In the most narrow sense, families are constructed through patterns of relationship formation, relationship breakup, and childbearing. These patterns have changed during the past several decades, resulting in greater variability across families.

4. Policies and programs targeted to a single ideology about families may be problematic for those they intend to serve. Policies and programs may assume a level of support that is not forthcoming, or they may miss aid from individuals who exist outside traditional family boundaries.

5. Parent-adult child relationships are influenced by both gender and experience. Because young women and men typically experience many transitions, their relationships with their middle-aged parents are often in a state of change.

6. The ties within and across generations are built and nurtured primarily by women. This unpaid work of kinkeeping is seen as women's responsibility.

What Is a Family?

The ideology of family suggests a household with two adults, a woman and a man, who are married to each other, and their biological children who are younger than 18 years of age (Barrett & McIntosh, 1982). In reality, few households look this way. Instead, families often extend beyond this narrow age range, embrace more than two generations, and reach outside a household.

Policymakers seem to have a relatively narrow definition of family. They frequently define family as young children and the parents who live with them (Bould, 1993). They presume that family members, in addition to living together in the same household, are related by blood, marriage, or adoption. Definitions such as this one, whether fully articulated or simply implicit in policy and practice, have implications for individuals and family members across the life span.

Policymakers may have assumptions not only about who is in a family but also about what help is available from those family members. Policies and programs that assume the availability of willing and able coresidential relatives to help older persons may lead to inadequate care if family members provide less assistance than expected. Family members who live in the same household as a frail, older adult cannot always be relied on for help. Programs with assumptions of such help are not always practical and, indeed, may pose difficulties for older family members who are unable to get the support that they need.

Some dependent older persons receive assistance from relatives or fictive kin who live outside the household. The failure to recognize the interpersonal resources available to older adults may blind formal service providers to those who are helping and who need support to continue to give help. Policies that neither recognize nor support such help may incorrectly assume that an older adult cannot remain at home. Both types of policies, as we will see in Part V, may leave older persons who are unwell at risk for neglect or abuse.

Our definition of family is quite broad. We include individuals within the same household even when they are not connected by blood, marriage, or adoption. We include heterosexual couples who live together as family, whether or not they have biological children, and although they may not be legally married. We think of lesbian and gay persons not only as individuals but as having families as well. We do not see gayness and family as mutually exclusive (Allen & Demo, 1995). In the reading "The Last Diamond of Summer" in Part I, B. K. Loren's grandfather lived for many years with his wife—Loren's grandmother—

and his wife's partner, Margaret. Loren's mother tells her, "We were a family." Lesbians and gay men, like others in society, create a network of family relationships as they age (Kimmel, 1992).

A broad definition of family actually is quite common in the United States. It exists among American Indians, African Americans, and Mexican Americans, who have long included fictive kin as family members (e.g., Horowitz, 1983; Johnson, 1995; Weibel-Orlando, 1990). It is not unusual, for example, for African Americans to have loose, rather than rigid, boundaries distinguishing biological mothers from *bloodmothers* (mothers related through kinship) and *othermothers* (those welcomed into families as fictive kin). Instead, mothering occurs in a variety of settings involving a variety of family and "nonfamily" members (Collins, 1991).

The first reading in Part I, "Four Models of Adolescent Mother-Grandmother Relationships in Black Inner-City Families," by Nancy Apfel and Victoria Seitz, illustrates such variability in kinship. These young adolescent mothers sometimes raise their children alone, with limited help from other family members; they sometimes raise them in conjunction with other family members; and they sometimes give responsibility for their children completely to their own mothers, to bloodmothers, or to othermothers. Through their study, Apfel and Seitz illustrate how variations in African American family patterns reflect ways in which family members come together to meet needs that cannot be met through traditional structures (Bould, 1993). The forms these variations take for the families in Apfel and Seitz's study are consistent with family members' beliefs about how to take care of an adolescent who has a young child.

Asian Americans also have demonstrated flexibility in family composition and responsibility for each other. Chinese laborers, for example, developed nonkin ties when U.S. policy prohibited the immigration of their relatives from China (Glenn, 1983). Beginning in 1882, it was illegal for Chinese family members to immigrate to the United States unless it could be shown that they had been born here. This policy continued until the mid-1950s. In effect, the U.S. government prohibited family relationships for Chinese workers. In place of relatives, therefore, they relied on immigrant associations that provided access to others who could serve as kin for them. Similar practices occur today among members of racial and ethnic groups who come to the United States without their family members. They create relationships equivalent to traditional family ties with nonbiological, nonlegal, nonadopted associates.

White Americans, as well, often extend their family boundaries. In the early 1900s, for example, working-class immigrants from Italy who did not have relatives in this country connected with *paesanos* or other peasants who had emigrated to the United States from the same village in Italy. Similarly, it is not unusual for people today to have a "second mom," a friend who is "like a brother to me," or even a family whose house they consider to be a second home.

Not everyone agrees that families can be so variable, however. College students are more likely to define as a family a married couple without children than a cohabiting couple without children (Ford, 1994). For some, then, being married is a key feature of family life. Marital status is less important in naming a couple as a family if the couple has young children, however. Students are likely to say that a heterosexual cohabiting couple is a family when biological children are living with the couple and that a household consisting of a single parent and biological children is a family. Especially for young men, parenthood and/or marriage are distinguishing features of family life. College student women are more likely to extend family definitions beyond the traditional.

In "Social Demography of Contemporary Families and Aging," Christine L. Himes suggests problems in equating families with households. She shows how families are developing more complex, cross-household connections because of relatively high rates of divorce and remarriage across adulthood. A related problem is assuming that never-married persons, many of whom live alone, are socially isolated and lack families. In "Forgotten Streams in the Family Life Course," Katherine R. Allen and Robert S. Pickett demonstrate the fallacy of this perspective. They show that despite their relative invisibility, never-married women in their 80s have had purposeful family ties throughout their entire lives. A perspective that sees families as complex, diverse, and dynamic has room to include a variety of family forms.

According to sociologist Judith Stacey (1993), any normative definition that prescribes particular membership in families can be sustained for only a brief time. Families inevitably change. Recognizing variability within and across families helps us understand that experience within any one family is not the same for all family members. Women's family experiences differ from those of men, and one's position and generation in a family also shape one's experience of it. Young children and sometimes frail old family members, for example, relative to middle-aged adults, often have limited choices about how their daily lives are structured.

Thus, experience within families varies by age and gender and across families by race, ethnicity, sexual orientation, and social class. There is, for example, no one African American or Asian American or American Indian family (e.g., Tatum, 1987). Indeed, there is no "monolithic family" (Thorne, 1982, p. 2). Instead, there are many family forms.

Our study of families, particularly those in middle and later life, has convinced us that families are more than households and biological or legal connections (Bould, 1993). Yes, families do have commonalities: They consist of two or more individuals who may or may not live together and who share a history with and a commitment to each other

(Bould, 1993; Weston, 1991). But they also are tremendously diverse. Regardless of family structure, gender, and generation, being a part of a family is a central component of identity and a major way through which individuals maintain connections throughout their adult lives.

How Does the Transition to Adulthood Shape Parents' Relationships With Children?

The transitions experienced by young adult children influence the connections between the generations, and they do so against a backdrop of generally positive intergenerational ties. Members of both generations report strong feelings of attachment and connection to each other regardless of life stage, marital status, parental status, problems at work, and so on. These positive feelings occur during a relationship that lasts for 50 years or longer, with children as adults for most of that time (Rossi & Rossi, 1990).

Although both report intense feelings, parents have stronger connections to their children than their children have to them. This finding is so well established in the literature that it has a name: the *developmental stake* (Lynott & Roberts, 1997). The older generation has more of a stake in the younger generation than the reverse. So it is not unexpected that adult children tend to report stronger feelings for their children than they do for their parents. And those grandchildren are less connected to their parents than they will be to any children of their own.

Although children's feelings for their parents are not as intense as their parents' feelings for them, they are very intense indeed. The parent-child relationship is particularly strong and compelling across all stages of adult life and is an important source of support for both generations.

Aid from parents to children is common throughout adulthood. Until parents are in the stage that has come to be called old-old age (85 and older), adult children continue to receive more aid from their parents than they give in return. This help comes in many forms: care of a sick or out-of-school child, help with transportation, big-ticket items given by parents as gifts that help their young adult children financially, and so on. This help occurs in families regardless of race, ethnicity, or social class (Benin & Keith, 1995).

In the final reading in Part I, "Intergenerational Solidarity and the Structure of Adult Child-Parent Relationships in American Families," Merril Silverstein and Vern L. Bengtson describe contemporary intergenerational connections as a *latent kin matrix*. Latency implies that parents and adult children have the potential to be mobilized to respond when needed, even if they are not very involved with each other at the present time. From this perspective, the same relationship may change through time, with more aid exchanged when needed. Furthermore, relationships within families differ from each other as well. Some inter-generational ties are characterized by long-standing, close emotional connection and high levels of contact. Others are characterized by life-long patterns of limited contact and emotional distance. These are only the two extremes of five variations in intergenerational relationship patterns. All variations have the potential for responses when needed, whether family members are motivated by affection or from a sense of duty.

Silverstein and Bengtson note that on average, African American and Hispanic adults report relationships with parents that are emotionally closer than those reported by Whites. For the most part, however, regardless of race or social class, families seem ready and able to help when relatives are in need. This is true despite strong expectations in the United States that adults, including young adult children, should be independent (Johnson, 1995; Ward & Spitze, 1996). One of the first family transitions that middle-aged parents expect is the launching of their children. The language used to describe this transition assumes that when children reach a certain age, they are quickly and resolutely sent forward into the world by their parents to be on their own. As you probably know, the reality is quite a bit more complex. As Apfel and Seitz show, some children go out on their own before they reach the legal age of adulthood. Others leave the parental home before age 18 but continue to depend on their parents in a number of ways. Some return home after losing a job or ending a marriage. Among middle-class families, it is common for young adult children to move out of their parents' home but to continue to be dependent on them throughout the college years. For some, this dependence extends through graduate school!

Young adulthood is the stage when people are expected to make choices that will shape their experiences until the end of their lives. This is the period when individuals not only leave their parents' homes but also make what is meant to be a lifelong commitment to a partner, as well as choices about a desired occupation or area of paid work. Today, women as well as men are expected to make a commitment to the paid labor force. Contrary to work patterns in the middle of the 20th century, a majority of adult women under age 65 work for pay, as do most mothers of young children and mothers of infants. Our interest is in the way these transitions influence the relationships between these young adult children and their middle-aged parents.

Young Adult Transitions and Relationships With Parents

Generally, the relationships between middle-aged parents and their adult children tend to improve as children leave home, cohabit, marry, and take on full-time employment (Aquilino, 1997; White & Rogers, 1997). Children's movement into these adult roles leads to greater emotional closeness and less conflict between the generations. It seems to help parent-child relationships when children move into the roles their parents occupy, such as establishing an independent residence, becoming a spouse, and making a long-term commitment to an occupation. Children who make these transitions successfully, and who make them at a point considered to be "on time," foster these stronger ties with their parents. Those who struggle with these transitions face a different picture. Children who have difficulty keeping a job, for example, are a source of stress to their parents (Suitor, Pillemer, Keeton, & Robison, 1995). Those who leave home or become parents early—or who wait too long to leave home or to have children—similarly strain their connections with their parents. Most adult children, however, make these transitions successfully during the range of time considered appropriate for them.

In the early stage of these transitions, young adults' identities are in flux, and decisions are somewhat unstable. Think of how many times college seniors have changed their majors or how many serious relationships they have had! This dynamic phase of life for young adults creates challenges for their relationships with their middle-aged parents. In "One Week Until College," Sandi Kahn Shelton vividly portrays the anxiety and uncertainty of this period. Her daughter, Allie, seems caught between wanting to have left home long ago and the fear that things she has known and understood will never be the same again. Shelton seems unable to figure out how to connect with her daughter in these last months before Allie leaves for college.

Although there may be considerable tension during early stages of these transitions, most relationships between parents and young adult children will weather this tension and will continue to be important to and valued by both of them throughout the remainder of their lives. In other words, relationships typically exhibit a pattern of continuity throughout adulthood. Although they may have their ups and downs, good relationships tend to stay that way, and only rarely do poor relationships improve.

The picture is more complex for Caroline Hwang. In "The Good Daughter," Hwang describes her position as the child of immigrant parents. She was born in the United States two years after her parents emigrated from Korea. Her parents struggled to see that she was American in every way and that she took advantage of what the United States had to offer. From Hwang's perspective, however, her parents seem unaware that she does not fit in with her peers as they had hoped. As an Asian American, she is reminded constantly that she is not part of the dominant White majority. She does not feel more comfortable as a Korean, however. She learned little about her racial and ethnic heritage and is even unable to pronounce her last name correctly. Nevertheless,

Hwang believes that her parents want her to marry a Korean American and, eventually, to produce Korean American grandchildren. Hwang also feels unable to pursue the occupation she believes her parents expect for her. The connection between these two generations seems filled with contradictions, and Hwang seems to have many challenges ahead, both in making the choices that she must make and in her relationships with her parents.

Forming Primary Partnerships

One transition experienced by most young adults is marriage. A child's marriage adds new dimensions to the relationships with parents and, perhaps, new tensions as well. Parents may have to take on the major expense associated with the wedding itself and with helping the young couple establish a new household. Parents now have a daughter- or son-in-law in addition to their own child. Relationships with kin in the United States are structured primarily through women's ties. This means that these new daughters-in-law will play key roles in maintaining the connections across the generations.

There is some evidence that sons' contact with parents actually increases after they marry (Rossi & Rossi, 1990). New daughters-in-law may help sons keep in contact with their mothers and fathers, which sons did not do as much on their own. Contact with newly married daughters, however, seems to decline. Newly married daughters seem to be working at building connections with their husbands' parents. Meanwhile, parents seem to be connecting with and helping their unmarried daughters. Alice and Peter Rossi (1990), who conducted an extensive study of parent-adult child relationships across the life span, speculate that family members tend to help unmarried women because they are perceived to be needy. Those who are married are perceived to be getting the help they need from their husbands.

As you will see in Part II, adult children may form partnerships with persons of the same gender. When they inform their parents of their relationship, they also may be providing information that they are lesbian or gay. For some, this information will forever strain the parent-child tie, but other parents will welcome their child and their child's partner into the family. For still others, it may take time for a warm and supportive relationship to emerge.

The marriages and other partnerships of some young adult children end within a few years of having been formed. Such change in the marital status of adult children has an influence on the connection between the generations. Silverstein and Bengtson show that divorced children have weaker ties to their parents than married children do. This is especially true of daughters with marital problems (Kaufman & Uhlenberg, 1998). Parenthetically, the marital status of parents also is important in relationships with young adult children, especially the ties between fathers and their children. Divorced mothers, widowed fathers, but especially divorced fathers have weaker connections to their adult children than do continuously married parents.

When Children Become Parents

Relationships with parents change again when children have children of their own, but the direction of that change may surprise you. Parents are less emotionally close to and report more conflict with their children who are parents than with those who are not (Aquilino, 1997). Alice and Peter Rossi (1990) suggest that having young children takes time and energy away from relationships with one's parents. Furthermore, although the role of parent may give the two generations one more thing in common, it also brings with it a potential area of disagreement (Aquilino, 1997). In the first reading in Part I, Apfel and Seitz describe the situation of Marty and her mother, Mae. The two have always had a difficult relationship, and now new tensions are caused by Mae's concerns about how her daughter is behaving as a mother. Parenting in this case seems to be another domain about which the two can disagree.

After becoming parents themselves, daughters seem to become more distant than sons from their parents (Kaufman & Uhlenberg, 1998). Having a child seems to bring a son and his mother a little closer together, but it has the opposite effect for the connection between daughters and their fathers. As the Rossis (1990) argue, young mothers have many more demands on their time and energy than do young fathers, and these demands interfere with their ability to sustain connections with others. In their study, children who have never had children of their own are more closely connected to their parents and spend more time with them throughout adulthood. These adult children are not alienated, as some might assume. Katherine Allen and Robert Pickett show this in their study of never-married daughters.

One social change evident in the last decades of the 20th century has been the disentangling of marriage from parenthood. Through time, more and more people have been having children without first being married. This has been true for adolescents, for many women in their 20s, and, although the actual numbers were small, for women in their 30s and early 40s as well (Siegel, 1995). High divorce rates, which almost inevitably lead to different residences of children from a parent—usually a father—also characterize this period. This is another way in which parents and their adult children are different. Marrying later, being more likely to have children outside marriage, and ending more marriages through divorce are three demographic patterns more characteristic of younger adults than of older adults.

Not all young adults have children. Indeed, the proportion of individuals of childbearing age who either postponed having children or decided not to have children at all increased substantially during the last decade of the 20th century, especially among Whites (Heaton, Jacobson, & Holland, 1999). This followed a period of younger child-bearing in the 1980s. Christine Himes discusses both patterns in "Social Demography of Contemporary Families and Aging." More persons seem to change their minds about parenthood than was true in the past, from wanting to have children to not wanting them, as well as from not wanting children to desiring to be parents. It appears that the uncertainty that characterizes young adulthood is lasting for a longer time today, which may pose a challenge for connections with their parents.

Commitment to Paid Work

Even if they were employed as adolescents, the work in which children engage in adulthood has greater significance in establishing independence from parents. In young adulthood, middle- and upper-middle-class children are expected to make long-term commitments to a specific type of work, perhaps within a particular segment of the economy. For example, a young woman might parlay her degree in computer science with a minor in business into an administrative position in a technical support department of a major firm. Although she may change jobs throughout her work history, first within this firm, then across companies, the expectation is that she will be engaged in paid labor in a context tied both to computers and to business.

The picture for persons in the working classes is less clear. The number of industrial jobs in the United States and the availability of trades for skilled workers have declined dramatically. Fewer positions are available, and those that are available offer limited, if any, job security; provide meager, if any, benefits; are highly vulnerable to fluctuations in the economy; and may not pay a living wage.

For persons who are poor, particularly those with minimal education, the picture is worse. They may have access to only low-wage jobs in the service sector, with little opportunity for advancement, no job security, and little chance of experiencing a sense of mastery in the labor force arena. Fortunately, people in the working classes, and those with less income and education, report stronger ties across the generations (Lynott & Roberts, 1997). This means that young adults in these families can count on parents, grandparents, and adult siblings to help out during periods of economic and other stresses. As is shown throughout this volume, however, the poorest families may have difficulty responding to such needs because of their own limited resources.

Regardless of social class, parents want their children, especially their sons, to be in stable employment, earning a sufficient wage to be independent and to support any dependent family members. They do not want to have to worry about them (Suitor et al., 1995). This may be why, when sons increase their hours in paid work, their relationships with their fathers seem to improve (Kaufman & Uhlenberg, 1998). Things are more complicated for daughters, however. When daughters work longer hours in the labor force, relationships with their fathers deteriorate. Why might this be so?

Men are more traditional than women in their ideas about families and family relationships. As we discussed earlier, college student women have more flexible definitions of family than their male classmates do. Similarly, fathers seem to expect more traditional behavior from their adult children than mothers do. Kaufman and Uhlenberg (1998) suggest that fathers want their sons to have strong, effective connections with the paid labor force but are less likely to desire paid work careers for their daughters.

The employment of middle-class women is one major way in which society has changed. Few middle-class women over the age of 60 today were employed when they had young children. Instead, most young mothers who were employed were those who were poor or working class, many of whom were women of color. Their families desperately needed their economic contributions to survive. Today, even middle-class women work for pay. In part, they do so because as women have become more educated, their interest in experiencing a sense of mastery through paid work has increased. They also work, in part, because during the past 30 years, one income has become less and less able to support a worker, a dependent spouse, and young children.

Because women's employment patterns have changed across cohorts in the United States, the paid work of young adult women today is an area of potential conflict across generations within families. Rossi and Rossi (1990) suggest that one reason women's ties in families are stronger than men's is their historically lower labor force commitment. Less time in paid work gives women more time to maintain connections with kin. They speculate that the increasing attachment of women to the paid labor force carries with it the risk of undermining the strong female intergenerational bonds that characterize kinship systems in the United States. At the current time, however, investment by adult children in paid work seems more important to ties between sons and their parents than to daughters and their parents (Suitor et al., 1995).

The transitions of young adulthood have long-term implications, as Himes demonstrates. The characteristics of older persons today, and the nature of their family supports, reflect the choices and decisions they made decades ago. The same will be true 50 and 60 years from now for the young adults who today make choices about commitments to partners, to parenthood, and to paid work. Families change through time and will continue to do so in ways that have implications for intergenerational connections. For example, young parents today have fewer children than their own parents did. Alice and Peter Rossi (1990) suggest that the smaller families characteristic of the early 21st century could lead to an intensification of the relationships between parents and adult children. As always, however, it is wise to remember the variability among families. Not all young families today are small, and not all middle-aged parents will respond in the same way to the decisions and transitions of their adult children.

Regardless of changes in broad social patterns, women are likely to continue to play an important role in maintaining connections within and across generations. Irrespective of age or stage in the life cycle, women report stronger connections to family members than men do (Lynott & Roberts, 1996). The more we study links across generations, the more evidence we have that women are key.

How Are Relationships Across Generations Shaped, Preserved, and Anchored Throughout Adulthood?

We introduced Part I by describing the many ways in which families differ from each other, mostly in whether they live together and who is considered to be a family member. Here, we see that regardless of residence or membership, families also differ in what Silverstein and Bengtson, in our last reading, call *solidarity*.

Some parent-child ties fit our ideals about relationships across generations: They are emotionally close, the intergenerational partners agree with each other on social views, they live near each other, they have frequent contact, and they exchange aid across the generations in both directions. Other parent-child ties demonstrate few of these characteristics. A variety of other combinations exist somewhere between these two ends of this continuum. Silverstein and Bengtson emphasize the (latent) potential of intergenerational bonds to be mobilized in times of need.

None of the five relationship types that Silverstein and Bengtson describe accounts for a majority of parent-child connections. Relationships between mothers and their adult children in particular differ from those between fathers and their adult children. As indicated earlier, family relationships are more central for women than for men. The mother-daughter tie is particularly strong. Think of B. K. Loren's relationships with her parents, described in "The Last Diamond of Summer." Her mother visits her in her new hometown, unaccompanied by her father. Loren does not feel welcome in her parents' home because her father disapproves of her being a lesbian. Other examples of the centrality of mother-daughter ties are found in the readings as well. In "One Week Before College," Allie, Sandi Shelton's daughter, lived with her mother, rather than with her father, after her parents' divorce. During the Great Depression, adult daughters, rather than adult sons, were expected to help care for their aging family members, as shown by Katherine Allen and Robert Pickett in "Forgotten Streams in the Family Life Course."

Silverstein and Bengtson's descriptions of variations in intergenerational ties support the view that women's ties are stronger than men's. Whereas more than one in four adult children, especially daughters, have relationships with their mothers that can be described as tight-knit, the same number have relationships with their fathers that are best described as detached. Female family members see each other and talk with each other more than male family members do. For example, about half of all adult daughters see their mothers weekly, whereas only one third of adult sons see their mothers as often. Rates of contact with fathers for both daughters and sons are much lower. The Rossis (1990) suggest that at all ages, women have a greater stake than men do in maintaining family connections within and across generations. Women also are more likely to need financial assistance and emotional support from family members. In part, this is because they are less likely than men to be in the paid labor force. Furthermore, when they are employed, they are more likely to be in lower-paying jobs with intermittent job commitment. These characteristics translate into less pay, fewer benefits, and a lifetime of depressed income.

People of color similarly face obstacles to enhanced income such that minority women, through time, are increasingly needy relative to White women and especially relative to men. Thus, women are more financially dependent than are men. In consideration of this, together with women's greater emotional investment in relationships, it is no wonder that women's family ties are less influenced by changes in proximity, marital status, parenthood status, job history, and so on than are men's family ties (Rossi & Rossi, 1990). Women are more flexible than men in their intergenerational connections—more willing to forget past difficulties and to work through current issues. No surprise, then, that B. K. Loren's mother, but not her father, will travel to Colorado to visit her. The Rossis find that men have more precarious or contingent family bonds than women do. Transitions such as divorce in either generation and moving farther away chip away at the family connections of men, but their effect on women's ties is negligible.

2

Four Models of Adolescent Mother-Grandmother Relationships in Black Inner-City Families

Nancy H. Apfel
Victoria Seitz

The present study is designed to elaborate on the roles black inner-city grandmothers play in their adolescent daughters' transition to parenthood. From our longitudinal research and contact with these families four conceptual models are proposed. Vignettes from maternal and grandmaternal interviews are offered as examples of four distinctly different modes of adaptation to adolescent parenthood. Practitioners who work with adolescent parents will often find that the influence of the young mother's mother—the grandmother—is powerful. Her advice may be heeded by an adolescent mother more than that of a professional (Zuckerman, Winsmore, & Alpert, 1979). Most teen mothers and their children are part of a family system which has its own history of interaction and interdependencies. This family history and structure affect the way in which a family meets developmental challenges (Brubaker, 1986, 1990). The family in the midst of the crisis of adolescent parenthood is often in need of, and may be uniquely receptive to,

sensitive intervention (Bryan-Logan & Dancy, 1974; Russell, 1980).

Method

Subjects

As part of an ongoing study (Seitz, Apfel, & Rosenbaum, in press), interviews were conducted at 18 months postpartum with 119 black inner-city adolescents who were less than 19 years old when they gave birth to their first-born child. The adolescents' ages at delivery ranged from 13 to 18 years old with an average age of 16.8.

The mothers of these adolescent mothers also were interviewed during this same time period. If the young mother's own mother was deceased or unavailable to the adolescent, the adolescent was asked if anyone had been a mother-substitute for her. If so, this person was interviewed. Ninety-five percent (113) of the teen mothers had a mother or surrogate involved in her life; these women will be referred to as "grandmothers" or "surrogate grandmothers," speaking from the baby's point of view. Ninety-one percent (103) of the available grandmothers, or surrogate grandmothers agreed to be interviewed. Eighty-eight of these interviews were with biological grandmothers, 15 were with surrogates. The ages of the interviewed biological grandmothers at 18 months after the birth of their daughters' firstborns, ranged from 28-55 years (median age 39); 40% were high school graduates.

Procedures

Interviews of both the mothers and the grandmothers were similar, with questions concerning parenting practices and beliefs, daily routines, child care arrangements, divisions of child care tasks, household composition, whether emergencies had occurred, and who had helped the young mother cope with them.

Each was asked to describe a typical day in their lives in detail. Specifics about who was caring for and interacting with the child throughout the day—feeding, dressing, bathing, playing with, and visiting—were probed. The daily comings and goings of the mother and grandmother were described. As what the adolescents and their mothers said about how the infants were being raised was examined, the following classification was derived. The strengths and weaknesses of each adaptational approach are discussed.

Results

At 18 months postpartum, the following models of familial adaptation were discerned: (1) Parental Replacement, (2) Parental Supplement, (3) Supported Primary Parent, and (4) Parental Apprentice.

The Parental Replacement Model

In this model, which occurred in about 10% of the families, the mother of the adolescent mother assumes total responsibility for rearing the baby. In so doing, she becomes the psychological parent to her daughter's child. Her daughter, although biologically the mother to the child, has minimal parenting responsibilities.

Parental Replacement can occur for a variety of reasons. It can happen by mutual agreement, with the young mother leaving the child for her mother to raise while she goes on to college, or into the army, or to a job. In some cases the daughter lives with her family, but assumes little of the responsibility for her child and maintains the life-style of her nonparenting peers. In other families the mother is irresponsible and negligent in her early parenting, with the result that the grandmother and/or social service agencies decide that the young mother's behavior jeopardizes her child's well-being and the grandmother has to step into the main caregiver role. The replacement process can be gradual, when the young mother abandons her mother with the child by absenting herself for longer and longer periods, or abrupt when she suddenly leaves both her mother and baby.

Gerri: only a biological mother. Gerri became pregnant when she was 17 years old. Her distress at being pregnant was evident to the medical staff at the clinic she attended for prenatal care. In the hospital after she delivered her baby boy, the staff noticed that Gerri was unresponsive to her son's cries, but that her mother, Jane, would pick up and comfort the baby. This was the start of a pattern of behavior in which Jane became the primary nurturer of her grandchild.

At 18 months postpartum Gerri was attending a 4-year college in another state. Her 38-year-old mother, Jane, who had a one-year-old child of her own, and the 18-month-old Donny were living in the housing project where Gerri grew up. Gerri's mother spoke proudly of Gerri's school achievements and how she called Gerri's college regularly to check on her grades.

During the summer vacations, Gerri would return home to be with her mother, child, and younger siblings. During the interview she referred to taking care of her own child as doing "baby-sitting" for her mother.

Jane commented in her interview that one day Gerri might return and want to have Donny live with her permanently. Jane seemed to accept this possibility with equanimity, as if it would be a natural course of events.

Benefits. A primary benefit of the Replacement Model is that the mother may continue on a developmental track that avoids some of the potential pitfalls of premature parenthood. Free from the responsibilities of parenting a child, the mother can return to school or vocational training with a primary focus on her own future, increasing the likelihood that she will eventually complete her education and be self-supporting.

Another strength of the Parental Replacement model comes from the clarity about who is the psychological parent to the child, at least for a particular period of time. In addition, in this model the child has the potential advantage of being raised by a more mature parent, who may have better parenting skills than adolescent parents (Elster, McAnarney, & Lamb, 1983; Roosa, Fitzgerald, & Carlson, 1982).

Risks. The risks of the Replacement Model partially relate to the process by which the replacement occurs. When it is a mutually agreed upon plan without conflict, the prognosis would appear to be good for all concerned. When it occurs because the young mother has failed at parenting, the risks are higher that the child has suffered and that the mother could feel loss, anger, guilt, and depression. If the grandmother feels abandoned by her daughter, or the daughter feels supplanted by her mother, there can be tension and even estrangement between grandmother and mother. In such cases, the young mother is at risk of losing both her child and her mother. Loss of

her mother, in particular, may occur at a developmentally significant time for the adolescent who still needs parental guidance and nurturance as she tries to define herself. The adolescent may prematurely leave the extended family household and as a consequence lose its financial support as well (Hofferth, 1984).

In this particular family, the grandmother's acceptance that her daughter may eventually rear her grandson appears to reflect her belief that the primary caregiver of a child can change without difficulty for the child, grandmother, or mother. If the young mother returns and claims her child one day, the child's subsequent adjustment could be difficult. On the other hand, preparing children for the possibility that another mother figure might be caring for them some day may be an adaptive strategy to cope with potential adversity. Several grandmothers in this exclusively black sample commented in their interviews that it was not a good thing to have a mother and baby too exclusively attached to each other. This may reflect a cultural difference in beliefs about whether the mothering bond should be exclusive and unchanging (Stack, 1975).

To take on the rearing of her grandchild, a grandmother may have to make considerable sacrifices in her life course. This is welcomed by some, accepted with resignation by some, and rejected by others. In addition, by virtue of her age, the grandmother is more at risk than her daughter to have ill health interfere with her ability to carry out this charge over the many years the child would depend on her.

The Parental Supplement Model

The Parental Supplement model occurs when the care of the child is shared between the grandmother and her daughter. Often the teen's siblings or other relatives also help. There may be one steady child care provider or many providers. The organization of such an arrangement varies: In some households child care depends on who is present, whereas in others it is divided by tasks (e.g., the grandmother prepares food and feeds the baby). In still other households, the arrangement is by time division; thus, the young mother attends school from 8:00 a.m. to 3:00 p.m. and her mother does child care for this time each weekday. In some of these arrangements it is assumed that the mother will take care of the child when she is home. In other families, even if the mother is home, her mother (the grandmother) will feed, or bathe, or clothe the baby. This Parental Supplement Model was the most common form of adaptation in the sample, occurring in slightly more than 50% of the families. The young mother may live with her family or apart—the distinguishing feature of the Parental Supplement Model is that the child's care is regularly shared.

> *Pam: paying her dues, with help from her Mom.* Pam had her child Toya when she was 16 years old and a sophomore in high school. At the 18 months postpartum interview, Pam was a senior in high school, attending school for 6 hours a day Monday through Friday. After school each day she would return home, take care of her child, and do homework for the next day.
>
> Pam's 37-year-old mother and her older sister took care of Toya while Pam was at school. The grandmother commented, "At first it was hard to manage baby-sitting; I changed my schedule from days to nights, now I'm used to it. I know Pam would love to go out more, but the baby ties her down." There was the clear assumption that the daughter was to be the primary caregiver of her child when she returned home from school, and it was expected that she return home promptly each day.

Families that fall into this model of Parental Supplement appear to have as their goal the management of a crisis. Family energy is devoted to getting through the present with its new complications. The pervasive feeling is that the damage of premature parenthood to the girl's present and future should be contained as much as possible. One or several family members are mustered to assist in caring for the child so that the total responsibility does not rest on the young mother. In these families the young mother may attend school, work, or do neither, but the family assumption is that she should be helped with child care.

The Parental Supplement Model was the most complex, as well as the most prevalent, adaptation of grandmothers and their daughters to adolescent parenthood. It appeared that both the number of caregivers and family's ability to plan for child care have implications for how successfully the child and the young mother will fare in this arrangement. Some families had two, three, or even more family members involved in child care, usually the teen mother, her siblings, and her mother. Similarly the degree of planning for the day varies widely. Some families had achieved a smooth predictable routine with multiple caregivers, while in other families each day differed for each family member (sometimes causing stress for all involved).

Benefits. One primary benefit of the Supplemental Model is that the new mother can continue with her education, reducing her risk of later welfare dependency or poor employment. There is at least one other adult to help out with inevitable childhood sicknesses and emergencies of parenthood. Protection is provided to the young mother so that she is not facing all the realities of adulthood in one sudden transition. From the child's point of view, there is another caregiver who is older and more experienced at child rearing than the child's mother.

The success of the Supplemental Model would seem to rest on the organization and understanding among the participants in the arrangement. In situations in which the number of different caregivers is small, in which the collaboration is relatively harmonious and predictable, and in which one caregiver feels strong affective ties to the child and takes primary responsibility, the likelihood is high that a child could thrive in such an arrangement.

Risks. This Supplemental Model carries the long-range risk that the adult family members may not work toward the goal of molding a talented parent out of their teenager. An additional problem is that the child could become more attached to the grandmother, revealing this in ways that discourage the young mother in her caregiving attempts.

A more immediate risk in this model is the potential for confusion about who is responsible for the child's care. This confusion can lead to grandmother-mother conflict pervading their daily interactions. The resulting anger and tension can be corrosive to familial relationships. A family with multiple caregivers and poorly defined responsibilities could even be unaware when the baby is receiving dangerously inadequate care because of their scattered child care arrangements. This has to be considered a risk for the baby.

Supported Primary Parent Model

In this model, which occurred in about 20% of all the families, the young mother is primarily responsible for the full-time care of her child. She may receive family support in the form of regular communication, visiting, financial contributions, occasional baby-sitting and help with household tasks. Half of this group lived independently, so that their households were separate from, but closely linked to, their families. The other half of this category of adolescent mothers lived with their mothers, but they differed from Supplemental Model families because of the adolescents' nearly full-time involvement in the care of their children.

The assumption made by families in the Supported Primary Parent model is that the adolescent is able to make a rapid transition to full-time parenthood with minimal guidance and supervision. There are reciprocal influences on how a family makes this adjustment. The young mother may willingly choose to be the primary caregiver of her child, or her par-

ents' work may be their priority, making them unavailable for child care even though they share a household. Several grandmothers expressed the belief that if they withheld their child care services, their daughter would not "romanticize the responsibilities of motherhood and make the same mistake again." There were also families who were weary due to multiple crises and who simply did not have the emotional or financial resources to provide more help. On the other hand, some young mothers wanted to strike out on their own as a statement that they had "come of age." Some wanted to live with the father of their baby or a new boyfriend, with or without their mother's approval. In other families conflict and lack of warmth forced the young mother away from her family.

Marty: having trouble caring for her baby as grandmother stands by. From the time of Aaron's birth, Marty and Aaron lived in an apartment in the same building as her parents; this allowed daily visits between the households. Mae worked full-time in a city government job; but after work each day she dropped in on her daughter and grandson to take him for a walk or to take him to her apartment for a visit. She was concerned about the care that Aaron was receiving from Marty and would talk to her daughter about the injuries and sicknesses to which he seemed prone. By the time he was 18 months old, Aaron had been hospitalized three times with two bouts of pneumonia and with an injury. During the 18-month postpartum interview, Mae expressed concern that her daughter was pregnant again and needed to think seriously about how she would manage to take care of two children.

Marty's relationship with her family was turbulent before her pregnancy, expressed by her repeated running away from home. During this transition to parenthood and grandparenthood, Marty's mother had provided some support, but there was also an undercurrent of tension and disapproval, and a warranted concern about Marty's parenting. It was questionable whether Marty could be receptive to her mother's suggestions and attempts to assist.

Benefits. Although the vignette describes a young mother and child with a poor prognosis for successful parenting, there were adolescent mothers in this Supported Primary Parent model who were doing well. Given that in this model the adolescent mother is expected to be the primary parent who provides the majority of the child's care, the mother-child relationship may be strengthened. The blurring of role distinctions between mother and grandmother is less likely to happen than in the Parental Supplement Model. The adolescent may use her mother, or some other maternal figure, as a consultant, companion, and helpmate, but the boundaries of responsibility for her child are more clearly drawn and the young mother carries this charge. There is less risk that the young mother would not identify with the role of parent, or that her mother (the grandmother) would interfere with her feelings of attachment to her own child. A number of grandmothers in this model even expressed a deference to their daughter's understanding and ability to comfort their grandchild.

The Supported Primary Parent Model can be a harmonious and stable arrangement, satisfactory to both mother and daughter whether they live together or apart. A number of young mothers who lived apart from their nuclear family would visit their mother's household daily, sharing meals and talking together. In other cases the grandmother would visit her daughter and grandchild regularly. The regular visiting and warm contact can provide a nurturant environment that appears to be sufficient support for some young mothers.

When the young mother lives at home with her parents, but is responsible for the majority of the child care while her mother is at work during the day, she too can be receiving sufficient support. At night the grandmother returns home and plays with the child, chats with her daughter, and perhaps cooks dinner for the whole family.

Risks. The primary risk in this model of adjustment is that the young mother's immaturity could prevent her from adapting to the responsibilities of parenting without more intense grandmother support and mentoring. There is the risk that problems could escalate into a crisis, with neglect, abuse, or abandonment of the child. When such a crisis occurred, the grandmother in some families had to assume total responsibility for raising the child or children of the young mother. Thus, the family's adaptation pattern to adolescent parenthood had to shift from Supported Primary Parent to Parental Replacement. It would seem probable that the caregiving failure preceding the shift would be damaging to the baby's well-being and to the mother's sense of herself as a parent.

It is also less likely that a young mother in this arrangement could develop the skills necessary to be financially independent while being fully responsible for her child. The adolescent mothers in this model are subjected to another risk. Due to their minimal opportunity to observe and model others in the parenting role, these adolescent mothers may not become as competent in parenting their young children.

The Parental Apprentice Model

A fourth model of adaptation to grandparenthood, found in almost 10% of our sample, is the Parental Apprentice. In the Parental Apprentice Model, the grandmother acts as a mentor to her daughter, whom she views as an "apprentice mother." The grandmother does not assume that her daughter will have inborn maternal behavior that will emerge on cue without help from outside influence. Nor does she assume that her daughter's previous experience in taking care of siblings and other children will provide all the information that she needs to be a competent parent. These grandmothers attempt to facilitate their daughter's transition to parenthood, and to support and educate the young mother, without supplanting her in the parenting role.

The task of the grandmother in this model is to be responsive and sensitive to her daughter's knowledge and ability level in parenting, and to lead her to higher levels of skill and confidence. Then the grandmother must gradually relinquish the parenting role to her daughter. The tasks of mothering are broken down into manageable subtasks that the daughter practices under her mother's watchful eye. The total job of mothering is not expected to be carried by the young mother, instead, she manages certain tasks, gaining confidence and competence. The Apprenticeship Model could be viewed as a developmentally higher level of adjustment made by grandmothers to their "premature grandparenthood." These grandmothers acknowledge their daughters' inexperience and youth, but also articulate the belief that their daughters can become capable parents.

Irma: a mother in training. Sarah was born in October. Irma continued to live with Marion and her stepfather. For the first months, Marion took care of her grandchild during school hours until her daughter completed high school, a semester early, the following January. When Irma was home, she cared for her child under her mother's watchful eye. Irma reflected on how she learned to parent. "I didn't understand what a mother meant until I became one. It's not an easy job."

In helping Irma establish an independent household about a year and a half after Sarah's birth, Marion stood behind her belief that "You can't be a woman in your mother's house. Your place gives you responsibility. With your own mother you act like a kid." In the same way that she had taught Irma how to parent, she began to teach her how to manage a household.

An assumption seems to be made by apprenticing grandmothers that the adolescent mother needs education in parenting, as well as emotional, financial, and child care support. This is not to imply that the grandmothers who were successful at apprenticing their daughters into motherhood were not disappointed and distressed about the pregnancy. But they seemed to be able to surmount these initial reactions.

Benefits. A benefit of the Apprentice Model is that the adolescent is more likely to become a confident, competent mother, well attached to her own child, and her child to her. Tensions between grandmother and daughter about who is the real parent to the child are less likely to occur since the overt purpose of these grandmothers is to create competent mothers, not to take over the mothering role themselves. This group also would seem to have a lower risk that the daughter will eventually fade out of the mothering role, leaving the grandmother as the primary caregiver. A benefit for the child is the influence of a mature watchful grandmother who creates a more secure environment with the potential of long lasting stability if the parenting education is successful.

A further benefit of the Apprentice Model is an enhanced relationship between the young mother and her own mother. Both mother and daughter often seemed, in their separate interviews, to be mutually appreciative of each other. The warmth, trust, communicativeness, and lack of conflict between mother and daughter seemed to relate to successful apprenticeship. Also some grandmothers may be more gifted than others in imparting information uncritically about parenting, making it easier for the daughter to accept the mentoring.

Risks. The risks of this model come from the emphasis on mothering, which may put the young mother's academic and economic future in jeopardy. Although some of the apprenticing mothers were working at both their parenting and their academics, for some it may have been too much to handle and their schooling was in jeopardy.

There is also the risk that a grandmother's attempts at apprenticeship will fail. Apprenticeship requires interaction between two parties—one has to be receptive, the other, skilled. Not all daughters were willing apprentices, nor were all grandmothers equally talented in instruction.

Summary and Implications

Each of these models suggests a system of beliefs, articulated or tacit, of how to care for an adolescent who has a baby. These expectations could be expressed as follows: "I am raising your child for you." (Parental Replacement Model); "We are all raising this child." (Parental Supplement Model); "This is your child and he's your responsibility to raise." (Supported Primary Parent); and "I will act as your mentor as you learn how to raise your child." (Parental Apprentice).

There are two aspects of familial support that discriminate among these four models. The first is the degree of child care provided by the mother. Using this variable one can view these models as a continuum, ranging from minimal maternal child care in the Parental Replacement Model (where the grandparent is rearing the child) to maximum maternal child care in the Supported Primary Parent Model (where the young parent is rearing the child with some degree of emotional and material support). In the middle range of maternal responsibility for child rearing are the other two models, Parental Supplement and Parental Apprentice, distinguished by the second significant variable of family support, training in parenting skills.

The belief that it is necessary to educate a young mother in parenting skills is evident in a small but important group of grandparents—the Parental Apprentice Model grandparents. These grandparents appear to engage in long-range planning to prepare their daughters for eventual independence as parents.

The grandmothers outside of the Parental Apprentice model do not articulate, nor do they seem to have the underlying belief in teaching parenting skills. These grandparents seem to assume that since their daughters have been baby-sitting for siblings for years, and there is nothing unique about caring for one's own firstborn child, further instruction is unnecessary.

Other grandmothers expressed the belief that parenting skills were inborn and therefore unnecessary to teach. One grandmother aptly summed up this belief, "It (parenting) comes naturally to a woman."

Several grandparents in the Parental Supplemental Model articulated a wish that their daughters eventually would not need so much assistance, but they seemed to be unaware of an educational strategy that might help them to accomplish this goal. While the Supplemental Model grandmothers provided child care assistance regularly and often, the grandmothers in the Supported Primary Parent Model treated the fledgling mothers as most grandmothers in our society treat their more mature married daughters with children, by providing only occasional baby-sitting. They appeared to assume that an adolescent mother can manage the majority of the child care with minimal guidance and education.

Nevertheless, each of these models, except the Parental Replacement Model, has the potential for a successful transition to parenting for the young mother. The Parental Supplement and the Supported Primary Parent Models seem to have more inherent risks that the transition might go awry. The model with the highest potential for creating a well-functioning mother out of an adolescent would appear to be the Parental Apprentice Model.

References

Brubaker, T. H. (1986). Developmental tasks in later life: An overview. *American Behavioral Scientist, 29,* 381-388.

Brubaker, T. H. (1990). Families in later life: A burgeoning research area. *Journal of Marriage and the Family, 52,* 959-981.

Bryan-Logan, B., & Dancy, B. (1974). Unwed pregnant adolescents: Their mothers' dilemma. *Nursing Clinics of North America, 9*(1), 57-68.

Elster, A., McAnarney, E., & Lamb, M. (1983). Parental behavior of adolescent mothers. *Pediatrics, 71,* 494-503.

Hofferth, S. (1984). Kin networks, race, and family structure. *Journal of Marriage and the Family, 46,* 791-806.

Roosa, M. W., Fitzgerald, N. E., & Carlson, N. A. (1982). Teenage and older mothers and their infants: A descriptive comparison. *Adolescence, 17*(65), 1-17.

Russell, C. S. (1980). Unscheduled parenthood: Transition to "parent" for the teenager. *Journal of Social Issues, 36,* 45-63.

Seitz, V., Apfel, N., & Rosenbaum, L. (in press). Effects of an intervention program for pregnant adolescents: Educational outcomes at 2 years postpartum. *American Journal of Community Psychology.*

Stack, C. (1975). *All our kin: Strategies for survival in a black community.* New York: Harper & Row.

Zuckerman, B., Winsmore, G., & Alpert, J. (1979). A study of attitudes and support systems of inner city adolescent mothers. *The Journal of Pediatrics, 95*(1), 122-125.

3

One Week Until College

Sandi Kahn Shelton

My daughter, Allie, is leaving for college in one week. What this means for today—when it's still not time to say good-bye—is that it's impossible to make a path through her room. The floor is cluttered with bags from Filene's and J. Crew: They're filled with extra-long sheets for her dormitory bed, fleece blankets still in their wrappers, thick dark blue towels, wash-cloths, new pairs of jeans and sweaters, baskets of shampoo and loofahs.

She won't talk about going.

I say, "I'm going to miss you," and she gives me one of her looks and finds a reason to leave the room.

Another time I say, in a voice so friendly it surprises even me: "Do you think you'll take down your posters and pictures and take them with you, or will you get new ones at college?"

She answers, in a voice filled with annoy-ance, "How should I know?"

My daughter is off with friends most of the time. Yesterday was the last day she'd have until Christmas with her friend Katharine, whom she'd known since kindergarten. Soon, very soon, it will be her last day with Sarah, Claire, Heather, and Lauren.

And then it will be her last day with me. My friend Karen told me, "The August before I left for college, I screamed at my mother the whole month. Be prepared."

Yet I stand here in the kitchen, watching my daughter make a glass of iced tea. Her face, once so open and trusting, is closed to me. I struggle to think of something to say to her, something friendly and warm. I would like her to know that I admire her, that I am excited about the college she has chosen, that I know the adventure of her life is just about to get started, and that I am so proud of how she's handling everything.

But here's the thing: The look on her face is so mad that I think she might slug me if I open my mouth.

I can't think what I have done. One night not long ago—after a particularly long period of silence between us—I asked what I might have done or said to make her angry with me. I felt foolish saying it. My own mother, who ruled the house with such authoritative maj-esty, would never have deigned to find out what I thought or felt about anything she did. But there I was, obviously having offended my daughter, and I wanted to know. I felt vulnera-ble asking the question, but it was important.

She sighed, as though this question were more evidence of a problem so vast and fundamental that it could never be explained, and she said, "Mom, you haven't done anything. It's fine."

It *is* fine. It's just distant, that's all. May I tell you how close we once were? When she was two years old, my husband and I divorced—one of those modern, amiable divorces that was just great for all parties involved, except that I had to quit my part-time job and take a full-time position. When I would come to the day-care center to pick Allie up after work, she and I would sit on the reading mattress together, and she would nurse. For a whole year after that divorce, we would sit every day at five o'clock, our eyes locked together, concentrating on and reconnecting with each other at the end of our public day. In middle school, when other mothers were already lamenting the estrangement they felt with their adolescent daughters, I hit upon what seemed the perfect solution: rescue raids. I would simply show up occasionally at the school, sign her out of class, and take her somewhere—out to lunch, off to the movies, once on a long walk on the beach. It may sound irresponsible, unsupportive of education, but it worked. It kept us close when around us other mothers and daughters were floundering. We talked about everything on those outings, outings we kept secret from the rest of the family and even from friends.

Sometimes, blow-drying her hair in the bathroom while I brushed my teeth, she'd say, "Mom, I really could use a rescue raid soon." And so I would arrange my work schedule to make one possible.

Anyone will tell you that high school is hard on the mother-daughter bond, and so it was for us, too. I'd get up with her in the early mornings to make her sandwich for school, and we'd silently drink a cup of tea together before the six-forty school bus came. But then she decided she'd rather buy her lunch at school, and she came right out and said she'd prefer to be alone in the mornings while she got ready. It was hard to concentrate on everything she needed to do with someone else standing there, she said.

We didn't have the typical fights that the media lead us to expect with teenagers: She didn't go in for tattoos and body piercings; she was mostly good about curfews; she didn't drink or do drugs. Her friends seemed nice, and the boys she occasionally brought home were polite and acceptable.

But what happened? More and more often, I'd feel her eyes boring into me when I was living my regular life, doing my usual things: talking on the phone with friends, disciplining her younger sister, cleaning the bathroom. And the look on her face was a look of frozen disapproval, disappointment . . . even rage.

A couple of times during her senior year I went into her room at night, when the light was off but before she went to sleep. I sat on the edge of her bed and managed to find things to say that didn't enrage or disappoint her. She told me, sometimes, about problems she was having at school: a teacher who lowered her grade because she was too shy to talk in class, a boy who teased her between classes, a friend who had started smoking. Her disembodied voice, coming out of the darkness, sounded young and questioning. She listened when I said things. A few days later, I'd hear her on the phone, repeating some of the things I had said, things she had adopted for her own, and I felt glad to have been there with her that night.

I said to myself, "Somehow I can be the right kind of mother. Somehow we will find our way back to closeness again."

We haven't found our way back. And now we are having two different kinds of Augusts. I want a romantic August, where we stock up together on things she will need in her dormitory. I want to go to lunch and lean across the table toward each other, the way we've all seen mothers and daughters do, and say how much we will miss each other. I want smiles through tears, bittersweet moments of reminiscence, and the chance to offer the last little bits of wisdom I might be able to summon for her.

But she is having an August where her feelings have gone underground, where to reach over and touch her arms seems an act of war. She pulls away, eyes hard. She turns down every invitation I extend, no matter how lightly I offer them; instead of coming out with me, she lies on her bed reading Emily Dickinson until I say I have always loved Emily Dickinson, and then—but is this just a coincidence?—she closes the book.

Books I have read about surviving adolescence say that the closer your bond with your child, the more violent is the child's need to break away from you, to establish her own identity in the world. The more it will hurt, they say.

My husband says, "She's missing you so much already that she can't bear it."

A friend of mine, an editor in New York who went through a difficult adolescence with her daughter but now has become close to her again, tells me, "You're a wonderful mother. Your daughter will be back to you."

"I don't know," I say to them. I sometimes feel so angry around her that I want to go over and shake her. I want to say, "Talk to me! Either you talk to me—or you're grounded!" I can actually feel myself wanting to say that most horrible of all mother phrases: "Think of everything I've done for you. Don't you appreciate how I've suffered and struggled to give you what you need?"

Late at night, when I'm exhausted with the effort of trying not to mind the loneliness I've felt all day around her, I am getting ready for bed. She shows up at the door of the bathroom, watches me brush my teeth. For a moment, I think wildly that I must be brushing my teeth in a way she doesn't approve of, and I'll be upbraided for it.

But then she says, "I want to read you something." She's holding a handbook sent by her college. "These are tips for parents," she says.

I watch her face as she reads the advice aloud. "'Don't ask your student if she is homesick,' it says. 'She might feel bad the first few weeks, but don't let it worry you. This is a natural time of transition. Write her letters and call her a lot. Send a package of goodies. . . '"

Her voice breaks, and she comes over to me and buries her head in my shoulder. I stroke her hair, lightly, afraid she'll bolt if I say a word. We stand there together for long moments, swaying.

I know it will be hard again. We probably won't have sentimental lunches in restaurants before she leaves, and most likely there will be a fight about something. But I am grateful to be standing in the bathroom at midnight, both of us tired and sad, toothpaste smeared on my chin, holding tight—while at the same time letting go of—this daughter who is trying to say good-bye.

4

The Good Daughter

Caroline Hwang

As the child of immigrants, I'm torn between my parents' dreams and my own.

The moment I walked into the dry-cleaning store, I knew the woman behind the counter was from Korea, like my parents. To show her that we shared a heritage, and possibly get a fellow countryman's discount, I tilted my head forward, in shy imitation of a traditional bow.

"Name?" she asked, not noticing my attempted obeisance.

"Hwang," I answered.

"Hwang? Are you Chinese?"

Her question caught me off-guard. I was used to hearing such queries from non-Asians who think Asians all look alike, but never from one of my own people. Of course, the only Koreans I knew were my parents and their friends, people who've never asked me where I came from, since they knew better than I.

I ransacked my mind for the Korean words that would tell her who I was. It's always struck me as funny (in a mirthless sort of way) that I can more readily say "I am Korean" in Spanish, German and even Latin than I can in the language of my ancestry. In the end, I told her in English.

The dry-cleaning woman squinted as though trying to see past the glare of my strangeness, repeating my surname under her breath. "Oh, Fxuang," she said, doubling over with laughter. "You don't know how to speak your name."

I flinched. Perhaps I was particularly sensitive at the time, having just dropped out of graduate school. I had torn up my map for the future, the one that said not only where I was going but who I was. My sense of identity was already disintegrating.

When I got home, I called my parents to ask why they had never bothered to correct me. "Big deal," my mother said, sounding more flippant than I knew she intended. (Like many people who learn English in a classroom, she uses idioms that don't always fit the occasion.) "So what if you can't pronounce your name? You are American," she said.

Though I didn't challenge her explanation, it left me unsatisfied. The fact is, my cultural identity is hardly that clear-cut.

My parents immigrated to this country 30 years ago, two years before I was born. They told me often, while I was growing up, that, if I wanted to, I could be president someday, that here my grasp would be as long as my reach.

To ensure that I reaped all the advantages of this country, my parents saw to it that I became fully assimilated. So, like any American of my generation, I whiled away my youth strolling malls and talking on the phone, rhapsodizing over Andrew McCarthy's blue eyes or analyzing the meaning of a certain upperclassman's offer of a ride to the Homecoming football game.

To my parents, I am all American, and the sacrifices they made in leaving Korea—including my mispronounced name—pale in comparison to the opportunities those sacrifices gave me. They do not see that I straddle two cultures, nor that I feel displaced in the only country I know. I identify with Americans, but Americans do not identify with me. I've never known what it's like to belong to a community—neither one at large, nor of an extended family. I know more about Europe than the continent my ancestors unmistakably come from. I sometimes wonder, as I did that day in the dry cleaner's, if I would be a happier person had my parents stayed in Korea.

I first began to consider this thought around the time I decided to go to graduate school. It had been a compromise: my parents wanted me to go to law school; I wanted to skip the starched-collar track and be a writer—the hungrier the better. But after 20-some years of following their wishes and meeting all of their expectations, I couldn't bring myself to disobey or disappoint. A writing career is riskier than law, I remember thinking. If I'm a failure and my life is a washout, then what does that make my parents' lives?

I know that many of my friends had to choose between pleasing their parents and being true to themselves. But for the children of immigrants, the choice seems more complicated, a happy outcome impossible. By making the biggest move of their lives for me, my parents indentured me to the largest debt imaginable—I owe them the fulfillment of their hopes for me.

It tore me up inside to suppress my dream, but I went to school for a Ph.D. in English literature, thinking I had found the perfect compromise. I would be able to write at least about books while pursuing a graduate degree. Predictably, it didn't work out. How could I labor for five years in a program I had no passion for? When I finally left school, my parents were disappointed, but since it wasn't what they wanted me to do, they weren't devastated. I, on the other hand, felt I was staring at the bottom of the abyss. I had seen the flaw in my life of halfwayness, in my planned life of compromises.

I hadn't thought about my love life, but I had a vague plan to make concessions there, too. Though they raised me as an American, my parents expect me to marry someone Korean and give them grandchildren who look like them. This didn't seem like such a huge request when I was 14, but now I don't know what I'm going to do. I've never been in love with someone I dated, or dated someone I loved. (Since I can't bring myself even to entertain the thought of marrying the non-Korean men I'm attracted to, I've been dating only those I know I can stay clearheaded about.) And as I near that age when the question of marriage stalks every relationship, I can't help but wonder if my parents' expectations are responsible for the lack of passion in my life.

My parents didn't want their daughter to be Korean, but they don't want her fully American, either. Children of immigrants are living paradoxes. We are the first generation and the last. We are in this country for its opportunities, yet filial duty binds us. When my parents boarded the plane, they knew they were embarking on a rough trip. I don't think they imagined the rocks in the path of their daughter who can't even pronounce her own name.

5

Forgotten Streams in the Family Life Course: Utilization of Qualitative Retrospective Interviews in the Analysis of Lifelong Single Women's Family Careers

Katherine R. Allen
Robert S. Pickett

Theories of women's development within the family have tended to exclude women who do not experience the typical events of marriage and motherhood. The familial roles of adult women, such as wife, mother, grandmother, and widow, have been defined and studied in normative terms, but women who do not marry and who remain childless have been contrasted to their traditional peers as "deviant" (Uhlenberg, 1974). Thus, our perspectives have excluded variation from traditional pathways and have relegated nonparticipants in the procreative family life cycle to the residual category of "never-married."

The "phantom" lives of lifelong single women are examined here within the context of women's traditional and variant family careers. The approach taken combines the theoretical perspective of the life course and the qualitative research strategy of retrospective interviewing. This theoretical and method-

ological linkage provides a broader base than the family life cycle concept to approach differentiation in women's lives as variation rather than deviation. The research question guiding this inquiry is: What similarities and differences in the family life course may be identified by never-married and widowed women from the 1910 birth cohort? To answer this question, the analysis compares similarities and discontinuities in the women's lives during three broad periods: childhood, the transition to young adulthood, and adulthood.

The Life Course Perspective

The life course perspective is an interdisciplinary approach to studying individual and family change over time (Elder, 1977, 1981; Hareven, 1982). It offers a dynamic view of family process and incorporates the earlier ideas of pioneers in the developmental approach to the family (Hill and Mattessich, 1979; Hill and Rodgers, 1964; Rodgers, 1973). The life course notion incorporates the timing and transitions of age cohorts within the context of changing historical circumstances (Allen and Pickett, 1984; Elder, 1977; Hareven, 1977; Ryder, 1965).

The historical dimension of the family life course perspective provides an appreciation of the multiple dimensions of time (historical, social, family, and individual) that impinge on the lives of individuals and their families (Hareven, 1977, 1982).

Methodology

The Sample

The sample consisted of 30 women from the 1910 birth cohort who were homogeneous in nearly every respect except for their marital and parental careers. They were white, native-born, working-class women, born between 1907 and 1914, and in their seventies at the time of the interviews. The basic difference among these women was in their family careers. Fifteen women were widowed at the time of the study. They had married only once, had at least one child who survived to adulthood, became grandmothers, and became widowed after a marriage that lasted 20 years or more. The other 15 women did not marry and did not bear children. These two groups represented the most typical and the most atypical of women aged 65 and over, respectively (Glick, 1977).

The interviews were conducted by the first author from January to June 1994 in a metropolitan area in upstate New York. Participants were selected systematically from the total of 122 senior citizen clubs and centers in the city and county. The selection of sites was based on the attempt to locate subjects with working-class backgrounds. Sites were selected from all geographic areas of the city and county to include subjects from rural and urban communities.

Processes and Transitions in the Family Life Course

Harsh Realities of Life During Childhood

The historical experience of the American working class marked the lives of these 30 women. The combination of forces beyond their control, including gender, birth cohort, and socioeconomic status, set up early experiences that focused their expectations toward the harsh realities of life. At the time these women were born, people delayed or sacrificed their personal desires and individual transitions and placed the needs of their families first, as dictated by the prevailing theme of the familistic ideology (Hareven, 1977). Older members of the working class had insecure employment, were employed in hard physical labor, and had few work-related benefits to cushion disability, injury, or the death of the main wage earner (Katz, 1983). As daughters of working-class families, the women in this sample also endured hardship by being subjected to the social-historical effects of immigrant status. Nineteen women were the children or grandchildren of European immigrants, primarily from Italy, Germany, and Ireland. The sense of ethnic identity they developed reflected the insecurity of their early years, as the daughter of Italian immigrants noted:

> Those days when we were kids, they were all from their own country, and they all followed their own race, how they lived. They didn't bother with nobody else.

As working-class females, their educational and occupational opportunities were severely limited. They experienced the working conditions and precarious opportunities that plagued their elders:

> In my time, there were only three things I could have been that I know of. One was a teacher, one was a nurse, and one was a secretary.

Another major factor shaping the life course of these women was the early experience of loss. As children, six of the never-married women and three of the widows survived the death of a parent. In addition, two widows lost contact with their fathers when their parents divorced. Physical and mental illnesses were common in the families of all the subjects. Thus, the permanent or temporary loss of parents was a shared experience in their early lives; these vicissitudes required their families to adopt coping strategies characteristic of American working-class life in the late 19th and early 20th centuries (Elder, 1977; Hareven, 1977, 1982; Katz, 1983). The familistic ideology operated as a safety net by providing kinfolk as substitute caretakers for children whose parents died, divorced, or were institutionalized. As a consequence of being taken care of by adults other than their parents for some portion of their early lives, the women described close relationships with grandparents, aunts, older siblings, nuns, and other adults, most of whom were female. One widow explained,

> My mother and father separated for a while, never legally, and we all lived together in this rooming house. Then, my mother got TB when my sister was born, and she had to go up to the sanitarium for a year. So, my grandmother had to take care of us. My aunt took my sister because she was ill, and my grandmother took my brother and I.

Being cared for by women in times of family hardship was a lesson these women learned early in life. They carried forth this lesson of family commitment and caregiving into their adult lives, when the single women became caretakers of aging parents, siblings, nieces, and nephews, and the married women cared for their husbands, children, and grandchildren.

Discontinuities in Family Responsibilities During Young Adulthood

One factor that explains discontinuities in establishing a family of procreation versus remaining in the family of orientation is the intersection of the Great Depression with a critical period in the women's individual development. They were completing the transition to adulthood by the onset of the Great Depression, an adverse historical period that devastated many families and individuals economically and psychologically as well (Elder, 1974, 1981; Erikson, 1975). The Depression was one factor in ruling out marriage totally for the lifelong single women, whose labor was needed by their families of orientation.

The Depression was a factor, as well, in delaying the event of marriage for the five widows who married late, as typified in the experiences of a woman who married at age 30 in 1939:

> I went with him when the Depression was on, and after a couple of months, he asked me to marry him. I would have, but we both got out of a job at that time and then, three years later, he got back. He worked in a steel mill then. So we got married.

In addition to economic considerations, responsibilities toward the family of orientation took precedence in their early adulthood and delayed the opportunity to marry, as one woman who married in 1941 noted:

> Well, I thought there for a while I was going to be an old maid because I was 29. There again, I

was close to my mother. I took care of her, and she died of cancer, and I was home.

In contrast, then, to the 10 widows who married on time, the never-married women and the late-marrying widows shared the common experience of being in service to their families of orientation in a nurturant or economic capacity during the Great Depression.

The second factor that explains intracohort discontinuities is the way in which the women and their families interpreted the familistic ideology. The explanation for delayed marriage and permanent singlehood is related to the women's perception of their responsibilities to their parents during young adulthood. While two single women offered an account for not marrying by citing a broken engagement, the never-married women, in general, described not marrying as a process of remaining in their parents' home and going to work to help support themselves and their families:

> I brought the children up, and I used to take care of the house and the kids, make up the beds. See, my mother was never too well. She had very serious operations. I thought we were going to lose her so many times. . . . That is why I stayed home so much.

In addition, being the only daughter left at home to care for a widowed mother was common among the never-married women:

> I had to take my mother into consideration. No, I couldn't do anything. She had to be my prime concern. . . . So there was just no question about it. . . . It was my responsibility because my older brother was married, and my other brother was in school, so I was elected.

Remaining single had very little to do with the stereotype that women must be married in order to be fulfilled. Rather, marriage was avoided by the never-married women and delayed for five of the widows primarily because their family-of-orientation responsibilities came first. At a critical time in the life course,

when chances of marriage were greatest, the context of their individual lives denied the opportunity to marry.

During much of their young adulthood, the five widows who married late paralleled the lives of the permanent singles. They described themselves as "almost old maids" because family-of-orientation responsibilities kept them at home. For four of these women, marriage followed the death of a parent. In the fifth case, a woman who married against her parents' wishes when she was 30 years old thought that her mother's feelings, nevertheless, influenced her decision to marry:

> She didn't want me to get married. But see, I was 30, and I thought if I don't marry this guy, I mean everybody should get married, and I liked him immensely.

This passage reveals, as well, the implicit understanding that there is a certain point in time when it is appropriate to marry—if one plans to do so at all.

By contrast, widows who married in their late teens and early twenties did so because of opportunity and expectation. They recalled that their transition to early marriage was a time when their friends were also getting married:

> Like all my friends got married, because we all hung around together. I was the first one in my group to get married. And, then, they all spoiled my baby. They used to come to the house, and I was the only one with a baby. But, then, eventually, they got children, too, so our lives were all the same.

Another widow who married on time described the beginning of her marriage as a "liberation" from her mother's home. She stated that she left home as soon as she could to begin a household with her husband:

> With my large family and there wasn't much money in the house, we had to do everything ourselves, and I was the one who had to do

most of it. I never resented it, but I didn't realize until I got married what I did do before. It was an entirely different type of life for me. . . . Somebody now tried to do things for me.

However, the theme of hardship in childhood that was carried forth to young adulthood was still evident in the lives of women who did marry early. As young wives and mothers, their experiences revealed the struggles that young families endured.

I had all these kids, and there was never any money. My husband was not educated and just made it to the eighth grade. He was a trucker when I married him. He worked on a nursery. He ran a gas station and did whatever there was to do. He hauled milk from the farmers to the dairy. So, he was struggling all the time to put a roof over our heads and clothes on our backs and food in our mouths, so life was not easy.

Responsibility to the family was a lesson that was driven home to all members of the sample, regardless of eventual marital status. The familistic ideology they inherited from the past meant that they learned the lesson of subordinating their own needs to the survival of their families. Their lives were shaped by the influences of historical circumstances, social class, family composition, and gender. These influences testified to the childhood legacy that had become integrated into their adult lives: hardship, individual sacrifice, family survival, and women's involvement in caretaking. The content underlying the legacy was the same, but the expression of this legacy in adulthood was different: half of these women remained attached to their families of orientation by a process of events and transitions that kept them at home and prevented their opportunity to marry, and the other half eventually found their way to marriage and began their own families of procreation.

Thus, marital and parental status differentiated their lives in adulthood, revealing different streams in the family life course, but both groups of women exercised the mandates of the familistic ideology and became caretakers of their families.

Discontinuities in Family Caregiving

Both widows and never-married women described their lives in terms of the caretaking roles they performed in their families. Widows were connected in essential ways to their families of procreation. They cared for husbands, and they extended their family roles to descending generations as they become mothers, grandmothers, and great-grandmothers. As one widow remarked,

My grandson is the most important person to me. It used to be my son, but he moved away, so his son has taken his place for me.

The experience of caring for aging parents was not a common one for widows in this sample; only four widows did so. Of the four, only one widow assumed major responsibilities for the care of her parents, and she assumed this role after her husband died.

In contrast, lifelong single women were connected in essential ways to their families of orientation. Twelve never-married women took care of aging parents until their parents' deaths. Caring for aging parents was described as a responsibility that kept them tied to the family, whether as a voluntary process or as a duty. Fourteen of the never-married women functioned in a surrogate-mother role to their nieces and nephews or within an occupational capacity as a baby nurse or housekeeper. As adults, they expressed their childhood legacy by becoming the maintainers of the original family. As one woman noted,

I believe I was born for a certain purpose here on earth. . . . My purpose has been to take care of all these kids that have come along. Of course, they call me their second mother. I'm not as close as they would have been to their real mother, but I take care of those kids.

Never-married women maintained their families in a variety of roles through their relationships with ancestors, lateral kin, and younger kin. They were caretakers of parents, aunts, and uncles. They were companions and caretakers of siblings. They served as surrogate mothers to the descendants of siblings. They were also the "bearers of the family history" by maintaining the family heirlooms and weaving into their own life histories the stories about their ancestors. Their roles were active and essential. They kept people alive, they provided relief from day-to-day responsibilities of married siblings, and they kept the past alive.

This study reveals the common experience, among all the participating women, of allegiance to family cohesion and survival. Although the actual expression of this allegiance differed in adulthood according to marital and parental status, the underlying theme of family commitment as revealed in caretaking roles characterized the women's lives in this sample.

Conclusion

The broader context of caretaking reveals the process by which women, as individuals, extend and maintain families. Clearly, the linear progression from family of orientation to family of procreation characterized in the family life cycle concept reveals only one stream in the family life course. The experiences of lifelong single women reveal another. Awareness of their experiences broadens the notion of family life to include lifelong participation in the family of orientation and emphasizes, as well, the centrality of family in women's lives.

References

Allen, Katherine R., and Robert S. Pickett. 1984. "Historical perspectives on the life course of elderly women born in 1910." Journal of Applied Gerontology 3: 161-170.

Elder, Glen H., Jr. 1974. Children of the Great Depression. Chicago: University of Chicago Press.

Elder, Glen H., Jr. 1977. "Family history and the life course." Journal of Family History 2: 279-304.

Elder, Glen H., Jr. 1981. "History and the family: The discovery of complexity." Journal of Marriage and the Family 43: 489-519.

Erikson, Erik H. 1975. Life History and the Historical Moment. New York: Norton.

Glick, Paul C. 1977. "Updating the life cycle of the family." Journal of Marriage and the Family 39: 5-13.

Hareven, Tamara K. 1977. "Family time and historical time." Daedalus 106: 57-70.

Hareven, Tamara K. 1982. "The life course and aging in historical perspective." Pp. 1-26 in Tamara K. Hareven and Kathleen J. Adams (eds.), Aging and the Life Course: An Interdisciplinary Perspective. New York: Guilford.

Hill, Reuben, and Paul Mattessich. 1979. "Family development theory and life-span development." Pp. 161-204 in Paul B. Baltes and Orville G. Brim, Jr. (eds.), Life-Span Development and Behavior (Vol. 2). New York: Academic Press.

Hill, Reuben, and Roy H. Rodgers. 1964. "The developmental approach." Pp. 171-211 in Harold T. Christensen (ed.), Handbook of Marriage and the Family. Chicago: Rand McNally.

Katz, Michael B. 1983. Poverty and Policy in American History. New York: Academic Press.

Rodgers, Roy H. 1973. Family Interaction and Transaction: The Developmental Approach. Englewood Cliffs, NJ: Prentice Hall.

Ryder, Norman, B. 1965. "The cohort as a concept in the study of social change." American Sociological Review 30: 843-861.

Uhlenberg, Peter. 1974. "Cohort variations in family life cycle experiences of U.S. females." Journal of Marriage and the Family 36: 284-292.

6

Social Demography of Contemporary Families and Aging

Christine L. Himes

Among the elderly the most common living arrangement for men is to be living with their wife—about 75 percent of men over age 65 in 1990 were living with their spouse. The living arrangements of women are slightly different. The greater chance of a woman outliving her husband means that elderly women are more likely than men to be living alone. This pattern becomes especially noticeable after age 75, when over one-half of all women are living alone. Older women in the African American and Hispanic populations are also less likely to live with a spouse as they age; however, the trend is not toward living alone but toward living with relatives—children, siblings, or other family members.

The Census definition of a family unit is useful since most statistics on families are collected for households, but it is not sufficient because many of a person's family members are not residents of the same household and many households consist of other types of relatives. The picture of the families of older persons can be broadened by looking at each of the demographic processes—mortality, fertility, and marriage—that affect family structure. An examination of the trends across time and dif-

ferences across ethnic groups in these processes reveals their importance in explaining the variation in family structures.

Mortality

Life expectancy at birth has been increasing steadily in the United States (National Center for Health Statistics, 1992). For the white population, life expectancy at birth in 1940 was 62.1 years for males and 66.6 years for females. By 1989 (the latest year available) life expectancy had reached 72.7 years for white males and 79.2 years for white females. This increase in longevity has been more dramatic in the nonwhite population. Vital statistics data indicate that among the nonwhite population, life expectancy between 1940 and 1989 increased by nearly 16 years to 67.1 years for males and by 20 years to 75.2 years for females.

This lengthening life expectancy has resulted in two major changes in family structure and function. First, more generations are alive at any one time, increasing the vertical spread of families (Watkins, Menken and

Bongaarts, 1987). Second, the longer life expectancy has resulted in a greater proportion of years of life spent with chronic health problems (Verbrugge, 1984; Crimmins, Saito and Ingegneri, 1989).

Since increased longevity brings with it an increase in the number of years spent with disabilities, an older person will most likely receive any needed assistance at a later age and for a longer period of time. Family members, especially adult daughters, have been the traditional providers of care for impaired elderly (Stone, Cafferata and Sangl, 1987). The need to provide care for a parent for longer periods of time and at later ages will place a larger responsibility on other family members who may themselves be beginning to suffer from age-related impairments.

Fertility

Fertility trends over the past 40 years have been the subject of considerable attention. A rise in birthrates between 1945 and 1965 resulted in a very large group of children—the baby boom—who are now entering middle age. The very size of this group has focused attention on their needs and influenced political and economic decisions of the entire nation. In particular, there is concern in certain circles about the ability of the nation's Social Security system to meet the needs of this large group as it reaches retirement age. However, before retirement the members of the baby boom generation will experience the aging of their parents, who are just now entering the older ages. The influence of this experience may serve as a motivation for concentrated efforts to expand care for the elderly.

Understanding the pattern of past fertility is very important for determining the number of adult children of the elderly. The most important fertility change over time has been in the proportion of women who remain childless. There is a striking difference over time and between white and African American women in the proportion childless (U.S. Bureau of the Census, 1975). Among white women aged 65 to 69 in 1990, about 10 percent had not borne a child compared to 17.5 percent of African American women of the same age. The low birthrates during the 1930s result in an increase in the childless population at older ages. In the age group 85 to 89, 19.5 percent of white women and 28.1 percent of African American women were childless. In contrast, among women who began childbearing during the 1950s, childlessness was rare; 7 percent of white women and 11 percent of African American women between the ages of 55 and 60 in 1990 were childless.

Current fertility patterns are also important to the families of the elderly through their effect on the numbers and age distributions of grandchildren. The recent increase in early childbearing creates young parents and young grandparents. These young parents, often single mothers, are frequently in need of greater assistance than parents who bear their children later (Tienda and Angel, 1982; Furstenberg, Brooks-Gunn and Morgan, 1987). These young parents often turn to their own parents as a primary resource for financial and emotional assistance and support (Eggebeen and Hogan, 1990).

Marriage

The third demographic process involved in the formation and structure of families is marriage and marital dissolution. Despite recent declines, marriage continues to be a nearly universal experience among Americans, and the vast majority of persons currently over age 65 have been married (U.S. Bureau of the Census, 1991). In 1990, only 4.9 percent of white women and 4.0 percent of white men over age 65 had never married. These percentages are slightly higher among the African American population; 5.3 percent of women and 5.6 [percent] of men had never married. The percentage of Hispanic elderly never married indicates a different type of marriage pattern: 5.4 percent of Hispanic women over age 65 have never married, a figure similar to that for white and African American populations, but only 2.6 percent of elderly Hispanic men have never married.

Although marriage rates are declining at younger ages, the proportion of the older population who have never been married has actually decreased over the past 20 years. This pattern represents the high rates of marriage that existed in the past. Groups of people reaching age 65 in the next 10 years, those age 55 to 64 in 1990, will have experienced even higher rates of marriage than those currently over age 65. However, this pattern apparently will reverse further in the future if the younger age groups continue their lower rates of marriage as they age.

Not all marriages endure into old age. Some may dissolve because of divorce or the death of a spouse. The divorce rate in the United States has generally declined since experiencing sharp increases in the late 1970s and early 1980s (National Center for Health Statistics, 1991). However, there has been little variation in the divorce rate for men and women over age 65. Among the elderly, divorce continues to be a relatively rare experience; approximately two out of 1,000 married men over age 65 will divorce each year and less than two out of 1,000 married women.

Many divorced persons, particularly men, will remarry. As a result, few older persons are single because of divorce. Based on data in the Current Population Survey (U.S. Bureau of the Census, 1991), just under 5 percent of white men and women over age 65 were divorced and unmarried in 1990. The chances of divorce are higher, and the chances of remarriage lower, in the African American population, and the proportions of older African Ameri-

cans who are divorced reflect this difference; 8 percent of elderly African American men and 9 percent of elderly African American women are divorced and single.

The past high rates of marriage, coupled with lower rates of divorce, create a situation in which the current population over age 55 is more likely to have a spouse available in the household than will be the case in the future—offsetting some of the gains in longer life expectancy. The higher mortality of men and the tendency for women to marry men of an older age create a disparity in the presence of spouses for men and women. Elderly African American women are much more likely than any other group to be living without a spouse. Twenty-five percent of African American women over age 65 are living with a husband compared to 40 percent of white women and 40 percent of Hispanic women. A similar disparity is seen in the probability that an elderly African American man is living with his wife. Fifty-four percent of African American men live with a wife, while 76 percent of white men and 73 percent of Hispanic men are living with a wife.

The families of the elderly are affected not only by the rates of marriage and divorce they experience but also by the experience of their children. The trend toward later ages at marriage and lower proportions of young adults marrying results in an increase in the proportion of adult children between 18 and 34 who are living with their parents (U.S. Bureau of the Census, 1991). In 1990, 11.5 percent of young adults 25 to 34 years old lived with their parents, compared to 8 percent in 1970. Over one-half of young adults aged 18 to 24 were members of their parents' household in 1990. Most of these adult children had never married and were childless—97 percent of those 18 to 24 and 80 percent of those 25 to 34. However, 13 percent of the older age group living with their parents also had children living with them, creating three-generation, or more, family households.

Future Implications

In the near future, elderly people will have a greater number of family members—a result of past decreases in mortality, high levels of fertility, and high levels of marriage. This network of family may be a strong source of support for older persons. However, the changing demographics of younger families are increasing the possibility that younger family members will turn to older members for support. Other factors, such as the increased participation of women in the labor force and the greater mobility of family members, are also likely to have an impact on the ability of families to interact and exchange support. Recent decreases in the rates of marriage and fertility, along with increasing rates of divorce, are creating more complicated family structures. Future elderly may have more vertical distribution in family members, that is, they may be more likely to have grandchildren and great-grandchildren, but each generation is likely to be smaller.

References

Crimmins, E. M., Saito, Y. and Ingegneri, D., 1989. "Changes in Life Expectancy and Disability-Free Life Expectancy in the United States." *Population and Development Review* 15(2):235-67.

Eggebeen, D. J. and Hogan, D. P., 1990. "Giving Between the Generations in American Families." *Human Nature* 1(3):211-32.

Furstenberg, F., Brooks-Gunn, J. and Morgan, S. P., 1987. *Adolescent Mothers in Later Life*. Cambridge: Cambridge University Press.

National Center for Health Statistics, 1991. "Advance Report of Final Divorce Statistics, 1988." *Monthly Vital Statistics Report* 39(12, Supplement).

National Center for Health Statistics, 1992. "Advance Report of Final Mortality Statistics, 1989." *Monthly Vital Statistics Report* 40(8, Supplement).

Stone, R., Cafferata, G. L. and Sangl, J., 1987. "Caregivers of the Frail Elderly: A National Profile." *Gerontologist* 27:616-26.

Tienda, M. and Angel, R., 1982. "Determinants of Extended Household Structure: Cultural Pattern or Economic Need?" *American Journal of Sociology* 87:1360-83.

U.S. Bureau of the Census, 1975. "Women by Number of Children Ever Born." *1970 Census of the Population, Final report PC(2)-3A*. Washington, D.C.: Government Printing Office.

U.S. Bureau of the Census, 1991. "Marital Status and Living Arrangements: March 1990." *Current Population Reports, Series P-20, No. 450*. Washington, D.C.: Government Printing Office.

Verbrugge, L., 1984. "Longer Life but Worsening Health? Trends in Health and Mortality of Middle-Aged and Older Persons." *Milbank Memorial Fund Quarterly* 62:475-519.

Watkins, S. C., Menken, J. A. and Bongaarts, J., 1987. "Demographic Foundations of Family Change." *American Sociological Review* 52(3):346-58.

7

The Last Diamond of Summer

B. K. Loren

The sweet smell of columbine, lilac, and wild rose trickled through the spring air. My grandmother stood, in high-heeled shoes, on the very top of the makeshift pitcher's mound in the center of the green meadow that surrounded our mountain home. She ignored her tight, restrictive dress, bent slightly forward at the waist, squinted and nodded at our nonexistent catcher, then wound up and released the pitch. It swooshed over home plate. With a swing and a crack, I sent it sailing like a rainbow over the meadow.

We played until the spring twilight was the color of honey and the crescent moon rocked in the dark blue cradle of two shadowed peaks.

"One more," I called.

"One more," she called back. The crisp sound of her voice cut the thin mountain air like the music of a river.

If I gave her a line drive, she caught it. If I sent a pop fly out to left field, she ran after it, high heels and all, and most times, she made it back to the infield in time to hold me at third.

That was 1962.

By 1963, she was dead.

Even if I had known that the summer of 1962 would be the last summer I would spend with my grandmother, I don't think that her memory would be any clearer than it is now. I inhaled every moment of that summer as if it were simultaneously my first and last breath. My grandmother's cheek, smooth and warm against mine when we snuggled up to chase away evening chill; the smooth scent of her perfume; the way her hands curved around a baseball in a way that mine had yet to learn; these moments make up my most vivid childhood memories.

As I grew older, I began to wonder about the connection I had with my grandmother. I did not know my mother's mother very long. She never lived with us, and I can't remember ever spending the night in her house.

I do remember visiting her though. And I remember that she felt like a "buddy." She understood me in a way that I felt no one else did. My grandmother was the only adult who did not reprimand me for being so active and competitive. She played baseball *with* me. She understood why, when I was in ballet class, I liked to run as fast and leap as high as I could— instead of running *gracefully* to make all the moves look delicate and lacy. She slipped me a dime before each ballet class because she knew I hated to attend them—and she knew it made my mother happy when I did attend. Still, the palmed dime and the understanding nod when I had to do "The Flying Dutchman" over and over again did not really account for the impact she had on my dreams and memories.

Twenty-four years later, I sat in a restaurant with my mother. She had traveled from Colorado to see where, and if, I had made a home for myself in California. I had succeeded and it was great to share it with her; but it was not like my home in Colorado. I had trekked across those mountains on skis, hiked them in summer, climbed many of their peaks, kayaked the rivers that ran through them and biked their deepest back trails. I knew the sky and its birds, where they nested and when they migrated. That land was my religion. And now, I felt vaguely exiled. I could not return home and feel altogether welcomed because my father disapproved of my lifestyle as a lesbian—and my mother disapproved of his disapproval. Still, I wondered, occasionally, if she also felt a little ashamed.

So there, with a cheap restaurant candle flickering dimly between us, casting amber shadows across the table, I asked her.

"Mom, are you ashamed of me?"

I will never forget the look on her face. I had listened to my mother tell the story of losing her first child to sudden infant death syndrome, watched her bail my brother out of jail, and listened to her on the phone while she consoled her friends who were sick or dying. But I don't think I had ever seen her look so shocked, so hurt, as she did in that moment.

"Why on earth would you think that I was ashamed of you?" Her voice cracked.

"Well, I thought you might be ashamed because I am in love with a woman."

My mother paid the bill and walked briskly out of the restaurant.

"Are you angry?" I asked, following behind her to the car.

"No," she said.

"Where are you going?"

"Home. I brought something I want to show you."

At home, my mother pulled some old leather photo albums from her suitcase. Faded black and white photos were affixed to pages worn thin by time. I opened the leather cover and turned each page slowly, careful not to pull the paper from its tattered binding. Photos fell like autumn leaves into my lap. I held them individually. I recognized my grandmother, but I had never before seen her in this light. I looked from the photos to my mother.

"Your grandmother was like you," she said. "She lived with Margaret for twenty-five years."

I was silent for a long time. When I could talk again, I was only able to mutter, "What about Grandpa?"

"He was fine with it. He loved your grandmother, and she loved him. But they were not in love like Margaret and Grandma. Nonetheless, we were a family. We all loved each other and were very happy."

"And that's how you were raised, Mom?"

She nodded her head, then held my hand. "Don't ever think that I am ashamed of you."

A quarter century later, I finally understand the summer of 1962. I was bonded with my grandmother by invisible ties that, in her day, were unspeakable. But her love for Margaret, and for the rest of her family, was strong in the face of that silence. It endured, as we all endure. In a world that paves shopping malls over wildflowers, and superimposes false restrictions on the delicate terrain of our deepest emotions, we have learned to make safe places for what we truly love; we have learned to endure.

8

Intergenerational Solidarity and the Structure of Adult Child-Parent Relationships in American Families

Merril Silverstein
Vern L. Bengtson

Introduction

Recently there has been much scholarly debate concerning the decline of the contemporary American family (Popenoe 1988; Stacey 1990; Skolnick 1991; Bengtson, Rosenthal, and Burton 1995). This debate centers on whether the family has become ill equipped to handle the problems and dependencies—and to ensure the well-being—of its members. Proponents of the "family decline" hypothesis primarily focus on the negative consequences of changing family structure—resulting from divorce and single parenting—for the psychological, social, and economic well-being of dependent children (see Popenoe 1993). Further, they maintain that social norms legitimating the pursuit of individual over collective goals and the availability of alternative social groups for the satisfaction of basic human needs have fatally weakened the institution of the family as an agent of socialization and a source of nurturance (Lasch 1977).

A broader conceptualization of the contingencies inherent in family relations (as exemplified by the modified-extended family) has been termed the *latent kin matrix*—"a web of continually shifting linkages that provide the potential for activating and intensifying close kin relationships" (Riley 1983, p. 441). Increasing heterogeneity in intergenerational family structures—due to divorce/remarriage, the prolongation of intergenerational ties, and geographic dispersion—and the more voluntaristic, less contractual basis for maintaining intergenerational relations are taken as evidence for growing uncertainty in the function of kinship ties. An important feature of the latent matrix is that family members may remain dormant for long periods of time and only emerge as a resource when the need arises (Riley and Riley 1993). If family relationships alternately shift between latency and activity, then it is important to consider the latent *potential* of kinship relations—insofar as it triggers or enables manifest functions—before making pronouncements about the utility of the contemporary family.

Intergenerational Solidarity

Building on theoretical and empirical advances in the social psychology of small group and family cohesion (Hechter 1987; Homans 1950; Heider 1958; Jansen 1952; Rogers and Sebald 1962; Hill and Hansen 1960; Nye and Rushing 1969), our previous research has codified six principal dimensions of solidarity between generations (Bengtson and Schrader 1982; Roberts, Richards, and Bengtson 1991). These dimensions comprise (1) structure (factors such as geographic distance that constrain or enhance interaction between family members), (2) association (frequency of social contact and shared activities between family members), (3) affect (feelings of emotional closeness, affirmation, and intimacy between family members), (4) consensus (actual or perceived agreement in opinions, values, and lifestyles between family members), (5) function (exchanges of instrumental and financial assistance and support between family members), and (6) norms (strength of obligation felt toward other family members).

We are guided by the following research questions: How many types are needed to represent adequately the diverse forms of adult intergenerational relationships in American society? How can these types best be characterized, and what is their representation in the population? Considering gender differences, do the same types emerge for relations of adult children with mothers as for relations with fathers? If so, are there differences in the distribution of types between the two kinds of relationships? Are demographic characteristics of adult children and parents associated with the type of relationship they are likely to have with each other?

Method

Sample

We address the research questions raised above using data from a nationally representative survey undertaken by the American Association of Retired Persons (AARP) in collaboration with a research team from Harvard University and the University of Southern California. The survey involved a sample of 1,500 adults ages 18-90 years old from randomly selected households in the 48 contiguous states, who were interviewed by telephone in July and August of 1990. One resident from each contacted household was randomly selected for interview; residents of institutions and group quarters were not part of the sampling frame.

Since our analysis focuses solely on the relations of adult children who live apart from their parents, we exclude the 3.8% of adult children in the sample who live with their mothers and 1.5% who live with their fathers. Thus, the operational sample consists of 971 adult children who have at least one surviving noncoresident parent. Of these, 61% have two living parents, 28% have only a living mother, and 11% have only a living father. Adult children in the sample evaluated a total of 1,564 parental relations, 864 (55%) with mothers and 700 (45%) with fathers.

Measures of Intergenerational Solidarity

Adult children in the sample were asked a series of questions about the nature of their relationship with each surviving biological parent. These questions, reflecting five of the six dimensions of intergenerational solidarity, form the building blocks of our typology. Normative solidarity is not considered in the typology because it is measured in the AARP survey as a *generalized* sense of responsibility for older par-

TABLE 8.1 Latent Classes of Intergenerational Relations

Class	Definition
Tight-knit	Adult children are engaged with their parents based on all six indicators of solidarity.
Sociable	Adult children are engaged with their parents based on geographic proximity, frequency of contact, emotional closeness, and similarity of opinions but not based on providing assistance and receiving assistance.
Obligatory	Adult children are engaged with their parents based on geographic proximity, and frequency of contact but not based on emotional closeness and similarity of opinions. While only about one-third of children in this class are engaged in providing and receiving assistance, this proportion is slightly higher than that for the sample as a whole.
Intimate but distant	Adult children are engaged with their parents on emotional closeness and similarity of opinions but not based on geographic proximity, frequency of contact, providing assistance, and receiving assistance.
Detached	Adult children are not engaged with their parents based on any of the six indicators of solidarity.

ents and not as the responsibility felt by each respondent for his or her own parents.

Measurement Model of Intergenerational Types

The five derived classes typify various sociological models of contemporary families (see Table 8.1). The *tight-knit* class is most characteristic of the traditional (or corporate) extended family, while the *detached* class is most emblematic of the isolated extended family (Parsons 1944). Relationships in the other three classes are connected on some but not all the dimensions of solidarity, representing "variegated" forms of child-parent relations. The *sociable* and *intimate but distant* types are forms of the modified extended family in which functional exchange is absent, but where high levels of affinity may hold the potential for future exchange (Rosenmayer 1968; Litwak 1985). Yet, in intimate-but-distant relations, goodwill

between the generations translates neither into action nor interaction. That these two types of relations are functionally independent, in spite of being otherwise integrated, may be related to the lack of *need*, or a preference for intergenerational autonomy. Interestingly, we also found evidence for an *obligatory* type of extended family that is structurally connected and has an average level of functional exchange but lacks strong positive sentiment. We attribute the structural and functional integration of generations in the absence of affinity to a sense of duty on the part of the adult child.

Distribution of Intergenerational Types and Gender of Parent

For adult child-mother relations, the most common type is the tight-knit, with nearly one in three (31%) of such relations falling into this, the most cohesive group. The next most common type, consisting of more than one-quarter

(28%) of adult child-mother relations, is the sociable, followed by the intimate but distant (19%), the obligatory (16%), and last, the detached (7%).

Where detached relations are relatively rare among child-mother relations, they are the most prevalent among adult child-father relations, comprising more than one-quarter (27%) of all such relations. The sociable is the next most common child-father type (23%), followed by the tight-knit (20%), the obligatory (16%), and the intimate but distant (14%).

The most striking contrast between the two distributions is that the detached type is *least* common among child-mother relations and *most* common among child-father relations. Additionally, child-mother relations are more likely than child-father relations to be either tight-knit, sociable, and intimate but distant and less likely to be obligatory. Taken together, these gender-related patterns demonstrate that adult intergenerational solidarity is stronger with mothers than with fathers.

Differentiating Among Types of Intergenerational Relations

Relations with mothers. Turning first to the effects of child's gender, we note that daughters are more likely than sons to have a tight-knit relationship with their mothers and are less likely than sons to have an obligatory relationship.

Parental marital status is also related to the type of relationship adult children are likely to have with their mothers. Marital disruption in the parental generation appears to weaken the strength of the maternal bond. Adult children are more likely to have obligatory and detached relations with divorced/separated mothers than they are with married mothers. In addition children have a higher probability of having obligatory relationships with widowed than with married mothers.

Age has a linear effect on the three types of relationships with mothers. Older adult children are less likely than younger adult children to have tight-knit relations and more likely than younger children to have sociable and detached relationships with mothers. However, there are no significant quadratic effects of age in these equations, providing little evidence for a resurgence in relationship quality with the aging of the child.

Divorced children are less likely than married children to have intimate but distant relations. Otherwise, marital status of child exerts little influence on relationship qualities.

Race and ethnicity variables are associated with types of maternal relationships. Both blacks and Hispanics are less likely than non-Hispanic whites to have obligatory relationships with their mothers, and blacks are less likely than whites to have detached relationships. This suggests that intergenerational contact and exchange between generations in minority families may be based more on altruistic than on obligatory or utilitarian motivations—affirming the cohesive strength traditionally ascribed to black and Hispanic families (McAdoo 1981; Burton 1996) and the matrifocal tilt of intergenerational relations in such families (Taylor and Chatters 1991).

Income is inversely associated with having tight-knit relationships with mothers. That adult children with lower income have a greater likelihood of having this, the most cohesive type of relationship, is consistent with research showing stronger family orientations among lower- and working-class individuals (Kulis 1991). Homeownership is associated with four out of the five types of maternal relationships. Homeowners are more likely than those who rent to have tight-knit and sociable types of relations and less likely to be intimate but distant or detached. Homeownership may reflect the preference of adult children to purchase a home based on its proximity to parents with whom they desire to have regular interaction and exchanges (O'Bryant 1983).

Respondents who have at least one dependent child in the household have a significantly lower probability of being intimate but distant with their mothers. Given inequality in child-rearing duties between men and women, we also tested for interactions between gender of adult child and having a dependent child in the household. Significant effects were found for predicting the probability of having tight-knit relations with mothers. Confirming our expectation, the interaction term (not shown) indicates that when a dependent child is in the household, daughters are more likely than sons to have tight-knit relationships with mothers. It is likely that mothers are providing services that help their daughters cope with the demands of raising children.

Relations with fathers. Gender of child does not significantly predict membership in any of the latent classes. However, father's marital status is an important predictor of relationship type. Adult children are less likely to have tight-knit, sociable, and intimate-but-distant relationships and are more likely to have detached relationships with divorced/separated fathers than with married fathers; indeed, relations with divorced fathers are 33% more likely to be detached. In addition, relations with widowed fathers tend less to be tight-knit and tend more to be detached compared to relations with married fathers.

Age is also a significant predictor of paternal relationship types. As with relations with mothers, older children are less likely than younger children to have tight-knit relations with fathers and more likely to have sociable and detached relations with them. Further analyses of adjusted predicted values reveal that the probability of being detached from fathers is low in young adulthood (.13 at 21 years old), increases with age, peaking in middle age (.27 at 43 years old), after which it begins to decline as the adult child reaches old age (.13 at 68 years old).

Neither race/ethnicity nor child's marital status predict child-father type. However, higher income is associated with a greater probability of being intimate but distant with fathers. This is consistent with the greater geographical dispersion and lower affiliation with extended family typically found among those with higher social class.

In addition, homeownership differentiates child-father relations. As in the analysis of child-mother relations, owning a home is associated with a higher probability of having tight-knit and sociable relations with fathers and a lower probability of having intimate-but-distant and detached relations with them. However, having a dependent child in the household does not predict type of relationship with fathers nor does this variable significantly interact with adult child's gender.

Discussion

We began this article by suggesting that contemporary social commentaries that paint the family as an institution in decline have used too broad a brush to characterize intergenerational family relationships. Portrayals of the family solely in terms of lost functions fail to capture the diversity, as well as the latent potential, embedded in such relationships. Using the conceptual model of intergenerational solidarity as a theoretical guide, we have identified five underlying types of intergenerational family relationships.

Several aspects of the resulting typology are noteworthy in light of the current decline-of-family debate. First, none of the types constitute a majority of relationships or represent a "typical" relationship: for example, among child-mother relations, the most common type—the tight-knit—comprises less than one-third of total relations, while for child-father relations the most common type—the detached—comprises about one-quarter of total relations. Given the heterogeneity of types, we conclude that it is misleading to generalize about a "modal" type of intergenerational family, as is often done on both sides of the debate.

Second, the prevalence of "variegated" types (i.e., those other than tight-knit and detached) represent a majority of relations with mothers (62%) and with fathers (53%). Several of the "variegated" types in particular—the sociable and the intimate but distant—evoke earlier sociological models of intergenerational kinship structures, collectively labeled "modified-extended," where family members are geographically dispersed but not necessarily emotionally or socially distanced. While functional exchanges are less prominent in these types of families, a reservoir of latent solidarity may motivate or enable the exchange of assistance should it be needed in the future.

There are also important sources of heterogeneity in the distribution of types with respect to gender, marital status, and age. Most notable is the importance of parents' gender in structuring intergenerational relationships. We found a wide schism in the types of relations that adult children maintain with their mothers and with their fathers. Indeed, almost four times as many children are detached from their fathers as from their mothers, supporting claims that it is the "disappearance of fathers" that is responsible for family decline (Furstenberg and Nord 1985). It is likely that the weakness of child-father relations in adulthood has its antecedents in early family socialization, including gender-specific allocation of nurturing roles to women and in custody decisions that favor mothers over fathers (Hagestad 1986; Rossi 1984; Rossi 1993).

The gender of the adult child plays less a role than predicted. While daughters are more likely to be tight-knit and less likely to have obligatory relations with mothers, there are no differences between daughters and sons in relations with fathers. These results suggest that there is a unique salience to the mother-daughter bond and that paternal relations are relatively weak with both sons and daughters.

The divorce or separation of parents weakens intergenerational relations with both mothers and fathers, as it is positively associated with each relationship being detached, and, for fathers, it is also inversely associated with having a relationship characterized by strong affinity. Thus, the magnitude of the effects of marital disruption are more pronounced in relations with fathers than in relations with mothers; the effect of parental divorce/separation on the likelihood of having detached relations is about five times greater with fathers than it is with mothers. These results echo other findings documenting the deleterious effects of parental divorce on intergenerational relations with fathers (Umberson 1992; White 1992). Widowhood also erodes relationships of children more so with fathers than with mothers. The potential for the dependencies associated with widowhood to strain close family relationships (Ferraro and Barresi 1982; Morgan 1984) is heightened among widowed fathers who generally lack the skills necessary for household management (Umberson, Wortman, and Kessler 1992). In addition, since widowed fathers have a greater chance of remarrying than widowed mothers (Goldscheider 1990), widowers may be more likely than widows to have dual family allegiances. Taken together, our results concerning the effect of marital disruption on intergenerational relations suggest the tenuous role played by divorced and widowed fathers in the lives of their biological children (Amato et al. 1995; Cooney and Uhlenberg 1990) and foreshadow possible deficits in their social support portfolio when they reach old age (Goldscheider 1990).

With respect to age, our results suggest that there is a realignment of child-parent relations with the aging of the child. Consistent with the life-course theoretical perspective (Bengtson and Allen 1993; Elder 1984; Elder and O'Rand 1995), younger adult children are more likely than older children to have integrated relations with their mothers and their fathers and less likely to have detached relations with them. Young adults who have just been launched from the parental household are in the most need of social and tangible resources from parents, while in middle age, children occupy career and parenting roles that may limit their ability to invest in parental relationships. Children in young adulthood are enmeshed with their parents to satisfy emotional and material needs resulting from their transition to independence, and middle-aged children disengage from their parents because alternative family and occupational demands may supersede functional integration with them.

Further, we found a curvilinear relationship between age of child and whether relations with fathers are detached. When the child passes beyond middle age (and when their fathers pass into advanced old age) the likelihood of being detached is as low as it was in young adulthood. This pattern suggests that adult children reconcile with their elderly fathers at a stage of the fathers' lives when support needs are at a maximum and when intimate family relationships become most salient—an interpretation consistent with socioemotional selectivity theory in developmental social psychology (Carstensen 1992).

Conclusion

In summary, our findings portray adult intergenerational relationships in American families as diverse but reflecting five principal types based on affinal, structural, and functional dimensions of solidarity. At the broadest level, heterogeneity in intergenerational relationships can be attributed to historical trends over the past century, such as geographic and economic mobility of generations, the surge in divorce rates, increasing numbers of later-life families, and a shift away from the family of orientation as the basis for everyday social life

in adulthood. For intergenerational families, particularly in paternal relations, these trends may have increased the uncertainty associated with enactment of supportive roles. On the other hand, our research demonstrates that adult children, especially daughters, serve as significant elements in the kin matrix of mothers. This suggests that the primacy of the mother-daughter bond—rooted in biosocial mechanisms of early socialization—extends through much of the adult life course (Rossi 1984).

References

Amato, Paul R., Sandra J. Rezac, and Alan Booth. 1995. "Helping between Parents and Young Adult Offspring: The Role of Parental Marital Quality, Divorce, and Remarriage." *Journal of Marriage and the Family* 57:363-74.

Bengtson, Vern L., and Katherine R. Allen. 1993. "The Life Course Perspective Applied to Families over Time." Pp. 469-98 in *Sourcebook of Family Theories and Methods: A Contextual Approach*, edited by Pauline G. Boss, William J. Doherty, Ralph LaRossa, Walter R. Schumm, and Suzanne K. Steinmetz. New York: Plenum Press.

Bengtson, Vern L., Carolyn Rosenthal, and Linda Burton. 1995. "Paradoxes of Families and Aging." Pp. 234-59 in *Handbook of Aging and the Social Sciences*, edited by Robert Binstock and Linda George. New York: Academic Press.

Bengtson, Vern L., and Sandi S. Schrader. 1982. "Parent-Child Relations." Pp. 115-85 in *Handbook of Research Instruments in Social Gerontology*, vol. 2. Edited by David J. Mangen and Warren A. Peterson. Minneapolis: University of Minnesota Press.

Burton, Linda M. 1996. "Intergenerational Patterns of Providing Care in African-American Families with Teenage Childbearers: Emergent Patterns in an Ethnographic Study." Pp. 79-96 in *Adult Intergenerational Relations: Effects of Social Change*, edited by Vern L. Bengtson, K. Warner Schaie, and Linda M. Burton. New York: Springer.

Carstensen, Laura L. 1992. "Social and Emotional Patterns in Adulthood: Support for Socioemotional Selectivity Theory." *Psychology and Aging* 7:331-38.

Cooney, Teresa, and Peter Uhlenberg. 1990. "The Role of Divorce in Men's Relations with Their Adult Children after Mid-Life." *Journal of Marriage and the Family* 52:677-88.

Elder, Glen H., Jr. 1984. "Families, Kin, and the Life Course: A Sociological Perspective." Pp. 80-136 in *Advances in Child Development Research: The Family*, edited by Ross Parke. Chicago: University of Chicago Press.

Elder, Glen H., and Angela M. O'Rand. 1995. "Adult Lives in a Changing Society." Pp. 452-75 in *Sociological Perspectives on Social Psychology*, edited by Karen S. Cook, Gary Alan Fine, and James S. House. Needham Heights, Mass.: Allyn & Bacon.

Ferraro, Kenneth F., and Charles M. Barresi. 1982. "The Impact of Widowhood on the Social Relations of Older Persons." *Research on Aging* 4:227-47.

Furstenberg, Frank, and C. W. Nord. 1985. "Parenting Apart: Patterns of Childrearing after Marital Disruption." *Journal of Marriage and the Family* 47:893-905.

Goldscheider, Frances K. 1990. "The Aging of the Gender Revolution." *Research on Aging* 12:531-45.

Hagestad, Gunhild. 1986. "The Family: Women and Grandparents as Kinkeepers." Pp. 141-60 in *Our Aging Society*, edited by Alan Pifer and Lydia Bronte. New York: Norton.

Hechter, M. 1987. *Principles of Group Solidarity.* Berkeley and Los Angeles: University of California Press.

Heider, F. 1958. *The Psychology of Interpersonal Relations.* New York: John Wiley.

Hill, Reuben, and D. A. Hansen. 1960. "The Identification of Conceptual Frameworks Utilized in Family Study." *Marriage and Family Living* 12:299-311.

Homans, G. F. 1950. *The Human Group.* New York: Harcourt, Brace, & World.

Jansen, L. T. 1952. "Measuring Family Solidarity." *American Sociological Review* 17:727-33.

Kulis, Stephen S. 1991. *Why Honor Thy Father and Mother? Class, Mobility, and Family Ties in Later Life.* New York: Garland.

Lasch, Christopher. 1977. *Haven in a Heartless World: The Family Besieged.* New York: Basic Books.

Litwak, Eugene. 1985. *Helping the Elderly: The Complementary Roles of Informal Networks and Formal Systems.* New York: Guilford.

McAdoo, Harriett P. 1981. *Black Families.* Beverly Hills, Calif.: Sage.

Morgan, Leslie A. 1984. "Changes in Family Interaction Following Widowhood." *Journal of Marriage and the Family* 46:323-31.

Nye, F. I., and W. Rushing. 1969. "Toward Family Measurement Research." In *Marriage and Family*, edited by J. Hadden and E. Borgatta. Itasca, Ill.: Peacock.

O'Bryant, Shirley L. 1983. "The Subjective Value of 'Home' to Older Homeowners." *Journal of Housing for the Elderly* 1:29-43.

Parsons, Talcott. 1944. "The Social Structure of the Family." Pp. 173-201 in *The Family: Its Function and Destiny*, edited by R. N. Anshen. New York: Harper.

Popenoe, David. 1988. *Disturbing the Nest: Family Change and Decline in Modern Societies.* New York: Aldine de Gruyter.

Popenoe, David. 1993. "American Family Decline, 1960-1990: A Review and Appraisal." *Journal of Marriage and the Family* 55:527-55.

Riley, Matilda W. 1983. "The Family in an Aging Society: A Matrix of Latent Relationships." *Journal of Family Issues* 4:439-54.

Riley, Matilda W., and John W. Riley, Jr. 1993. "Connections: Kin and Cohort." Pp. 169-90 in *The Changing Contract across Generations*, edited by Vern L. Bengtson and W. Andrew Achenbaum. Hawthorne, N.Y.: Aldine de Gruyter.

Roberts, Robert E. L., Leslie N. Richards, and Vern L. Bengtson. 1991. "Intergenerational Solidarity in Families: Untangling the Ties that Bind." Pp. 11-46 in *Marriage and Family Review.* Vol. 16, *Families: Intergenerational and Generational Connections, Part One*, edited by S. K. Pfeifer and Marvin B. Sussman. Binghamton, N.Y.: Haworth.

Rogers, E. M., and H. Sebald. 1962. "Familism, Family Integration, and Kinship Orientation. *Marriage and Family Living* 24:25-30.

Rosenmayer, L. 1968. "Family Relations of the Elderly." *Journal of Marriage and the Family* 30:672-80.

Rossi, Alice S. 1984. "Gender and Parenthood." *American Sociological Review* 49:1-18.

Rossi, Alice S. 1993. "Intergenerational Relations: Gender, Norms, and Behavior." Pp. 191-212 in *The Changing Contract across Generations,* edited by Vern L. Bengtson and W. Andrew Achenbaum. Hawthorne, N.Y.: Aldine de Gruyter.

Skolnick, Arlene. 1991. *Embattled Paradise: The American Family in an Age of Uncertainty.* New York: Basic Books.

Stacey, Judith. 1990. *Brave New Families.* New York: Basic Books.

Taylor, Robert J., and Linda M. Chatters. 1991. "Extended Family Networks of Older Black Adults."

Journal of Gerontology: Social Sciences 46:S210-S217.

Umberson, Deborah. 1992. "Relationships between Adult Children and Their Parents: Psychological Consequences." *Journal of Marriage and the Family* 54:664-74.

Umberson, Deborah, Camille B. Wortman, and Ronald C. Kessler. 1992. "Widowhood and Depression: Explaining Long-Term Gender Differences in Vulnerability." *Journal of Health and Social Behavior* 33:10-24.

White, Lynn K. 1992. "The Effect of Parental Divorce and Remarriage on Parental Support for Adult Children." *Journal of Family Issues* 13:234-50.

1   Young adult children sometimes create tensions in the lives of their parents. B. K. Loren's father will not welcome her, as a lesbian, into his home, and her mother is unhappy with her father's attitude. How do you think their attitudes and the intergenerational and marital relationships might change if and when B. K. and a woman partner have a child?

2   Caroline Hwang is a heterosexual woman who hopes someday to marry and have children. How do you think her relationship with her parents would be affected if she married a White American? What if she married a Chinese or Japanese American?

3   In the United States, divorce weakens contact and emotional closeness between fathers and their children. Given that most help to older adults who need it is provided by family members, how might divorce earlier in their adult lives affect men in their 80s and 90s who need care?

4   Some Asian Americans, such as the Vietnamese, have high rates of multigeneration households, containing children, parents, grandparents, and sometimes even aunts, uncles, and cousins. This pattern is not common for Japanese Americans. Why might different Asian American groups vary in their coresidential practices? What would you think about living with your parents and grandparents?

5   Women are key links in intergenerational relationships. Think about your relationship with your parents and about your parents' relationships with their parents. In what ways do women nurture and support these ties?

6   Rossi and Rossi (1990) argue that the increasing attachment of women to the labor force may undermine intergenerational ties. Can you identify any examples from your own life, or the lives of people you know, that support or contradict this view?

SUGGESTIONS FOR FURTHER READING

1   Bould, S. (1993). Familial caretaking: A middle-range definition of family in the context of social policy. *Journal of Family Issues, 14,* 133-151.

Family policy assumes that family members live together, in a static or unchanging family structure, and that family members are related by blood, marriage, or adoption. It further emphasizes minor-aged children and their coresidential parents. Bould argues that a fluid definition of family that recognizes emotional ties and acknowledges that family members do not always behave toward each other as expected is essential for effective family caregiving.

2   Tax, M. (1981). *Families.* New York: Feminist Press.

This children's book, available in Spanish and English, tells us everything that six-year-old Angie knows about families, which turns out to be a great deal. Angie demonstrates that despite their variations in structure, all families have things in common.

3   Weston, K. (1991). *Families we choose.* New York: Columbia University Press.

Anthropologist Kath Weston proposes the term *chosen* family to explain the links she finds between lesbians and gay men and the networks they create that function as kin ties.

4   Dill, B. T. (1988). Our mothers' grief: Racial ethnic women and the maintenance of families. *Journal of Family History, 13,* 415-431.

Dill describes the early family histories of African American, Chinese American, and Mexican American workers in the United States, illustrating how government policy created for these people of color a conflict between our ideology of what a family is and the everyday reality of family life.

5   Horowitz, R. (1983). *Honor and the American dream: Culture and identity in a Chicano community.* New Brunswick, NJ: Rutgers University Press.

Horowitz illustrates how kin ties in Mexico have been expanded to include *compadres,* or godparents, who help create an expanded family network. This expansion occurs across socioeconomic classes in Mexico and provides additional resources for support in times of need.

6   Martínez, D. (1997). *Mother tongue.* New York: Ballantine.

This novel tells about a young American woman who finds identity and commitment through her relationship with a refugee from El Salvador. Twenty years later, she tries to help their son, who never knew his father, develop an understanding of his father's culture and heritage. In the process, she better understands herself.

7 Rossi, A. S., & Rossi, P. H. (1990). *Of human bonding: Parent-child relations across the life course.* New York: Aldine de Gruyter.

Alice and Peter Rossi describe their multifaceted study of parent-child relationships at all ages of the life span. Their findings demonstrate the primacy and strength of the parent-child relationship over other kin ties and the importance of women in maintaining links between and across generations.

8 Dangarembga, T. (1988). *Nervous conditions.* Seattle, WA: Seal Press.

Tsitsi Dangarembga's novel tells the story of the childhood and coming of age of a young girl in Africa. She takes advantage of a rare opportunity to be educated at a British boarding school in a nearby city and, in the process, becomes a person no longer comfortable with her family or her culture.

SUGGESTIONS FOR BROWSING THE WEB

1 *www.lovemakesafamily.org/*

Featuring photos and text of interviews from the award-winning book and exhibit "Love Makes a Family," this site shows a variety of lesbian, gay, bisexual, and transgendered persons and their families.

2 *www.webcom.com/~intvoice/*

"Interracial Voice" is an independent Web site designed for people of mixed race and interracial community. It provides information on interracial advocacy groups and features in-depth interviews with people of mixed race.

3 *www.popexpo.net/english.html*

"6 Billion Human Beings" is a Web adaptation of an exhibit from the Musée de l'Homme in the Muséum National d'Histoire Naturelle in Paris. Although this Web site takes a decidedly antipopulation growth stance, it enables you to see demographic patterns in different regions of the world and how those patterns may affect life in the future.

4 *www.norc.uchicago.edu/online/emerge.htm*

"The Emerging 21st Century Family" features a report from the National Opinion Research Center at the University of Chicago describing the most recent trends in rates of marriage and childbearing, labor force participation, and sexual behavior, as well as views about gender and sexual practices.

---

1   *Breaking Away* (1979)

This movie is an engaging, funny story of four working-class, 19-year-old young men who are unsure what to do after high school. It focuses on Dave Stohler, whose ups and downs about his future are reflected in his relationships with his mother and father, and in their relationship with each other as well. Parenthetically, this film is beloved by bicyclists.

2   *Guess Who's Coming to Dinner* (1967)

Two young adults, one African American and one White, struggle with their parents over their forthcoming marriage. Made during the 1960s, this film is about a topic that continues to be controversial today.

3   *October Sky* (1999)

This delightful film portrays a son's dream to be a "rocket scientist" and his father's wish for him to carry on the family tradition of coal mining.

4   *The Wedding Banquet* (1993)

A Taiwanese American gay man, along with his White American partner, goes to great lengths to make his parents believe that he is heterosexual. This funny, poignant film examines both cultural identity and parent-adult child relationships.

PART II

Connections Across the Generations in Midlife

In midlife, ties to family members beyond the household remain strong and are often a major source of personal identity and life meaning. Both stability and change can be seen in these relationships. Intergenerational helping patterns continue, for example. Parents who paid for college and helped buy that first car often continue to help adult children with major household expenses. They also participate in caring for grandchildren if and when they arrive. When children divorce, parents often provide financial help, a place to stay, and emotional support and advice. As adult children shift from young adulthood to middle age, many continue to look to their parents for approval and encouragement. Adult children also provide help and assistance to their parents during this time.

Relationships undergo change, as well, as you saw in the introduction and in Part I. In many cases, parents and children begin to understand each other beyond their familial roles. For example, family members may gain appreciation for one another as competent individuals in the workforce. Parents become aware of skills and talents that they had not recognized in their children. At the same time, adults with young children of their own may gain greater appreciation of how their parents balanced work and family responsibilities as they were growing up.

Family life transitions that typically occur in midlife also lead to change. These transitions include becoming grandparents, beginning parental care, and experiencing the death of a family member. Most of the time, these transitions take place in predictable ways and at predictable times. As you can see by the way this reader is organized, however, these transitions can occur unexpectedly or off time. The grandmothers whose daughters became mothers in adolescence, which you read about in Part I, are an example.

In Part II, we examine individual mastery in paid and unpaid work and its relationship to family life, becoming a grandparent, and the death of a family member. As always, we call attention to the personal and sociohistorical context in which these events occur.

Key Issues

We discuss the following key issues in our introduction to the readings in Part II:

1. Parents and their adult children grow in their understanding of one another with adult children's transitions, including establishing a commitment to paid work, accepting one's sexual identity, and becoming a caregiver.

2. The need for connection and approval between generations continues throughout the life span, contributing to purposeful and satisfying relationships.

3. Family caregiving occurs throughout the life course, with parent care predominant in midlife. Regardless of when it occurs, however, gender, ethnicity, and social class shape the experience of family caregiving.

4. The grandparent role is important in midlife for many, but not all, grandparents. Variability in grandparenthood is influenced by age, gender, ethnicity, and social class.

5. Demographic shifts during the last century have affected our experiences with death, but there continues to be a wide range of grief responses to both normative and nonnormative losses.

What Is the Connection Between One's Identity as an Adult and One's Identity as a Family Member?

When children become adults, we, as a society, expect them to do productive work, whether it is paid or unpaid. We also anticipate that they will marry and form new households. With these transitions, adult children acquire roles in common with their parents' roles, such as employee, spouse or partner, parent, and even widow or retired person. As they obtain more life experiences themselves, adult children often gain new understanding of their parents as individuals. This can be seen in two of the readings in this section: Darrell G. H. Schramm's new insights about his father in "Father's Sorrow, Father's Joy," and Sandra Cisneros's new connections with her father in "Only Daughter."

Regardless of age and life choices, adult children frequently look to their parents for approval and support. This support is often forthcoming, as seen in the writings of Sandra Cisneros and Darrell Schramm. Cisneros has chosen and pursued work that takes her into a different world from that of her working-class, Mexican American parents. Her father does not quite understand her interest in education and a professional career over marriage and family. Despite her success, Cisneros still finds it important for her father to know her as a writer as well as a daughter and to approve of and be proud of her work.

The reading by Darrell Schramm focuses less on work and more on his changing understanding of his relationship with his father. As a child, he experienced his father as distant and unsympathetic. He felt his father was especially critical of him. Only with age did he recognize that his father had always accepted and loved him. Coming out to one's family as a gay man is often difficult. Those in both generations may experience feelings of shame, fear, disappointment, rejection, ambivalence, anger, and uncertainty. Popular myth would have us believe that families will disown their gay and lesbian children. This rarely occurs. Instead, through time, family members generally renegotiate their relationships, incorporating this new identity and associated ties (Laird, 1998). As both Darrell Schramm and his father accept his identity as a gay man, they develop a new closeness and deeper understanding of each other.

Who Provides Care in Families, and What Are Some of the Consequences of Caregiving?

Caregiving is a fundamental part of family life. Family members provide care to each other in routine, day-to-day family tasks, such as child care and housework, offering emotional support, and providing food and shelter (Dressel & Clark, 1990). In gerontology, however, we more often think of caregiving as help and assistance given to dependent adults. In these situations, caregiving tasks are defined more narrowly. Caregiving refers to basic activities such as helping someone bathe or dress, move from bed to wheelchair, or balance a checkbook. Most women provide this type of care at some point in their lives.

At any given time, about 20% of all adults are caregivers for someone with a disability or chronic illness (Marks, 1996). Most of the time, caregiving occurs intermittently and for short periods. Demographic patterns discussed earlier and the changing nature of caregiving needs and tasks, however, mean that the most recent cohorts of women are providing more care than those in the past (Moen, Robison, & Fields, 1994).

Not surprisingly, the likelihood of being a caregiver increases with age. Furthermore, most care is provided to older people. Family caregivers provide about two thirds of all community-based care needed by older persons. The vast majority do not use formal, paid services to supplement that care (Mezy, Miller, & Nelson, 1999). Instead, people who need assistance rely on family members.

Here in Part II, we focus on middle-aged children caring for aging parents. Emily K. Abel sets the stage in her chapter, "Historical Perspectives on Caregiving: Documenting Women's Experiences." Caregiving in the 19th century was generally considered women's work, and it was performed in the home. Without running water, electricity, and washing machines, the labor of caregiving was physically more challenging than it is today. More than the physical aspects of care has changed, however. Today, people are living longer because infectious diseases are no longer the killers they once were. Now, much of the care provided involves the management of chronic disease and disability, and caregiving may extend for months and even years. For example, persons with Alzheimer's disease gradually lose their memories and the ability to process information and make appropriate decisions. As the disease progresses, they become more and more dependent in all aspects of life, requiring constant supervision. Ultimately, the disease leaves them unresponsive and unable to move. Those with Parkinson's disease, cardiopulmonary disease, and other illnesses often experience steady declines in their abilities to function physically. Many will be bed bound for major portions of the last year of their lives (Mezy et al., 1999). Diseases such as these, then, lead to long periods of intensive caregiving for family members.

Caregiving continues to be women's work. Women spend more time helping more family members, friends, and neighbors than do men. In addition, compared with men, women help more kin, including in-laws, and a greater number of persons overall. When women and men are similar in health status, employment, and income, they are more similar in who they help (Gallagher, 1994). The types of help and the range of tasks performed, however, are still greater for women and follow traditional ideas about gender. For example, women are more likely to provide the personal care of bathing, dressing, grooming, and toileting, whereas men perform tasks related to home maintenance and managing finances.

Although women are more likely to be caregivers, men do perform many caregiving tasks. In a chapter from *Looking After: A Son's Memoir*, John Daniel describes helping his mother with her shower, a caregiving activity typically thought of as women's work. Daniel's mother is in her mid-80s and is experiencing decline in both physical and cognitive functioning. In addition to bathing, she needs emotional support and help with many activities of daily living, which Daniel provides. Older people today have fewer children than in the past, and ideas about gender seem to be changing. As we look to the future, we may find that John Daniel's caregiving experience is typical for many sons (Hirshorn & Piering, 1998-1999).

Employment and caregiving are issues of growing importance, particularly in midlife. Employed women are more likely than employed men to be caregivers. Employed women regularly help older family members with transportation, shopping, housekeeping, and meals, along with checking in by phone, visiting, and giving emotional support (Neal, Ingersoll-Dayton, & Starrels, 1997). In general, women provide two more hours of care a week than do men and frequently identify themselves as primary caregivers. Employed caregiving women add more than an extra workweek of nonpaid work to their monthly load (Gerstel & Gallagher, 1994).

Caregiving takes an enormous financial toll on many families. Caregiving women often find that they must reduce paid work hours or leave the workforce altogether. Those who leave rarely return to paid employment once caregiving responsibilities are over, nor is lost income recovered (Pavalko & Artis, 1997). In all, employed caregivers lose more than $11 billion in wages every year. Furthermore, the annual costs of unpaid, informal care for people with Alzheimer's disease alone is nearly $40 billion (Mezy et al., 1999). As the population continues to age, we can expect the economic and emotional burden of caregiving on families to increase. We need social policies and programs that will support families who are involved in this vital and often unrecognized work.

In recent years, middle-aged women have been called a "sandwiched generation" when they are caught between the needs of their children and those of their parents. Only a minority of middle-aged women and men are actually in this position, however (Neal, Hammer, Rickard, Isgrigg, & Brockwood, 1999). In most cases, children are no longer dependent when their parents assume parent care responsibilities. Still, parents of young adults may be providing some financial assistance. Those providing care to more than one generation do have unique needs and challenges that should not be minimized. In "Last Christmas Gift From a Mother," Lois F. Lyles relates how she helped provide care to her mother who was dying of cancer. She vividly describes the tasks of caregiving and the difficulties and blessings of this work. Her 12-year-old son was with her during this time. Lyles does not address the challenges of balancing child and parent care directly. She does indicate, however, the presence of other family members in the household who likely assisted in the care of both mother and son.

As described by Peggye Dilworth-Anderson in "Extended Kin Networks in Black Families," African American families have traditionally served their members through an extensive collection of relatives providing mutual aid and support among generations. Family in this case is not limited to those with blood ties. Close friends often become part of the family as fictive kin. When assessing family resources, therefore, it is important to consider these fictive kin ties. Multigenerational households are more common in Black families than in the dominant culture, and they facilitate care across generations. Although African American families have traditionally provided extensive care to one another, many are faced with extraordinary challenges that may undermine such care in the future. African American families have higher rates than White families of single female-headed households, unemployment, and poverty. Given the lack of resources available to many African American women, Dilworth-Anderson expresses concern about the ability of some in the middle generations to provide care to their older parents in the future. This concern is supported by recent research. Consistent with their traditional cultural norms, older African Americans have higher expectations than older Whites that younger generations should care for older generations. At the same time, however, the levels of actual support received are similar in the two groups (Lee, Peek, & Coward, 1998).

Much of the research literature focuses on the stress of caregiving and its often negative consequences, such as ill health of caregivers, increased levels of depression, and the lack of personal time. Yet when caregivers are asked if there is anything good about caregiving, most identify positive outcomes such as developing closer relationships, greater understanding, and more patience. Positive relationships between caregivers and care receivers reduce the overall strain and tension related to caregiving (Archbold, Stewart, Greenlick, & Harvath, 1990; Walker & Allen, 1991). At the same time, positive relationships do not overcome all the strain. This is particularly true for caregivers who lack social and economic resources. The affection and love felt by Lois Lyles and John Daniel for their mothers are apparent in their writings. Although caring for their mothers was emotionally difficult for them, each identified areas of personal growth and a deeper understanding of their mothers as rewarding outcomes. For them, the process of helping dependent parents was a positive, life-changing experience.

How Important Is
Grandparenthood in Midlife?

Almost all parents eventually become grandparents, although the timing of this transition varies widely. On average, first grandchildren are born when grandparents are in their late 40s. In the study by Apfel and Seitz (Part I), however, mothers ranged from age 28 to age 55 when their teenaged daughters had children. Some already were grandmothers. Age at first grandparenthood may occur as late as the eighth decade. Furthermore, more than 40 years may pass between the birth of a first and last grandchild.

Think about the things you did with your grandparents when you were very young. Now think about some of the activities you have done together more recently. As you can imagine, relationships with grandchildren will be influenced by grandparents' age and stage of development, as well as by the age and other characteristics of the grandchild. You do different things with a toddler than you do with an adolescent, and still other things with adults. In addition, as grandparents age, they usually experience other role transitions and changes in health status that influence the types of things they are able to do. It is not too surprising, therefore, that many grandparents have different kinds of relationships with a first grandchild than with a last grandchild. In thinking about grandparents in middle age and then in later life, it is important to keep the influence of age in mind. Given the length of time that grandparents and grandchildren spend together, we need to remember that like parent-child relationships, relationships between grandparents and grandchildren are dynamic and evolving.

Historical changes in the 20th century, such as greater longevity and decreasing fertility rates, were discussed in the introduction and in Part I of this book. Like other family relationships, these population changes have influenced the experience of being a grandparent or a grandchild. Compared with children in earlier times, children today are more likely to have all four grandparents living when they are born, and most will have at least two living grandparents when they reach adulthood (Szinovacz, 1998; Uhlenberg & Kirby, 1998). The role of grandparent is more distinct from parenting than it was in the past because grandparents are more likely to have completed their own active parenting. Although there is tremendous variability, people entering middle and old age today are healthier, are better educated, and typically enjoy greater economic security than those early in the 20th century. As a result, the nature of grandparenting has changed, making it possible for families to construct their own definitions of what it means to be a grandparent.

Meaning

Most grandparents indicate that their relationships with grandchildren are meaningful and satisfactory. This is true for the grandparents studied by Sarah Cunningham-Burley in "The Experience of Grandfatherhood." Grandparents often find meaning from seeing new generations emerge in their families. For older adults, grandchildren provide a sense of continuity with the past and knowledge that the family will extend into the future. Grandparents also describe grandparenthood as stirring up memories of their own past. They may remember special times they spent with their grandparents and seek to re-create those experiences with their grandchildren. Similarly, memories of their own parents as grandparents provide additional models of grandparenting within families—sometimes models of how not to be a grandparent. Some of the grandfathers with whom Sarah Cunningham-Burley talked hoped to avoid the mistakes they felt their own parents had made as grandparents. A special relationship with a grandchild is another source of meaning. The grandfathers you will read about find meaning in relationships with their grandchildren that are different from those they had with their own children. These grandfathers have more time for enjoyment without the demands of being the family provider.

Many grandparents find satisfaction in being a resource to their children and grandchildren, passing on knowledge, skills, and family stories. This role is particularly important in ethnic minority populations in which grandparents pass on language, tradition, and culture. This aspect of grandparenthood is central for many of the American Indian grandparents described by Joan Weibel-Orlando in Part III. Transmitting one's culture, however, may be difficult when adult children and grandchildren increasingly embrace the customs of the dominant culture, as suggested by Caroline Hwang in Part I.

The proximity of grandparents to grandchildren affects their relationship. When they live nearby, grandparents see grandchildren frequently. Maternal grandmothers in particular are likely to participate in child care when grandchildren are young. These grandparents commonly attend school events and other activities of their grandchildren. Living at a distance means less contact and involvement. Although relationships at a distance may be more symbolic, even geographically distant grandparents report positive ties and feelings of closeness to grandchildren.

Gender

The grandparent experience is different for women and men. Consistent with other aspects of family life, grandmothers are more likely to be involved with child care, nurturing grandchildren, and planning and orchestrating family gatherings. Grandmothers are more likely to assume caregiving responsibilities, whether for their parents or for their grandchildren. Family relationships are often of paramount concern to them. Grandfathers, by contrast, tend to focus on practical issues, such as education, jobs, and responsibility for and managing money (Hagestad, 1985). Grandfathers are sometimes involved in activities more actively with their grandsons than with their granddaughters. For example, grandfathers and adolescent grandsons spend more time together exchanging help and services than do other grandparent-grandchild pairs (Cherlin & Furstenberg, 1986).

Grandmothers often talk more than grandfathers about their family life, as you will see in Cunningham-Burley's chapter. In another study, college students asked their grandparents to share stories. Grandmothers talked more than twice as long as grandfathers, and the content of their stories was different. Grandmothers told stories about family history, whereas grandfathers told stories of their own triumphs as young men or stories with a moral message (Nussbaum & Bettini, 1994).

As Cunningham-Burley suggests, however, differences between grandmothers and grandfathers should not overshadow their many similarities. The grandparent role is significant to grandmothers and grandfathers alike, and most grandparents indicate a high level of satisfaction with the role. Both share stories with their grandchildren even if the content of those stories is different. Both see their grandchildren about the same amount, although visits are probably arranged by grandmothers and mothers. Both grandmothers and grandfathers come to the aid of their children in need, although they provide help in different ways.

What Is the Role of Death of a Family Member in One's Identity and in One's Connections to Other Family Members?

Normative Loss

Today, most deaths occur after age 75. They usually happen in hospitals or nursing homes instead of at home. The death of a child or young person has become relatively rare in Western societies. The combination of death at an older age and change in the location of death has altered death from the more intimate experience typical of the early 20th century. Parental death is the most common death experience in midlife, frequently occurring when adult children are between the ages of 49 and 64. Adult children are often grandparents themselves before experiencing the loss of a parent. In addition, because most 30-year-olds still have a living grandparent, the death of a grandparent is increasingly an experience of middle age as well.

Death is not limited to middle or later life, however. Fatal accidents or terminal illnesses occur at all stages of life. In addition, death occurs earlier in life for minorities and the poor. Lois F. Lyles's mother ("Last Christmas Gift From a Mother"), an African American, died in middle age, arguably as a consequence of a life of poverty. As a Southern Black woman, devoted to family and others, she would not consciously seek out care and attention for her own body. The well-documented history of poor treatment of people of color in the health care system also may have contributed to her reluctance to seek early intervention for breast cancer.

The death of a parent is often seen as less traumatic than other deaths, such as those of a child or a spouse, in part because death in old age seems to be "more fair." At the same time, however, the loss of a parent or parents can have a profound effect on the surviving child regardless of age. We have already seen that the parent-child bond is the strongest and the longest lasting intergenerational tie. At any age, parents are generally identified as the most influential individuals in a person's life (Moss & Moss, 1989). The death of a parent, therefore, often means the loss of a significant and valued relationship that has grown and matured through time. A unique link with one's past is gone forever. Relationships with siblings and long-time friends can compensate only partially for this loss.

Although it is a difficult transition, parental death can promote coping with many developmental issues of midlife (Moss & Moss, 1989). With the death of a parent, adult children often reconsider their own goals and life expectations. They also evaluate the relevance of their parents' lives to their own, taking comfort in a fulfilling life or feeling greater sadness or loss if fulfillment is lacking. Darrell G. H. Schramm ("Father's Sorrow, Father's Joy") describes his grief at the death of his father. When he recognizes in himself the characteristics he valued in his father, he is comforted. He also realizes with satisfaction that his love for his partner is an extension of his love for his father.

Lois F. Lyles recounts the process and emotional pain of caring for her mother as she was dying. The experience was overwhelming. For a time, she actually lost sight of her mother in this increasingly dependent and demanding person. Yet her mother knew that this intense caregiving experience ultimately would contribute to Lyles's personal growth.

The loss of a parent has been associated with coming to terms with one's own mortality. The adult child becomes "next in line" for death and may begin to view life as time left to live. We will revisit this issue in Part V of this reader through the work of Laura Carstensen.

Grief from the death of a parent often goes unrecognized and unsupported (Moss & Moss, 1989). In part, this occurs because parental death is considered a normative life event. Perhaps more important, we, as a society, do not deal well with issues of grief and loss. In the dominant culture, few rituals or rules guide our response to death. We often are at a loss for words and do not understand the impact of death on acquaintances, friends, or even close family members. This will be apparent in the study by Debra Umberson included in Part III. She describes the all-too-frequent experience of adult children who do not receive the support they need from their spouses following a parent's death.

Nonnormative Loss

Although fewer than 6% of all deaths in the United States take place before the age of 35, this number represented nearly 140,000 individuals in 1995 (Bern-Klug & Chapin, 1999). These off-time deaths are devastating to all family members but particularly to parents because of the strong parent-child bond. People feel that life is unfair when a child or young person dies, in part because lives are cut short without fulfilling their potential. We anticipate that people will live until old age, and we do not expect parents to outlive their children.

Middle-aged and older people often reflect on the successes or failures of their children in evaluating their own lives. The loss of a child, particularly an only child, may make this aspect of life review especially difficult and painful. Furthermore, a child's death may mean a loss of social heirs and family continuity. Increasing longevity may make the loss of a child in one's old age a more common experience, especially for women. Nearly 10% of parents over the age of 65 experience the death of one of their children. Consequences of this late-life loss may include health problems, functional decline, and psychological distress (Lesher & Bergey, 1988).

When someone dies, the focus of support is on parents, partner, and children, although other family members also are affected. Today, for example, when a child or young adult dies, it is likely that grandparents are among the survivors. Grandparents share many of the grief reactions that parents experience, although given the unique strength of the parent-child bond, perhaps to a lesser extent. Grandparents do report anguish at their own impotence in helping their adult children in the face of overwhelming grief.

Regardless of age at the time of death, however, child loss is a traumatic experience symbolizing the loss of one's future and perhaps the loss of identity as a parent. In the first reading in Part II, Camille Peri ("Dancing With Death") recounts the story of the death of her close friend, Toby, a young man in his 30s. Toby's mother describes his illness and how she and her husband, along with Toby's wife, participated in his care. Many years later, ties to their son continue, as do feelings of loss and grief.

Responses to Bereavement

The extreme experiences of bereaved parents have resulted in growing recognition that grief from the death of any close relationship rarely ends. Although most people are resilient and learn to live with their losses, grief becomes part of the self. Furthermore, connections with those who have died continue to be important aspects of life. This is clearly the case for Toby's parents in "Dancing With Death." We will see this continuing connection again when we discuss widowhood in Parts IV and V. Examples of continuing bonds include the stories that grandparents and adult children tell about their parents and grandparents who have died. These stories are part of the family's legacy.

Various family rituals are another way of remembering and connecting with the past. Birthdays, holidays, and other family times may become bittersweet as family members think of those who died recently or a long time ago. Faced with important life decisions, we often wonder what someone we loved would have done given the same choices. We also imagine what they would have wanted or expected of us. Bereaved parents continue privately or publicly to remember their children. In Camille Peri's "Dancing With Death," Toby's father included his son in his paintings, especially as Toby was dying and in the months immediately following his death. Many years later, he remarks that there continues to be a part of his son in every painting he does.

Responses to the death of a close family member vary tremendously from one person to the next. Emotions may change from moment to moment. Dale Lund (1996) compared grief to a roller-coaster ride with many emotional ups and downs occurring frequently and at high speed. Somewhat paradoxically, bereaved family members are more resilient than anticipated and, at the same time, experience grief longer than is usually recognized in or allowed by the dominant culture. We do not "get over" the loss of significant relationships in a matter of weeks, months, or even years. One of the reasons that John Daniel wrote a memoir about his mother was to help him deal with his sometimes overwhelming grief at her death.

As family gerontologists, we know that there is great variability in grief responses. Much of what we know, however, is based on the experiences of White middle-class or working-class women. When we expand our attention to men and to multiple cultures and ethnic groups, we find even greater variability in grief. We tend to underestimate the grief experienced by men. Furthermore, lack of knowledge about or sensitivity to differences in customs and rituals may compound the bereaved family members' experience. For example, in some cultures, it is important to have an open window for the spirit when it leaves the body. This is difficult to accomplish in modern hospitals, especially if staff members are insensitive to this belief. Wailing or song may be appropriate grief reactions in some cultures. These responses may be difficult to understand and accommodate for those whose tradition requires more stoic, reserved behaviors. How the body is prepared for burial, beliefs in an afterlife, levels of family involvement, and appropriate ways to refer to the person who has died all are areas of difference requiring sensitivity and openness by those who wish to help.

Social and emotional support is a critical factor in adaptation to traumatic life events. Support may take the form of practical help such as filling out forms, packing up or distributing belongings, bringing food, and helping with funeral arrangements. Emotional support is also important. People feel supported emotionally when their grief is acknowledged, when they feel cared for, and when they are able to express feelings as they desire—in ways consistent with preferred cultural norms. Because death has become an uncommon occurrence before old age, people often do not know how to help those who grieve. Kelly Osmont (1988) provides some guidance in a poem she wrote following the death of her 19-year old son, Aaron. Part of this poem is excerpted below.

> Listening with your heart to "how I am doing" relieves
>   the pain,
> for when the tears can freely come and go, I feel lighter.
> Talking to you releases what I've been wanting to say aloud,
>   clearing space
> for a touch of joy in my life. (p. 17)

Self-help groups, including bereavement support groups, have become pervasive during the past two decades. Although support groups do not appeal to everyone, they are helpful for many. Research studies have found few differences in adaptation to bereavement between those who attend support groups and those who do not. Almost every community has some type of organized bereavement group, offered through hospitals, hospice programs, churches, and senior centers, for example. Sometimes, specific relationship losses are targeted, such as widow-to-widow programs. Others focus on losses from specific illnesses such as cancer. Some groups are informal and continuing, whereas others are more structured and short-term. Regardless of the format or focus, the purpose of these groups is to provide a range of emotional and social support to those who grieve.

9

Dancing With Death

Camille Peri

It was at Toby's wedding that Rose [Toby's mother] first noticed something wrong. Toby and Ellen, an animator and producer, had met at ILM [George Lucas's Bay Area film studio, Industrial Light and Magic] and moved to Los Angeles, where they were married in 1989. "I remember looking at him at the ceremony and his back was shaking," says Rose. "He was pale and his eyes were kind of bulging. I wondered if he was high and for a minute I was irritated. Then I thought, Well, it's his wedding."

The autumn after the wedding, Toby thought he had an ulcer; his doctors examined his upper body and found and removed a tumor in his lung. But by his first wedding anniversary, he still didn't feel well. The following month, they discovered cancer "everywhere," according to Rose—under his navel; in his rectum, the stomach walls, the portal veins to his liver. Rose remembers flying out to California to see him as if in a dream. "He just laid his head in my lap and said he was frightened. He looked so thin. I said, 'You'll be all right. We're going to get you well.'"

Toby's doctors had told his father, Bob, and Ellen that the cancer was terminal, but Rose couldn't believe it. "I felt like my stomach had dropped out," she says. "You hear things like they'll have one percent chance of surviving if it gets to the organs and you think, Well, my child is going to be in that one percent."

At Ellen's invitation, Rose and Bob moved in with them and began to take care of Toby during the day while Ellen worked. Rose remembers a night soon after, when Toby was in excruciating pain. "I wished it was my pain. I remember rocking him, saying, 'We're going to get through this.' And I believed we would—I had to." But by the time they got him to a hospital, he was almost unconscious. The oncologist told them he had three months to live. "He said, 'I don't want to see you back here again. Let him die in peace.'"

They did not talk directly about his death again. Instead, they lived with a kind of wordless understanding, taking their cues from Toby. Miraculously, he continued working as a cameraman on a television pilot. After he grew

---

This chapter is an abridged version of the original by Camille Peri.

too weak to walk, Rose and Bob would help him to a director's chair on a crane. He finished filming three weeks before his death.

Bob had transferred his art studio to Toby and Ellen's house. He was in the middle of a series for the Scottish Ballet production *What to Do Until the Messiah Comes.* His paintings suddenly became charged with anguish, the dance an allegory of Toby and Ellen's life. Toby would sit near his father, strumming his guitar while he watched Bob paint. One day he lifted an eyebrow and said, "Dad, if I die, I know you're going to paint me."

Ultimately, Rose and Bob believe, Toby died of starvation. His six-foot-two frame had shrunk to ninety-eight pounds, the skin stretched so tight on his face he could no longer close his mouth. "Two nights before his death, he came into our room and said, 'Mom, can I lie down there with you and Dad?'" Rose recalls. "He never left. Maybe he just wanted to crawl back into the womb. We'd just hold each other and reminisce. He said, 'Mom, if I kick the bucket, these are the things I remember.' He talked about how much he loved Ellen and Bob and me, about ILM; he talked about you. Then he said, 'If I live, these are the things I want to do,' and he talked about directing a movie, having children."

Rose says she can still see Toby's face in the moments before he died. "He looked at me with those big brown eyes—I remember they seemed bigger than ever because that was almost all that was left of him. He opened his mouth as if he was about to say something to me and then he closed his eyes and died. Maybe he was just taking a breath, maybe he didn't have anything to say. But that will haunt me until I die."

The family had all been there; she and Ellen were hugging him when he died. "We were talking with him until the last breath, telling him we loved him and not to be afraid," Rose recalls. "The only thing we didn't do was go with him. And I would have gladly taken his place."

Parents never completely stop feeling responsible for their children; when a child dies, they still feel somehow to blame, no matter how old the child or what caused his death. For five years, Rose tells me, she reviewed Toby's life and found guilt in even the smallest details—from whether she let him eat too much candy as a child to a family fight that was a turning point in his life. Toby had been out drinking with high school friends when he flipped his parents' jeep. "Fortunately, no one was hurt, but Bob blew up," Rose recalls. "He said, 'After graduation you're out of here.' I think it was too soon—he had just turned eighteen and he wasn't ready. Intellectually, I know it didn't cause the cancer, but maybe it had some impact, weakened his immune system. Maybe I should have stood up to Bob more."

Alone in San Francisco, Toby got a room in a transient hotel. "He'd call and say, 'I'm thinking of coming home.' I'd say, 'Come back,' but Bob would say, 'Stick it out a little longer. I'm sure you'll find work.' He was talking from his own experience: When he was eighteen, he went to New York with his portfolio, stayed for a week, and came home. He didn't want Toby to have that regret." If Toby had lived, I realize, this would be part of his success story, what made him, but now it is forever tinged with sadness.

Bob did paint Toby. His work now hangs in their home: huge, grief-wreathed portraits of a young man whose gaze stays clear and serene while disease destroys his body. They are both beautiful and raw, filled with a palpable rage and tender, bereaved love. And for a year after Toby's death, they were almost all Bob could do.

"When a woman loses a child, she loses her past, present, and future," he says. "A man loses his future. Toby was an extension of me." The only way for Bob to reclaim him was through painting. "As long as I have pictures of somebody, I have them. I don't know that I could ever go back and do them now. I don't think I could do a realistic picture of his face anymore. But he's still there, in some way, in every painting I do."

"For the first few years, I thought, Toby's just gone for a while. He'll be back," says Rose. The first time she saw him was on a stage in London, shortly after his death, when she was shooting photos of dancers in rehearsal. "The light was falling on his face and hair, but his body was partly hidden in the curtains," she recalls. "He was wearing his glasses, like he used to. My heart was pounding. I grabbed the telephoto lens to get a better look, but he was gone." Later, she found out it was the ballet's young composer. "But that used to happen a lot—I'd see a young man and think it was him."

Researchers trying to ascertain the endpoints of grief have yet to determine if there is a limit to parents' mourning. Rose would say there is not. "It softens after about seven years," says Rose. "It never goes away."

A woman carries a baby in her body and when that child dies, no matter how old he or she is, the mother feels that something has been cut out from inside her—the loss is as profound and permanent as becoming a parent. I asked Rose how childbirth and child death changed their lives.

Rose thinks back to Toby's birth. "I remember holding him when he was a newborn, being scared to death. Here was this tiny human being that I was responsible for, and the love and commitment is for life, even after he's married and has children. And when you lose that child, it takes a part of you out that never returns—a part of your heart. A light goes out forever. You just learn to live with the loss."

10

Historical Perspectives on Caregiving: Documenting Women's Experiences

Emily K. Abel

This chapter shows that women's diaries and letters provide a rich source of data on caregiving throughout the 19th century. The great majority of 19th-century women routinely engaged in caring for the sick and the dying and filled their personal writings with accounts of those activities. These accounts provide a unique perspective from which to examine caregiving today.

19th-Century Caregiving

Although some men participated in nursing care, the reigning ideology assigned the work of caring exclusively to women. Between 1820 and 1865, popular writers expounded a new doctrine that exalted women's special sphere. At the heart of this ideology lay the belief that women were innately different from men. The traits that are central to caregiving—including responsiveness to the needs of others, patience, and an ability to adapt to individual change—became part of a new cultural definition of womanhood (Cott, 1983; Ryan, 1982; Welter, 1964). Women also were believed to have a spe-

cial obligation to safeguard the health of their families (Motz, 1983; Verbrugge, 1979).

Few medical services relieved women's burdens. As Rosenberg (1987) writes, "Most Americans in 1800 had probably heard that such things as hospitals existed, but only a minority would ever have had occasion to see one" (p. 18). The situation had not changed greatly 70 years later. When the first government survey was conducted in 1873, the nation boasted only 120 hospitals, most of which were custodial institutions serving the deserving poor (Vogel, 1980). Middle-class patients rarely entered hospitals. Although low-income people had few options, those with families to care for them avoided these institutions whenever possible. Even surgeries were performed at home, most frequently in the kitchen (Rosenberg, 1987; Starr, 1982).

Other institutions also were sparse. Although tuberculosis was common throughout the century, the sanitarium movement was not launched until the 1880s (Bates, 1992). Reformers began to establish special institutions for the mentally ill as early as the 1820s and 1830s, but many families were reluctant to entrust ill relatives to their care (Dwyer, 1987; Grob, 1973;

Rothman, 1971; Tomes, 1984). In the absence of nursing homes, the sole facilities for the elderly were poorhouses; only the most desperate, however, sought refuge within their walls (Katz, 1986).

Family members also received little help from health professionals. Skepticism about medical interventions deterred some caregivers from relying on physicians. Throughout the 19th century, many women had little confidence that physicians could deliver better care than they themselves. In addition, some families could not afford the fees that physicians charged. For those without telephones and automobiles, summoning a physician involved considerable time and effort. Outside urban areas, physicians frequently were inaccessible (Blake, 1977; Cassedy, 1977).

Family caregivers had even less contact with nurses. Nursing did not begin to organize as a profession until after the Civil War. Most graduates of the first nursing schools worked as private-duty nurses providing care to patients' individual households. But hiring nurses was an option only for the very affluent (Reverby, 1987).

The Value of History

Of course, one could argue that the vast differences between the 19th century and the late 20th render irrelevant the experiences of 19th-century women for those who wish to understand contemporary caregiving. Because infectious diseases were rampant and antibiotics nonexistent, most 19th-century caregivers tended children with acute illnesses rather than elderly people with chronic health problems. To be sure, many women did have extensive responsibilities for both spousal and parental care. But because life expectancy was less than 50 years throughout the century (Siegel & Taeuber, 1986), women often cared for husbands and parents long before they reached old age. Nevertheless, an exploration

of caregiving in the past can highlight some of the distinctive features of modern caregiving.

Diaries and Letters

Diaries and letters have limitations as well as advantages. Many journal entries and letters consisted of short, matter-of-fact statements that chronicled daily events rather than revealing intimate thoughts. Because caregiving was often too commonplace to warrant detailed descriptions, many women simply noted that they had "visited" the sick or "sat up" with the dying. When they were most intensively involved in rendering care, women often failed to write at all. Because some women used diaries and letters to justify their actions or construct ideal self-images, we cannot accept their statements at face value. Although some full-length diaries are available, many journals are too fragmentary to enable us to place the entries in a meaningful context. An even more serious problem is that diary and letter writers tended to be overwhelmingly white, middle-class, and Eastern. A variety of historians have sought to correct this imbalance by uncovering the accounts of pioneer women, immigrant women, and women of color, but members of the most impoverished and oppressed groups remain seriously underrepresented. Finally, those who use the past to understand events today court the danger of "presentism." As Fee and Fox (1988) explain, this means "distorting the past by seeing it only from the point of view of our own time, rather than using primary sources to understand how other people organized and interpreted their lives" (p. 4).

Analyzing Documents

The Content of Care

When policy makers idealize the care delivered by family members, they often are thinking primarily about its emotional dimension. Because relatives have a close bond with a patient, they are believed to be especially well qualified to comfort and reassure. This also is the aspect that brings the greatest gratification to caregivers. In the 19th century, as in the late 20th, some women found satisfaction in catering to their patients. "I had the great pleasure of supplying all her needs and fancies," wrote Louisa May Alcott when her beloved mother was ill in 1874 (Cheney, 1982, p. 272). After her mother's death three years later, Alcott wrote in her journal, "My only comfort is that I could make her last years comfortable, and lift off the burden she had carried so bravely all these years" (Cheney, 1982, p. 300). To a friend she commented, "I could not let anyone else care for the dear invalid while I could lift a hand for I had always been her nurse & knew her little ways" (Myerson & Shealy, 1987, p. 230). The century's attitudes about the significance of personal ties helped to elevate the emotional component of care. According to dominant medical beliefs, the mind and the body were closely related. The solace that family members offered could not only facilitate healing but also ensure a peaceful death (Rosenberg, 1979).

Care of the soul was as important as care of the psyche. Women sought to ensure that the dying were adequately penitent, "sensible" of their situation, and prepared to face death openly (Saum, 1975). In the summer of 1863, Eliza Webber, her sister Emma, and her brother Alpha left their home in Glover, Vermont, to seek their fortunes as itinerant booksellers in upstate New York. When typhoid fever struck Alpha soon after their arrival, Eliza wrote to reassure her parents: "I think him perfectly prepared to die, we read in the Bible everyday to him. The Methodist and Presbyterian Ministers have been in a number of times and have prayed with him. He is so patient and satisfied with all that we do" (letter of Eliza Roxanna Webber Denny, July 22, 1863).

Women were especially likely to consider themselves entrusted with responsibility for their husbands' spiritual well-being. The wife of a merchant in Fulton, Missouri, Samuella Curd was more successful than many women in exerting a pious influence over her husband. She had been married for two years and had just given birth to her first child when her husband entered the final stages of tuberculosis. The pleasure she took in her husband's growing faith helped to mitigate her deepening gloom about his physical deterioration.

When caregivers provided spiritual and emotional support, they acted in accordance with prevailing conceptions about women's roles. But most aspects of care were less compatible with reigning notions about female identity. In many cases, caregiving entailed arduous and unpleasant physical labor. "It is hard to have the care of a poor sick man day after day, week after week," wrote Mary Ann Webber to her son in 1871 when her husband was seriously ill (letter of Mary Ann Webber to Alpha Webber, 1871). She had to dress him, help him in and out of bed, assist him in walking, and bathe him. As he grew progressively weaker, her burdens multiplied. Although she was familiar with heavy farm work, lifting a bedridden man several times a day taxed her strength.

Caregiving also involved what frequently is called "dirty work" (Douglas, 1966). Caregivers cleaned up excrement and vomit, washed bloodstained sheets and bedclothes, and removed chamberpots, "the most disagreeable item in domestic labor," according to one influential writer of household treatises (Catharine Beecher, quoted in Strasser, 1982, p. 95). Lucy Sprague Mitchell (1953) later described one of the tasks entrusted to her when she nursed her tubercular father and aunt:

> I began to empty the cuspidors. Every room except mine had at least one cuspidor partly filled with water. . . . I knew cleaning the cuspidors was dangerous work, for no maid was ever allowed to touch one. . . . I half resented this job, but who else was there? I thought. It was an unpleasant job, too, and I often sent my breakfast down the toilet as a finish. (p. 105)

In addition, caregiving augmented the demands of household labor, which were staggering even in the best of times. Without indoor plumbing and major appliances, housework was difficult and unremitting. Family sickness meant that women had to cook special meals, haul additional water, and carry extra loads of wood. Moreover, because health advocates preached the virtues of cleanliness in the sickroom, women's household chores were considered critical ingredients of medical therapeutics. Before the acceptance of the germ theory, scrubbing the sickroom and thoroughly washing patients' sheets and clothes were considered the best defenses against infection. But laundry was the most hated task of women. It was a day-long ordeal that demanded that women carry 50 gallons of water, lug pails of wet clothes, scrub each item, expose their hands to caustic soaps, and rinse and hang the laundry to dry (Strasser, 1982, p. 195).

In October 1884, Sarah Gillespie described her workload when caring for her brother, who had suffered a serious accident:

> I can't tell how many washings & ironings I have done. But a doz. pillow slips had to be changed each day besides sheets & clothes & I [remember] washing & ironing 23 slips one day when I came home & then baking a doz pumpkin pies & making cake & washing all the dishes making the beds & to see to everything else. (diary of Sarah Gillespie Huftalen [SGH; State Historical Society of Iowa in Iowa City], Oct. 19, 1884)

Caregivers also performed work that we now consider the exclusive province of skilled medical providers. The words women chose to describe their activities suggest that they saw themselves functioning as doctors and nurses. "We doctored her ourselves and got her all right in two or three days," wrote Gwendoline Kincaid of her daughter Cora in 1899 (Hampsten, 1979, p. 26). When her sister lay dying in 1842, Catharine M. Sedgwick com-

mented, "We are all by turns her nurses" (Dewey, 1871).

Because surgeries were performed at home rather than in hospitals, women frequently served as assistants. In 1871, a physician operated on the thumb of a woman who was staying at a friend's home in Idaho. The friend later commented, "By the time it came to the tying of the stitches she struggled so that the doctor asked me to tie them while he held her and I did" (Reid, 1923, p. 52).

In most instances, however, women did not act as subordinates of physicians. I have noted that many women had no more than fleeting contact with doctors. Even women who summoned physicians regularly relied extensively on their own medical knowledge and skills. Alone, or with the assistance of family and friends, women dressed wounds, applied poultices and plasters, dispensed drugs, and administered special tonics. Two weeks before the death of her mother in March 1888, Sarah Gillespie wrote in her diary,

> Her bed-sores are very painful—one which is a trifle better now is 3 in. deep & 2½ in. in diameter. I have to cut out the "puss" & cleanse them often & it fairly makes my veins refuse to carry the blood sometimes. (SGH, March 15, 1888)

When patients were seriously ill, "watching" was a crucial component of caregiving. The watcher sat by the patient's bed, looking for signs that might indicate the approach of death or the need to administer new treatment. In the absence of stethoscopes and thermometers, it was necessary to monitor changes in the color of the skin, the rapidity of the pulse, and the character of the breathing. After her mother suffered a stroke in the spring of 1886, Sarah Gillespie frequently "sat up" to forestall more "sinking spells." She often slept just one or two hours. On June 2, she slept from 11:30 p.m. to 12:30 a.m. and from 2:15 to 3:45 a.m. (SGH, June 3, 1886). On June 28, she wrote that she undressed and went to bed for the first time in six weeks (SGH, June 28, 1886).

Caregiving responsibilities continued after the patient's death. Although family and friends hoped for an eternal life of the soul, they themselves had to take care of the corpse. Because professional funeral services were not available until the end of the century (Farrell, 1980), many women found themselves responsible for laying out the dead. The wife of a small farmer in Arkansas, Nannie Jackson visited her friend Mrs. Hornbuckle for a few hours after the death of her son on April 13, 1891. After dinner, Nannie went back to the home of the bereaved mother to "sit up" with the body. Returning home before breakfast the following day, she again "went up to Mrs. Hornbuckles & stayed a few minutes [and] got the material." Nannie then went to the home of another friend, who helped her "make the pillow and face cover" for the coffin (Bolsteri, 1982, pp. 66-67).

We can see that women who delivered care during the 1800s were not simply angels of mercy. Caregiving demanded strength, resourcefulness, and skill, not just warmth and compassion. Although women found fulfillment in responding to the needs of intimates, they also exercised medical judgment, lugged heavy pails of water, and prepared corpses for burial. The prodigious labor required by households with sick members occasionally left little time for ministering to patients' emotional and spiritual needs. Even when physicians were accessible, women controlled medical decisions. And despite widespread notions of female modesty, women routinely cleaned up excreta, vomit, and blood. In short, the demands of caring for sick and disabled people in the 19th century required women to develop high-level skills and brought them into sustained contact with some of the most fundamental aspects of human existence. Women's experiences during the 19th century add weight to the recurrent feminist argument that we should accord greater recognition to the work of care.

Continuity and Change

A series of historical changes have profoundly altered the content and meaning of care since 1900. The growing secularization of society has meant that women devote less attention to safeguarding the spiritual health of the dying. Because many infectious diseases have disappeared and the life span has lengthened, caregivers are much more likely today to focus on elderly people suffering from chronic conditions. With the advent of mass-produced labor-saving devices, few contemporary caregivers have such difficult and unremitting household chores as 19th-century women. The emergence of a formal system of health care delivery has simultaneously lightened many aspects of caregiving and undermined the sense of mastery that women previously enjoyed.

But historical analysis can reveal continuity as well as change. Although hospitals and funeral homes isolate family members from some aspects of sickness and death, caregivers still must confront basic life experiences. Despite the decreased prominence of religion, many family members continue to try to ease dying people into acceptance of the inevitable. And even though family caregivers today are far less likely than their 19th-century counterparts to draw on their own fund of medical knowledge, their work still requires considerable skill.

References

Bates, B. (1992). *Bargaining for life: A social history of tuberculosis, 1876-1938.* Philadelphia: University of Pennsylvania Press.

Blake, J. B. (1977). From Buchanan to Fishbein: The literature of domestic medicine. In G. B. Risse, R. L. Numbers, & J. W. Leavitt (Eds.), *Medicine without doctors* (pp. 11-30). New York: Science History.

Bolsteri, M. J. (Ed.). (1982). *Vinegar pie and chicken bread: A woman's diary of life in the rural south 1890-1891.* Fayetteville: University of Arkansas Press.

Cassedy, J. H. (1977). Why self-help? Americans alone with their diseases, 1800-1850. In G. B. Risse, R. K. Numbers, & J. W. Leavitt (Eds.), *Medicine without doctors* (pp. 31-48). New York: Science History.

Cheney, E. D. (Ed.). (1982). *Louisa May Alcott: Her life, letters, and journals.* Boston: Roberts.

Cott, N. F. (1983). *The bonds of womanhood: Women's sphere in New England, 1780-1835.* New Haven, CT: Yale University Press.

Dewey, M. E. (Ed.). (1871). *Life and letters of Catharine M. Sedgwick.* New York: Harper.

Douglas, M. (1966). *Purity and danger: An analysis of concepts of pollution and taboo.* London: Routledge & Kegan Paul.

Dwyer, E. (1987). *Homes for the mad: Life inside two nineteenth-century asylums.* New Brunswick, NJ: Rutgers University Press.

Farrell, J. J. (1980). *Inventing the American way of death, 1830-1920.* Philadelphia: Temple University Press.

Fee, E., & Fox, D. M. (1988). Introduction: AIDS, public policy, and historical inquiry. In E. Fee & D. M. Fox (Eds.), *AIDS: The burdens of history* (pp. 1-11). Berkeley: University of California Press.

Grob, G. N. (1973). *Mental institutions in America.* New York: Free Press.

Hampsten, E. (1979). *To all enquiring friends: Letters, diaries, and essays in North Dakota, 1880-1910.* Grand Forks: University of North Dakota.

Katz, M. B. (1986). *In the shadow of the poorhouse: A social history of welfare in America.* New York: Basic Books.

Mitchell, L. S. (1953). *Two lives: The story of Wesley Clair Mitchell and myself.* New York: Simon & Schuster.

Motz, M. F. (1983). *True sisterhood: Michigan women and their kin, 1890-1920.* Albany: State University of New York Press.

Myerson, J., & Shealy, D. (Eds.). (1987). *The selected letters of Louisa May Alcott.* Boston: Little, Brown.

Reid, A. J. (1923). *Letters of long ago.* Caldwell, ID: Caxton.

Reverby, S. M. (1987). *Ordered to care: The dilemma of American nursing, 1850-1945.* New York: Cambridge University Press.

Rosenberg, C. E. (1979). Florence Nightingale on contagion: The hospital as moral universe. In C. E. Rosenberg (Ed.), *Healing and history: Essays for George Rosen* (pp. 116-136). Kent, UK: William Dawson.

Rosenberg, C. E. (1987). *The care of strangers: The rise of America's hospital system.* New York: Basic Books.

Rothman, D. J. (1971). *The discovery of the asylum: Social order and disorder in the new republic.* Boston: Little, Brown.

Ryan, M. (1982). *Empire of the mother: American writing about domesticity, 1830-1860.* New York: Institute for Research on History and Haworth Press.

Saum, L. O. (1975). Death in the popular mind of pre-Civil War America. In D. E. Stannard (Ed.), *Death in America* (pp. 30-48). Philadelphia: University of Pennsylvania.

Siegel, J. S., & Tauber, C. M. (1986). Demographic perspectives on the long-lived society. *Daedalus, 115*(1), 77-118.

Starr, P. (1982). *The social transformation of American medicine: The rise of a sovereign profession and the making of a vast industry.* New York: Basic Books.

Strasser, S. (1982). *Never done: A history of American housework.* New York: Pantheon.

Tomes, N. (1984). *A generous confidence: Thomas Story Kirkbridge and the art of asylum-keeping, 1840-1883.* Cambridge, UK: Cambridge University Press.

Verbrugge, M. H. (1979). The social meaning of personal health: The Ladies' Physiological Institute of Boston and vicinity in the 1850's. In S. Reverby & D. Rosner (Eds.), *Health care in America: Essays in social history* (pp. 45-66). Philadelphia: Temple University Press.

Vogel, M. J. (1980). *The invention of the modern hospital: Boston, 1870-1930.* Chicago: University of Chicago Press.

Welter, B. (1964). The cult of true womanhood, 1820-1860. *American Quarterly, 18,* 151-174.

11

Only Daughter

Sandra Cisneros

Once, several years ago, when I was just starting out my writing career, I was asked to write my own contributor's note for an anthology I was part of. I wrote: "I am the only daughter in a family of six sons. *That* explains everything."

Well, I've thought about that ever since, and yes, it explains a lot to me, but for the reader's sake I should have written: "I am the only daughter in a *Mexican* family of six sons." Or even: "I am the only daughter of a Mexican father and a Mexican-American mother." Or: "I am the only daughter of a working-class family of nine." All of these had everything to do with who I am today.

I was/am the only daughter and *only* a daughter. Being an only daughter in a family of six sons forced me by circumstance to spend a lot of time by myself because my brothers felt it beneath them to play with a *girl* in public. But that aloneness, that loneliness, was good for a would-be writer—it allowed me time to think and think, to imagine, to read and prepare myself.

Being only a daughter for my father meant my destiny would lead me to become someone's wife. That's what he believed. But when I was in fifth grade and shared my plans for college with him, I was sure he understood. I remember my father saying, "*Que bueno, mi'ja,*

that's good." That meant a lot to me, especially since my brothers thought the idea hilarious. What I didn't realize was that my father thought college was good for girls—for finding a husband. After four years in college and two more in graduate school, and still no husband, my father shakes his head even now and says I wasted all that education.

In retrospect, I'm lucky my father believed daughters were meant for husbands. It meant it didn't matter if I majored in something silly like English. After all, I'd find a nice professional eventually, right? This allowed me the liberty to putter about embroidering my little poems and stories without my father interrupting with so much as a "What's that you're writing?"

But the truth is, I wanted him to interrupt. I wanted my father to understand what it was I was scribbling, to introduce me as "My only daughter, the writer." Not as "This is my only daughter. She teaches." *El maestra*—teacher. Not even *profesora.*

In a sense, everything I have ever written has been for him, to win his approval even though I know my father can't read English words, even though my father's only reading includes the brown-ink *Esto* sports magazines from Mexico City and the bloody *¡Alarma!*

magazines that feature yet another sighting of *La Virgen de Guadalupe* on a tortilla or a wife's revenge on her philandering husband by bashing his skull in with a *molcajete* (a kitchen mortar made of volcanic rock). Or the *fotonovelas*, the little picture paperbacks with tragedy and trauma erupting from the characters' mouths in bubbles.

My father represents, then, the public majority. A public who is disinterested in reading, and yet one whom I am writing about and for, and privately trying to woo.

When we were growing up in Chicago, we moved a lot because of my father. He suffered periodic bouts of nostalgia. Then we'd have to let go our flat, store the furniture with mother's relatives, load the station wagon with baggage and bologna sandwiches, and head south. To Mexico City.

We came back, of course. To yet another Chicago flat, another Chicago neighborhood, another Catholic school. Each time, my father would seek out the parish priest in order to get a tuition break, and complain or boast: "I have seven sons."

He meant *siete hijos*, seven children, but he translated it as "sons." "I have seven sons." To anyone who would listen. The Sears Roebuck employee who sold us the washing machine. The short-order cook where my father ate his ham-and-eggs breakfasts. "I have seven sons." As if he deserved a medal from the state.

My papa. He didn't mean anything by that mistranslation, I'm sure. But somehow I could feel myself being erased. I'd tug my father's sleeve and whisper: "Not seven sons. Six! and *one daughter*."

When my oldest brother graduated from medical school, he fulfilled my father's dream that we study hard and use this—our heads, instead of this—our hands. Even now my father's hands are thick and yellow, stubbed by a history of hammer and nails and twine and coils and springs. "Use this," my father said, tapping his head, "and not this," showing us those hands. He always looked tired when he said it.

Wasn't college an investment? And hadn't I spent all those years in college? And if I didn't marry, what was it all for? Why would anyone go to college and then choose to be poor? Especially someone who had always been poor.

Last year, after ten years of writing professionally, the financial rewards started to trickle in. My second National Endowment for the Arts Fellowship. A guest professorship at the University of California, Berkeley. My book, which sold to a major New York publishing house.

At Christmas, I flew home to Chicago. The house was throbbing, same as always; hot *tamales* and sweet *tamales* hissing in my mother's pressure cooker, and everybody—my mother, six brothers, wives, babies, aunts, cousins—talking too loud and at the same time, like in a Fellini film, because that's just how we are.

I went upstairs to my father's room. One of my stories had just been translated into Spanish and published in an anthology of Chicano writing, and I wanted to show it to him. Ever since he recovered from a stroke two years ago, my father likes to spend his leisure hours horizontally. And that's how I found him, watching a Pedro Infante movie on Galavision and eating rice pudding.

There was a glass filmed with milk on the bedside table. There were several vials of pills and balled Kleenex. And on the floor, one black sock and a plastic urinal that I didn't want to look at but looked at anyway. Pedro Infante was about to burst into song, and my father was laughing.

I'm not sure if it was because my story was translated into Spanish, or because it was published in Mexico, or perhaps because the story dealt with Tepeyac, the *colonia* my father was raised in, but at any rate, my father punched the mute button on his remote control and read my story.

I sat on the bed next to my father and waited. He read it very slowly. As if he were reading each line over and over. He laughed at all the right places and read lines he liked out loud. He pointed and asked questions: "Is this So-and-so?" "Yes," I said. He kept reading.

When he was finally finished, after what seemed like hours, my father looked up and asked: "Where can we get more copies of this for the relatives?"

Of all the wonderful things that happened to me last year, that was the most wonderful.

12

The Experience of Grandfatherhood

Sarah Cunningham-Burley

The Study

The study aimed to examine the meaning and significance of grandparenthood, in depth, from the point of view of people becoming grandparents for the first time. A sample of eighteen couples were interviewed over a period of one year, once before and twice after the birth of their first grandchild. The couples all lived in Aberdeen, and had their families either living within the city or its environs. They were aged between 42 and 55 years, except one couple in their mid-sixties. Most were working class, with only two couples having middle-class occupations. All the grandfathers were in full-time employment. All but one of the grandmothers were working, at least part-time. Contact was made via the daughter or daughter-in-law while she was attending the antenatal clinic. This prospective strategy enabled the process of becoming a grandparent to be explored, from the early anticipations of the first interviews, through the excitement of the birth itself, to the routines developed by the time the child was 6 to 9 months old.

Constructing Grandfatherhood

An analysis of the grandfathers' role in the interview setting showed that it would be easy to discount men in family research, or to construct their role in families only from a woman's point of view. The grandmothers certainly spoke much more in the interview setting. They also seemed to be much more involved in speaking about grandparenthood on other occasions as well. For them, much of the experience was something tangible.

The grandfathers, however, were much less involved in such verbal interchanges, and treated the interviews very differently. They laughed and joked, came and went, and tended to be somewhat peripheral to the proceedings. In short, the interviews were rather dominated by the grandmothers. It is important to understand this difference between the grandmothers and grandfathers, for it informs how grandfatherhood is socially constructed. On the whole the grandfathers did not seem to find it so easy to express how they felt about grandfatherhood. However, one should not interpret this as a lack of involvement in grandparenthood.

Dilemmas of Grandparenthood

Both the grandmothers and grandfathers recollected past experience, and from this made an assessment of both the differences between grandparents past and present, and between parenting and grandparenting. The grandfathers were more likely to stress the different environment of today and how this meant that you had fewer grandchildren, and more time to spend with them. The grandmothers were more likely to say that people had more resources these days, especially money: grandparents were able to do more today.

Many respondents used recollections of their own parents as grandparents to illustrate what they felt that one should or should not do as grandparents. Rather than producing a clear definition of the grandparental role, the grandparents' recollections seemed to highlight some inherent dilemmas in the grandparental role.

The grandfathers were more likely than the grandmothers to talk about arguments which they had had with their own parents and parents-in-law about their role with the grandchildren. This tended to make them seem more sceptical. While agreeing that grandparents today could do more, they did not think this was wholly positive in the way that the grandmothers did. While grandparents were able to do more than before, they were also constrained. Both the grandfathers and the grandmothers said that they should not interfere with the new family, or spoil the grandchild. They should not impose their desire to grandparent on the young couple (Cunningham-Burley, 1985).

The grandfathers particularly seemed to be aware that by the very nature of their role they may end up making the same mistakes as their own parents as grandparents did sometimes. Learning from past experience seemed to be important. However, the grandparents thought that there may be a certain inevitability to their actions. While all said that they should not interfere, they also realized that grandfatherhood was something new to them, so that they would not be sure how they would react.

The accounts of the differences between grandfathering and fathering reflected both change and continuity. These contradictory components pertained both to the grandfathers' experiences and to the meanings which they attached to grandfatherhood. There was an important variety in the grandfathers' accounts, which should not be lost in the search for general patterns. While at one level grandfatherhood was like "starting all over again," it was also different from fathering.

SCB: Is it very difficult being a father and being a grandfather?

GF: Oh-oh-yes definitely. Having said what I said you try to bring your own up in a . . . in the way I believe is right, whether it be right or wrong, you know, but I think a grandchild's different. He's just a . . . something to love, I suppose, have a bit of fun with, it's up to him (the son) to bring it up, him or her, whatever you like. You haven't got the same pressure on you that to see that it goes on the right path, you know, just here for fun.

The grandfathers' recollections of their own fathering were dominated by the experience of not having the time to be with their young children. As grandfathers they felt that they would be able to spend more time with their grandchildren than they did with their own children, and enjoy their development.

Having more time seemed to constitute an essential difference between fathering as it was then, and grandfathering as it is now. Having more patience also was significant. This was related to having more time but also to having less "parental" responsibility for the child, and to being older and more lenient oneself. The responsibilities of fathers and grandfathers were seen as quite different.

In many ways then, grandfatherhood could be enjoyed more than fatherhood, although one grandfather noted that "it's not as exciting as your own children," making it difficult to generalize. While a difference between being a parent and being a grandparent was often expressed by the respondents, the essence of these differences remained ill-defined. Some said that they could not remember what they felt like becoming or being a father, or speculated that they must have felt about the same. Thus, comparing fatherhood and grandfatherhood was one method through which the grandfathers expressed what becoming a grandfather was like.

Grandfathers and Social Change

The grandfathers often worked long hours when they were fathers, and both the grandmothers and grandfathers generally said that the grandfathers were not very involved in child-care because of this. However, the grandmothers also felt that the role of fathers had changed since then. As will be noted below, there were exceptions to this, namely, those grandfathers who were "involved" fathers. Both the grandmothers and grandfathers had a lot to say about the changing role of fathers across the generations. This is of interest to a fuller understanding of the grandfathers' experience of grandfatherhood, and the constraints and contradictions within it. It also highlights some interesting gender differences, which underlie how family life is accounted and described by men and women.

The respondents' own recollections of early married life reflected a harder time, with less help from relatives. Wages did not go far. The respondents told of how, as young parents, they could not afford to go out, and that life

was a struggle. This was not the case for the younger generation: life had changed, and was easier. The grandparents themselves contributed to that change by providing material goods for the new family, and helping out in various ways. They would do all these things because they knew it was hard bringing up a family whatever the circumstances. They were glad of the opportunity to help out, and the impact of these changes was generally seen as good.

Within this broad consensus about the changing social environment of family life, the grandmothers and grandfathers differed greatly in their assessment of the role of grandfathers. Although the respondents did discuss the role of mothers, it was the role of fathers which came under greatest scrutiny. It was within these discussions that diverse assessments were made of the grandfathers' fathering, and reference made to their grandfathering. In this way it is interesting to see how the grandmothers and the grandfathers account for change differently, and locate the role of fathers, and grandfathers within divergent perceptions of social change.

By implication if not by direct comparison, the grandmothers thought that the grandfathers, when they were fathers of young children, did not do as much as their sons or sons-in-law are perceived to do.

A few of the grandfathers were described as being exceptionally good fathers, by the grandmothers, because they went beyond what they considered to be the then accepted role, and became involved with their children. They played and had fun with their families, and it was expected that they would be the same as grandfathers.

These days, however, "good" fathers were not just those who happened to be good with children anyway, or who enjoyed being involved: today fathers were expected to help with the baby, and share this new responsibility.

The grandparents talked about why things were different these days, drawing both on personal experience and general knowledge.

Each grandfather's experience was different and accounts for the subtle variety in their expressions about the meaning and significance of grandfatherhood and fatherhood. Those grandfathers who were described as having been "good fathers" (because they helped out in the home, went shopping, or more especially played with or looked after the infants) could account for their own sons' behaviour as being learned. This occurred in two cases: Mr McCallum said that none of his boys would complain about helping out; Mr Sinclair explained that his sons had been taught to help their wives and to be involved with their children. Change and continuity could be accounted at a personal level or beyond the immediate family experience.

Others said that times had changed, even when within their own family the trend of increased paternal involvement was seen to have begun with the respondents' own child-rearing. This could be done once individual personal experience was considered atypical.

It was clear from this study that most of the grandfathers had the opportunity to behave differently as grandfathers than they did as fathers, or as their own fathers did as grandfathers. Yet, this was because they were grandfathers, not because fathering as an institution had changed for them. Having more time, money and patience were cited as important. They did not have to worry about bringing the child up or making ends meet. To them grandfatherhood was in many ways totally new: it was different from being a father, yet different from past grandparents' roles. Grandmotherhood was perhaps more taken-for-granted: they saw the family during the day more, since most of the grandmothers worked part-time rather than full-time. However, the grandfathers certainly spent time with their grandchildren, and many activities were joint activities in the evenings or at weekends. Only one grandfather said that he felt left out, although as I have noted elsewhere lesser grandparental involvement in the early months of grandparenthood was perhaps taken for granted (Cunningham-Burley, 1984). Yet, the grandfathers did seem to enjoy grandfatherhood, and through comments made both by them and the grandmothers, an understanding of the experience of grandfatherhood can be developed.

The Experience of Grandfatherhood

In the early stages of grandfathering, the grandfathers' role was not clear cut. They did not become immediately involved in helping out, in knitting, or in talking about their grandchildren to friends—all activities which the grandmothers spoke about frequently. Not only were these activities associated with grandmothers but also with babies. Some of the grandfathers said that they would wait until the child was older.

As noted earlier, many of the grandfathers had not been involved with their children as babies. However, it was also recognized that they might end up being more involved with their grandchildren as babies than they had anticipated. This was because they had, for example, more time now than they had as fathers. Grandfatherhood brings with it the potential to do things differently.

In the case of those grandfathers who had been involved as fathers, grandfatherhood brought with it the chance to do things again. The constraints which the grandfathers felt affected their fathering (that is not having enough time), coupled with ageing effects (having more patience) were the very enabling features of grandfathering. They could be different, and enjoy their grandchildren in a different way from their own children.

Grandfatherhood did seem to be important to the grandfathers in the sample, they just found it difficult to express how they felt:

e.g. Mr Henderson: Everybody asks you, "How do you feel being a grandfather?"

But you can't say . . . I don't feel any different yet it is a different feeling. Don't ask me to put it into words for you.

As the following example demonstrates, this does not mean that the experience of grandfatherhood was not something meaningful to them:

> e.g. **Mr Findlay:**   I would not show it as much as my wife. I never show my feelings outwardly—but inwardly I'll probably be just as excited or more excited.

In addition to grandfatherhood being a chance to be involved with children either again or for the first time, becoming a grandfather held other meanings. Although the grandfathers did not talk about doing very much in terms of grandparental activities at this early stage, they still described grandfatherhood as important, in a symbolic way. It is part of life, and thus both significant and important.

Conclusion

An individual grandfather may have quite different experiences with different grandchildren, as his grandchildren get older, or as he himself ages. The research reported here has shown that each grandfather has a unique history of family relationships, although there were common threads across the sample. Grandfatherhood is bound up with experiences of fatherhood past and present. Its special features are that it is different from parenting, because of having more time, money and patience, yet different from grandparenting in the past because today's grandparents can do more for and with the family and child. The fathering role was seen to have changed much more than the mothering role. Although this was welcomed by the grandmothers, it caused some trouble for the grandfathers: their own parenting was implicitly called into question, and they had to develop a role for themselves in a new family setting. Unlike Russell (1985) I did not find that the grandfathers regretted their own fathering, but saw it as appropriate for the time, and within the constraints of their working lives. The grandmothers, it seemed, could take much more for granted in developing their grandmaternal roles. In spite of these difficulties the grandfathers were enjoying the experience of grandfatherhood, not only in the practical sense of being with their grandchildren, but at a symbolic level as becoming a grandfather was part of the way life developed and progressed.

References

Cunningham-Burley, S. (1984) "'We Don't Talk about it . . .' Issues of Gender and Method in the Portrayal of Grandfatherhood," *Sociology*, 18(3): 325-38.

Cunningham-Burley, S. (1985) "Constructing Grandparenthood: Anticipating Appropriate Action," *Sociology*, 19 (3): 421-36.

Russell, G. (1985) "Grandfathers: Making Up for Lost Opportunities?" in R. A. Lewis and R. E. Salt (eds) *Men in Families*. Beverly Hills: Sage.

13

Father's Sorrow, Father's Joy

Darrell G. H. Schramm

As an adult I once studied a photograph of him standing beside me when I was perhaps four years old. His smile is a pencil line, his arms straight—they are close to but not touching me as I stand on the running board of a 1940s Packard.

It was a winter morning when the photo was taken, the sun having melted the night-frost or the thin lick of snow that skirts a Midwestern house like a ruffle even when the rest of the ground is free of any precipitation. My little fist is clenched; it must have been cold.

Studying that picture, I thought, "He could have held my hand." But he didn't. We stood smiling pleasantly for a camera's eye, unmoved by anything but the social obedience that demands a subject stand still for a photograph. "He could have held my hand. In all those years of growing up, he could have touched me just once to show he was glad to have fathered me, his first son."

What wasted years before we both understood, before we became true father-and-son. All those years growing up, I believed wrongly that his silence and restraint were measuring me against himself and the other men of our German clan, that the silence meant rejection or denial, that love is voiced only in words.

It was after my sixth birthday when he asked me if I'd accompany him to the pasture where he was going to "take care of" one of our cows that had broken her foot stepping into a gopher or prairie-dog hole. I sensed we were on an adventure, driving through the prairie grass, for normally we walked the pasture, usually to herd the cows home for milking. Not until Dad had pulled up beside the cow, still standing near the fatal gopher hole, and pulled a rifle from the trunk did I realize with a sudden terror what was about to happen.

"Aren't you coming out of the car?" Dad asked me in German.

I could only shake my head. When I saw him raise the gun, I quickly rolled up the windows, ducked below the steering wheel, and squeezed my eyes shut while plugging my ears with my fingers. And I was in pain, a new pain I'd never before felt.

I heard the gun go off, then heard the car door open. "What's wrong with you?" Dad

---

This chapter is an abridged version of the original by Darrell G. H. Schramm.

asked me. "Afraid of a gun?" (Or had he said "Afraid of *the* gun?" The difference matters to a child's interpretation.) I thought he was mocking me, belittling my horror. Still I refused to look at the spot where the milk cow had stood. We drove back to the farmhouse in silence.

Those were the years, too, at ages six and seven, when I took to wearing aprons, pretending I was a girl as I played in the barnyard, the cornfield, the loft, the house. Sometimes I'd even tie my shirt around my head, letting it fall in back, making believe I had long hair. If ever Dad commented on my games, he never spoke a word to me. Silence can be the voice of approval or acceptance also, but what does a child know of that?

At age eight I exchanged my aprons for my mother's discarded skirts, wearing them until I was eleven, even in the backyard after we'd moved to town. I didn't notice that Dad—not only Mom—allowed me this freedom until I outgrew it.

When I was eleven, we moved from North Dakota to northern California, where Dad began to work at construction sites long distances from home. Consequently, he would often be gone during the week, home only on weekends. More and more he seemed on the periphery of my life. Little teasings—taunts I thought they were—come back to me: when I refused to eat hot chili peppers, he would say, "Takes a man to eat these"; when I'd bend a nail while hammering, he'd say, "Hold the hammer like a man"; when I'd speak enthusiastically about my male friends, he'd ask, "Do you have a girlfriend yet?" Though he never barked, snapped, or scolded, I was convinced that he disapproved. I was not like my younger brothers or my many male cousins. Except for track and tennis, I participated in and cared about no sports. I read novels and poetry and listened to classical music. And I was an adolescent who secretly loved boys my own age. How could he approve?

Yet one memory of my teenage years stands out like an exclamation mark to contradict the censure I felt from my father. Though unable to afford it, my parents sent me to a Christian boarding school in Oakland, birthplace of Robert Duncan, childhood home of Gertrude Stein. I'd come home for a short holiday during my sophomore year but had seen little of Dad, who worked long shifts at the Oroville Dam. And he'd already gone to work long before the time I had to return to the city. Ticket in my hand, I was slowly moving in line toward the door of the Greyhound bus when a Pontiac squealed to a stop behind it. Dad jumped from the car. Had I forgotten something? No, he'd just come from work during his break. "Well, uh, you be good and don't do anything I wouldn't do," he said. Then he leaned toward me and kissed me good-bye.

All the way back to Oakland I kept thinking, "Maybe he loves me after all."

But the years shuffled on, each year seeming to put more distance between us.

When I was thirty-three, I met Chris. When we met, we were both living in San Francisco. We'd been visiting and dating each other constantly for about ten months when, for Thanksgiving, I drove home to southern California where my parents had moved a few years before.

The evening I arrived at their Santa Maria home, Dad and I were seated across from each other, he in his rocker and I on the sofa, a wide empty space between us. After one or two perfunctory remarks about the weather, we lapsed into our usual silence. I picked up a magazine, *Family Circle* or *Woman's Day* most likely, and fluttered through it. Suddenly the room thundered. Dad had burst out, "Why in hell don't you talk to me like my other boys do!" and stormed from the room. I was stunned. For a long time I sat listening to the echoes rumbling in my heart.

The next morning on our way to buy fresh eggs at a farm outside town, I said, "Dad, before I return to San Francisco, I have to tell you something."

"So whyn't you tell me now?" he asked quietly, glancing at me from the steering wheel. His face seemed gentle.

"Because I'm scared. I need more time."

Accepting my reason, he began speaking of the farmer we were about to visit, of how he himself still enjoyed eating farm-fresh eggs, of how he sometimes missed farm life. . . .

. . . I was pacing when Dad walked into the room. "Whyn't you sit down?" he asked me.

"I'm too nervous," I said, then stopped abruptly a few feet from him. Looking at him, I went on with a rush. "Dad, I'm in love with someone I'd like to spend the rest of my life with. It's a man. I'm in love with another man."

The sky didn't fall, lightning didn't strike me, hell didn't open at my feet. But Dad, my father, opened his arms. Taking a couple of steps toward me, he put his hands on my shoulders and said, "You're my son. As long as you never turn on your mother and me, you'll always be my son." And then he held me against his chest.

The next time I drove home for a visit, Chris was with me. Dad welcomed him immediately.

Over the next decade, Chris and I invited my parents to San Francisco to spend weekends with us. And they came. Sometimes while my mother and I fixed meals, Dad joined Chris outside for a smoke. Seeing Chris as an extension of myself, he gave Chris as much attention and affection as he gave me.

We had come a long way, my father and I, and we had only a short way yet to go. That following spring, I resigned from my teaching position of eleven years in order to work on a book of poetry and to complete a long short story I'd been struggling with for years. I would go to Europe, traveling with Chris for a month, then stay on to write. Late that summer, shortly before Chris and I were to leave, Dad had a heart attack. Mom called me after he'd been hospitalized and seemed to be doing well. He'd told her from his hospital bed that I was

not to cancel my trip nor change my plans on his account. Still skeptical, I called his nurse, who reassured me that so far all signs were in his favor, that there was no vascular damage. When I spoke to Dad, he insisted he was all right, that I was to take my trip, to follow through what I had begun. He sounded cheerful as he wished me a safe journey. Later, when I called home from Scotland, he was still doing well.

Once Chris had returned to the States, I traveled for two weeks in Italy, then went to Spain, where I settled in a white, hilltop town. When the Loma Prieta earthquake struck the San Francisco area, I was in Sevilla. For two days I tried to get through by telephone without any luck. On the third day I connected with Chris's sister, who immediately assured me that everyone I cared about in San Francisco was safe and fine.

"But there's still some bad news," she said. "Oh, Darrell, I'm so sorry. Your father died."

I hung up slowly, walked to the nearby Plaza Nueva, sat under a lamp, and wept.

This man, my father, had loved much, silently and deeply, had given of his love through work and sacrifice, without comment or complaint.

And I remembered, too, our last words to each other, long-distance words. "Dad," I'd said over the telephone, "I love you."

"I love you too, son," he said. "And give my love to Chris, okay?"

"Dad, it's good to hear your voice."

There was a pause, and then Dad's voice broke as he said goodbye. I believe he knew even then.

I, a man who loves men and the land, shall have no sons to carry on the love of sons and the land. But sometimes, digging in my garden, I remember him; and sometimes, seeing Chris smoke a cigarette on the back porch, I remember him; but most of all I remember him when, loving Chris and aware of my own body, I know that I am his flesh and his love continuing.

14

Last Christmas Gift From a Mother

Lois F. Lyles

Nightgown

The pink and white flowered gown I wear to bed is three years old, and threadbare. It had been witness to my first experience of loving a good man. Both the gown and the good man are still with me.

Now my gown is again a witness. It carries a black smudge (the watery mascara from the blotting of my midnight tears) just above the ruffle at the hem. I cannot cry in the daytime. I must, like my relatives, look at my mother in the hospital bed and pretend nothing is wrong. Besides, I must try to be cheerful, to keep her spirits up.

Sometimes she, either from pain or from fear of the axe of doom hovering over her neck, explodes in a tempest of nervous tears. Then my father, scowling, exclaims, "Aw, Minnie, don't cry!"

Twice when she and I have been by ourselves in the room, we have cried together. She doesn't mind my tears, I know, and hers don't bother me. When nobody is looking at us, we can cry, and then it is all right.

It's not all right when I am at the house; if I cry there, father or son is sure to reproach me for the weakness of sorrow. So, at night, I go into my room and shut the door. I pull my old, warm gown, first the gown of love, and now of grief, over my head. The soft white flannel balls into my palm as soon as the room is dark and my feet have slid between the cool bedsheets. In a few minutes, the flannel is damp. Can I get a witness? I've got my gown.

Waiting on the Sick

Mama is down, I am up. Up, and up, and up. She wants vaseline for her char-dry lips, her Saint Francis church bulletin, her rosary. The vase on the dresser must be moved out of the way of the black-faced digital clock. Two twenty-five, New Year's afternoon. She stares at the red numerals, each like an imp or an infernal flame, as the five becomes a six; the six, a seven.

"Water the plants, Lois."

Nervously, I dribble water into the flowerpots. I work fast. She has approximately one request every three minutes.

"Thank you, darling. I feel so worthless and useless. Why can't I do anything?"

"Mama, you are not worthless. You are a beautiful person. You still look beautiful to me," I say, and mean it. She was my childhood idol. Her soulful-eyed, smooth-haired beauty was my first acquaintance with romance.

"No, I'm not," she whimpers; then says, "Thank you, darling."

"Mama, whatever happens, I'm with you, and I'm for you."

She cries. Her misery makes me recall how my fear of death had once made me, to my mortal shame, abandon a sick woman I loved. I am the namesake of Mama's sister Florence, who died of cancer four summers ago. Florence is my middle name. Mama must be thinking of Aunt Flo, too, for she says, "I took care of Sister when she went up to her bedroom three days before she died and never came downstairs again. I remember she was amazed that I would wash her down there, you know, her private parts. She didn't want me to have to do that." After pausing, my mother adds, "I thought, Lois, it would help you after this is over, to be with me now when I need you, and do things for me."

I am astonished at her, the good mother. She has called me to her sickbed, not so much to help her as to help *me*. I, in childhood, was never hungry, never homeless, never seriously ill; and was never exposed to the sight of physical suffering. My parents had made sure of all that. But an easy ride of a life is only a half-truth. Now Mama's gift is to let me know her pain. She is letting me see if I am strong enough to grapple, by proxy, with Death.

Her Names

The phone cries unceasing alarm. Three nurses, a nurse's aide, an oncologist, a dermatologist, the family physician, a lawyer, a social worker, the medical insurance people. Nephews, nieces, sisters, daughter Mary, friends. "Anything I can do? So sorry. Call me if you need anything. So sad." So sorry to hear about Miz Lyles, about Minnie, about Auntie Minnie, about Nanny, about Mary (this last, the name my mother chose to call herself after she, upon retirement, developed her own business; she had always hated "Minnie").

She has some other names. To my son, whom she reared, she is alternately "Ma" and "Grandma." To "the Frye bunch," my sister's four, she is "Big Grandmommy," in contrast to Mrs. Alberta Frye, "Little Grandmommy."

Mama is hunched over in the wheelchair as I, moaning under my breath and clutching her shoulders, sit behind her on the bed. The emergency medical technicians, all in blue shirts and trousers, seem to take up too much space in this bedroom, that, for the first time, is receiving the scrutiny of strangers.

"What's her name?" the big, blond technician asks.

"Mrs. Lyles."

"First name?"

"Minnie."

He bends toward her and trumpets, "Minnie, can you hear me?" His Southern accent grates on my ears.

"Her name is *Mrs.* Lyles." I stare at the man.

"I'm sorry!" He twirls the end of his thick yellow moustache between thumb and index finger. "She is a very sick woman. What's more important, that I check her condition, or that I call her by her proper name?" The young man's brow knits, and he shakes his head.

I think, "He's young, White, she never would have let him call her by her first name. *They* always did that to us, down South."

Dog

My mother is a dog. She snarls, rather than talks. She seemed all right at first, but a relapse came after the temporary stroke. That her speech is half-gone frightens and hurts me above all else. I have always loved the richness, cadence, clarity of the human voice.

My mother is a dog. It is easier to think of her that way. Since the stroke, I have not kissed her hands or face. Did I promise that I'd always be her support, no matter what happened? Well, I lied. I am afraid of her now. *Liar, liar*, I taunt myself. You only loved a woman beautiful or whole.

This is early morning on a bad day. All the days now are bad. Since the stroke. When was that? What's today? I remember dinner last night, that's all.

Now I have to watch her when she eats the way you watch a baby. Her hair dangles in the plate and crumbs of meat and vegetables stick to the white strands. *Now I have to chop and mash her food, just like a baby's. Only she's not a baby.* With her left hand, she claws for the bread on her lap tray. "Why can't I use my left hand? Why is everybody well but me?" she moans. The bread, clawed to fragments, spatters all over her pajamas.

"Mom, don't try to use your left hand. It's weak. Use your right."

Still, her left hand scratches over the slick surface of the plastic tray, seeking the recalcitrant remnants of bread.

"Mom!" I move her left hand to her thigh, hold it there. *Be still.*

Night is worse than mealtimes. I am up every few hours to help her take her pills. She is getting too weak to swallow them. To medicate her, I get my hand behind her back, and heave her into a sitting position. Then I support her shoulders against my chest so that she will not fall. She is boulder-heavy. How can one little body just under five and a half feet long, weighing under a hundred pounds, be so maliciously, grossly heavy? *Dead weight.*

She is calling me. I wake up in the dark, hearing her. How long has it been since I gave her the midnight pills? "Lo-was. Lo-was." I run across the hall. In the light of the pink, chartreuse, and indigo figures flickering on the TV screen, Mama is lying on the floor, her legs splayed out over the bathroom lintel, her head just underneath the bed.

"Mama! Mama!" I bend over her, tugging at her to get her all the way out into the bedroom and sitting up.

"I wanna use the toilet," she growls, slowly, sullenly, like a drunk. I try to help her up, but she is all dull, insensate weight.

"Daddy! Daddy!"

Together he and I lift her back onto the bed, but she tries to roll out. "Gotta use the bathroom," she insists.

"No, Ma!" I run to the linen closet, get towels, shove them under her. Dad and I tell her it is better to mess the bed than fall and get hurt. But she is obstinate. Her leg keeps pummeling the side of the bed.

"Minnie, if you've got to go, just cut loose." Dad is frowning, exasperated.

"No. I'm not gonna go in the bed. Can't do that."

"Mama!" Dad and I lean over her and press back her squirming hips and thighs.

"Put these chairs up against the bed," Dad says. He is pulling up one of the chairs we have brought in here for visitors. Soon Mama is imprisoned by three high-backed chairs. *This is what you do to keep a baby from rolling out of bed,* I think. She still begs us to let her get up.

"Tomorrow I'll have to get a bedpan," Dad says. He pads downstairs.

In a little while, the bitter odor of urine is on the air. I pull the wet towels from under her and remove the wet pajama bottoms. Her sex is a forlorn, desiccated rose in a desert of loose, sandy flesh. Her privates simultaneously repel, shame, and fascinate me. I cannot remember ever having seen my mother's nakedness. *This is the body from which I came.*

Gingerly, I wash her genitals and thighs, and change her clothing. What about the soaked bedding? Moving her to the other side of the bed is a task for a weightlifter. How do you move a helpless woman?

"Ma, you gotta move to the other side of the bed," I say. I stand cupping my jaw in my right hand, looking down at her, but not meeting her eyes. Since the temporary stroke, I have avoided looking her full in the face.

A dovelike touch greets my hand. I bend over her.

"Ma, what is it?"

Her right arm curves gracefully as a swan's neck around the back of my head, and her hand settles politely on my neck.

"Oh! You remembered!" I look in her eyes now, as she tries to raise her shoulders. *She* had remembered; I had not.

The first time the nurse had come, I'd asked, *How do I help her sit up?* And the nurse had explained, *Mrs. Lyles, put your arm around your daughter's neck. Lois, slip your left hand behind her back, and hook your right around her waist. Then, ease her up gradually.*

I smile at Mama. *My mother is not a dog.*

15

Extended Kin Networks in Black Families

Peggye Dilworth-Anderson

The family within the African American culture provides a template and filter for the expression of traditions, beliefs, symbols, language, ways of thinking, and rules for interacting within black cultures. It provides the foundation for understanding what it means to be black (Spencer and Adams-Markstrom, 1990). The family also provides a window into the dynamic and static aspects of the culture that are put into play within a group as it shifts and reshapes in response to the needs of its members.

What Is Family in the Black Community?

The traditional black communities define family relationally. Although most kin are related by blood, this is not a requisite. Family membership is not determined only by blood but also by the nature of the relationship between individuals. Fictive kin can, therefore, be as important in the black family as those related by blood. Boundaries are also permeable and flexible in black families. People can move in and out of several families and have numerous siblings or "play" siblings and parents. The

family is both temporal and stable, depending on the conditions of individuals within it and the degree to which the kin network can absorb members. These traditional families foster parent-care and the absorption of dependent and needy generations (Herkovits, 1970; Gutman, 1976). This particular orientation has served the elderly blacks very well, especially in regard to creating a mutual aid system between themselves and other members of their families.

Emergence of the Mutual Aid System

The mutual aid system in extended black families is rooted within a larger cultural context that evolved from the "brother" and "sister" concept in the African American community (Frazier, 1932; Franklin, 1948). This concept emerged out of the idea of survival in a hostile and oppressive society where blacks viewed themselves as "making it" only through the concerted efforts of groups of people. This way of thinking provided a belief system and a context for extended kin relations to emerge. The individual was not socialized—nor afforded the opportunity—by his underground community and the mainstream society to "make it" on his own.

Extended black families provide care and support to children, older people, and other needy adult members. Aged blacks and their adult children share goods and services with one another, and adult children are their parents' primary caregivers (Martin and Martin, 1978; Mutran, 1985; Taylor and Chatters, 1991).

Mutran (1985) reports that aged blacks receive as well as give support to their extended families. They give advice and economic support to their adult children more often than do whites, and assist their children by providing services to their grandchildren. In fact, current research shows that black grandparents are playing significant roles in the parenting of their grandchildren by serving as surrogate parents (or coparents) in their socialization and rearing. Many of them share homes with their grandchildren and frequently support them financially (Foster, 1983; Hogan, Hao and Parish, 1990; Wilson et al., 1990).

However, the ability of the black extended family to continue its system of providing support to its members will be challenged by changing demographic conditions. Black families are now faced with increasing unemployment, greater numbers of single parent households, more poverty among women, and more early childbearing families. Although these changes are evident in white families, black families experience them at a higher rate (Jaynes and Williams, 1989). For example, black males are almost three times more likely to be unemployed than are whites—11 percent and 4 percent, respectively. Furthermore, 40 percent of black as compared with 25 percent of white families have no employed person in the household. Among female-headed households, the problem is even more severe. Almost 60 percent of households headed by black females, as compared to 48 percent headed by white females, have no employed person in the household. With slightly over 50 percent of

black families headed by females today, the issue of poverty among families with young children, which is related to employment, is an increasing concern. Sixty-eight percent of black female heads of household with children under the age of 18 are in poverty, as compared to 48 percent of their white counterparts. These poor black women, many of whom are unskilled, with low levels of education, and with more children to take care of as compared to white females, look to their extended family for support, especially to (given the history of their roles in the family) grandparents.

The Future of Black Extended Families

Black mothers in the work force, many of whom are single, without adequate childcare, and earning 5 percent less than their white counterparts, will continue to need whatever financial and other assistance their extended families can offer. Like those of the past, black grandparents today remain central figures in the survival process and may assume roles to protect, maintain, nurture, and serve as role models to different generations, especially young children.

Older grandparents (those over age 65), like the younger women in the family, have very low incomes; many who are still employed have low-wage jobs. In addition, many have health problems and live in substandard housing (Horton and Smith, 1990). Moreover, roles that were always stressful for grandparents have become increasingly so as their adult children experience increasing rates (compared to whites) of poverty and joblessness, and as teenage fertility rates and the number of single parent households rise among blacks—along with the number of multigenerational households (Farley and Allen, 1987).

Competing demands of different dependent generations in the family will greatly challenge black women's ability to care for their children and older parents. Again, young single mothers who will have a history of poverty will be the expected caregivers of the growing older population in the black community—and these single mothers will themselves need as much or more support as the aged for whom they will be expected to care.

Summary and Discussion

One would assume that the cultural expectation in most black families is that the kin network will continue providing care and support to dependent members. However, the ability to maintain this traditional way of responding will be challenged by the status, situation, and condition of those who serve in the caregiving and supportive roles (Barresi and Menon, 1990). Changing sociodemographic characteristics of black families indicate that a large proportion of the pool of kin-keepers and caregivers will be poor and needy.

It is hoped that black families in the future will become more resilient and flexible in attempting to find ways to address the social and economic conditions that threaten the existence of the extended kin network. They will probably develop diverse ways of surviving and coping. Researchers studying and practitioners working with black families need to be sensitive to the diverse ways in which black families will try to address the challenges they face.

References

Barresi, C. M. and Menon, G., 1990. "Diversity in Black Family Caregiving." In Z. Harel, ed., *Black Aged.* Newbury Park, Calif.: Sage.

Farley, R. and Allen, W. R., 1987. *The Color Line and the Quality of Life in America.* New York: Oxford University Press.

Foster, H. J., 1983. "African Patterns in the Afro-American Family." *Journal of Black Studies* 14:201-32.

Franklin, J. H., 1948. *From Slavery to Freedom: A History of American Negroes.* New York: Alfred A. Knopf.

Frazier, E. F., 1932. *The Negro Family.* Chicago: University of Chicago Press.

Gutman, H., 1976. *The Black Family in Slavery and Freedom, 1750-1925.* New York: Pantheon Books.

Herkovits, M., 1970. *The Myth of the Negro Past.* Boston: Beacon Press.

Hogan, D., Hao, L.-X. and Parish, W., 1990. "Race, Kin Networks, and Assistance to Mother-Headed Families." *Social Forces* 68:797-812.

Horton, C. P. and Smith, J. C., 1990. *Statistical Records of Black America.* Detroit, Mich.: Gale Research, Inc.

Jaynes, D. J. and Williams, R. M., 1989. *A Common Destiny: Blacks in American Society.* Washington, D.C.: National Academy Press.

Martin, E. P. and Martin, J. M., 1978. *The Black Extended Family.* Chicago: University of Chicago Press.

Mutran, E., 1985. "Intergenerational Family Support Among Blacks and Whites: Response to Culture or to Socio-Economic Differences." *Journal of Gerontology* 40:382-89.

Spencer, M. B. and Adams-Markstrom, C., 1990. "Identity Processes Among Racial and Ethnic Minority Children in America." *Child Development* 61:290-310.

Taylor, R. and Chatters, L., 1991. "Extended Family Networks of Older Black Adults." *Journal of Gerontology,* 46:S210-17.

Wilson, M. N. et al., 1990, "Flexibility and Sharing of Childcare Duties in Black Families." *Sex Roles* 22:409-25.

16

Looking After:
A Son's Memoir

John Daniel

I never looked forward to helping my mother with her shower. She wasn't the least self-conscious about baring her body in my presence, but something in me shrank from it. To be with her in her nakedness seemed too intimate for a grown son. And some other part of me, the child who wants always to be cared for and never burdened with responsibility, felt put upon and put out. Why was I having to do this? It seemed an indignity, and it touched an open wound. I had no child to bathe, to make faces at, to splash and laugh with. Most likely I never would. What I had was a frail and failing old woman who couldn't take a shower on her own.

Talking her into it was the first challenge. "Oh, I don't need a shower," she would say. "I just had one yesterday, didn't I?"

"You haven't had one for a week."

"But I don't *do* anything. Why do I need a shower?"

It wasn't only bad memory and lapsing judgment that made her resist, of course. It was also that the shower was strenuous for her, and she didn't want to acknowledge, or couldn't, that she needed help with anything so simple. In her own mind, the mind I believe she inhab-

ited most of the time, she was perfectly capable of taking a shower by herself if she wanted to. In this mind she was still the woman she had been five years ago, a woman who came and went and drove a car, a woman who lived on her own on the coast of Maine and was only temporarily exiled in a distant place. This woman was honestly perplexed when we bought her a cane and asked her, over and over again, to use it. What need had Zilla Daniel for a cane? Somewhere inside her she was not only an able-bodied woman but still a Sea Scout, climbing the rigging in a bright clear wind.

But in her present mind she knew, whenever she leaned far forward in a chair and tried to stiff-arm herself to her feet, whenever she steadied herself with a hand on the wall as she shuffled to the bathroom, just how incapable she had become. She knew, and she hated it. How could she not have hated it? And if she had to bear it, she didn't want me or Marilyn or anyone else to have to help her bear it. She wanted to carry herself on her own stooped shoulders. I can still hear her making her way to the toilet with her left hand pulling her nightgown tight behind her, disgustedly whispering *No, no* to her bladder that could not hold back what it should have held back. As if she were castigating an unbroken puppy, but without the tolerance she would have granted an innocent thing.

Standing for any length of time was hard for my mother, and so the shower was a kind of siege. She would grip the soap tray with both hands as I got the water temperature right—"*Aaant!*" she would holler, "too cold!"—and soaped a washcloth to scrub her sway-spined back. Even the soap met resistance.

"Sai Baba says not to use soap," she informed me early on. "It's just one more thing that has to come off."

"Well, it does come off," I answered, peeling open a bar of Dial. "It rinses off."

"My dear, it leaves a *residue*. Plain water is enough."

"Mother, for God's sake. This isn't the ashram. You need soap to get clean."

"Yes, Father," she said with a scowl.

Eventually we worked out a mulish compromise. We used Ivory, which we both agreed was the most natural. I washed her back and buttocks with a soaped washcloth; she held the cloth a few seconds in the shower spray before washing her front. One hand on the soap tray for support, she briefly swabbed her sagging breasts, her abdomen, the thinly gray-haired pubic region from which I once emerged, and the smooth, still-young skin of her upper thighs. Then I helped her down to the bath stool, where she rested a while and washed her lower legs and feet. The skin of her shins was dry and papery, perpetually blotched with dark purple—not impact bruises but bruises of age.

As I lathered shampoo into her wet white curls, her head would bow from the pressure of my fingers. I'd ask her to hold it up and she would for a second or two, then it would slowly sink again. It must have taken a major effort just to hold herself as upright as she did in her last years. All the while she was slowly bending, slowly folding, curling toward the fetal comfort of the grave.

She squeezed her eyes shut as I rinsed her hair in the shower stream. She scrunched up her face, stuck her lips out, and sputtered through the soapy runoff. It was in that recurring moment of her life with us, her hair flattened to her head, darkened a little with the soaking spray, that I could almost see my mother as a girl—swimming the cold swells off Hancock Point, splashing and laughing, shouting something toward shore, laying into the water with strong even strokes that would take her where she wanted to go.

She would let me stop rinsing only when she could rub a bit of her hair between finger and thumb and make it squeak. Then I would steady her out of the shower stall, her two hands in mine. It felt at moments like a kind of dance, a dance that maybe I knew how to do and needed to do.

I helped my mother down into a straight-backed chair and left her in the bathroom with towels, clean underwear, and a little space heater to keep her warm. She took her time, as with everything. Often it was half an hour or longer before she emerged in her dressing gown, her hair beginning to fluff, her face smiling. No matter how hard she might have resisted the idea, a bath or shower always seemed to renew her: Soap or no soap, the old woman came forth cleaner of spirit.

"She was pure as the driven snow," she usually quoted, gaily, then a pause: "But she drifted."

I guess I came out of the bathroom cleaner of spirit myself. Soap or no soap, whatever the tenor of our conversation, I appreciate now what a privilege it was to help my mother with her shower. I wish I'd seen it more clearly at the time. We don't get to choose our privileges, and the ones that come to us aren't always the ones we would choose, and each of them is as much burden as joy. But they do come, and it's important to know them for what they are.

One morning as my mother came out of her shower she paused at the bottom of the stairs. I was reading the paper in the living room.

"Do you feel them sprouting?" she said, smiling in her white gown.

"Do I feel what sprouting?"

"Your wings," she said. She stood there, barefooted and bright, smiling right at me and through me, smiling as though she weren't feeble of body and failing of mind but filled with an uncanny power that saw things I could only glimpse.

"Mother, I don't have wings," I said.

But she was still smiling as she headed up the stairs, gripping the banister hand over hand, hauling herself up fifteen carpeted steps to her room and her bed made of sea-weathered posts and boards, where she would read for a while, gaze out her window at sky and tree-tops, then drift into sleep.

1   Darrell Schramm talks about the difficulty of sharing his sexual identity with his father. Sandra Cisneros describes her effort to share her work identity with her father. How do these aspects of identity influence the parent-child relationships of each author?

2   What type of caregiving do you anticipate you will be doing? How do you expect it to compare with the caregiving described by Emily Abel? What types of support do you think you might need as a caregiver?

3   Family time is often restricted by participation in the paid workforce. At the same time, the proportion of very old people who are at risk for dependency is increasing rapidly. How does paid work influence the connections between adult children and their parents and between adult children and their grandparents?

4   Why do you think men might want to have a more involved relationship with their grandchildren than they did with their children? What might make it difficult to achieve this expanded relationship? Can you identify parallel differences in the relationships between mothers and children and between grandmothers and grandchildren?

5   Lois Lyles and Camille Peri each described the death of a family member to cancer. Think about where each woman was in her life course. How were the experiences portrayed in these families similar? How were they different? How could you support these family members in their grief?

6   How do you think relationships with siblings in middle age contribute to continuity between older and younger generations?

1   Laird, J. (1998). Invisible ties: Lesbians and their families of origin. In C. J. Patterson & A. R. D'Augelli (Eds.), *Lesbian, gay, and bisexual identities in families: Psychological perspectives* (pp. 197-228). New York: Oxford University Press.

Using personal experience and stories from clinical practice, Joan Laird challenges the myth that lesbians are estranged from their families of origin. She describes these myths as reflected in popular culture. Her own research reveals a wide range of family experiences; most feel powerful connections to family.

2   Daniel, J. (1996). *Looking after: A son's memoir.* Washington, DC: Counterpoint.

John Daniel writes about his often eccentric mother and their changing relationship as she reaches very old age. As his mother becomes more frail, she moves cross-country to live near and ultimately with Daniel and his wife. He chronicles the often draining experience of looking after his mother, the strains that caregiving places on him and his wife, and the great sadness he experiences at her death.

3   L'Engle, M. (1974). *The summer of the great-grandmother.* San Francisco: Harper.

Madeleine L'Engle describes her mother's failing health and loss of cognitive functioning. As the great-grandmother enters a large and multigenerational household, L'Engle talks about the pain and stress of caregiving and how she, her family, and friends mobilized to provide her mother and each other the support they needed through these difficult yet triumphant days.

4   Quindlen, A. (1994). *One true thing.* New York: Dell.

This novel describes changes in the relationship between an adult daughter and her mother during the mother's terminal illness. As the daughter gains insights into her mother's character, their relationship changes and grows stronger.

5   Walker, A. J., & Allen, K. R. (1991). Relationships between caregiving daughters and their elderly mothers. *The Gerontologist, 31,* 389-396.

This study focused on variations in the mother-daughter relationship when mothers experienced a decline in physical functioning. Almost half of all pairs were characterized by mutual rewards, concern for one another, and lack of conflict. About a third experienced both costs and rewards within their relationship. Conflict characterized the relationships of the remaining 20%.

6   Cherlin, J. A., & Furstenberg, F. F. (1986). *The new American grandparent: A place in the family, a life apart.* New York: Basic Books.

This book reports on a study of grandparents of adolescents. The authors describe changes in the role and experiences of grandparents during the last century. They found that most grandparents take great pleasure in the role. Furthermore, grand-parents prefer their current relationships with their grandchildren, characterized by companionship and independence, over their more formal relationships with their own grandparents.

7   Horowitz, J. (1996). *Tessie and Pearlie: A granddaughter's story.*
    New York: Scribner.

    Horowitz writes about her relationships with her 90-year-old grandmothers, their immigrant history, their advice, their family stories, and their recipes. Throughout, family is central.

8   Irish, D. P., Lundquist, K. F., & Nelsen, V. J. (1993). *Ethnic variations in dying, death, and grief: Diversity in universality.* Washington, DC: Taylor & Francis.

    Aimed at professionals who work with persons who are dying, this book includes beliefs and mourning rituals of distinct ethnic populations written by people who share the cultural traditions they describe.

9   Schwiebert, P., & DeKlyen, C. (1999). *Tear soup: A recipe for healing after loss.* Portland, OR: Grief Watch.

    Although this has the look of a children's book, the message is for people of all ages. With beautiful illustrations, the story describes how Grandy deals with a big loss by making her own tear soup. The book shows how everyone faces loss in a different way and suggests how to support people who must make their own tear soup.

SUGGESTIONS FOR BROWSING THE WEB

1   *www.pflag.org*

    This not-for-profit organization—Parents, Families and Friends of Lesbians and Gays (PFLAG)—provides support, education, and advocacy for gay, lesbian, bisexual, and transgendered persons, their families, and friends. Information on local chapters also is available from this site.

2   *www.compassionatefriends.org*

    Parents who experience the death of a child of any age may find information and support through the Compassionate Friends. The primary goal of this not-for-profit organization is to assist families in the positive resolution of grief following a child's death. It also provides information on how to help someone through the bereavement process.

3   *www.aarp.org/confacts/programs/gic.html*

AARP's Grandparent Information Center provides information for grandparents, ranging from how to build stronger relationships with grandchildren to ensuring safety when grandchildren come to visit.

4   *www.caregiver.org*

This Family Caregiver Alliance Web site provides a variety of information for and about family caregivers. A key feature of the site is the Resource Center (click on Resources), which features practical advice and information to assist caregivers, as well as an on-line support group.

SUGGESTIONS FOR VIDEOS TO RENT FROM YOUR LOCAL VIDEO STORE OR BORROW FROM YOUR PUBLIC LIBRARY

---

1   *Joy Luck Club* (1993)

A tale of four young Chinese American women and their relationships with their mothers and each other, the story highlights the lives of mothers who grew up under extremely difficult circumstances in China and their assimilated American daughters.

2   *One True Thing* (1998)

Based on Anna Quindlen's novel of the same title, this film examines family ties and intergenerational relationships when a daughter leaves her job to take care of her terminally ill mother. In the process, the daughter learns a great deal about herself and her mother.

3   *Ordinary People* (1980)

An upper-middle-class family deteriorates after the death of the elder son. Variation in grief response is illustrated as each family member faces this tragedy in a different way. With the help of a psychiatrist, the surviving son experiences healing and new closeness with his father.

4 *Steel Magnolias* (1989)

This story of long-term friendships portrays how intergenerational relationships are affected when adult children make choices that differ from those their parents would make for them.

PART III

The Centrality of Intimacy in Later Midlife

In Part III, we focus on the intimate relationships of middle-aged and older adults and on the variety of ways in which grandparenthood is enacted in later life. We also discuss the diversity of kin ties among different racial and ethnic groups and the significance of kinkeeping to maintaining extended family connections. Sibling relationships in adulthood also are highlighted. Finally, we show how the death of a parent affects an adult child's life and marital relationship. The key ideas we address are these:

- Marriages and other partnerships in middle and later life tend to be happy and satisfying.

- Individuals continue to value emotional connection and sexual intimacy in close relationships.

- Families vary in their kinship structures by race and ethnicity.

- Women are primary agents for creating and maintaining relationships with family members.

- There is variability in the way grandparenthood is enacted.

- Sibling ties provide opportunities for closeness and connection in midlife.

- The loss of a parent is a major midlife transition.

How Are Marriage and Close Partnerships Central in Midlife? How Are These Relationships Problematic?

Most marriages in middle and later life are happy ones, having evolved from many years of shared experiences—both joyous and challenging. These enduring marriages provide companionship and support for couples. In general, relationships that have been vital and rewarding continue to be satisfying in later life. Relationships that have been difficult and unsatisfying are likely to remain so during middle and later years (Brubaker, 1991). The predominance of happy marriages in later life can be explained by the survivor effect (Troll, Miller, & Atchley, 1979). Marriages that are happy tend to survive into later life; marriages that are unhappy end in early adulthood. Of course, some unhappy marriages do continue into old age (Heaton & Albrecht, 1991).

Heaton and Albrecht (1991) identify several factors associated with enduring unhappy marriages. First, these marriages are more likely to continue if they already have a long history. Years of investment in a relationship add to its stability, particularly for women. Midlife divorce can be especially costly for women who have contributed to their husbands' career success and who perceive few alternatives to their current marriages. The beliefs that marriage is a lifelong commitment and that life would be less satisfying outside marriage contribute to the stability of unhappy marriages as well. Finally, women and men who feel that they have little control over their lives are less likely to leave an unfulfilling marriage than are those who have a sense of control.

What are the characteristics of enduring, happy marriages? Happier marriages are ones with high levels of intimacy and affection and few marital problems (Alford-Cooper, 1998; Klagsbrun, 1985). When conflicts arise, partners communicate, compromise, and attempt to give more than they receive. In other words, a spirit of generosity pervades these relationships. John Gottman (1999) reports that enduring, happy marriages are likely to consist of people who make room for each other in their thoughts and allow their partners to influence them during times of decision making. Frances Klagsbrun (1985) suggests that marriages remain strong when partners have an ability to change and to tolerate change, as well as to trust and to foster trust. Partners in strong marriages are mutually dependent or interdependent on one another.

In the second reading in this part, you will learn about a happily married couple through an excerpt from Anne Tyler's novel, *Breathing Lessons*. The couple's patterns of interaction demonstrate a long history of give-and-take.

Gottman (1999) describes several styles of successful marriages, all of them characterized by more positive than negative interactions. *Volatile couples* exhibit high levels of emotion in both their arguing and their making up. Partners in volatile couples are emotionally engaged. These couples tend to see each other as equals and respect each other's independence. *Validating couples* have a strong ability to listen to and understand each other's feelings and views. These couples tend to compromise during times of conflict and see themselves as good friends. Partners in validating couples tend to maintain traditional spheres of responsibility, with the husband as the final decision maker. *Avoidant couples* minimize, rather than resolve, their differences. Bonds in these couples are strong, but levels of companionship and sharing are low.

Gottman (1999) describes two less successful styles of marriage as well, characterized by more negative than positive interactions. Both styles are characterized by hostility, but one style consists of engaged partners and the other of detached partners. *Hostile-engaged couples* argue often with intensity but do not use humor and affection to balance their interactions. *Hostile-detached partners* fight regularly at low levels of intensity and show little support or affection. David Halle's article, "Marriage and Family Life of Blue-Collar Men," illustrates a number of men who express dissatisfaction with marriage in midlife.

In general, we know little about long-term intimate partnerships. It seems that marital satisfaction changes through the life course, with greater satisfaction for younger and older couples and less satisfaction for persons in middle age. One study (Levenson, Carstensen, & Gottman, 1993) showed that couples in their 60s and 70s had lower levels of conflict and higher levels of pleasure in their marriages compared with couples in their 40s and 50s. Although this curvilinear pattern describes a common pathway, there are many types of intimate relationships.

Long-term committed partnerships are common among people in same-sex relationships, particularly for women (Peplau, 1991). Monogamy is as common for lesbians as it is for heterosexual relationships. For gay men, long-term relationships are somewhat less common. Between 40% and 60% of all gay men, however, are in committed partnerships.

Partners in same-sex relationships face many challenges. Lesbian and gay relationships, for example, are still illegal in some parts of the United States. In some ways, lesbians and gay men are invisible to mainstream society and, thus, are harder to study (Laird, 1993). Research that does exist, however, supports the idea that same-sex relationships are similar to heterosexual relationships. For example, lesbians and gay men can have validating, volatile, and avoidant relationships, as well as stable unhappy relationships.

How Do Families Vary in Their Kinship Patterns?

As we noted earlier, families include not only those members who live in the same house but also those who live elsewhere—next door or across the country. These broader kin ties have become more complex. Because our society is mobile, grandchildren sometimes grow up in communities distant from those in which their grandparents live. The same is true for aunts, uncles, and cousins. Nevertheless, families recognize relationships with these extended kin as significant and maintain connections with them through the use of telephones, the Internet, and face-to-face visits.

As a society, we tend to agree on which kin relationships are more or less fundamental to our lives. For example, we believe that parent-child and marital or partner relations are central, grandparent-grandchild and sibling relations are somewhat less central, and ties with aunts, uncles, and cousins are even less central (Rossi & Rossi, 1990). Although there is normative agreement about the relative importance of kin ties, there is also variability in these norms, especially among racial and ethnic groups (Johnson, 1995). For example, some cultural patterns emphasize vertical connections, such as those of Asian, Puerto Rican, and early-immigrant Italian families. Vertical connections lead to strong ties among grandparents, parents, children, and grandchildren. Other cultural patterns emphasize horizontal ties, such as those of Irish Americans, leading to strong marital bonds and connections among siblings and friends.

Kinship patterns are strongly influenced by the historical context in which they evolve and by the social context within which they endure. For example, American Indians, particularly those who live on reservations, have maintained many traditional kinship patterns, some of which are described in the reading by Joan Weibel-Orlando. Also, African Americans have kinship traditions that have been transformed by their experiences with slavery and racism. Diverse groups of immigrants, both in the past and in the present, have developed kin patterns that combine traditions from their countries of origin and those of their chosen country (DeGenova, 1997).

Most immigrants to the United States continue to value traditional family practices from their homelands. They tend to have high regard for their older family members and a strong sense of obligation to kin. Another theme in immigrant families, according to Colleen Johnson (1995), is change in kinship values across generations. For example, in China, the common pattern of kinship, particularly in rural areas, is for older adults to live with their grown children. In the United States, however, older Chinese Americans tend to live on their own, but near their offspring. Through time, younger immigrant family members are less likely than older family members to uphold traditional cultural values. Furthermore, the value they place on family ties may decline, and the value they place on individual interests may increase consistent with dominant U.S. values. These values include a sense of duty between older adults and their children that coexists with emphasis on both autonomy and individualism. The emphasis on individuality eventually is adopted by many members of the younger generations in immigrant families.

The ability to maintain patterns more consistent with traditional cultural values is enhanced by living in an ethnic neighborhood. For example, Chinese Americans in the "Chinatown" section of any major urban city are more like their counterparts in China than are Chinese Americans who are interspersed with White Americans. American Indians who live on reservations are more traditional in their values and patterns than those who live in urban areas. Similarly, Amish Americans maintain distinct communities that encourage family solidarity through adherence to religious practices and discourage assimilation into mainstream American culture. Until World War II, Japanese Americans maintained relatively traditional Japanese kinship patterns. Japanese Americans, however, were interned in camps during World War II. Following their release after the war, many lived in isolation from each other, rather than in ethnic communities. Consequently, today, they are much more like the dominant White pattern in their kin connections than are members of other Asian American cultures. Cultural values are more traditional when persons remain embedded in ethnic neighborhoods, religious institutions, and community associations (Johnson, 1995).

One way in which immigrant and other families have adapted their kinship patterns to their experiences of mobility or economic stress has been to form what Johnson (1995) describes as *opportune families*, that is, families that are not consistent with a traditional definition. An opportune family arises for reasons associated with values or beliefs, in response to stresses, or because of the circumstances in which people find themselves. For example, several of the grandparent-grandchild relationships described by Joan Weibel-Orlando portray opportune family patterns. They spring from both stressful situations and a desire to pass on cultural values and beliefs.

African American families also have patterns reflecting opportune family systems. Apfel and Seitz's study of adolescent daughters and their mothers in Part I and Dilworth-Anderson's chapter on African American kin networks in Part II illustrate opportune family systems. In general, African American families are more kin oriented than are White families and are more flexible in their definitions of who is and who is not included in their family. Fictive kin are unrelated individuals who are treated as if they were related. African American families are more likely to follow a fictive kin pattern, a type of opportune family, to survive circumstances of extreme economic stress. As Dilworth-Anderson cautioned, however, there is a limit to how long families can continue to function effectively under duress.

Another way that culture influences kinship systems is by contributing to differing patterns of marriage, divorce, and childbearing. For example, relative to non-Hispanic Whites, Hispanics in the United States have high rates of marriage, low rates of divorce, and high rates of fertility. This means that they have more stable marriages and larger numbers of children per family. In "Silent Dancing," Judith Ortiz Cofer's family is a wonderful example of an intense kinship pattern within a Puerto Rican American family. The story depicts a large and loving family, some of whom live on the mainland and some of whom live on the island. It is hard to imagine Mama not surrounded by relatives of all ages.

How Do Families Maintain Connections Across Kin?

Whatever their ethnic background, older adults are usually well integrated into an extended network of kin ties. The presence of a kinkeeper is a key factor in maintaining connection with these larger kin networks (Rosenthal, 1985). Kinkeeping, in broad terms, involves the effort or work undertaken to encourage family connections across households—on both sides of the family (DiLeonardo, 1987). Kinkeepers communicate with family members via telephone calls, visits, and, to a lesser extent, cards and letters. They often take responsibility for organizing family gatherings, such as reunions and holiday dinners, and they perform much of the labor required for these events. They also provide emotional, practical, and financial support to family members in need (Logan & Spitze, 1996). Kinkeepers are important family historians as well, telling and retelling family stories and sometimes writing down important family events (Martin, Hagestad, & Diedrick, 1988; Rosenthal, 1985). Kinkeeping provides the glue to hold extended family networks together.

How common is it for families to have a kinkeeper? In a study by Caroline Rosenthal (1985), 52% of the respondents identified a kinkeeper within their extended family, and an additional 16% said that a kinkeeper had been in their family in the past. Regardless of the presence of someone particularly noted for kinkeeping activities, most members of families engage in some level of kinkeeping. Those who grew up in families that emphasized the importance of kin ties report higher obligations to their extended families in adulthood and are engaged in higher levels of kinkeeping activities (Rossi & Rossi, 1990; Waite & Harrison, 1992). In other words, parents who encourage their children to have close connections with kin during childhood tend to have adult children who encourage close connections with extended family members as well.

The position of kinkeeper is usually held by a woman and often is passed on from mother to daughter. Women bring their spouses and children into contact with their own extended family, as well as with their husband's family. Not surprisingly, then, most people report feeling closer to grandmothers and aunts than to grandfathers and uncles. As you will see later in this section, sisters play a pivotal role in promoting sibling ties as well.

How Important Is Grandparenthood to One's Identity, and What Role Do Grandparents Play in Kin Connections?

In Part II, we discussed how grandparenthood is an important role for people in midlife. Although the experience may begin in middle age, we emphasize that grandparenting continues into old age. Most grandparents spend nearly half of their lives in the role. Here, we describe three major styles of grandparenting: *companionate, remote,* and *involved* (Cherlin & Furstenberg, 1986).

Most grandparents, especially White middle-class grandparents, are companionate ones. These grandparents spend time with their grandchildren engaging in fun activities, such as going to the park, fishing, attending plays, and watching their grandchildren participate in sports. They are affectionate, indulgent friends for their grandchildren. Companionate grandparents play a unique role because they do not participate in discipline or other child-rearing duties, leaving these responsibilities to their grandchildren's parents. This *norm of noninterference* appears to be agreeable to parents and grandparents alike. The grandparents from Scotland described by Sarah Cunningham-Burley in Part II seem to fit this style of grandparenting.

The companionate style of grandparenting is a recent one and may have developed, in part, because modern grandparents lead independent lives, both socially and financially, from their children and grandchildren (Cherlin & Furstenberg, 1986). Most midlife grandparents participate in the paid workforce, earning their highest wages during this time. The unpaid work of caring for family members, generally done by women in midlife, is time-consuming as well. Participation in paid and unpaid work, volunteer activities, and leisure requires time and attention that compete with other activities, such as time with grandchildren. Finally, grandparents often feel that they have raised children already. They want a new type of relationship with their grandchildren, one with more fun and less responsibility.

A second style described by Cherlin and Furstenberg is remote grandparenting. Remote grandparents limit interactions with their grandchildren and find little meaning in the role (Neugarten & Weinstein, 1964). About a third of all grandparents fall into this category. Remote grandparents are similar in style to the detached parent-child relations described by Silverstein and Bengtson in Part I. Remote grandparents can be found among all racial and ethnic groups. You will see examples of remote grandparents in the Weibel-Orlando reading.

Detachment in parent-adult child ties seems to foster remote behavior in grandparent-grandchild ties. For example, relationships between grandparents and grandchildren are weaker and less satisfactory if a history of strain and conflict exists between grandparents and their adult children (Whitbeck, Hoyt, & Huck, 1993). Ties between grandparents and grandchildren are strongest when ties between mothers and grandparents are strong (Rossi & Rossi, 1990). This is true, in part, because mothers facilitate or fail to nurture these relationships, depending on the quality of their ties to grandparents. Of course, grandparents influence these interactions through the quality of their investment in relationships with mothers. Because of the strength of the mother-daughter bond, mothers tend to be more involved with their own parents than they are with their parents-in-law. As a result, grandchildren often report being closer to maternal grandparents than to paternal grandparents. Even as adults, however, grandchildren pattern their helping behavior and affection after their mothers' behaviors, favoring their maternal grandparents.

Involved grandparenting is the third style described by Cherlin and Furstenberg (1986). Involved grandparents tend to live close to their grandchildren, or even in the same household. They are actively immersed in their grandchildren's daily lives. About 16% of grandparents are involved grandparents. They are characterized either by authoritative behavior, similar to parental behavior, or by assuming the parenting role in lieu of their adult children. Most grandparents raising their grandchildren clearly are involved grandparents (Pebley & Rudkin, 1999).

Ethnic minority families are more likely than Whites to have involved grandparents, although Whites exhibit this style as well. Historically, African American grandparents provided important financial and emotional resources to ensure family survival and well-being. Today, with increasing numbers of female-headed households and continuing high rates of poverty, unemployment, and under-employment, involved grandparenting remains an effective response for some low-income African American and other families.

Hispanic families, also, tend to have more involved grandparents. Relative to White and African American grandparents, Mexican American grandparents have more contact, greater satisfaction with contact, and greater expectations for intergenerational assistance (Williams & Torrez, 1998). They also have a far greater desire to live in the same community or household with their children and grandchildren.

Many Asian American grandparents are also involved, a style that is fostered by their tendency to live in extended households.

For example, about one in five Chinese Americans and almost two in five of Asian Indian American elders live with their children and grandchildren (Kamo, 1998). Older Japanese Americans, who have a longer history in this country, have living arrangements that are more like those of White Americans. About 6% of older Japanese Americans and about 5% of White grandparents live with their children and grandchildren.

American Indians sometimes are involved grandparents as well, as illustrated in Joan Weibel-Orlando's study. Although she found a few examples of remote or detached grandparenting, most grandparents were actively involved in their grandchildren's lives. For some, this means taking in their grandchildren for extended periods to teach them their tribe's way of life. Grandparents in her study provide an example of how styles of relating can vary within a racial-ethnic group, depending on the individual preferences of the grandparents, the relationships they have with their own children, and the larger social environment.

How Important Are Sibling Relationships in Later Life?

Most people in their 50s, 60s, and 70s were born into families with three or more children. The majority of these children are still alive today, meaning that adults in midlife are likely to have living siblings. Although sibling relationships are usually considered secondary to parent-child and marital relations (Rossi & Rossi, 1990), sibling ties are the longest lasting of all family connections. Most people feel a sense of solidarity with their siblings, regardless of how often they see one another. Even so, there are only a handful of studies about sibling ties, probably because these ties are seen as secondary to others (Goetting, 1986). Parents will confide in an adult child, for example, before they will confide in a sibling. Having a spouse, children, or a parent makes support from siblings less likely (Miner & Uhlenberg, 1997). Nevertheless, a pattern of affectionate family interaction increases the likelihood that siblings will exchange aid and emotional support with each other (Miner & Uhlenberg, 1997). Overall, family closeness promotes sibling solidarity, similar to relationship processes that promote family cohesion among other extended kin.

Relationships among siblings are quite variable and are influenced by many factors (Antonucci & Akiyama, 1995). For example, sibling ties vary in closeness during the life course. Middle age is a time when sibling relationships seem to resurface in importance (Bedford, 1995). Connections with siblings, especially those between brothers, tend to fall off during early adulthood, during which time individuals focus on commitment to a primary partner, paid work, and raising children.

After age 45 or so, people tend to rate their sibling ties both more positively and as more important (Connidis & Campbell, 1995; Rosenthal, 1985).

Another important source of variation in sibling ties is gender (Bedford, 1995). Older adults tend to rate their relationships with their sisters as more important and more intimate than those with their brothers. The reading by Ingrid Connidis and Lori D. Campbell describes patterns of "Closeness, Confiding, and Contact Among Siblings in Middle and Late Adulthood." They show that sister-sister ties are more active than sister-brother or brother-brother ties. Not surprisingly, however, more conflict is reported between sisters than in other sibling combinations. This may be because conflict is more likely in relationships that are more intense. Despite this conflict, sisters and sisters-in-law are key sources of emotional support for adults, second only to mothers and daughters (Bedford, 1995).

Another way in which sisters promote family ties is by kinkeeping. When sibling relationships are considered important, families are more likely to have a kinkeeper (Rosenthal, 1985). Kinkeepers help siblings, especially brothers, maintain contact with each other and develop and observe family rituals such as holiday dinners and gift exchanges. The desire to maintain connections with siblings is a motivation for families to identify a kinkeeper who will maintain same-generation or horizontal ties. Because parents often serve as the connecting link among siblings, a parent's death can be a catalyst for the identification of a sibling kinkeeper.

Sibling relationships vary by race or ethnicity as well. The exchange of aid among siblings is greater for African Americans than for Whites (Bedford, 1995). Furthermore, African Americans report feeling closer to siblings than do Whites and are more likely than Whites to live within two miles of their siblings (Miner & Uhlenberg, 1997). As noted earlier, African Americans emphasize collateral or horizontal ties, as do Irish Americans (Johnson, 1995). This emphasis on horizontal ties leads to stronger bonds among siblings and friends. Because vertical ties are stronger among Asian, Hispanic, and White (other than Irish) groups, families in these groups place less emphasis on sibling relations and friendships.

Socioeconomic status also influences sibling relationship variability. Evidence suggests that those in the working class report closer and more intense sibling ties than those in the middle class. In the fifth reading in this section, Connidis and Campbell, using education as a proxy for social class, show that persons with more education have less contact with their siblings. Persons who are highly educated, however, are more likely to report an especially close connection to one sibling. That is, they are likely to confide in a single, chosen sibling rather than to have similarly high levels of confiding across all siblings.

One of the major findings of Connidis and Campbell's study is related to the influence of marital status on sibling relationships. Never-married, divorced, and especially widowed older adults are more likely than are continuously married adults to have close ties to siblings. These close ties are reflected in frequent contact but not necessarily in emotional closeness. Similarly, siblings without children confide more in their sisters and brothers but do not report being closer emotionally. These findings reflect the idea that the more roles an individual occupies and the more social obligations one has, the less close one's involvement with siblings will be.

Sibling relationships are influenced not only by the number of roles one performs but also by life transitions. For example, sibling ties are influenced by the transition to caring for aging parents. In the sixth reading in this section ("Shared Filial Responsibility"), Sarah H. Matthews and Tena Tarler Rosner explore how siblings, especially sisters, are brought into closer connection with each other when a frail, aging parent needs aid. The resulting interaction can be both positive and negative (Bedford, 1995). Sisters report more positive interactions with each other during caregiving than do brothers or sister-brother pairs. Sometimes, however, working out caregiving responsibilities leads to strain for caregivers, especially sisters, adding to any stress they experience from caregiving itself.

The way that family members orchestrate care for an older parent is influenced more by gender than by any other variable (Keith, 1995). In part, we as a society have beliefs about caregiving that define it as the work of women. In Sarah Matthews's (1995) study of sisters, brothers, and caregiving, a brother explains his lesser involvement in caregiving this way: "My sister, she's a woman, so she's better at cleaning, plus I don't have time for it" (p. S314). This brother illustrates how beliefs shape behavior and promote women's caregiving responsibility. Matthews also found that parents prefer daughters, rather than sons, to be caregivers, and parents have expectations of more help from daughters. Daughters, then, are likely to organize and coordinate sibling care for both sisters and brothers.

How Does the Death of a Parent Affect One's Life and Relationships in Midlife?

The death of a parent has important implications for individuals and their families in midlife, as shown previously in Part II. In her poem, "What Remains," Marge Piercy poignantly describes the profound sadness she experiences after the death of her mother. She describes her mother as her longest and oldest love—a common feeling for daughters to have about their mothers—and tells of her journey to bring her mother's ashes home. She promises to remember their time together always. She also talks of their continued connection when she says, "Yet just as I knew when you really died, you know I have brought you home." This poem illustrates the intense feelings of bereavement that children can experience after the death of a parent.

After the loss of a parent, marital relationships seem to suffer. Debra Umberson's article, "Marriage as Support or Strain? Marital Quality Following the Death of a Parent" identifies the processes that may bring about a decline in marital quality following bereavement. She identifies four areas of marital strain: (a) failed social support, (b) a partner's unwillingness or inability to communicate about the death, (c) a partner's lack of empathy, and (d) excessive expectations and demands. Her study suggests that following a parent's death, individuals may expect but not receive additional support from their partner.

17

Marriage and Family Life of Blue-Collar Men

David Halle

As the important material aspects of the lives of family members increasingly are handled outside the home, the expectation has grown that their deepest emotional relations should occur within it. As a result, the principle of the modern nuclear family can conflict with other principles of how to live interpersonal life—for instance, relations based on work and relations with friends of the same and of the opposite sex. This often causes problems for husbands and wives whatever their social class, though occupation and education may influence the form such conflicts take.[2]

Certain characteristics of blue-collar husbands do add a distinct flavor to their marriages. They have somewhat low status as "factory workers" and modest levels of formal education. And they have jobs, not careers. The impact of these features should not be ignored. Yet for a balanced picture it is important to place these distinguishing features in the context of the similarities between these marriages and those of the middle class.

The account that follows is based on research among the entire blue-collar labor force of a New Jersey chemical plant, owned by Imperium Oil and Chemicals (a pseudonym).[5] The research was designed to address a question that has long dominated discussion of the

working class in advanced industrial societies. To what extent are blue-collar workers "middle-class" in the sense that their lives and beliefs overlap with those of white-collar workers? (The latter can be divided into an "upper-white-collar sector," composed of managers and professionals, and a "lower-white-collar sector," composed of clerical, secretarial, and sales workers.)

I chose to study a group of workers whose position is strategic for this debate, for if any blue-collar group is "middle-class," then these workers should be. Their wages and benefits are well above the average for blue-collar workers in America, they are protected by a union, and the chemical complex where they are employed is typical of the kind of modern technological setting that is said to have transformed blue-collar work.

The research took place during a seven-year period, from late 1974 until late 1981. The total number of blue-collar workers fluctuated, from a high of 126 to a low of 115. All these workers are men, for blue-collar work is dominated by males.[6] I investigated their views through long and frequent informal conversations, individually and in groups, at and outside the workplace. I recorded these conversations as soon afterward as possible. During the long time I knew them, I talked with almost all these workers about marriage and family life. Seventy-nine were willing to discuss these questions at enough length for me to feel justified in including their views in the analysis that follows. Of this group, fifty-nine are currently married, and the rest are divorced, separated, or bachelors.

Most wives of Imperium workers are, like many women in America, in lower-white-collar occupations: secretaries, clerical workers, or salespeople. But an interesting and important minority of Imperium wives are professionals or managers. I knew the wives of most workers from the annual Christmas party and other social occasions. Although my discussion concentrates on blue-collar men, I have included data on their wives where it is pertinent and where I have enough information to justify doing so.

Marital Contentment and Discontent

Almost all the married men have in mind a general judgment about the quality of their marriages—the extent to which marriage is a source of satisfaction. The basic question underlying this judgment is whether they are glad or sorry to be married. This question naturally occurs to everyone, for the existence of divorced persons among their fellow workers, kin, or friends is a constant reminder that marriages can be terminated.[7]

Thirty-five percent say that they are glad to be married and speak with enthusiasm about their wives. Another 25 percent have mixed feelings. Some have gone through a long period of serious difficulty, often coming close to divorce. Others experience major problems, but also important satisfactions, in their marriages. The third and largest group, 40 percent of the husbands, are unhappily married. Relations with their wives are in general a source of considerable frustration and anger.

What reasons do those men give who do not, or did not, get along with their wives? What problems have they encountered?

The Principle of the Modern Nuclear Family Versus Other Principles

The modern marital ideal of shared companionship as well as shared sex is one of which all these workers are aware and to which most subscribe. But in practice many find it hard to achieve. Thus, the most frequent problem in these marriages is conflict between spending leisure time with wives and spending it in other ways.

Leisure Relations With Male Friends

The main, but not the only, reason for conflict is the lack of common leisure interests. An important part of men's leisure activities are of a kind not easily shared with women. This motif touches most men's marriages, and for at least half it creates serious problems, constituting a recurring source of dispute, anger, and resentment.[8] Consider a worker in his mid-forties: "Susan [his wife] keeps saying, 'Why don't we go away together? Just you and I.' But that's boring. I like to go fishing and drink a few beers when I'm on vacation, but she doesn't want to do that."

The two most common joint leisure activities for husband and wife are eating at restaurants and visiting friends. But visiting friends is often a joint activity only in a formal sense. On such occasions the company tends to divide along gender lines. The men do talk with the women, but they spend far more time talking with each other.

Mindful of this dominant problem, those workers who are happily married commonly stress the importance of spending leisure time with their wives. This is widely viewed as the key to marital harmony:

I don't care what they [the other workers] say, marriage is a beautiful thing. But you have to work at it. You can't just leave your wife alone, like a lot of these guys.

I'll tell you what makes a good marriage. It's when you do things together. Like, my wife comes fishing.

Indeed, despite the difficulties just outlined, there is a sizable group of husbands (just under half) for whom the lack of shared leisure time is not a serious problem. For some that is because the husbands have given up their contacts with the male leisure culture. They come home after work and, as they sometimes put it, "don't socialize with the other guys." Others develop leisure pursuits that they can share with their wives. Dancing is a common one.

The limited nature of their shared leisure pursuits is not a problem for some couples, because they are willing to allow each other considerable latitude. The wife does not mind if her husband spends several hours a day in the tavern, and the husband is content to let his wife spend time with her female friends or kin.

Work and Workaholism

A desire to spend leisure time with male friends is not the only reason workers are not with their wives as much as the wives might like. Some men are "workaholics." They will repeatedly, over many years, spend as much extra time in the factory as they can. Many workers are tempted by the additional money overtime brings, but only a few will, throughout their lives, work overtime on every possible occasion.

Sexual Friendships
With Other Women

Other men spend less time with their wives because they are having extramarital affairs. Given the geographic separation of work and home, this is not difficult. Also, as men get older, the gender ratio becomes increasingly favorable. For a worker in his forties and older, there is a plentiful supply of available women—divorced, widowed, or never married.

Thus, for many of these workers the principle of the nuclear family conflicts with the principle of male friendships, and for some it conflicts with the principle of work or the principle of sexual friendships with other women. The modern marital ideal that husband and wife should be each other's closest friend as well as sexual partner is hard to achieve regardless of occupation. As with leisure, occupation may make some difference to the way couples experience this ideal. But if it does, it does not separate working class from middle class, but those with jobs from those for whom work is a central interest, especially those with careers. And those with jobs include not only most blue-collar workers, but also most lower-white-collar workers and a portion of the upper-white-collar sector.

For these blue-collar workers, in jobs, not careers, friendships at work—"buddies"—are vital, for it is such camaraderie that makes a dull setting tolerable. And a work context involving cooperation and a union strengthens such ties. There is some tendency for this work-related culture to spill over into life outside work and to compete and interfere with wives' claims to a share of their husbands' leisure time. (This tendency should not be exaggerated. About half the married workers go straight home after work. And not all blue-collar settings involve cooperation and dense friendships at work.)

On the other hand, absorbing work and a career can intrude on marital life in a variety of ways that most of those in jobs are largely free of. Their husbands' lack of careers protects the wives of blue-collar workers from such difficulties.[9] Thus, the difference between a career and a job may change the likely order of conflict between the principle of the nuclear family and other principles. For those in careers it may be the principle of work that interferes most often with the principle of the nuclear family. For blue-collar workers in jobs, it may be the principle of male friendships.

The Social Status of the Husband

The second most common problem, cited by 30 percent of the married men, concerns the tendency of some wives to complain that their husbands' social status is too low. This complaint typically conveys a number of ideas. There is the obvious truth that blue-collar workers lack a college degree and whatever status this confers. There is the related notion that they lack the qualifications and aspirations for the kind of jobs that require college education and beyond, notably upper-white-collar jobs. One worker expressed this as follows: "You know, women are terrible. Here I am, just a working slob, and I've got a house and the mortgage all paid off. And still my wife says I should be looking higher. And *she* doesn't work. I hate work."

There is also the view that workers lack the social tastes, interests, and skills that education is supposed to confer. Particularly prone to give offense is men's earthy language and forthright manner. Tastes that wives perceive as unrefined are also a source of argument.

Further, employed wives of blue-collar workers tend to have jobs that arguably carry higher status than their husbands' jobs. Most blue-collar workers' wives, if employed, are in clerical and secretarial jobs that, though typically poorly paid, are still "office jobs." And a minority are in upper-white-collar managerial or professional employment.

The impact of this is softened because the income of men at Imperium usually exceeds their wives'. Given the importance of income as a determinant of status in the United States, this clearly offsets any tendency of husbands to feel inferior, even if from other points of view their occupation carries lower status. Indeed, workers often pointedly contrast their income

with that of white-collar occupations. Consider the mechanic with a ninth-grade education who said proudly: "My daughter told her teachers how much her father earned without an education! They didn't believe it so I Xeroxed a pay stub for her to show them!"

Still, in a society that has for so long stressed that occupation is of primary importance for the husband but only secondary importance for the wife, the relatively low status of factory work as compared with office work can create special problems for the marriages of blue-collar workers.[10]

Yet the difficulties created in these marriages by the tendency for wives' dissatisfaction with their husbands' job, education, or social demeanor should not be exaggerated. About a third of the married men find this a problem, but that leaves a larger group who do not.

Problem Drinking

Heavy drinking that constitutes or verges on alcoholism is the third most frequent difficulty men cite in their marriages. Seventeen workers mentioned it as a problem.

These men commonly make a distinction between an alcoholic and a heavy drinker. An "alcoholic" is someone whose drinking persistently interferes with his ability to come to work or to perform minimally on the job. A "heavy drinker," on the other hand, enjoys spending time in the tavern and drinking beer at home but can usually still perform the routine activities of living and working. But this is a distinction that, some men believe, their wives do not always appreciate. As one worker complained: "Mary [his wife] reads a guy in the newspaper who says if you need a cocktail before dinner every night then you're an alcoholic, and she believes it. Then she yells at me because I have a beer before dinner."

Mostly it is the men who drink too heavily (for their spouses' liking), but sometimes it is the women.

Heavy drinking and problem drinking ("alcoholism") are obviously not confined to blue-collar workers, nor are they most concentrated among them. In a national sample, Don Cahalan and associates found that heavy drinking is about as widespread among managers and professionals as among blue-collar workers.[11] Beer and the tavern are part of traditional working-class culture, but the world of business and management also involves a considerable amount of drinking, though with differences of nuance—less beer in the tavern, more drinks over expense-account meals.

So far this article has explored the main difficulties that occur in these marriages. There are several reasons for this focus. First, more marriages have problems than do not. Second, workers tend to be more articulate about their troubles, for these provoke thought and reflection. Workers are less likely to be able to explain why their marriages are successful than why they are not.

Yet one theme persistently occurs when workers are discussing the benefits of being married—the idea that their wives rescued them from the wild lifestyle of the male culture, a lifestyle that they believe would in the end have been their downfall. A worker: "Marriage? Well, it's discipline. You know, a wife will straighten a guy out. She'll make sure he comes home instead of going out drinking every night, and he'll start to think of his responsibilities."

Marriage After the Children Leave Home

The Companionate Marriage

As men grow older, their marital and leisure lives enter a stage marked by a much-improved economic situation. Their children have grown up; their wives usually take jobs; and their mortgages are (or are almost) paid off. At work men have accumulated twenty or thirty years of seniority, which protects them against cutbacks in the labor force (though not against a plant closure) and entitles them to several weeks' annual vacation, as well as to a pension when they retire.

At the same time, workers begin to develop physical ailments that slow their mobility. By this time, too, everyone knows fellow workers who have died suddenly, and the lesson of life's brevity is not lost. As they enter their late forties, sometimes even earlier, workers often remark that they do not know how much longer they have to live—they might die tomorrow.

In this stage some of the married workers who once spent most of their leisure time with male friends now spend more time with their wives, either because physical ailments have curtailed their sporting activities, or because their buddies have died or moved away, or because they fear being alone in old age. The wife becomes more of a companion. Joint travel, in America and abroad, adds color to the marital relation. A worker in his mid-fifties commented on his own marriage and those of other older workers: "You know, with most of them [the older workers] it isn't even what you might call love. It's—well, when you've been with someone for a long time you get like this" (locking his hands together).

Such marriages come to resemble those where husband and wife have always spent considerable time together, for there too the spouses tend to rely even more on each other for companionship as they grow older. One worker in his early fifties, whose marriage had always been happy, commented on this change. His younger son was in college:

You know, before we got married I used to like to go out with my wife. We'd eat and have a couple of drinks. Then after we got married we figured, "Why not stay home?" So we didn't bother to go out for drinks. We'd have our drinks at home. But we used to socialize. I couldn't imagine not going out Saturday night. My wife had four or five girl friends and I had my friends, and we'd do a lot in couples.

But then gradually it began to stop. You know, people got involved in their own families. One night you'd ask one couple and they'd be caught up with something with the kids, maybe something at school. And then they'd ask you and you'd be doing something and someone would get offended and you'd stop seeing each other. It happened to everyone I know. I don't know why, it's a pity. Like the last few years on Saturday evening we'll watch TV.

This tendency for husband and wife, as they grow older, to see each other increasingly as companions is not confined to the marriages of blue-collar workers. The "companionate" marriage is common among older couples regardless of social class.[17]

As these workers grow older, such differences as once existed between their marriages and those of the white-collar sector decrease further. Men's retirement removes a crucial factor that differentiates marriages—the occupation of the husband. Both blue- and white-collar spouses become preoccupied with a similar series of problems concerning financial security, physical health, and making the most of their remaining years.

The Discontented

On the other hand, some couples finally split up. With the children grown, an important reason for remaining in an unhappy marriage disappears. Whether happily or unhappily married, most men derive considerable pleasure from watching their young children develop. A divorce would risk loss, or considerable reduction, of this contact, since custody usually goes to the wife. Workers who are divorced often speak with regret about their inability to see their young children as much as they would like. Some have lost all contact except for occasional formal matters. Men who have stayed in unhappy marriages to enjoy

their children have less incentive to remain after the children leave home.

The absence of young children also removes certain economic barriers to divorce. Wives no longer must stay home to care for them, so they can obtain full-time jobs, and thus some economic independence. The children's growing up frees the husband in a different way. He no longer has to fear heavy child-support payments if he quits the marriage.

Yet by no means all the workers who are unhappily married obtain a divorce when the children have left home. Forty percent of Imperium husbands are unhappily married, and the children of half this group are no longer in high school. These husbands consistently fail to get along with their wives. Why do they stay married?

For both husbands and wives there is a psychological dimension—fear of change, fear of independence. And there are still economic considerations. The wives doubt that they can maintain the same standard of living. As one wife commented about some of the Imperium wives who were unhappily married and did not have jobs:

> They're scared. They don't know what they can do. You take a woman in her fifties, and she hasn't done anything [hasn't had a job] all her life. What's she going to do? And if they [husband and wife] break up, she *may* get something [alimony and property settlement], but she doesn't know, she can't be certain.

There is also an important economic reason why many of these men remain in unhappy marriages. They fear alimony payments and property division. In particular, men are very reluctant to lose their houses. In New Jersey property is usually divided equally between the husband and the wife after a divorce, and the husband must often pay alimony. And even though many men in America default on such payments after a few years, Imperium workers contemplating divorce face serious economic uncertainties.

Ironically, the house, which represented economic independence, becomes a source of marital dependence.

Desertion, a traditional method of at least avoiding alimony payments, is not feasible, since men are to a large extent locked into their jobs. Unhappily married workers sometimes talk about disappearing out West as a way of freeing themselves without incurring crippling financial penalties. But loss of their relatively well-paying jobs and their seniority and pensions is a strong deterrent:

> When you get married, you lose your freedom. And the divorce laws in New Jersey are brutal. Take Bill [a divorced worker in the plant]. He's still paying six years later [after the divorce], and if he doesn't, she sends the police around. And he lost his house. He can only afford a room in Elizabeth.

This motif illustrates a subtle way in which such men's position in the class structure and their level of income and wealth (but not their occupation) influence their married life. Since they have relatively well-paying jobs and usually houses, they have real assets to lose in any divorce settlement. Yet their income is not high enough for them to recover easily from a settlement. At their income level alimony and property division are severe economic blows.

Conclusion

Consider now the main overlaps between the lives of blue-collar and upper-white-collar employees outside the workplace. Better-paid blue-collar workers earn as much as or more than many white-collar workers. This enables workers at Imperium to move from older neighborhoods to areas that contain a greater occupational mix, especially to post-World War II suburbs in which their close neighbors are rarely other Imperium workers. And their income enables better-paid blue-collar workers to buy the same houses and consumer goods and services as many white-collar employees and to engage in many of the same leisure activities.

Life outside work bears the mark of other forces, in addition to income level, that cut across collar color. Residential America is visibly divided by race, into black and Hispanic areas on the one hand and white areas on the other. This is potentially explosive. There are also differences of gender. For example, interest in sports such as football, baseball, hunting, and fishing is concentrated among males (though some women do follow such sports and though other sports, such as jogging and swimming, are less divided by gender). Gender operates in another way. Many wives in America share certain similarities that transcend their husbands' occupations. They are concentrated in unpaid housework, poorly paid clerical and service jobs, and certain professions such as teaching, nursing, and social work. And they, rather than their husbands, tend to be responsible for most of the housework and child-care. Finally, there are the effects of age and stage in the marital cycle. For example, the presence of young children often curtails the leisure lives of parents (though usually more for the mother than the father).

Finally, to mention such overlaps is not to imply that life outside work is integrated. For example, in their marriages both blue- and white-collar Americans face the task of reconciling the principle at the heart of the modern nuclear family—the idea of husband, wife, and children as each other's closest friends, a cohesive emotional unit based on relations of "love" rather than the often-exploitative relations seen as pervading the outside world—with other principles of interpersonal life. The principle of the modern nuclear family coexists uneasily with the principle of work and work relations (for those in careers, for example, leading to conflicts between absorbing work and home life; for those with jobs, perhaps leading to conflicts between friendships at work and home life; for anyone working shifts, leading to possible difficulties at home). It coexists uneasily with the principle of same-sex friendships, (leading to conflicts over how much leisure time spouses will spend together and how much separately with their own friends). And it coexists uneasily with the principle of friendships between men and women, including sexual relations.

Notes

[Only the notes that are included in the excerpted material appear here.]

2. For a discussion of the emotional overload that the modern "companionate family" places on spouses and children by separating members from the community, see Philippe Ariès, "Family and the City," in Alice S. Rossi (ed.), *The Family* (New York: Norton, 1978); Lawrence Stone, *The Family, Sex and Marriage in England, 1500-1800* (New York: Harper & Row, 1977).

5. For the entire study see David Halle, *America's Working Man* (Chicago: University of Chicago Press, 1984).

6. Men are concentrated in blue-collar craft and laboring jobs, whereas both sexes are about equally represented in blue-collar operative work. See Donald Treiman and Kermit Terrell, "Women, Work and Wages: Trends in the Female Occupational Structure Since 1940," in Kenneth Land and Seymour Spilerman (eds.), *Social Indicator Models* (New York: Russell Sage Foundation, 1974); Patricia Roos, *Gender and Work* (New York: State University of New York Press, 1985).

7. Thus, what most workers are reporting here is not quite the same as whether they have a psychological sense of well-being ("happiness") with their wives and children. Still, when workers ask themselves if they are glad or sorry to be married, the question whether the time they spend with wife and children brings about such a psychological state is important, for increasingly in America "happiness" in this sense is seen as the goal of marriage.

Measuring "happiness" as a psychological state of well-being, akin to pleasure, is fraught with difficulties, as has often been pointed out. See, for instance, Edwin Lively, "Toward Concept Clarification," *Journal of Marriage and the Family* 31 (1969):108-14.

8. A number of works have discussed the struggle between the blue-collar husband and his wife, most intense at the start of the marriage, over whether the husband will continue to spend most of his leisure time with his friends or will now spend it with his wife. See Herbert Gans, *The Urban Villagers: Group and Class in the Life of Italian-Americans* (New York: Free Press, 1962), pp. 70-71, and Mirra Komarovsky, *Blue-Collar Marriage* (New York: Random House, 1962), pp. 28-32.

9. For this point see also Komarovsky, *Blue-Collar Marriage* p. 332.

10. The classic statement of the view that if the prestige of a wife's occupation approaches (or worse, equals or exceeds) her husband's, a destructively competitive element is likely to be injected into the marriage is Talcott Parsons, "The Kinship System of the United States," *American Anthropologist* 45 (1943):22-38. A more recent theory also predicts marital trouble if the status of the wife's occupation, especially as measured in income, considerably exceeds that of the husband's. However, this theory suggests that a wife's occupation may approach, equal, or even moderately exceed that of her husband without causing marital problems so long as her occupation enhances rather than detracts from the status of the family as a whole. See Valerie Oppenheimer, "Sociology of Women's Economic Role in the Family," *American Sociological Review* 42 (1977):387-406.

11. See Don Cahalan, Ira Cisin, and Helen Crossley, *American Drinking Practices: A National Study of Drinking Behavior and Attitudes* (New Brunswick, N.J.: Rutgers Center of Alcohol Studies, 1969); Don Cahalan, *Problem Drinkers* (San Francisco: Jossey-Bass, 1970); Don Cahalan and Robin Room, *Problem Drinking Among American Men* (New Brunswick, N.J.: Rutgers Center of Alcohol Studies, 1974).

17. See Clifford Sager, *Marriage Contracts and Couple Therapy: Hidden Forces in Intimate Relationships* (New York: Brunner-Mazel, 1976), chap 6.

18

Breathing Lessons

Anne Tyler

But to look at Serena's movie, would you guess what had come just before? They seemed an ordinary couple, maybe a bit mismatched as to height. He was too tall and thin and she was too short and plump. Their expressions were grave but they certainly didn't look as if anything earth-shattering had recently taken place. They opened and closed their mouths in silence while the audience sang for them, poking gentle fun, intoning melodramatically. "'Love is Nature's way of giving, a reason to be living . . .'" Only Maggie knew how Ira's hand had braced the small of her back.

Then the Barley twins leaned into each other and sang the processional, their faces raised like baby birds' faces; and the camera swung from them to Serena all in white. Serena sailed down the aisle with her mother hanging on to her. Funny: From this vantage neither one of them seemed particularly unconventional. Serena stared straight ahead, intent. Anita's makeup was a little too heavy but she could have been anybody's mother, really, anxious-looking and outdated in her tight dress. "Look

at you!" someone told Serena, laughing. Meanwhile the audience sang, "'Though I don't know many words to say . . .'"

But then the camera jerked and swooped and there was Max, waiting next to Reverend Connors in front of the altar. One by one, the singers trailed off. Sweet Max, pursing his chapped lips and squinting his blue eyes in an attempt to seem fittingly dignified as he watched Serena approaching. Everything about him had faded except for his freckles, which stood out like metal spangles across his broad cheeks.

Maggie felt tears welling up. Several people blew their noses.

No one, she thought, had suspected back then that it would all turn out to be so serious.

But of course the mood brightened again, because the song went on too long and the couple had to stand in position, with Reverend Connors beaming at them, while the Barley twins wound down. And by the time the vows were exchanged and Sugar rose to sing the recessional, most of the people in the audience

---

This chapter is an excerpt form of the novel by Anne Tyler.

were nudging each other expectantly. For who could forget what came next?

Max escorted Serena back down the aisle far too slowly, employing a measured, hitching gait that he must have thought appropriate. Sugar's song was over and done with before they had finished exiting. Serena tugged at Max's elbow, spoke urgently in his ear, traveled almost backward for the last few feet as she towed him into the vestibule. And then once they were out of sight, what a battle there'd been! The whispers, rising to hisses, rising to shouts! "If you'd stayed through the goddamn rehearsal," Serena had cried, "instead of tearing off to Penn Station for your never-ending relatives and leaving me to practice on my own so you had no idea how fast to walk me—" The congregation had remained seated, not knowing where to look. They'd grinned sheepishly at their laps, and finally broke into laughter.

"Serena, honey," Max had said, "pipe down. For Lord's sake, Serena, everyone can hear you, Serena, honey pie . . ."

Naturally none of this was apparent from the movie, which was finished anyhow except for a few scarred numerals flashing by. But all around the room people were refreshing other people's recollections, bringing the scene back to life. "And then she stalked out—"

"Slammed the church door—"

"Shook the whole building, remember?"

"Us just staring back toward the vestibule wondering how to behave—"

Someone flipped a window shade up: Serena herself. The room was filled with light. Serena was smiling but her cheeks were wet. People were saying, "And then, Serena . . ." and, "Remember, Serena?" and she was nodding and smiling and crying. The old lady next to Maggie said, "Dear, dear Maxwell," and sighed, perhaps not even aware of the others' merriment.

Maggie rose and collected her purse. She wanted Ira; she felt lost without Ira. She looked around for him but saw only the others, mean-

ingless and bland. She threaded her way to the dining alcove, but he wasn't among the guests who stood picking over the platters of food. She walked down the hall and peeked into Serena's bedroom.

And there he was, seated at the bureau. He'd pulled a chair up close and moved Linda's graduation picture out of the way so he could spread a solitaire layout clear across the polished surface. One angular brown hand was poised above a jack, preparing to strike. Maggie stepped inside and shut the door. She set her purse down and wrapped her arms around him from behind. "You missed a good movie," she said into his hair. "Serena showed a film of her wedding."

"Isn't that just like her," Ira said. He placed the jack on a queen. His hair smelled like coconut—its natural scent, which always came through sooner or later no matter what shampoo he used.

"You and I were singing our duet," she said.

"And I suppose you got all teary and nostalgic."

"Yes, I did," she told him.

"Isn't that just like *you*," he said.

"Yes, it is," she said, and she smiled into the mirror in front of them. She felt she was almost boasting, that she'd made a kind of proclamation. If she was easily swayed, she thought, at least she had chosen who would sway her. If she was locked in a pattern, at least she had chosen what that pattern would be. She felt strong and free and definite. She watched Ira scoop up a whole row of diamonds, ace through ten, and lay them on the jack. "We looked like children," she told him. "Like infants. We were hardly older than Daisy is now; just imagine. And thought nothing of deciding then and there who we'd spend the next sixty years with."

"Mmhmm," Ira said.

He pondered a king, while Maggie laid her cheek on the top of his head. She seemed to have fallen in love again. In love with her own husband! The convenience of it pleased her—like finding right in her pantry all the fixings she needed for a new recipe.

"Remember the first year we were married?" she asked him. "It was awful. We fought every minute."

"Worst year of my life," he agreed, and when she moved around to the front he sat back slightly so she could settle on his lap. His thighs beneath her were long and bony—two planks of lumber. "Careful of my cards," he told her, but she could feel he was getting interested. She laid her head on his shoulder and traced the stitching of his shirt pocket with one finger.

"That Sunday we invited Max and Serena to dinner, remember? Our very first guests. We rearranged the furniture five times before they got there," she said. "I'd go out in the kitchen and come back to find you'd shifted all the chairs into corners, and I'd say, 'What have you *done?*' and shift them all some other way, and by the time the Gills arrived, the coffee table was upside down on the couch and you and I were having a shouting quarrel."

"We were scared to death, is what it was," Ira said. He had his arms around her now; she felt his amused, dry voice vibrating through his chest. "We were trying to act like grownups but we didn't know if we could pull it off."

"And then our first anniversary," Maggie said. "What a fiasco! Mother's etiquette book said it was either the paper anniversary or the clock anniversary, whichever I preferred. So I got this bright idea to construct your gift from a kit I saw advertised in a magazine: a working clock made out of paper."

"I don't remember that."

"That's because I never gave it to you," Maggie said.

"What happened to it?"

"Well, I must have put it together wrong," Maggie said. "I mean I followed all the directions, but it never really acted like it was supposed to. It dragged, it stopped and started, one edge curled over, there was a ripple under the twelve where I'd used too much glue. It was . . . makeshift, amateur. I was so ashamed of it, I threw it in the trash."

"Why, sweetheart," he said.

"I was afraid it was a symbol or something, I mean a symbol of our marriage. We were makeshift ourselves, is what I was afraid of."

He said, "Shoot, we were just learning back then. We didn't know what to do with each other."

"We know now," she whispered. Then she pressed her mouth into one of her favorite places, that nice warm nook where his jaw met his neck.

Meanwhile her fingers started traveling down to his belt buckle.

Ira said, "Maggie?" but he made no move to stop her. She straightened up to loosen his belt and unzip his fly.

"We can sit right here in this chair," she whispered. "No one will ever guess."

Ira groaned and pulled her against him. When he kissed her his lips felt smooth and very firm. She thought she could hear her own blood flooding through her veins; it made a rushing sound, like a seashell.

"Maggie Daley!" Serena said.

Ira started violently and Maggie jumped up from his lap. Serena stood frozen with one hand on the doorknob. She was gaping at Ira, at his open zipper and his shirttail flaring out.

Well, it could have gone in either direction, Maggie figured. You never knew with Serena. Serena could have just laughed it off. But maybe the funeral had been too much for her, or the movie afterward, or just widowhood in general. At any rate, she said, "I don't believe this. I do not believe it."

Maggie said, "Serena—"

"In my own house! My bedroom!"

"I'm sorry; please, we're both so sorry . . ." Maggie said, and Ira, hastily righting his clothes, said, "Yes, we honestly didn't—"

"You always were impossible," Serena told Maggie. "I suspect it's deliberate. No one could act so goofy purely by chance. I haven't forgotten what happened with my mother at the nursing home. And now this! At a funeral gathering! In the bedroom I shared with my husband!"

"It was an accident, Serena. We never meant to—"

"An accident!" Serena said. "Oh, just go."

"What?"

"Just leave," she said, and she wheeled and walked away.

Maggie picked up her purse, not looking at Ira. Ira collected his cards. She went through the doorway ahead of him and they walked down the hall to the living room. People stood back a little to let them pass. She had no idea how much they had heard. Probably everything; there was something hushed and thrilled about them. She opened the front door and then turned around and said, "Well, bye now!"

"Goodbye," they murmured. "Bye, Maggie, bye, Ira . . ."

Outside, the sunlight was blinding. She wished they'd driven over from the church. She took hold of Ira's hand when he offered it and picked her way along the gravel next to the road, fixing her eyes on her pumps, which had developed a thin film of dust.

"Well," Ira said finally, "we certainly livened up *that* little gathering."

"I feel just terrible," Maggie said.

"Oh, it'll blow over," Ira told her. "You know how she is." Then he gave a snort and said, "Just look on the bright side. As class reunions go—"

"But it wasn't a class reunion; it was a funeral," Maggie said. "A memorial service. I went and ruined a memorial service! She probably thinks we were showing off or something, taunting her now that she's a widow. I feel terrible."

"She'll forgive us," he told her.

A car swished by and he changed places with her, setting her to the inside away from the traffic. Now they walked slightly apart, not touching. They were back to their normal selves. Or almost back. Not entirely. Some trick of light or heat blurred Maggie's vision, and the stony old house they were passing seemed to shimmer for a moment. It dissolved in a gentle, radiant haze, and then it regrouped itself and grew solid again.

19

Grandparenting Styles:
Native American Perspectives

Joan Weibel-Orlando

Grandparental roles among contemporary North American Indians are expressed across a range of activities, purposes, and levels of intensity. The ways these components fit together are so varied as to be identified as distinct grandparenting styles. These five grandparenting styles are identified below as: cultural conservator, custodian, ceremonial, distanced, and fictive.

Description of the Sample

The twelve Indian men and sixteen American Indian women in the sample ranged in age from fifty-six to eighty-three in 1984. Twelve people (seven women and five men) are Sioux and were living on the Pine Ridge Reservation in South Dakota when I first interviewed them. Fourteen participants live in the area traditionally known as Indian Territory in southeastern Oklahoma. Five of these (two men and three women) are members of the Creek and Seminole tribes. Six (three women and three men) are Choctaw, and one man and two women are Chickasaw.

The twenty-eight participants represent seventeen households. Five women and one man were single heads of households. Out of fourteen families who had biological grandchildren, only five did not have grandchildren living with grandparents. Of these five families, all had grandchildren who still lived on the West Coast or at least five-hundred miles away, with their parents.

Seven families live in the type of three-generational family setting Harold Driver (1969:236) described as the modal North American Indian household configuration. One family had at least one member from each of its four generations living under one roof. Eight grandparents were the primary caretakers for at least one grandchild. In seven cases, the parents of the grandchildren were not living in the primary caretaking households at the time of the interviews. In an eighth case, the mother lived at home but worked full-time. Here, the resident grandmother was the primary caretaker of the three grandchildren in the household during the workweek.

The number of grandchildren in the household ranged fairly evenly between one and five. One family cared for a great grandchild at least half of the day while his mother attended high school classes. All fourteen biological grandparents had other grandchildren who were not living in their homes at the time of the interview.

Grandparenting Styles

Five observed grandparenting styles are defined and illustrated by excerpts from life-history interviews with individuals who exemplify a particular grandparenting style. These grandparenting styles are not mutually exclusive categories. Rather, the grandparents who shared their life histories with me, over time, have manifested attributes of several caretaking styles both with the same children and across their assortment of other grandchildren, both biological and fictive. The case studies presented represent the individual's modal executions of grandparenting which constitute their most consistent grandparenting style.

Although this chapter deals mainly with women as grandparents, there are ten men in the study who interact on a continuing basis with their grandchildren, so it seems more precise to label these relational styles grand-parenting, rather than grandmothering, styles. The grandfathers, although present in the homes, are much less absorbed in the ordering of their grandchildren's lives than are their wives. Rarely, and in this study only in the case of two men who were religious leaders, did grandfathers take on assertive roles *vis-à-vis* their grandchildren's socialization. Today, as in the nineteenth-century accounts of North American Indian family life, raising children is women's work.

The Distanced Grandparent

Of the seventeen families in this study, only three are best described by the term distanced grandparent. In all three cases the grandchildren are living either on the West Coast with their parents or far enough away to make regular visits difficult. Nor do summer school vacations herald extended visits from the grandchildren in these families. Occasionally, the grandparents will make the trip west to visit their grandchildren. These visits, however, are infrequent and do not have the ritual qualities of the scheduled visits of the ceremonial grandparents. The distance between grandparent and grandchild is geographical, psychological, and cultural. For the most part, the distanced grandparents understand the lack of communication with their grandchildren as the effect of changed lifestyles on their children and grandchildren. As one Choctaw grandmother told me: "Oh, they've got their own thing in the city. You know, they have their friends, and their music lessons and school activities. They'd get bored out here if they couldn't get to a mall or the movies."

In one case, the grandfather had had a child from a failed first marriage whom he has not seen since her birth. He has been told that she has had children of her own whom he also has not seen. This instance of both geographical and psychological distance, while more common among American Indian men, is highly unusual and almost nonexistent among American Indian grandmothers. For example, one Sioux grandmother not only knew all of her grandchildren from her children's formal marriages or publicly acknowledged, long-term liaisons but also all of her biological grandchildren from her sons' informal sexual encounters. In fact, the issue of grandparental responsibility to a new grandchild was such a strong cultural tenet that she sought out the assistance of a medicine man in determining the truth when a young woman presented herself as the mother of one of her son's children and the young man refused to acknowledge the paternity of the child. Of importance to the Sioux grandmother was that the child would know who his family was and that she would not shirk her grandparental responsibilities to the child because of her son's indifference.

The distanced grandparent, then, is a relatively rare phenomenon among North American Indian families. It appears to be an artifact of an earlier (1950s to the 1970s) migration of American Indians into urban centers. The distancing is gradual, accumulative, and only exacerbated by the second and third generations remaining in the cities to work, go to school, and become acclimated to urban life when grandparents decide to return to their homelands upon retirement.

Most American Indian families would still view this relative lack of contact between extended family members as an aberration. American Indians speak proudly of their familistic propensities, often comparing themselves favorably to what they see as the more nucleated, individualistic, and isolated Anglo-American family configuration.

The Ceremonial Grandparent

Only two cases of this grandparenting style were identified. In both cases the grandchildren live some distance from the grandparents who, as with the distanced grandparents, have returned to their ancestral homes after living for many years in urban centers. The quality, frequency, and purpose of their family visits, however, distinguish their grandparenting style from the distanced grandparent. These families tend to visit with regularity. Every year, summer vacations are planned to include a sojourn with the grandparents. Flowers, gifts of money, clothes, or plane and bus tickets are forwarded to the grandparents at most holidays and birthdays.

When grandchildren visit grandparents, or vice versa, the host communities are alerted. The entire family attends a steady round of ethnic ceremonial gatherings and social activities at which announcements of their visits are made and applauded. Frequently, the public announcements make references to the distances traveled and the venerable ages of the visiting or visited grandparents. That these features of intergenerational visits are equally and enthusiastically applauded by the spectators underscores the importance of cultural values, such as family cohesion and reverence for one's elders, which are ritually enacted and legitimized by these public displays of the ceremonial grandparents.

Ceremonial grandparenting is expressed in other public forms as well. Grandparents are often asked to say prayers, lead honoring dances, or stand and allow the community to honor them in ceremonies which dramatize the traditional attitudes of respect and reverence for those who have had the spiritual power to live to old age. Families gain honor and visibility in their communities for fostering the health and well-being of their ancient members. Therefore, the ceremonial prerogatives of old age are sought out and perpetuated both by the elderly person as one way of maintaining a public presence and by the elderly person's family as one way of enhancing group membership and family status within their ethnic group.

Ceremonial grandparents provide ideal models of "traditional" (correct) intergenerational behavior for their children, grandchildren, and the community. In time-limited interactions with their grandchildren, the venerated grandparents embody and enact those behaviors appropriate to their age and prestige ranking in the community. By watching the ceremonial displays of age and family cohesiveness, the children learn the appropriateness of veneration of the elderly and how adherence to community mores qualifies older individuals for displays of respect and love in old age. The children are taught to display appropriate ceremonial behavior toward their elders: assisting the unsteady of gait to the dance floor, fetching food and cold drinks for them, and formally presenting them with gifts and performance in special ceremonies such as the Siouan powwows and giveaways and the Muskogean church "sings."

The Fictive Grandparent

Fictive grandparenting is an alternative to the lack or absence of biological grandchildren. All three examples of fictive grandparenting in this sample are women. Two of the women had biological grandchildren living on the West Coast whose parents would not relinquish their care to the grandmothers. Solutions to their grandchildless homes included a variety of ingenious strategies. One Sioux woman applied for and received foster home accreditation. During the first two years of her return to reservation life she harbored seven different, non-related children in her home for periods of four to eighteen months. At one time she had four foster children living with her at the same time.

One Choctaw woman, a teacher's assistant in the public school system, became involved in the development of teaching materials designed to introduce American Indian and non-Indian students to traditional Choctaw life. Simple readers and instructional sheets in English that provide study outlines for the acquisition of traditional Choctaw dances, games, and foods have now evolved into a full-fledged Choctaw language-learning course. The grandmother's skill as a Choctaw-speaking storyteller has allowed her access to dozens of kindergarten to third-grade children who fill the widening gap she recognizes between herself and her West Coast-based grandchildren.

> I think it is very important for the young children, both Choctaw and non-Indian, to learn about traditional Choctaw culture. In this way they have something to be proud of. They won't think of themselves the way the non-Indians think of them—dirty, dumb savages—but as people who had a rich and beautiful culture which they can be proud of and that was taken away from them for no good reason. I feel as if I am passing on my heritage to not only my grandchildren as it would have been done traditionally but to all of the grandchildren who will ever have me as a teacher. (Choctaw woman, sixty-five, Broken Bow, Oklahoma)

One grandchildless woman had an informally adopted son living with her who was young enough to be her grandchild. (She was eighty-three and he was twenty-five when interviewed in 1984 and still living in Los Angeles.) He subsequently accompanied her to Oklahoma when she decided to return to her hometown in 1985. "He needed a home. And he didn't want to live with his mother no more. And we didn't know where his dad was. And all I had was my daughter, who works all day and is practically blind, so she isn't much help around the place when she gets home at night. I needed someone around here who can look after me, drive me places, help me with the shopping, and all that. So I adopted him when he was around seventeen and he's been with me every since" (Creek woman, eighty-three, Los Angeles, California).

Fictive grandparenting was not initiated by any of the men in this study. That is not to say, however, that men do not facilitate these types of relationships upon occasion. In fact, some older men, particularly if they are in command of medicinal or spiritual lore, will apprentice young men who they later adopt as kin if there is no blood tie between. Older women tend to initiate fictive kin ties for the broader personal, emotional, social, cultural, and purely pragmatic reasons stated above.

The Custodial Grandparent

Three families in this study are best described by the term custodial grandparenthood. In all three cases, the grandchildren were children of daughters who had either died, had their children taken from them by the court system, or had been abandoned by the children's fathers and could not keep the families intact with their meager earnings or child welfare stipends.

In one family the grandmother was not only caring for a daughter's three children but also one son's child, as well as a great-grandchild, when I interviewed her. The custodial role essentially has been forced upon her by the misconduct or lack of interest of two of her children. She begrudgingly accepts the role as the duty of a moral Christian woman and in the best interest of her several troubled and abandoned grandchildren.

> When is it ever going to end, that's what I would like to know? All my life I've had these kids off and on. Especially with my daughter's kids. . . . Atoka has been with me since she was a year and a half. Her mother would go out and would be partying and someone was left with the child. But that person took off and left Atoka by herself. And the neighbors called me to tell me the child was all by herself, crying. The judge wouldn't let her [the daughter] have her back so he gave her to me. Lahoma, she's been with me since she was born, I guess. Pamela went with somebody. I think she was placed in a home, then she would come to stay with me for a while, then her mother would take her back, and then get into trouble again and the whole thing would start all over again. (Choctaw woman, fifty-seven, Broken Bow, Oklahoma)[2]

For the cultural conservator, having a houseful of grandchildren is an expected privilege of old age. In contrast, the custodial grandmother is often relatively young and unprepared to take on the caretaking responsibilities culturally appropriate to the status of grandmother. In this case the woman's perceptions of her custodial grandmothering range from an appreciation of the comfort and companionship she received from her favorite grandson to annoyance and frustration with having to assume the extra burden of her sixteen-year old granddaughter's unwanted pregnancy. These child-care responsibilities are particularly irksome as they are thought to be inappropriate to the current stage of her life career trajectory: "I shouldn't be doing this [taking care of children]. Not at my age. I should be just taking it easy and going here and there. Now Donny, he's no problem. He's

real sweet and bright—he's got a brain. He's a lot of company for me. But, then, there's my sixteen-year-old granddaughter. She's going to have a baby. And guess who's going to take care of that baby when it comes?"

The Cultural Conservator Grandparent

Rather than accept an imposed role, the conservator grandparents actively solicit their children to allow the grandchildren to live with them for extended periods of time for the expressed purpose of exposing them to the American Indian way of life. Importantly, the cultural conservator is the modal grandparenting style among the families in this study.

Six families are best described by this term. One Sioux woman, who had two of her grandchildren living with her at the time of the interview, exemplifies the cultural conservator grandparenting style. The enthusiasm about having one or more grandchildren in her home for extended periods of time is tempered by the realization that, for her own children who grew up in an urban environment, the spiritual magnetism of reservation life is essentially lost. She regards their disdain for tribal life with consternation and ironic humor and consciously opts for taking a major role in the early socialization of her grandchildren. She views her children as being just "too far gone" (assimilated) for any attempt at repatriation on her part. Her role as the culture conservator grandmother, then, is doubly important. The grandchildren are her only hope for effecting both personal and cultural continuity: "The second- or third-generation Indian children out [in Los Angeles], most of them never get to see anything like . . . a sun dance or a memorial feast or giveaway or just stuff that Indians do back home. I wanted my children to be involved in them and know what it's all about. So that's the reason that I always try to keep my grandchildren whenever I can" (Sioux woman, sixtyseven, Pine Ridge, South Dakota).

She recognizes the primary caretaking aspects of her grandmotherhood as not only a traditionally American Indian, but also as a particularly Lakota thing to do: "The grandparents always took . . . at least the first grandchild to raise because that's just the way the Lakota did it. They [the grandparents] think that they're more mature and have had more experience and they could teach the children a lot more than the young parents, especially if the parents were young. . . . I'm still trying to carry on that tradition because my grandmother raised me most of the time up until I was nine years old."

She remembers her grandparents' enculturative styles as essentially conservative in the sense that those things they passed on to their grandchildren were taken from traditional Sioux lore. The grandparents rarely commanded or required the grandchild's allegiance to their particular world view. Rather, instruction took the form of suggestions about or presentation of models of exemplary behavior. "Well, my grandfather always told me what a Lakota woman wouldn't do and what they were supposed to do. But he never said I had to do anything." She purposely continues to shape her grandmotherhood on the cultural conservator model of her own grandparents. "I ask [my children] if [their children] could spend the summer with me if there isn't school and go with me to the Indian doings so that they'll know that they're Indian and know the culture and traditions. [I'm] just kind of building memories for them."

Those cultural and traditional aspects of Sioux life to which this grandmother exposes her city-born grandchildren include a wide range of ceremonial and informal activities. The children go everywhere with her. An active participant in village life, she and her grandchildren make continual rounds of American Indian church meetings, senior citizens lunches, tribal chapter hearings, powwows, memorial feasts, sun dances, funerals, giveaways, and rodeos. The children attend a tribe-run elementary school in which classes are taught in both English and Lakota. The children actively participate in the ceremonial life of the reservation, dancing in full regalia at powwows and helping their grandmother distribute gifts at giveaways and food at feasts. Most importantly, those grandchildren who live with her for long periods of time are immersed in the daily ordering of reservation life. Through the grandmother's firm, authoritative tutelage, complemented by their gentle and affectionate grandfather, and through the rough-and-tumble play with rural age-group members who, for the most part, can claim some kinship with the urban-born visitors, they learn, as did nineteenth-century Sioux children (through observation, example, and experimentation), their society's core values and interactional style.

Conclusions

The five divergent perceptions and expressions of grandparenthood presented here are clearly consequences of the individuals' sense of personal control and initiative in shaping the style in which they would carry out their grandparenthood. Clear parallels to the distanced and custodial grandparenting styles can be found in the descriptions of contemporary American grandparenthood (Cowgill and Holmes 1972; Myerhoff 1978; Stack 1974; Burton and Bengtson 1985; Simic 1987). I suggest that those factors which prompt these interactional styles among American Indian families—migration, psychological estrangement between the parental generations, and relative psychological and economic stability of the parental household—also produce instances of these grandparenting styles among non-Indian families. Interestingly, neither style is the cultural ideal for either American Indians or non-Indians. The popular literature deplores the psychological distance between generations, yet also finds the child reared by grandparents as culturally and psychologically disadvantaged. While American Indians equally deplore the distanced grandparenting style, the child in the custody of a grandparent is seen as potentially advantaged by that experience.

The status, grandparent, is imbued with considerable sociostructural weight in that it, across cultures, automatically confers both responsibility and rewards to the individual upon the birth of the grandchild. The roles associated with grandparenthood, however, can be and are negotiated. Satisfaction with both status and role is an artifact of the individual's sense of creating a grandparenthood consistent with both personal and cultural expectations.

Note

[Only the note that is included in the excerpted material appears here.]
2. In all cases fictitious names have been used to protect the privacy of those people who so generously shared their life stories, current activities, and views on grandparenthood with me.

References

Burton, L. M., & Bengtson, V. L. (1985). Black grandmothers: Issues of timing and continuity in roles. In V. L. Bengtson & J. F. Robertson (Eds.), *Grandparenthood* (pp. 61-77). Beverly Hills, CA: Sage.

Cowgill, D. O., & Holmes, L. D. (Eds.). (1972). *Aging and modernization.* New York: Appleton-Century-Crofts.

Driver, H. E. (1969). *Indians of North America.* Chicago: University of Chicago Press.

Myerhoff, B. G. (1978). A symbol perfected in death: Continuity and ritual in the life and death of an elderly Jew. In B. G. Myerhoff & A. Simic (Eds.), *Life's career-aging: Cultural variations in growing old* (pp. 163-206). Beverly Hills, CA: Sage.

Simic, A. (1987). Aging in the United States and Yugoslavia: Contrasting models on intergenerational relationships. In J. Sokolovsky (Ed.), *Growing old in different societies: Cross-cultural perspectives* (pp. 82-91). Acton, MA: Copley.

Stack, C. B. (1974). *All our kin.* New York: Harper Row.

20

Silent Dancing:
A Partial Remembrance of a
Puerto Rican Childhood

Judith Ortiz Cofer

My grandmother's house is like a chambered nautilus; it has many rooms, yet it is not a mansion. Its proportions are small and its design simple. It is a house that has grown organically, according to the needs of its inhabitants. To all of us in the family it is known as *la casa de Mamá.* It is the place of our origin; the stage for our memories and dreams of Island life.

I remember how in my childhood it sat on stilts; this was before it had a downstairs. It rested on its perch like a great blue bird, not a flying sort of bird, more like a nesting hen, but with spread wings. Grandfather had built it soon after their marriage. He was a painter and housebuilder by trade, a poet and meditative man by nature. As each of their eight children were born, new rooms were added. After a few years, the paint did not exactly match, nor the materials, so that there was a chronology to it, like the rings of a tree, and Mamá could tell you the history of each room in her *casa*, and thus the genealogy of the family along with it.

Her room is the heart of the house. Though I have seen it recently, and both woman and room have diminished in size, changed by the new perspective of my eyes, now capable of

looking over countertops and tall beds, it is not this picture I carry in my memory of Mamá's *casa.* Instead, I see her room as a queen's chamber where a small woman loomed large, a throne-room with a massive four-poster bed in its center which stood taller than a child's head. It was on this bed where her own children had been born that the smallest grandchildren were allowed to take naps in the afternoons; here too was where Mamá secluded herself to dispense private advice to her daughters, sitting on the edge of the bed, looking down at whoever sat on the rocker where generations of babies had been sung to sleep. To me she looked like a wise empress right out of the fairy tales I was addicted to reading.

Though the room was dominated by the mahogany four-poster, it also contained all of Mamá's symbols of power. On her dresser instead of cosmetics there were jars filled with herbs: *yerba buena, yerba mala,* the making of purgatives and teas to which we were all subjected during childhood crises. She had a steaming cup for anyone who could not, or would not, get up to face life on any given day. If the acrid aftertaste of her cures for malingering did not get you out of bed, then it was time to call *el doctor.*

Mamá slept alone on her large bed, except for the times when a sick grandchild warranted the privilege, or when a heartbroken daughter came home in need of more than herbal teas. In the family there is a story about how this came to be.

When one of the daughters, my mother or one of her sisters, tells the *cuento* of how Mamá came to own her nights, it is usually preceded by the qualifications that Papá's exile from his wife's room was not a result of animosity between the couple, but that the act had been Mamá's famous bloodless coup for her personal freedom. Papá was the benevolent dictator of her body and her life who had had to be banished from her bed so that Mamá could better serve her family. Before the telling, we had to agree that the old man was not to blame. We all recognized that in the family Papá was as an *alma de Dios,* a saintly, soft-spoken presence whose main pleasures in life, such as writing poetry and reading the Spanish large-type editions of *Reader's Digest,* always took place outside the vortex of Mamá's crowded realm. It was not his fault, after all, that every year or so he planted a baby-seed in Mamá's fertile body, keeping her from leading the active life she needed and desired. He loved her and the babies. Papá composed odes and lyrics to celebrate births and anniversaries and hired musicians to accompany him in singing them to his family and friends at extravagant pig-roasts he threw yearly. Mamá and the oldest girls worked for days preparing the food. Papá sat for hours in his painter's shed, also his study and library, composing the songs. At these celebrations he was also known to give long speeches in praise of God, his fecund wife, and his beloved island. As a middle child, my mother remembers these occasions as a time when the women sat in the kitchen and lamented their burdens, while the men feasted out in the patio, their rum-thickened voices rising in song and praise for each other, *compañeros* all.

It was after the birth of her eighth child, after she had lost three at birth or in infancy, that Mamá made her decision. They say that Mamá had had a special way of letting her husband know that they were expecting, one that had begun when, at the beginning of their marriage, he had built her a house too confining for her taste. So, when she discovered her first pregnancy, she supposedly drew plans for another room, which he dutifully executed. Every time a child was due, she would demand, *more space, more space.* Papá acceded to her wishes, child after child, since he had learned early that Mamá's renowned temper was a thing that grew like a monster along with a new belly. In this way Mamá got the house that she wanted, but with each child she lost in heart and energy. She had knowledge of her body and perceived that if she had any more children, her dreams and her plans would have to be permanently forgotten, because she would be a chronically ill woman, like Flora with her twelve children: asthma, no teeth, in bed more than on her feet.

And so, after my youngest uncle was born, she asked Papá to build a large room at the back of the house. He did so in joyful anticipation. Mamá had asked him special things this time: shelves on the walls, a private entrance. He thought that she meant this room to be a nursery where several children could sleep. He thought it was a wonderful idea. He painted it his favorite color, sky blue, and made large windows looking out over a green hill and the church spires beyond. But nothing happened. Mamá's belly did not grow, yet she seemed in a frenzy of activity over the house. Finally, an anxious Papá approached his wife to tell her that the new room was finished and ready to be occupied. And Mamá, they say, replied: "Good, it's for *you.*"

And so it was that Mamá discovered the only means of birth control available to a Catholic woman of her time: sacrifice. She gave up the comfort of Papá's sexual love for something she deemed greater: the right to own and control her body, so that she might live to meet her grandchildren—me among them—so that she could give more of herself to the ones already there, so that she could be more than a channel for other lives, so that even now that time has robbed her of the elasticity of her body and of her amazing reservoir of energy, she still emanates the kind of joy that can only be achieved by living according to the dictates of one's own heart.

Claims

Last time I saw her, Grandmother
had grown seamed as a bedouin tent.
She had claimed the right
to sleep alone, to own
her nights, to never bear
the weight of sex again, nor to accept
its gift of comfort, for the luxury
of stretching her bones.
She'd carried eight children,
three had sunk in her belly, *náufragos,*
she called them, shipwrecked babies
drowned in her black waters.
Children are made in the night and
steal your days
for the rest of your life, amen. She said this
to each of her daughters in turn. Once she had made a pact
with man and nature and kept it. Now like the sea,
she is claiming back her territory.

21

Closeness, Confiding, and Contact Among Siblings in Middle and Late Adulthood

Ingrid Arnet Connidis
Lori D. Campbell

Our purpose in this article is to examine three dimensions of the adult sibling tie: emotional closeness, confiding, and contact. Today, about 80% of older individuals have at least one living sibling (Avioli, 1989; Connidis, 1989b; Shanas, 1979). This will be true for parents of the baby boom and the baby boom itself, but, with family size shrinking, children of the baby boom cohort will have fewer siblings in adulthood and old age (Connidis, 1989b; Troll, 1986). The increase in research on older siblings over the past decade shows a growing awareness of this relationship's potential as an integral part of family life for most people throughout their lifetime. Yet, because adult siblings fall outside the nuclear family structure, their place within the social support networks of older adults is usually overlooked (Goetting, 1986). However, exploring the sibling tie highlights the ongoing influence and role of the family of origin as well as the continuity of the family over time and through changing circumstances (Connidis, 1992).

These are important reasons for examining sibling ties in middle and older age. A more fundamental reason for doing so is to enhance our understanding of the larger family system by considering ties beyond the nuclear family. Sprey (1991) applied the concepts of system and structure to his analysis of family life, arguing that one cannot focus on feelings and attitudes as explanations of behavior: "Personal feelings and attitudes at best may account for necessary conditions of family coherence and solidarity. It does not make sense to attach any explanatory power to individual intentions or motivations." Instead, Sprey argued,

> Family systems in particular, because of their culturally ascribed and socially recognized status, *implicate* or entangle their members in a form of involuntary membership. . . . [I]ndividuals, because of their joint membership, and regardless of their personal feelings, may be expected to engage in supportive behavior when such is deemed necessary. Refusal to participate will be seen as a violation of both familial *and* social obligation. (p. 229)

Finch's (1989) distinction between private domains and public morality parallels Sprey's distinction between familial and social obligations. Finch (1989) argued that kin networks can be defined as "interlocking sets of 'inner circles' of kin" whose operations and negotiations are influenced (but not determined) by the larger public morality (p. 186; see also Finch & Mason, 1993).

Finch's concept of "legitimate excuses" embodies these ideas as they apply to negotiating family obligations. She argues that family members find great difficulty in simply refusing to support one another, given social expectations about family membership. Instead, avoiding or minimizing the provision of support requires a "legitimate excuse." The legitimacy of excuses is determined through negotiation with family members who are influenced by socially defined expectations.

The impact of socially defined expectations is emphasized by feminist scholars in their focus on the influence of gender and age on social relationships. They argue that one must consider the different vantage points of men versus women and of parents versus children on family life (Fox, 1988). In both cases, power differentials are basic to variations in the perspective on, and experience of, family life. In our view, marital status is another basis for differential power (see Simon, 1987) and, consequently, may influence the ability to claim legitimate excuses regarding commitments to the family of origin (older parents, siblings) among adult members.

When familial relationships are ranked according to level of obligation, the sibling tie is typically less binding than marriage or the parent-child tie and more binding than other familial ties (see, e.g., Rossi & Rossi, 1990). Thus the sibling tie, typified by "limited but enduring involvement" (Allan, 1977, p. 182), is contingent on competing ties within the family of procreation (Connidis, 1989b) and whether "closer" relatives such as a spouse or children are available (Troll, 1986). Today's middle-aged and older aged single adults, having typically neither a spouse nor children, have fewer legit-

imate excuses for avoiding obligations to their older parents or to their siblings. Similarly, the childless may be assumed to have greater obligations than those with children toward their siblings. Thus, like women, the single and childless may be more obliged to provide support to their family of origin. In turn, siblings may be more likely to turn *to* a single sibling than a married one, knowing that a single sibling does not have the competing demands of a spouse and/or children (a legitimate excuse).

Hence, although it is true, as Sprey (1991) observed, that all family members are implicated by virtue of family membership, Finch's concept of legitimate excuses emphasizes that some members are more implicated than others. We would also argue that personal feelings may be differentially significant to understanding support among family members, depending on where a relationship stands in the social hierarchy of familial obligation. If the socially defined obligation is lower, then feelings may matter more. Thus how one feels about a family member may be a more significant determinant of the patterning and activities of sibling relationships than of parent-child or spousal relationships (see, e.g., Matthews, 1987). Indeed, Allan (1977) concluded that the key factor for sibling solidarity is "the siblings' compatibility and liking for one another" (p. 181), and Leigh (1982) argued that affectional closeness is a crucial element of understanding sibling relationships.

In sum, the concept of legitimate excuses and the observed hierarchy of familial obligations discussed above lead us to examine the impact of gender, marital status, and parent status on emotional closeness, confiding, and telephone and personal contact among siblings. Given the lower ranking of obligations to siblings when compared to spouse, parents, and children, we also explore whether personal feelings, as indicated by emotional closeness, exert an independent influence on levels of confiding and contact among siblings. Finally, for all analyses we address a crucial methodological question: Do findings vary depending on whether one examines the sibling of greatest closeness, confiding, and contact or a composite measure representing the entire sibling network?

Several other factors are pertinent to sibling ties, including age (Bedford, 1989; Gold 1989), social class (Allan, 1977), geographic proximity (Connidis 1989a, 1989b, 1989c; Goetting, 1986; Lee, Mancini, & Maxwell, 1990; Matthews, Delaney, & Adamek, 1989; Suggs, 1989), and family size (number of siblings; see Bossard & Boll, 1956). Therefore, these variables are introduced as controls in our analyses.

Method

Sample

Our sample has several unique characteristics that enhance the contribution of our analysis. Among these are representation of four marital-status groups, including substantial numbers of single and divorced respondents, and of both parents and childless individuals.

Data for this analysis are taken from a study of the social support networks of 678 residents of London, Canada, a city of approximately 300,000. Respondents aged 55 years of age or older were interviewed in their homes for an average of 70 minutes during 1990-1991. A multistage quota sampling technique was employed to generate a sample in which single, divorced, and childless men and women, and widowed men are overrepresented across three age groups (55 to 64, 65 to 74, and 75 or older). For each subgroup of the sample (e.g., single women aged 65 to 74), a quota was set to ensure that all groups were represented in the sample.

Because of our focus on the sibling relationship, this analysis includes the 528 respondents who have one or more living siblings. When compared with the Canadian population (Statistics Canada, 1992), this subsample overrepresents the single (14%), the widowed (27%), the divorced or separated (32%), and the childless (41%), as well as men (46%), enhancing the comparative analysis of various groups within the sample. These respondents have from 1 to 12 siblings, with a mean of 2.56 siblings.

Measures

To test for differences in the results based on one sibling versus the entire sibling network, and within the confines of quantitative analysis, we employ two measures for each *dependent* variable. In the first, we use the score for the sibling to whom the respondent is emotionally closest, in whom the respondent confides the most, and with whom the respondent has the greatest contact. In the second, for those with more than one sibling, we use a mean score for the entire sibling network. For the one third of respondents who have only one sibling, there can be no variation in this dependent variable. However, this lack of variation is not simply an artifact of measurement, for it reflects the fact that, indeed, for these respondents, differentiating among siblings is not a possibility.

Summary and Conclusions

We begin by discussing the effect of gender, marital status, parent status, and emotional closeness on the various dimensions of sibling ties examined here. For all but confiding, *respondent's gender* is significant for both the sibling of greatest closeness or contact and for the sibling network overall. We find that women's ties with siblings are more involved than those of men, supporting previous research (Longino & Lipman, 1981; Mugford & Kendig, 1986).

The significance of gender is also evident in the impact of *sibling's gender* on emotional closeness and telephone contact. Here again, supporting other research (Connidis, 1989a, 1989c; Scott, 1983), we find that respondents with sisters only are closer on average to their siblings than those whose networks include brothers *and* sisters. Respondents whose highest contact sibling is a sister talk on the phone more often than those whose highest contact sibling is a brother. The fact that we find no significant difference between respondents whose siblings are all sisters and those whose siblings are all brothers suggests the need to follow the example set by Matthews et al. (1989) of studying sibling networks consisting of brothers only. It may be that tilted families (those with more brothers *or* more sisters) share a similarity in perspective that leads to greater closeness.

The fact that differences in contact based on sibling gender emerge only in the model examining the sibling of greatest contact shows the contribution of studying both the entire sibling network and the sibling with whom the respondent is most involved.

We do not find significant interactions between respondent's and sibling/s' gender. Thus women are closer to, and in greater contact with, their brother(s) *and* their sister(s) than are men, and, for both men and women, telephone contact is more frequent if the highest contact sibling is a sister. Our results show that, overall, women have a greater emotional investment in their ties to siblings and are more engaged in sibling ties, potentially influenced by a greater level of assumed obligation to be so.

The effects of *marital status* are variable, depending on the dimension of the sibling tie and the measure of the dependent variable. The only difference regarding emotional closeness is the finding of closer ties among those whose closest sibling is widowed than among those whose closest sibling is single. This may reflect greater emotional attachment to a sibling following that sibling's experience of a personal crisis (see Connidis, 1992).

As was true for gender, there are no marital-status differences for level of confiding. Instead, marital status has the greatest impact on personal contact. The significant interaction between marital status of the respondent and of the sibling seen most often shows that contact is most frequent between a single respondent and a single sibling. Also, overall personal contact with siblings is greater for the single than for all other marital-status groups. This is also true when all siblings are unmarried rather than all married. For telephone contact, single respondents are in touch with their siblings more often than are married respondents. Thus being single affects the overall level of involvement with both the sibling network and the sibling seen most often but does not appear to alter feelings about siblings.

This combination of results suggests that single individuals do not maintain greater contact with their siblings because of greater emotional commitment to them. Instead, their greater involvement is more likely an outcome of having fewer competing relationships. Their contact with siblings may be due to both a greater need for the tie and their greater assumed obligation toward siblings in the absence of other relationships (spouse, child) who could serve as "legitimate excuses." The balance between these two factors is a topic that requires further investigation.

The significant interaction between respondent's marital status and sibling's marital status also shows that being unmarried per se does not enhance involvement with siblings. The most personal interaction between siblings occurs among dyads involving at least one single member (single-single, divorced-single, and widowed-single), whereas the least interaction occurs between dyads of one widowed and one divorced sibling or two widowed siblings. Thus it is important that we distinguish among the various unmarried groups in analyses of family ties.

Parent status of the respondent is significant for personal contact and confiding only. Childless respondents confide more in their primary sibling confidant and in their siblings overall than do parents. However, respondents whose networks include parent and childless siblings confide in their siblings overall more than those whose siblings are all childless. Perhaps families in which some siblings have children and others do not exchange more confidences because there is a shared concern about the children among all the siblings (see Connidis, 1992). The parent siblings contribute the next generation of children, whereas childless siblings have greater opportunity to invest in their nieces and nephews than do fellow parent siblings.

Those with childless siblings only report more face-to-face contact with their siblings overall than do those whose siblings networks include parents. Counter to previous findings (Lee & Ihinger-Tallman, 1980; Scott, 1983), we do not find greater emotional closeness to siblings among the childless. Thus, like the single, the greater contact with siblings among the childless does not appear to be due to greater emotional attachment but, rather, greater opportunity and, possibly, obligation. However, the childless do appear to have a greater emotional investment in their siblings as indicated by higher levels of confiding.

Our findings show the powerful influence of *emotional closeness* on confiding, telephone contact, and personal contact among siblings. For both the sibling with the highest score and for siblings overall, those who feel closer emotionally to their siblings confide in them, talk to them on the phone, and see them in person more often than those who feel less close. This provides evidence of a link between feelings and behavior, supporting the view that contact with siblings is not based on obligation alone (see also White & Riedmann, 1992). As argued earlier, feelings may be especially important influences on the sibling bond, given its more voluntary nature when compared with spousal and parent-child ties.

Although not our primary focus, findings for some of our control variables provide addi-tional insights into the sibling bond. Regarding age, our results confirm growing attachment to siblings over time (Bedford, 1989; Gold, 1989). However, this refers to the sibling network as a whole, as age is not related to emotional closeness to the closest sibling. Counter to Allan's (1977) observation that working-class siblings are closer emotionally to one another than middle-class siblings, we find that higher education is associated with greater closeness to the closest sibling, although not to the sibling network overall. On the other hand, educational level is inversely related to contact with the sibling network overall. Possibly, this reflects the greater need for (or greater obligation toward) siblings among the less advantaged and, in the absence of need, the greater focus on the emotional side of a selected sibling tie among the more advantaged.

Other studies have found that geographic proximity is a significant predictor of contact but not of confiding or closeness (Connidis, 1989a, 1989b; Goetting, 1986). However, siblings who live nearer to one another are more likely to be considered close friends (Connidis, 1989c), and geographic proximity appears to enhance sibling closeness (Lee et al., 1990) and the maintenance of sibling ties (Matthews et al., 1989; Suggs, 1989). We find that geographic proximity does enhance emotional closeness to the sibling network overall, not to the emotionally closest sibling. Therefore, the emotionally closest sibling is not necessarily the sibling who lives nearest by. It is possible, however, that having a more proximate sibling creates greater closeness to the sibling network because there is shared information about the rest of the network between the two siblings who live nearer each other. This would parallel the observed role of parents, especially mothers, as conduits of family news about all siblings (Allan, 1977). Geographic proximity also enhances telephone and personal contact with the sibling network and with the sibling of greatest contact. Thus opportunity is an essential component of sibling contact.

The *number of siblings* one has affects all dimensions of the sibling tie examined here in a pattern that suggests greater opportunity for selectivity within larger families. The consistent finding regarding the sibling of greatest closeness, confiding, and contact is that number of siblings is positively related. Conversely, number of siblings is inversely related to overall contact with siblings by phone and in person, indicating considerable range in contact within larger sibling networks. Network size is unrelated to overall closeness and confiding. Therefore, larger families appear to afford a greater opportunity for forming a sibling relationship marked by special closeness, extensive confiding, and high levels of contact.

In conclusion, our analyses show that gender has greater consequences for sibling ties than does marital status, reflecting the gendered nature of relations in our society. Our findings provide evidence of the link discussed by Finch (1989) between the private domains of family and the larger public morality's emphasis on a woman's commitment to family.

Our results generally indicate that being single has limited implications for emotional bonds between siblings and a substantial bearing on contact, especially in person. This could be evidence of a greater responsibility or obligation of the single to stay in touch with their siblings or a greater sense of obligation by sibling networks to maintain contact with their single members. We expect that both of these possibilities apply, but we place greater emphasis on the single person's commitment to his or her siblings because the respondent's singlehood has a greater impact on contact than does the singlehood of siblings, as reported by respondents of all marital statuses.

Parent status has less of a bearing on sibling ties than do gender and marital status, but, here again, we see that those with fewer competing relationships tend to maintain more active bonds with their siblings (with the exception of greater confiding within networks of parent and childless siblings than networks of childless siblings only).

Our analyses have shown the benefits of observing sibling relationships from at least two points of view, in this case, by looking at the exceptional sibling tie (i.e., the closest, most confiding, and greatest contact tie) and at the overall sibling network (as indicated by mean scores). Examining the results in juxtaposition reveals more about sibling ties than would studying either of them individually. Apparent contradictions in outcome, such as different significant predictors for the same dimension of sibling ties, become additional data, allowing for more sophisticated interpretation of the results, much as divergence between qualitative and quantitative data does (Connidis, 1983; Jick, 1979; Lever, 1981). Our preceding discussion of the impact of number of siblings and of geographic proximity exemplifies this benefit.

Our findings point to several directions for further research. Perhaps most important among them is further study of the effect of emotional closeness on supportive behavior. This would provide useful insight into our understanding of the sibling tie as a source of instrumental support. Are stronger emotional ties necessary for the sibling tie to be supportive in this way? The importance of emotional closeness to confiding and contact signals the need to go beyond the demands of family membership per se to better understand what prompts supportive behavior between family members. This subjective aspect of family relationships is more open to observation when the concept of family is extended beyond the more obligatory nuclear ties between spouses and between parents and children. At the same time, the extent to which the greater contact with siblings of women, the single, and the childless is a function of their greater obligation to their siblings, of siblings to them, or a balance of the two requires further study.

References

Allan, G. (1977). Sibling solidarity. *Journal of Marriage and the Family, 39*(1), 177-183.

Avioli, P. S. (1989). The social support functions of siblings in later life. *American Behavioral Scientist, 33*(1), 45-57.

Bedford, V. H. (1989). Understanding the value of siblings in old age. *American Behavioral Scientist, 33*(1), 33-44.

Bossard, J. H. S., & Boll, E. S. (1956). *The large family system.* Philadelphia: University of Pennsylvania Press.

Connidis, I. A. (1983). Integrating qualitative and quantitative methods in survey research on aging: An assessment. *Qualitative Sociology, 6,* 334-352.

Connidis, I. A. (1989a). Contact between siblings in later life. *Canadian Journal of Sociology, 14*(4), 429-441.

Connidis, I. A. (1989b). *Family ties and aging.* Toronto: Butterworths Canada.

Connidis, I. A. (1989c). Siblings as friends in later life. *American Behavioral Scientist, 33*(1), 81-93.

Connidis, I. A. (1992). Life transitions and the adult sibling tie: A qualitative study. *Journal of Marriage and the Family, 54*(4), 972-982.

Finch, J. (1989). *Family obligations and social change.* Cambridge: Polity Press.

Finch, J., & Mason, J. (1993). *Negotiating family responsibilities.* London: Tavistock/Routledge.

Fox, B. (1988). Conceptualizing "family": Definitions and theoretical perspectives. In B. Fox (Ed.), *Family bonds and gender divisions* (pp. 3-6). Toronto: Canadian Scholars' Press.

Goetting, A. (1986). The developmental tasks of siblingship over the life cycle. *Journal of Marriage and the Family, 48*(4), 703-714.

Gold, D. T. (1989). Generational solidarity: Conceptual antecedents and consequences. *American Behavioral Scientist, 33*(1), 19-32.

Jick, T. D. (1979). Mixing qualitative and quantitative methods: Triangulation in action. *Administrative Science Quarterly, 24,* 602-611.

Lee, G. R., & Ihinger-Tallman, M. (1980). Sibling interaction and morale: The effects of family relations on older people. *Research on Aging, 2*(3), 367-391.

Lee, T. R., Mancini, J. A., & Maxwell, J. W. (1990). Sibling relationships in adulthood: Contact patterns and motivations. *Journal of Marriage and the Family, 52*(2), 431-440.

Leigh, G. K. (1982). Kinship interaction over the family life span. *Journal of Marriage and the Family, 44*(1), 197-208.

Lever, J. (1981). Multiple methods of data collection: A note of divergence. *Urban Life, 10,* 199-213.

Longino, C. F., Jr., & Lipman, A. (1981). Married and spouseless men and women in planned retirement communities: Support network differentials. *Journal of Marriage and the Family, 43*(1), 169-177.

Matthews, S. H. (1987). Provision of care to old parents: Division of responsibility among adult children. *Research on Aging, 9,* 45-60.

Matthews, S. H., Delaney, P. J., & Adamek, M. E. (1989). Male kinship ties: Bonds between adult brothers. *American Behavioral Scientist, 33*(1), 58-69.

Mugford, S., & Kendig, H. L. (1986). Social relations: Networks and ties. In H. L. Kendig (Ed.), *Ageing and families: A social networks perspectives* (pp. 38-59). Boston: Allen & Unwin.

Rossi, A. S., & Rossi, P. H. (1990). *Of human bonding.* New York: Aldine de Gruyter.

Scott, J. P. (1983). Siblings and other kin. In T. H. Brubaker (Ed.), *Family relationships in later life* (pp. 47-62). Beverly Hills, CA: Sage.

Shanas, E. (1979). Social myth as hypothesis: The case of the family relations of old people. *The Gerontologist, 19,* 3-9.

Simon, B. L. (1987). *Never married women.* Philadelphia: Temple University Press.

Sprey, J. (1991). Studying adult children and their parents. *Marriage and Family Review 16*(3/4), 221-235.

Statistics Canada. (1992). Catalogue. In *Age, sex, and marital status: The nation* (pp. 93-310). Ottawa: Minister of Industry, Science and Technology.

Suggs, P. K. (1989). Predictors of association among older siblings: A Black/White comparison. *American Behavioral Scientist, 33,* 70-80.

Troll, L. E. (1986). Introduction. In L. E. Troll (Ed.), *Family issues in current gerontology* (pp. 301-312). New York: Springer.

White, L. K., & Riedmann, A. (1992). Ties among adult siblings. *Social Forces, 71*(1), 85-102.

22

Shared Filial Responsibility:
The Family as the Primary Caregiver

Sarah H. Matthews
Tena Tarler Rosner

Research Design
and Respondents

The informants for this research are pairs of sisters—one employed, one not employed—representing 50 sibling groups that range in size from two to seven. In all cases at least one of their parents was aged 75 or older, and all but one parent were living in the community.

The 151 siblings implicated in the research—126 sisters and 25 brothers—ranged in age from 33 to 78, with a median age of 51. Two-thirds were married at the time of the interview.

The 62 parents in these families ranged in age from 73 to 97, with a median age of 79. With respect to financial strain, approximately two-thirds of the parents were described as "comfortable" or better and, except for 2 who were described as "having difficulty making ends meet," the others were described as having "enough to get by on." In several cases, the respondents considered their parent(s) to be independent, so that the questions were ones about which they had not thought concretely.

In one case, the widowed mother, who suffered from dementia, had been transferred to the nursing home of the retirement community in which she resided. The parents, then, ranged from totally independent to totally dependent and their adult children were confronted with a wide range of service needs.

Mobilizing Adult Siblings
to Meet Parental Needs

When a parent's continued independence was threatened by such things as physical or mental changes or widowhood, family members were mobilized into a "parent-care system" in which decisions regarding what actions were required were more likely to be made in concert. Siblings were likely to be in touch with one another more often to confirm perceptions and to discuss whether action was required. Although each sibling continued to have a unique bond with the parent, once parental needs became an issue, siblings often became more aware of one another's activities with respect to the parent in order to avoid duplicating or overlooking particular tasks.

Unlike the care of infants, for whom biology dictates "continuity of coverage" by caretakers (LaRossa and LaRossa, 1981), the amount of coverage required by elders is not clear-cut, so that these siblings had to decide what constituted the appropriate amount. An unstated principle of least involvement appeared to govern their actions: when a sensitizing situation was somewhat ambiguous, they opted for less rather than more involvement in their parents' daily lives. Least involvement functioned to preserve the independence of both generations for as long as possible. One way in which children became involved without establishing dependency was through monitoring. For example, one daughter said about her mother, who sometimes forgot to take her medicine, "I keep my eye open for swelling of the ankles." In another family a daughter indicated, "Knowing he's alone we do try to watch over the situation more than we were obliged to do when my mother was alive." What siblings seemed to resist was making their parents more dependent on them than was apparently necessary.

The principle of least involvement continued to affect siblings' behavior as the parent became increasingly needy. Attempts were made to preserve the psychological if not the actual independence of the generations. When adult children began to feel overwhelmed by their parents' needs, in most cases they hired help to take over specific duties, such as cooking, cleaning, and transportation. Unless the cost was negligible, in almost all of these 50 families the parent's money was used so that children were able to view hiring help as part of the parent's normal adult behavior—that is, paying individuals to perform tasks that the parent could not or did not want to do. In none of these cases, however, did children relinquish filial responsibility. Rather, they continued to provide emotional support and services to their parents.

Styles of Participation

The style that formed the core of the parent-care system was *routine:* regular assistance to the elderly parent was incorporated into the adult child's ongoing activities. Use of this style meant that a sibling was both predictable and available to do whatever needed to be done. Because parents varied with respect to what was needed, routine involvement included a wide range of activities: household chores ("I do Mom's cleaning, dusting, vacuuming, and laundry"); "checking" ("I call my mother twice every day"); providing outings ("Every Tuesday I take Mother shopping for the day"); running errands ("I've always done Mother's grocery shopping"); managing finances ("I pay all of Mother's bills"); and visiting ("Tuesday and Saturday afternoons I spend visiting her").

A second style was being a *backup*. Some siblings were not routinely involved in providing emotional support or concrete services but could be counted on when siblings who engaged in routine caregiving asked them to help. For example, one sister explained, "I do what my sisters instruct me to do." There was apparently no doubt that she would respond to her sisters' instructions, but she did not initiate involvement.

Circumscribed is a style of participation that is highly predictable but carefully bounded. For example, one respondent said of her brother, "He gives a routine, once-a-week call." This call was important to their parent and the brother could be relied upon by his siblings to make it, but he apparently was not available or expected to increase the scope of his participation in the provision of care to their parent. Siblings who adopt this style could be counted on to help, but there were clear limits to what they could be called upon to do.

In contrast to the predictable nature of the contributions associated with the preceding ones, the *sporadic* style describes adult children who provided services to parents at their own convenience. For example, one daughter said, "We invite Mom to go along when we take trips." Another said, "My brother does come in when he feels like it to take Mother out on Sundays, but it's not a scheduled thing." Even though sporadic involvement was unreliable, it was recognized as valuable to the parent.

The last style is *dissociation* from filial responsibility. The filial behavior of siblings who used this style was predictable in that they could not be counted on to assist in their parents' care. In one family of three daughters, for example, the two younger ones were involved routinely in helping their mother, while their older sister "is not included in our discussions or dealings with my mother. . . . She doesn't do anything." While in some families these children apparently had dissociated themselves from the entire family, this was not always the case. In one family the brother early in his life had broken off contact with his mother and coincidentally, therefore, from parent care, but not from contact with his siblings. His sister explained, "My brother has no interest at all and does not care about my mother to any extent. In the few times he comes in from out of town, we deliberately don't discuss Mother with him."

Factors Affecting Styles of Participation

Once a sibling group was mobilized to meet parental needs, three other factors—family structure, family history, and extrafamilial ties—affected both the inclusion of specific styles and the likelihood that a sibling would use a particular style.

Family Structure: Size and Gender Composition

The structural properties of sibling groups define the parameters within which their actions take place. Two structural properties—size and gender composition—affected the likelihood that a style would be included as well as which siblings were likely to adopt it. Although these are discussed separately, there clearly is a relationship between them.

The size of the sibling group was important with respect to its organization. In 23 of the families the two sisters who were interviewed were the only adult children. These sisters shared an expectation that they were jointly responsible for their parent(s). They did not necessarily contribute in exactly the same way, but each expected the other at least to back her up. In dyads, then, circumscribed, sporadic, and dissociative styles rarely occurred. It is important to keep in mind that in order for a family to be included in the research, two sisters had to volunteer to be interviewed. The fact that in these 23 pairs of sisters—the only children in their families—both used the routine style or, occasionally, one served as a backup, is at least in part an artifact of the research design. However, in a number of these pairs, sisters clearly were not fond of one another and, had there been more siblings with whom to share responsibility, they might very well have used different styles. Unanswered is the question of what would be the case in dyads comprising only brothers or a brother and a sister.

In the 27 larger groups of siblings additional styles usually were present. In one family of six, for example, the mother rotated throughout the year among three of her daughters' homes; two daughters apparently contributed to the parent-care system sporadically, as did the son who provided extra money when he was asked. Usually two siblings, especially in families of four or more siblings, coordinated their routine efforts, with other siblings' participation characterized by one of the other three styles. An adult child's legitimately taking a relatively less important part in filial duties, then, occurred almost exclusively in families in which there were more than two siblings. The consequences for adult children of having old parents clearly varied in these 50 families depending on the number of siblings with whom filial responsibility was shared.

Although each of the five styles was utilized by both brothers and sisters, gender affected the likelihood that a particular style would be adopted by one or the other. Twenty-one of the families included at least one brother. "Routine" involvement was common for daughters in the study but atypical for sons.

The "backup" style was primarily used by sisters. As a sister in one family commented, "I hold myself in reserve." While it is possible that some brothers might have described themselves similarly had they been interviewed, their readiness to help was more likely than their sisters' to be described as "circumscribed." Brothers often were described as limiting their filial activity to a specific task or area of expertise—for example, repairing household appliances or providing financial information.

Very few sisters were described as using the "sporadic" style; brothers often were. When sisters reported this type of contact by their brothers, they tended to look upon it as important to their parents but not as a significant contribution in meeting parental needs. If they used it themselves, it was because parental needs were minimal, so that the mobilization to a "parent-care system" had not taken place.

The last approach, "dissociation" from filial responsibility, was reported more frequently for sons. A daughter was less likely to dissociate herself unless there were at least four sisters in the family who apparently could dilute the effect of her absence. For a son, fewer siblings were necessary to "cover" his absence. In those few families of three sisters in which one sister dissociated herself from parent care, respondents either expressed anger or offered an elaborate explanation for her nonparticipation. By contrast, a brother's dissociation, regardless of family size, was presented merely as a fact, albeit a sad one.

Ties Among Family Members

In some families the style of participation adopted by a sibling was affected by alliances that existed among various members. Parent-child alliances apparently were set by the parent. A "favorite" child, for example, had a special relationship with a parent and in some families became obligated in unique ways. One son, for example, was his father's favorite child. True to his feelings, the father had sold his home to finance a business for his son and was now viewed by his sisters as their brother's responsibility. More commonly, favorite children were seen by their siblings as being in a position to exercise leverage with the parent in accomplishing some objective, such as "getting Mother to take a bath," and in several of those families that activity was the basis for adoption of the circumscribed style. Favorite children who were involved only sporadically, not surprisingly, were not always spoken of kindly by their routinely involved sisters.

In half of the families, conflicts among members were reported. The tension, varying in intensity from family to family and by respondents within a family, was reported in most cases to stem from events that had occurred before meeting filial obligations was an issue. Conflicts were reported between parents and children as well as between siblings. In families with more than two siblings, serious conflict did result in a sibling's physically and psychologically dissociating him- or herself from membership in the family and, incidentally, from filial responsibilities. In families in which there were only two sisters, the tension between them—even though in two cases it was intense—usually was kept within limits in order to preserve their working relationship. In a number of families in which respondents reported conflict, parents apparently relied on others to meet their needs. One parent, for example, had built a duplex with her own sister and the two lived side by side. One couple had moved into a life-care retirement community, where the widowed mother still resided. Another widowed mother lived in the house she had occupied since her wedding in a small town surrounded by relatives, neighbors, and friends whom she had known all her life (or theirs). Family conflict that threatens to undermine adult children's meeting filial obligations may lead parents to act to heighten their own security.

Over the course of the years, siblings viewed one another and their parents as having stable personality characteristics. These attributions affected their relationships with one another and sometimes affected the style of involvement that a sibling was likely to use. One sister, for example, said, "My sister is not a very good person in a crisis. She tends to fall apart. I'm not that way." Responding to a parental crisis, then, fell to her rather than to her sister. Another respondent, whose sister had complete decision-making power with respect to their mother, said, "When we talked about Mother's having to go to a nursing home, I collapsed. . . . My sister is a rock." The two sisters were in agreement that one sister was capable of making difficult decisions while the other was not. The personality that a sibling was assigned within the family, then, affected the part he or she was expected to play in meeting filial obligations, with some being seen as well suited to participate routinely and others expected to take less integral parts.

Regardless of the history of family relationships, within the context of meeting needs of old parents, issues that related to how members felt about one another apparently took a back seat to the more important issue of providing adequate care in an equitable fashion. Family history issues did continue to affect the way siblings related to one another, both generally and while they went about the business of meeting filial obligations. They had less effect on the organization of the parent-care system, however, than the other factors over which siblings had much less control, such as parental

needs and the size and gender composition of their family.

Extrafamilial Ties: Competing Commitments

Time as a limiting factor. Geographical proximity between an adult child and an old parent was one very important factor that affected a sibling's style of participation. The travel time involved, even if the differences between siblings were relatively small, often was presented as an important consideration in determining which siblings would be routinely involved. For example, one sister who lived 4 miles from her mother was more likely to respond to her calls because she was closer than her sister who lived 12 miles away.

Employment represented another competing commitment that affected siblings' availability. For some siblings, employment was seen as limiting the amount of time free to devote to a parent: "Since I went back to work, I definitely do less." This sister, however, continued to be involved routinely but exercised more control over what and when she would contribute. Typically, a job put constraints on *when* rather than *if* siblings did things for their parents and did not decrease the likelihood of routine involvement. In one family in which the mother lived with an employed daughter, the daughter came home every day at lunch to walk her mother's dog, took her mother to activities on scheduled evenings, and arranged necessary appointments on weekends.

Spouses. One of the most important competing ties that adult children had was to their spouses. This went beyond a simple time commitment to the issue of loyalty. Although this conceivably could have applied to children as well, children apparently were expected to accept their parents' priorities, so that the issue, in fact, rarely was raised by the respondents. Not surprisingly, given the relationship between gender and style of participation discussed above, the impact of ties to a spouse varied by whether the spouse was a husband or a wife. The 90 sons-in-law and the 21 daughters-in-law implicated in this research assumed one of three postures: active support, indifference, or antagonism. It is important to keep in mind that a posture developed not as a response to parent care per se but over the years of a marriage. Furthermore, a posture was not independent of the attitudes and expectations of the spouse. The point, then, is not that relationships between in-laws are problematic but that, when parents require services to maintain independence, an adult child has less flexibility with which to negotiate meeting everyone's needs and demands. The posture of a husband or wife, then, affected how easily an adult child could adopt a particular style of parent care.

The posture of active support by husbands and wives took two major forms: direct services to the parents-in-law and indirect services through support to spouses. Some took on responsibilities for their parents-in-law as if the role were not mediated. One respondent reported that her husband "looks at her as his own mother. 'Mother' is respected no matter what. . . . He includes her in everything." In fact, she lived with them and was considered an integral part of the household. This daughter did not feel caught between the needs of her parent and the needs of her husband.

Other spouses' actions made evident the mediated nature of their relationships to their parents-in-law but were nevertheless supportive of their husbands' and wives' filial behavior. While not actively sharing the responsibility, such spouses made it relatively easy for their wives and husbands to be involved in providing parent care by seeing it as a legitimate competing commitment. One respondent, for example, said, "My husband is wonderful and has put up with this [arrangement for caring for my mother] for many years, so

I'm lucky." In some cases, husbands were willing to substitute for their wives. For example, one respondent said, "If I can't make it to take her to the doctor, he will do that." Adult children with supportive spouses were more likely to be routinely involved in providing services to old parents.

Other husbands and wives apparently were indifferent to their spouses' filial activities, seeing it as unrelated to them. The only comment one respondent made about her husband throughout the interview was in response to a direct query about his involvement with her parents, "He talks to them on the phone when we talk." In another case, the daughter was in daily contact with her mother, for whom she provided emotional support as well as transportation and other specific services. Her husband, who did see his mother-in-law on holidays, apparently was removed from all the parent-care activity that his wife and her sister shared. One sister explained, "She's never had any relationship with her sons-in-law." These husbands did not appear to inhibit their wives' meeting filial responsibilities, and the sisters were engaged in routine parent care. However, potential for conflict existed when spouses adopted this posture. For example, one mother was living in the household of her daughter and son-in-law. The respondent explained, "My husband comes and goes freely as always. He wouldn't have put up with it if it had affected his working life. It is getting to him now." Her husband was about to retire and wanted to travel, something that would be impossible if the frail, dependent mother continued to live with them. Plans were being made for her to move to a nursing home. Adult children whose spouses assume this posture, then, might find themselves caught between responsibilities to a parent and a spouse when the demands of either increase.

There were daughters- and sons-in-law, however, who were described as being openly antagonistic toward their parents-in-law. For their spouses, meeting the needs of their parents and their husbands or wives was not only a matter of juggling priorities but of deciding which act of treason was easier. One daughter explained, "My relationship with my husband is such that if I spent his money on my family, I was a parasite." Her sister confirmed this: "Her husband never comes to see my mother. He has a block." The husband's hostile attitude made every filial activity a conflict-laden choice for her. Some spouses, then, impeded their wives'

and husbands' providing services and emotional support to their parents, making it difficult for them to provide routine care or to act even as a backup.

Reference

LaRossa, Ralph, and Maureen Mulligan LaRossa. 1981. Transition to Parenthood: How Infants Change Families. Beverly Hills, CA: Sage Publications.

What Remains

Marge Piercy

These ashes are not the fine dust I imagined.
The undertaker brings them out from the back
in a plastic baggie, like supermarket produce.
I try not to grab, but my need shocks me,
how I hunger to seize this officially
labeled garbage and carry you off.

All the water was vaporized,
the tears, the blood, the sweat,
fluids of a juicy, steamy woman
burnt offering into the humid Florida
air among cement palm trees with brown
fronds stuck up top like feather dusters.

In the wind the palmettoes clatter.
The air is yellowed with dust.
I carry you back North where you belong
through the bumpy black December night
on the almost empty plane stopping
at every airport like a dog at posts.

Now I hold what is left in my hands
bone bits, segments of the arched skull
varicolored stones of the body,
green, copper, beige, black, purple
fragments of shells eroded by storm
that slowly color the beach.

Archeology in a plastic baggie.
Grit spills into my palms:
reconstruct your days, your odyssey.

These are fragments of a smashed mosaic
that formed the face of a dancer
with bound feet, cursing in dreams.

At the marriage of the cat and dog
I howl under the floor.
You will chew on each other's bones
for years. You cannot read
the other's body language.
On the same diet you starve.

My longest, oldest love, I have brought
you home to the land I am dug into.
I promise a path laid right to you,
roses to spring from you, herbs nearby,
the company of my dead cats
whose language you already know.

We'll make your grave by piney woods,
a fine place to sit and sip wine,
to take the sun and watch the beans
grow, the tomatoes swell and redden.
You will smell rosemary, thyme,
and the small birds will come.

I promise to hold you in the mind
as a cupped hand protects a flame.
That is nothing to you. You cannot
hear. Yet just as I knew when you
really died, you know I have brought
you home. Now you want to be roses.

Marriage as Support or Strain?
Marital Quality Following the Death of a Parent

Debra Umberson

The impact of death on the family has received surprisingly little research attention considering the inevitability and frequency of such events and in light of evidence that bereavement often has strong adverse effects on individual well-being (Stroebe & Stroebe, 1987). One of the most common deaths faced by adults is the death of a parent. Demographers report that the death of a mother is most likely to occur when children are between the ages of 45 and 64 and the death of a father is most likely to occur when children are between the ages of 35 and 54 (Marks, in press; also see Winsborough, Bumpass, & Aquilino, 1991). Annually, approximately 5% of the United States population experiences this type of loss (Moss & Moss, 1984). This is a fairly recent historical development arising from increases in longevity. Uhlenberg (1980) reported that "a shift from 1900 mortality conditions to those of 1976 implies an increase in the proportion of middle-aged couples who have living parents from 48 to 86 percent" (p. 319). A parent's death may have a significant impact on these couples' relationships.

The present study considers how the death of a parent may affect adult children's marital relationships and how change in marital quality affects individual well-being. This is an important issue for several reasons. First, the death of a parent is a common life transition for adults that may be a significant predictor of change in marital quality. Second, because marital quality is strongly associated with global happiness (Glenn, 1990) and psychological well-being (Gove, Hughes, & Style, 1983), any significant change in marital quality has important implications for the general well-being of individuals. Third, the quality of marital relationships may be a help or a hindrance to an individual who is coping with a parent's death. For example, a strained relationship with one's spouse might exacerbate the effect of a parent's death on individual well-being, while a supportive spouse might help reduce the adverse effect of a parent's death on individual well-being. Finally, family scholars have called for more research that uses nationally representative data to address the impact of familial losses on individuals (Perkins, 1990).

The proposed analysis will increase our understanding of the impact of a death in the family on individuals and family relationships.

Background

Although parental death and marital relationships have not been considered specifically, previous theory and research has considered how certain types of bereavement affect social and personal relationships. This literature suggests that the death of a loved one is often associated with change in social relationships—sometimes in a positive direction, sometimes in a negative direction (Ferraro, Mutran, & Barresi, 1984). Some theoretical work suggests a compensation model by which the bereaved attempt to fill the void with increased involvement in other relationships (Moss & Moss, 1984; Palmore, 1968; see discussion by Ferraro et al., 1984). Others suggest a decremental model by which the strain associated with bereavement undermines social relationships (Palmore, 1968; see discussion by Ferraro et al., 1984). Bereavement research shows that supportive relationships are helpful to the bereaved in alleviating the psychological distress associated with bereavement (Stroebe & Stroebe, 1987). However, even attempts by others to provide support may be conducive to distress in some cases; support attempts from others are sometimes viewed by the bereaved as unhelpful or even critical, which may create additional strain for the bereaved individual (Wortman & Lehman, 1985). Most empirical research on bereavement and relationships pertains to the death of a spouse. The death of a spouse seems to affect the degree of social support and strain that characterizes relationships with friends and surviving family members (Ferraro et al., 1984; Umberson, Wortman, & Kessler, 1992).

Previous research has suggested a number of reasons why the death of a parent might affect marital relationships. First, the death of a parent is a stressful life event (Umberson & Chen, 1994), and a substantial literature has suggested that stressful life events affect marital quality.

Bereavement following the death of a parent might well impair the bereaved individual's usual ability to maintain family and work roles, thus leading to a decline in marital quality. On the other hand, the death of a parent may reduce other role commitments (e.g., providing care and time to an elderly parent) that have competed with the marital role in the past and this may enhance marital quality.

Second, a few studies on adult children's caregiving for parents with dementia provide evidence for the impact of a type of symbolic parental loss on marital quality. In a study of caregiving for parents with dementia, Suitor and Pillemer (1994) found that adult children's caregiving does not necessarily lead to a decline in marital quality. Marital satisfaction is most likely to decline when spouses do not provide emotional support specific to caregiving or are a source of interpersonal stress. Furthermore, spouses who have been through a similar caregiving experience are more likely to be a source of support to the caregiver and less likely to be a source of interpersonal stress (Suitor & Pillemer, 1993). These results suggest that a spouse who has experienced his or her own parent's death may be more supportive of a partner who loses a parent.

Third, the marital relationship provides a "backstage" (Goffman, 1959) on which individuals can express feelings of loss and grief even if they do not express those feelings at work or to persons outside the family. In this sense, one's spouse may be the only person to witness the degree of distress or depression experienced by the bereaved person. Some spouses may be unnerved by continuing grief and depression in a partner. This situation may impose pressures on the bereaved person's spouse to be a ready source of support during the period of grief, either providing couples with the opportunity to become closer and more supportive of one another or introducing strain into the relationship.

The Present Study

The present study analyzes an interactive array of many of these factors with data from a prospective, nationally representative sample to address three questions: (a) How does the death of a parent affect marital quality? (b) Does marital quality explain some of the adverse effect of a parent's death on adults' well-being? That is, is marital quality an intervening variable that mediates the impact of a parent's death on individual physical and psychological well-being? (c) Does the effect of a parent's death on individual well-being depend, in part, on the quality of the bereaved individual's marital relationship? That is, does marital quality interact with the death of parent to moderate the impact of a parent's death on individual physical and psychological well-being? Additional data from an in-depth interview study of recently bereaved adults are analyzed to address a fourth question: (d) Why does the death of a parent lead to change in marital quality?

Data and Methods

I use two types of data to assess the impact of the recent death of a parent on adults' marital relationships and well-being. In the first part of this study I analyze data from a national two-wave panel survey of individuals to address the first three questions above. The subsample analyzed in the present study is composed of 802 individuals: The 123 consistently married/cohabiting individuals who lost a biological parent between 1986 and 1989 and a comparison group of 679 married/cohabiting individuals who had at least one living biological par-

ent in 1989 and who had not experienced the death of a parent between 1986 and 1989.

The second part of the study addresses the final question above and is based on a qualitative analysis of in-depth interviews with 42 recently bereaved adults who were married at the time of bereavement. These data, described further in the qualitative data analysis section, allow me to analyze respondents' perceptions of their partners and marriages following the loss of a parent, and to identify some of the processes through which respondents perceive that their parent's death affected the marital relationship.

Results

The estimated effects of a parent's death on marital quality follow a somewhat different pattern depending on the sex of the deceased parent. The death of a mother is associated with a decline in social support from one's partner and an increase in negative behavior by one's partner. While the other marital quality measures are not significantly affected by a mother's death, all of the estimated effects of a mother's death on marital quality measures are in a direction that is consistent with the finding of decline in relationship quality. The death of a father is associated with an increase in relationship strain and frequency of conflict, and a decline in relationship harmony. Tests for the difference in the impact of a mother's versus a father's death yielded only one significant difference; a mother's death seems to have a stronger adverse effect on social support from one's partner than does a father's death.

The impact of a parent's death on marital quality seems to be very similar for men and women. A number of significant interactions suggest, however, that marital quality of some groups of individuals may be more adversely affected than others by the death of a parent. Race interacted only with a father's death in predicting relationship strain. The death of a father is associated with increased relationship strain and this effect is stronger for African Americans than for others. In general, the death of a parent is associated with a greater decline in marital quality for individuals with more education. Education—and income, in some cases following a mother's death—do not seem to buffer individuals' marital relationships following a parent's death.

Age interacts with a father's death in predicting partner's negative behavior. Among individuals aged 43 and younger, a father's death is inversely associated with partner's negative behavior. However, among individuals 44 and older, a father's death is positively associated with partner's negative behavior. The nature of this interaction differs depending on the sex of the parent who died. Generally, the death of a father increases strain and conflict for married individuals. However, the more years spent in the relationship, the less strain and conflict seem to result from the father's death. In contrast, a mother's death is associated with reduced conflict, but this advantage lessens for those with more years in their relationships. The results for a father's death seem to make more intuitive sense, in that more years in a relationship should lessen the impact of life events on marital quality. However, several findings in this study suggest that respondents may place greater demands on a marriage following a mother's death and that this may be even more true for individuals who have spent more time in their relationship.

The category of parental status that significantly interacts with a father's death varies, but for each of the significant interactions, the death of a father results in a greater decline in marital quality for childless individuals than for individuals with children. This may occur because a father's death has less impact on individuals who feel that their father lives on in their children.

Several additional interactions pertain only to a mother's death. A mother's death interacts with income in predicting partner's negative behavior and relationship conflict. The death of a mother is inversely related to both negative outcomes; however, this advantage lessens for those with higher levels of income. A mother's death also interacts with marital status in predicting relationship harmony: A mother's death results in a greater decline in relationship harmony for cohabiting individuals than for married individuals. This may occur because cohabiting relationships are less stable than married relationships and are, as a consequence, more vulnerable to life strains.

Although these survey results suggest that the death of a parent may have adverse effects on the marital relationships of bereaved adult children and that negative change in some dimensions of marital quality may contribute to psychological distress, alcohol consumption, and physical health decline, the findings do not convey much information about the actual processes through which filial bereavement is associated with decline in marital quality. In fact, the results from the quantitative analysis raised a number of additional questions that could not be answered with the national data. In particular, what are the reasons for a decline in marital quality following the death of a parent? The quantitative results led me to design a qualitative study to address this specific question as well as other bereavement issues. The results from the qualitative analysis are reported in the next part of this study.

In-Depth Interviews With Recently Bereaved Adults

The second part of this study is based on an analysis of in-depth interviews with 73 adults, aged 25 to 67, who recently experienced the death of a parent. The mean age of respondents was 39.8; 58.9% were female, 5.6% were Hispanic, and 5.6% were African American. All individuals who said they were in a significant relationship at the time of the parent's death were asked to describe how their partner dealt with the bereaved respondent following the loss, how the relationship may have changed as a result of the loss, and how the relationship has affected their recovery from bereavement.

Although a number of respondents provided appreciative and warm reports of a supportive spouse who made the bereavement process easier, many respondents provided detailed accounts that provide insight into the processes behind the quantitative reports of a decline in marital quality following bereavement. The four themes of marital strain and decline identified with the greatest frequency in the in-depth interviews were: (a) failed social support, (b) partner's unwillingness or inability to communicate about the death, (c) partner's lack of empathy, and (d) excessive expectations and demands by the partner. A fifth theme, identified less often but having important implications for marital quality following bereavement, was labeled as liberation.

Failed Social Support

The most common and consistent theme in the in-depth interviews was that the partner could not seem to provide the bereaved individual with the emotional support that was desired or needed. This often led to disappointment, and occasionally to anger, with the partner.

> I had some expectations that my wife would be more helpful, but she's been so burned out at work . . . I haven't gotten the full support there. . . . I've had . . . a layer of disappointment in that. (41-year-old male)

> I have to be all things to all people and sometimes I need someone to be there for me. . . . I'm

disappointed in the fact that he doesn't know how to comfort me. (57-year-old female)

Importantly, several respondents emphasized that their partner was usually a supportive person, but that the partner seemed unable to provide support of the type and degree desired by the bereaved person during the bereavement period.

> He's generally a sensitive person. . . . He just couldn't understand. I mean there was nothing he said or did. It was just—at the moment, I just feel like he wasn't giving me enough. (49-year-old female)

Unwillingness or Inability to Communicate

A theme closely related to failed social support is the inability or unwillingness of a partner to talk about the loss.

> The subject of my father's death in the months following [the death] was never brought up unless I [brought it up]. His uncertainty and uneasiness of dealing with me and this situation made me very intolerant of him in general. I was almost angry with him because he was very passive about this. (39-year-old female)

> I wanted him to initiate the conversations about my father sometimes—to let me know that he was thinking about him too. He also would just let the conversation end. He would ask, "What are you thinking about?" I would say, "My dad." He would say, "Oh," and then there would be silence. (31-year-old female)

Some respondents attributed their partner's communication failures to a lack of skill and recognized that their partner wanted to be supportive, while others attributed lack of communication to the partner's self-centeredness. Of course, many spouses are simply continuing a relationship-long pattern of interaction; it may be that dissatisfaction with these patterns becomes more salient during the period of bereavement, a time in which need may be high and disappointments more acutely felt (Umberson et al., 1992).

Lack of Empathy

Many bereaved individuals reported that their spouse did not understand the importance of the loss or could not comprehend the significance of losing a parent. This was frustrating to respondents and also illustrated to them that their spouse did not share the bereavement experience.

> [My wife] is not that close to her family . . . she has no comprehension of what I'm going through. . . . It's hard for her . . . she doesn't know why I don't want to do anything. . . . I don't hold it against her but she just doesn't understand. . . . If her parents were to die she would probably be over it in 3 or 4 weeks. (46-year-old male)

Respondents often attributed this lack of empathy to their spouse having not yet experienced the death of a parent. Many respondents indicated that it was impossible for any individual who had not yet been through such a loss to understand the meaning of the loss. As one woman told us, "People that haven't gone through it—they can't know." This theme is supported by previous research on caregiving for a parent with dementia. Suitor and Pillemer (1993) found that spouses who had experienced the decline of their own parent were more likely to be a source of support and less likely to be a source of interpersonal strain for the partner currently dealing with the cognitive decline of a parent.

Excessive Expectations

Strain often seemed to arise in marital relationships because the bereaved person failed to meet the partner's expectations for role performance or recovery from bereavement. There seemed to be two primary reasons that respondents sometimes failed to meet role obligations that resulted in marital strain. First, the strain of caring for a sick parent prior to the death, or for the surviving parent following the death, sometimes took its toll on relationships.

> She had an awful lot of stress on her having to do everything . . . because I was never there. . . . The kids had a doctor's appointment or had to get their hair cut. . . . I wasn't there to cut the grass. I feel like she resented my going [away to care for my father]. (41-year-old male)

Second, respondents sometimes became quite depressed or despondent following the death. In turn, they were unable to participate in their usual work, family, or relationship roles.

> She's been anxious about the fact that I'm not working. . . . She was very, very critical for a while this summer about the fact that I wasn't working . . . she was expecting more of me than I thought she should have. (41-year-old male)

> My sex drive diminished a great deal because of my grief. [My husband] took this personally. (26-year-old female)

These findings are similar to those of Suitor and Pillemer (1994), who found that when a husband perceives his wife's participation in caring for a parent with dementia as interfering with her domestic roles, the result is a decline in marital satisfaction.

In addition, expectations for recovery often exceeded respondents' experience of recovery.

> He has a hard time with me and my emotional feelings about my mom—I feel like he wishes I'd get over it and go on. (39-year-old female)

> My wife is ready for me to get on with my life. Period. (42-year-old male)

These findings correspond to previous research showing that depression in a spouse may lead to a decline in marital quality (McLeod & Eckberg, 1993).

Liberation

Several respondents reported that they became separated or divorced from their spouse following the parent's death. Increasing marital strain typically preceded these breakups. Interestingly, several respondents reported that marital dissolution occurred partly because they no longer had to worry about how their parent would view the breakup.

> I can tell you honestly—if my mom and dad were still here, I'd probably still be there with him . . . [because of] their expectations of me. . . . Once mom and dad were gone, that gave me a lot of freedom. (41-year-old female)

Conclusion

The present study shows that marital quality does appear to be affected by the death of a parent in a national sample, and in a negative direction. Compared with nonbereaved individuals, individuals who have recently experienced the death of a mother exhibit a greater decline in social support from their partner and an increase in their partner's negative behavior. Compared with nonbereaved individuals, individuals who have recently experienced the death of a father exhibit a greater increase in relationship strain and frequency of conflict, as well as a greater decline in relationship harmony. Although the pattern of significant effects is slightly different following a mother's death, compared with a father's death, the present results do not provide evidence that the death of a mother has clearly different effects on marital quality than does the death of a father. Generally speaking, the differences are more of degree than kind—mothers' and fathers' deaths are associated with some dimensions of marital quality decline. The estimated effect of a mother's versus a father's death is significantly different in predicting only one dependent variable—social support from one's partner. This may occur because mothers typically provide more social support to adult children than do fathers (Umberson, 1992). The loss of a mother might then lead adults to expect more social support from their partners in order to fill this void.

In sum, the present findings suggest that the life event of filial bereavement may place a great deal of strain on many marital relationships. Furthermore, negative change in some dimensions of marital quality seems to contribute to psychological distress, physical health decline, and alcohol consumption.

In-depth interviews were conducted with recently bereaved adults to address some of the questions raised by the quantitative results. These interviews shed light on some of the possible reasons for a decline in marital quality following a parent's death. Results suggest that this decline may occur because the partner fails to provide desired emotional support, the partner cannot comprehend the significance and meaning of the loss, the partner is disappointed in the bereaved individual's ability to recover quickly, because individuals have new support needs following the death of a parent and these needs may be difficult to meet, and because some partners feel imposed upon—particularly by continuing distress and depression in the bereaved person.

The period following a parent's death may be a time when individuals are in particular need of support from their partners. A partner's failure to provide that support, or strains that are initiated by the partner, may lead to a decline in marital quality for recently bereaved individuals. The effects of this common life event warrant further investigation by family sociologists and demographers as well as marital and family therapists.

References

Ferraro, K. F., Mutran, E., & Barresi, C. M. (1984). Widowhood, health, and friendship support in later life. *Journal of Health and Social Behavior, 25,* 245-259.

Glenn, N. D. (1990). Quantitative research on marital quality in the 1980s: A critical review. *Journal of Marriage and the Family, 52,* 818-831.

Goffman, E. (1959). *The presentation of self in everyday life.* Garden City, NY: Doubleday.

Gove, W. R., Hughes, M., & Style, C. B. (1983). Does marriage have positive effects on the psychological well-being of the individual? *Journal of Health and Social Behavior, 24,* 122-131.

Marks, N. F. (in press). Contemporary social demographics of American midlife parents. In C. D. Ryff & M. M. Seltzer (Eds.), *When children grow up: Development and diversity in mid-life parenting.* Chicago: University of Chicago Press.

McLeod, J. D., & Eckberg, D. A. (1993). Concordance for depressive disorders and marital quality. *Journal of Marriage and the Family, 55,* 733-746.

Moss, M. M., & Moss, S. Z. (1984). The impact of parental death on middle aged children. *Omega, 14,* 65-75.

Palmore, E. B. (1968). The effects of aging on activities and attitudes. *The Gerontologist, 8,* 259-263.

Perkins, H. W. (1990). Familial bereavement and health in adult life course perspective. *Journal of Marriage and the Family, 52,* 233-241.

Stroebe, W., & Stroebe, M. S. (1987). *Bereavement and health: The psychological and physical consequences of partner loss.* Cambridge: Cambridge University Press.

Suitor, J. J., & Pillemer, K. (1993). Support and interpersonal stress in the social networks of married daughters caring for parents with dementia. *Journal of Gerontology, 48,* S1-S8.

Suitor, J. J., & Pillemer, K. (1994). Family caregiving and marital satisfaction: Findings from a 1-year panel study of women caring for parents with dementia. *Journal of Marriage and the Family, 56,* 681-690.

Uhlenberg, P. (1980, Fall). Death and the family. *Journal of Family History,* pp. 313-320.

Umberson, D. (1992). Relationships between adult children and their parents: Psychological consequences for both generations. *Journal of Marriage and the Family, 54,* 664-674.

Umberson, D., & Chen, M. D. (1994). Effects of a parent's death on adult children: Relationship salience and reactions to loss. *American Sociological Review, 59,* 152-168.

Umberson, D., Wortman, C. B., & Kessler, R. C. (1992). Widowhood and depression: Explaining long-term gender differences in vulnerability. *Journal of Health and Social Behavior, 33,* 10-24.

Winsborough, H. H., Bumpass, L. L., & Aquilino, W. S. (1991). *The death of parents and the transition to old age* (Working Paper NSFH-39). Madison: University of Wisconsin, Center for Demography and Ecology.

Wortman, C. B., & Lehman, D. R. (1985). Reactions to victims of life crises: Support attempts that fail. In I. G. Sarason & B. R. Sarason (Eds.), *Social support: Theory, research and applications* (pp. 463-489). Dordrecht, The Netherlands: Martinus Nijhoff.

1 Halle describes the experiences and attitudes of blue-collar husbands regarding their marriages. Their wives are not represented in this study. How do you think they might react to some of the things their husbands stated? Do you think their wives are glad or sorry to be married, and why?

2 American Indians tend to show greater respect for older adults compared with respect for older adults shown by members of the dominant U.S. culture. In what ways do the different styles of grandparenting described by Weibel-Orlando demonstrate this value? In what ways are the styles similar to the pattern of grandparenting in the dominant culture?

3 Think of examples of family gatherings from your own experience that included many family members of different ages. Who arranged these gatherings? How do your experiences compare with the finding that women are kinkeepers and that kinkeepers serve to bring sisters and brothers together?

4 For a variety of reasons, women provide the majority of care for older Americans. Because of their responsibility for care, women are more open to government legislation to support caregiving. How important do you think is the availability of low-cost, high-quality, community-based care?

5 Family gerontologists write about how once parents die, midlife children become the oldest generation in the family network. How might the experience of losing both parents influence adult children's ideas about time, feelings about living relatives, and ideas about what to do with the remainder of their lives?

1 Tyler, A. (1988). *Breathing lessons*. New York: Berkley.

Maggie and Ira Moran remember their marriage of 28 years. In this Pulitzer Prize-winning novel, Anne Tyler vividly portrays marriage in everyday life, celebrating this couple's patterns of intimacy, conflict, and resolution.

2   Minkler, M., & Roe, K. M. (1993). *Grandmothers as caregivers: Raising children of the crack cocaine epidemic.* Newbury Park, CA: Sage.

Minkler and Roe describe the experiences of 70 grandmothers in Oakland, California, who were caring for their grandchildren because their own children were addicted to crack cocaine. The authors provide an in-depth, compelling examination of the antecedents and consequences of this caregiving and explore social policies that hinder support for these women and their grandchildren.

3   Dorris, M. (1987). *Yellow raft in blue water.* New York: Warner.

Dorris tells the story of three generations of an American Indian family: a daughter, her mother, and her grandmother. We see how changes in their lives, their family relationships, and each woman's unique personality influence their identities, their choices, and their relationships with each other.

4   Naylor, G. (1982). *The women of Brewster Place.* New York: Penguin.

Gloria Naylor relates the profound story of African American women whose relationships with men are challenged by poverty, racism, and patriarchy. Together, the women of Brewster Place develop a powerful network of support that provides the extended family connections on which they depend.

5   DiLeonardo, M. (1987). The female world of cards and holidays: Women, families, and the work of kinship. *Signs, 12,* 440-453.

DiLeonardo describes the unpaid work of kinkeeping and explores how women use their kinkeeping labor as a strategy to create closer connections among family members.

6   Delany, S., Delany, A. E., with Hearth, A. H. (1996). *Having our say: The Delany sisters' first one hundred years.* New York: Dell.

Two African American sisters recount their childhood, their connections with others, their commitment to work, and their many years of living together and taking care of each other.

7   Say, A. (1993). *Grandfather's journey.* Boston: Houghton Mifflin.

This beautifully illustrated Caldecott Medal winner is a tribute from a grandson to his grandfather. The children's book poignantly portrays the adventures and challenges experienced by Japanese immigrant families in the United States. Allen Say comes to know his grandfather by having the same experience as his grandfather of living in one country and longing for the other.

8 Vozenilek, H. (Ed.). (1992). *Loss of the ground-note: Women writing about the loss of their mothers.* San Diego, CA: Clothespin Fever Press.

Thirty-four women write powerfully about the enormity of losing one's mother, whether the relationship was one of support, of struggle, or both. In particular, they act in response to the dominant culture's values that remove death and mourning from everyday life.

SUGGESTIONS FOR BROWSING THE WEB

---

1 *www.aarp.org/mmaturity/sept_oct99/home.html*

This series of articles on "great sex" from AARP's magazine, *Modern Maturity,* reports on a study of the sexual lives of middle-aged and older adults in the United States.

2 *www.aoa.gov/aoa/magimage/magimage.html*

This site provides photographs of older persons from *Aging,* the no longer published magazine of the U.S. Administration on Aging. These photos reflect the diversity of the aging population in the United States across a variety of settings.

3 *www.aarp.org/confacts/programs/grandraising.html*

AARP's Web site for grandparents raising grandchildren provides information on legal issues, such as adoption and guardianship; financial concerns, such as local resources for low-income grandparents; medical care and insurance; child care; and issues related to children's education.

4 *www.xculture.org/resource/library/index.cfm#downloads?QID=*

This page from the Web site of the Cross Cultural Health Care Program (CCHCP) provides links to separate documents that you may download to your personal computer. The CCHCP's mission is to ensure health care that is culture and language appropriate. Community profiles are available for the following populations: Arab, Cambodian, Eritrean, Ethiopian, Lao, Mien, Oromo, Samoan, Somali, South Asian, Soviet Jewish, and Ukrainian.

1   *Shall We Dance?* (1996) (English subtitles)

A middle-aged accountant leaves the rigid conformity of his daily life to enter the world of ballroom dance. Through his tenacious desire to learn to dance, he finds happiness and freedom. Sugiyama is so engrossed in his lessons that his wife hires a private investigator to find out why he stays out late and comes home smelling of perfume. Ultimately, his long-term marriage is enhanced by his experiences.

2   *Shirley Valentine* (1989)

Shirley Valentine, a middle-aged woman who feels that life has passed her by, decides to travel to Greece in search of adventure. There she rediscovers and learns to love herself.

3   *Soul Food* (1997)

This film is a loving depiction of a large, extended, African American family. Held together by a strong yet tender matriarch, the family suffers when she falls ill. Her grandson steps in, however, and works to keep his mother, aunts, and uncles united.

4   *The Straight Story* (1999)

Seventy-three-year-old Alvin Straight travels on a riding lawn mower from Laurens, Iowa, to Mt. Zion, Wisconsin, to visit his ill brother. The two brothers have lost contact through the years, and Alvin decides that it is time for them to put aside their differences and renew their friendship.

PART IV

Transitions at Work and at Home in Early Old Age

How we are acknowledged and integrated in the world is influenced by our identification as paid workers. Work provides us with new and sustaining relationships and support, establishes our standard of living, and colors our personal sense of self and family. Job satisfaction does not lead entirely to life satisfaction, but it does play a significant role in how happy we are and how successful we feel.

We are aware of our potential as future workforce participants long before we reach adulthood. While spending most of our early lives in school, we are often asked what we plan to do when we are adults. Once grown, however, we may find that certain jobs are inaccessible, that stable positions are unavailable, or that working for pay is not a family expectation. Our paths through paid work are diverse and are shaped by our gender, by our racial or ethnic identity, and by our social class. Similarly, our individual and family relationships are influenced by our working lives as well, regardless of whether we receive paychecks.

Adults who enter early old age often change the ways in which they work. Retirement, typically defined as the end of paid labor activities and long a signal of the transition into old age, has been assumed to have a major impact on how individuals and families fare in later adulthood. For many adults in early old age, however, retirement ranks lower in stress and influence than does the loss of an intimate partner through widowhood. When a partner dies, the person left behind must deal with loss and, at the same time, confront the change from couple to individual identity.

In Part IV, we center our attention on the ways that work changes and may end for older family members. We also explore how older family members respond to the loss of a partner. The key issues we address in this section are these:

- The work lives of adults in early old age change in a variety of ways. Not every adult ends paid work activity at age 65.

- Retirement, viewed as a normative end to paid work experiences, is a recent historical phenomenon that is not available to all older women and men.

- Employed couples commonly experience retirement together, continue gendered patterns of unpaid work at home, and describe the retirement transition as less stressful than other life course changes.

- Unmarried women and women of color are especially vulnerable in retirement. Government programs that provide aid in older age cannot compensate adequately for a lifetime of labor force disadvantages.

- Caregiving, a form of unpaid labor, is performed primarily by women. The need to provide care may continue throughout adulthood.

- Losing a partner can be one of the most stressful life course changes for both women and men, particularly if it occurs early in adulthood.

- Kin relationships continue to hold great significance for women and men in early old age.

What Is the Role of Work Transitions in the Identity and Relationships of Young-Old Adults?

The meaning of retirement is ambiguous. It is sometimes difficult to determine when someone is retired. Are you retired even if you are working part-time? Are you retired if you receive retirement pension benefits and still get paid for services you provide to others? Are you retired if you do not work for pay but have spent all your life caring for family members and continue to do so at age 75? Consider a retired tailor's response to an inquiry regarding his current identity:

> I'm doing what I have always done. My thinking hasn't changed, so my attitude hasn't changed. You could say I'm still working. Am I retired now because nobody pays me for this? The only thing that happened was when I was sixty-five I took off my watch. (Myerhoff, 1978, p. 46)

Challenges in Understanding Retirement

Toni Calasanti (1996) suggests that the traditional model of retirement holds little meaning for retirees. Workers of color, in particular, are overrepresented in low-paying and unstable service sector jobs that require part-time, involuntary employment past typical retirement ages. Although women may be able to stop paid labor, they do not cease meeting unpaid work demands such as household duties and caregiving for family members. If retirement is an earned reward, a time when paid work history comes to an end and individuals live leisurely on pensions, then most women, people of color, and members of the working classes will be unrewarded. Gender, social class, and race structure participation in and retirement from paid labor.

Retirement is a recent phenomenon. In past times, only individuals with land and financial resources were able to retire (Quadagno & McClellan, 1989). Today, retirement is seen as a rite of passage for those in early old age with the understanding that a solid financial foundation will buoy them up once they leave the workforce. Although a majority of older adults may welcome a transition out of the paid workforce, individuals who are poor may never have such expectations because of economic insecurity.

The average length of life in industrialized countries has increased dramatically. In past centuries, individuals were not expected to live beyond what we see today as retirement age. Because people now live longer and both women and men across race and ethnic boundaries participate in paid work at high levels, adults stay in the workforce longer and more often, if possible, retire as couples.

Retirement is perceived as a normative life course event that happens at a certain age. In the United States, established social policies dictate when and how women and men will receive financial support once paid work ends. We now see retirement as a time when older workers can anticipate, structure, and plan their exit from work successfully. In reality, however, older women and men experience a wide variety of work changes. For some, a focus on meeting today's needs prevents planning for the future. Others obtain so much satisfaction from work that they forgo the opportunity to retire. Still others may prefer to ease into retirement by working modified schedules (Kunde, 2000). A few may begin again in a new occupational field.

The retirement experience for older workers and their families is shaped by a changing economy and by the availability of workforce opportunities. The expectation that an individual, typically a husband, would begin and end a career as a "one-company" man is no longer a reality. As more jobs are concentrated in the service sector and as technological innovation creates new ways of doing things, women *and* men are engaging in paid work differently from their parents (Moen, 1998). Today, it is not uncommon to move from one job to another and to work temporarily for organizations that promise little security in employment or pension plans.

Retirement and Family Relationships

Although traditionally thought to be an extremely stressful transition, in reality retirement has less of an influence on individuals and families than was once thought. In most cases, problems in retirement adjustment are due to issues related to physical health and financial security that may or may not be related to retirement. Individuals who garner most of their sense of self-satisfaction and identity through their role as workers may experience dissatisfaction in retirement. Through time, however, most retirees come to terms with the shift of identity from working to nonworking status (Atchley, 1993; Reitzes, Mutran, & Fernandez, 1998).

Retirement is intricately linked to family relationships. Family members who still have children living at home and lack financial resources may put off retirement. The decision to retire then is linked to family needs. Women often synchronize their retirement to that of their husbands' or leave the workforce early to care for a spouse, an adult child, or another relative with special care needs (Hatch & Thompson, 1992; O'Rand, Henretta, & Krecker, 1992). Men leave the paid labor force more typically when they reach a certain age, experience failing health, receive good pension packages, or have adult children living independently (Palmore, Burchett, Fillenbaum, George, & Wallman, 1985).

The diversity of today's families, as demonstrated in Part I, poses interesting dilemmas for individuals considering retirement. For instance, single women who experience divorce or widowhood in midlife may not have sufficient financial resources to consider retirement. An older worker who has remarried and has a second set of children may need to continue paid work to support these newer and younger dependents.

In this section's first reading, "Retirement and Marital Satisfaction," Robert C. Atchley finds that retirement is not a stressful event for married couples. Although he shows that some couples experience adjustment problems after retirement, these issues appear minor for couples who rate their marriages as satisfying. Atchley suggests that negative retirement outcomes may be a result of the circumstances that led to retirement, rather than the retirement transition itself. For example, if couples retire not by choice but because of labor market changes or poor health, individual and family well-being may suffer.

How Is Retirement Shaped by Earlier Life Conditions and Choices?

As noted earlier, older women's and men's paid work history is shaped by the decisions they make and the opportunities they encounter during the course of their lives. The ethnic identification and cultural ties of older family members make significant differences in retirement because people of color are more likely to experience poverty. In "Elderly Mexican American Men: Work and Family Patterns," Norma Williams demonstrates how work experiences influence the family relationships of older adults. The impoverished elderly Mexican American men in her study lacked opportunities for education and skill development. As a result, they were unable to obtain stable, well-paying work. These older fathers experience stress because of their inability to provide for their adult children. As a consequence, they feel isolated and neglected.

Family support is vital for older women and men as they encounter problems that may be present in old age. Hispanic elders may have interdependent kinship networks consisting of family members of all ages. Such networks have helped older family members demonstrate a *firmeza de carácter* (strength of character) as they cope with being old and poor (Paz, 1993). When the kin safety net falls short of meeting their needs, however, older family members may be left without help.

The experience of retirement is also gendered. Older women's workforce and retirement experiences are different from those of older men. Women have tended to enter the labor force early, withdraw to mother their children, and then resume paid work once their children are more independent (Belgrave, 1988). Women who are in early old age today have spent significantly less time in the paid workforce than men. Even if they worked for pay, they are not likely to have had the opportunity to collect benefits and pensions.

Given that racial and ethnic minorities and women face disadvantages in retirement, women of color are especially vulnerable to poor outcomes. Martha Ozawa (1995) points out that African American women have longer paid work histories than other women. When it comes to establishing eligibility for Social Security benefits, however, these longtime working women qualify for less money and are more dependent on this income than are White women. The types of jobs they have held during adulthood contribute to this vulnerability in later life. Compared with Whites, African American and Hispanic women spend a disproportionate amount of their paid work lives in low-wage service jobs such as housecleaning. In particular, older African American women are unique because approximately one fourth of them have worked in private households—positions with strong historical antecedents for women of color and relatively little financial reward (Ozawa, 1995).

Women also have different retirement experiences based on marital status. Widowed, divorced, and separated women seem especially vulnerable to difficulties in retirement (Keith, 1985). Once a marital disruption occurs, newly single women typically need to work but often earn low pay. In "U.S. Old-Age Policy and the Family," Madonna Harrington Meyer and Marcia L. Bellas illustrate women's economic vulnerability. They show that men are more likely to receive Social Security benefits, whereas women are more likely to receive spousal and widow benefits, which are lower. When older women are unable to secure stable retirement incomes, other family members may suffer enormously. Care for older persons with little retirement resources also will weigh heavily on the shoulders of women.

How Does Unpaid Work Extend Into Later Years?

As shown in Part II, women are the primary kinkeepers and caregivers for family members. In early old age, these caregiving responsibilities may be reflected in a continuous pattern of a mother's providing care for an adult child with a disability or a wife's providing care for an ailing husband. Because men tend to need care before women do, when a wife is present, caregiving falls within her job description. Husbands help their wives when available, but most older women are widowed. Older mothers and adult daughters provide most of the essential care to family members in need.

Two of the readings in this section focus on women's caregiving experiences. Nancy Hooyman and Judith Gonyea (1995) point out that mothers who provide continuous care for their adult children with disabilities commonly identify their commitment as one of parenting rather than caregiving. In contrast, women and men who care for spouses in later life more typically identify their roles as caregivers. In "Predictors and Outcomes of the End of Co-Resident Caregiving in Aging Families of Adults With Mental Retardation or Mental Illness," Marsha Mailick Seltzer, Jan S. Greenberg, Marty Wyngaarden Krauss, and Jinkuk Hong focus on older mothers who care for adult children with disabilities. As primary care providers, mothers are instrumental in determining when care ends and if and when children are moved into alternative residential situations. For mothers of adult children with mental retardation, the caregiving role continues until their physical condition precludes caregiving. Mothers of adult children with mental illness end care once children's behaviors become unmanageable. Even after children are no longer at home, aging mothers continue to have frequent contact with them. These mothers undertake long-term commitments in providing years of unpaid caregiving labor.

Spouses who provide care for each other in later life do so within the long-term context of the couple's relationship. Women and men differ in how they make meaning, perform activities, and interact with each other in marriage (West & Zimmerman, 1991). Family work is at the core of this negotiation. A division of labor exists in families on the basis of gender, whereby women are expected to nurture and emotionally support family members and men are expected to provide resources and instrumental aid (DeVault, 1991). In "Gender and Control Among Spouses of the Cognitively Impaired: A Research Note," Baila Miller shows how women and men interpret and manage caregiving relationships with spouses. Wives identify change in the spousal relationship as an outcome of caregiving. They also express uncertainty in asserting power and authority over their husbands. Men talk of caregiving stress as well but more often demonstrate a greater sense of control by focusing on the specific tasks and projects required of them as caregivers.

Older couples create sustaining patterns of interaction that continue into later life. When major changes occur, however, women and men are forced to renegotiate their marriage relationship. The uncertainty that women feel in assuming authority over their husbands with dementia illustrates how gender shapes marriage and caregiving.

How Do Older Adults Cope With Loss of a Relationship Partner?

In early old age, women and men face the potential loss of a significant intimate relationship through widowhood. Census data show that roughly 14 million adults in the United States lose a spouse in middle or late adulthood. Of the spouses that remain, 11 million are women (U.S. Bureau of the Census, 1993). Although more women experience widowhood, both women and men face enormous challenges as they care for their partners with long-term, debilitating illnesses or when they lose them completely. In contrast to the experiences of family members shown in Part II, widowhood at this particular phase in the life span is considered normative and is a significant marker of older age. Even when this life change is expected, the potential loss of an intimate partner does not precipitate much planning for future security (Holden & Kuo, 1996). Once the loss does occur, however, many women and men show great resiliency in how they retain their identity, keep close kin ties, and create a sense of community.

Widowhood influences the ways that women and men view themselves and their social relationships. Women may experience more distress if their identities have been based primarily on the role of wife and when they have spent considerable time supporting their husbands' activities. A lack of specific death rituals, as in times past, may also influence how women and men feel about widowhood and how long they identify as spouses without partners. For example, a widow who loses a partner may find support from others waning before she is ready to live independently. Alternatively, she may feel constricted by how others view her long after she is ready to identify less as a widow (Lopata, 1996).

In the excerpt "Two-Part Invention: The Story of a Marriage," Madeleine L'Engle poignantly describes her grief after the loss of her husband of 40 years. She affirms grieving as an engaging and important experience. At the end of her marriage, L'Engle finds that her sense of who she is will be forever intermingled with her husband: "I am who I am because of our years together, freed by his acceptance and love of me." While acknowledging her vulnerability, L'Engle shows great strength as she keeps family members close and plans new activities.

As is the case with every life transition, widows and widowers are similar to each other in how they reconstruct their sense of who they are when a partner dies. After losing a spouse, many women and men express feelings of loneliness. Coping with the general activities of daily living, such as cooking and managing finances, is also challenging to newly widowed women and men. The first six months following death are the most critical. Most bereaved spouses report that their partners' deaths marked the most stressful period of their lives. On average, the overall impact of bereavement on the physical and mental health of older spouses is not as devastating as might be expected. Within two years, most have adjusted and are learning new life skills for living alone (Lund, 1993). When widows and widowers have strong social support from adult children, other family members, and friends, the loss of a spouse may not be so severe.

Paul McCartney, interviewed for the first time after the death of his wife, Linda, explained that her death represented the loss of the most significant member of his social support network:

> This is why this year has been so devastating for me—because she was the only person I ever talked to like this in my whole life. I never talked like this to my mum and dad, even though I was very close to them. (Hynde, 1998, p. 4)

Losing a wife is particularly severe for men who are less likely to have close relationships outside marriage.

Because men more typically do not perform many critical tasks in maintaining a home, they may view remarriage as a means to having someone care for them in old age. As Rosemary Blieszner (1994) points out, women may be better equipped to handle widowhood because they typically possess the social and household skills needed to remain independent. Although women may see remarriage as an avenue to greater financial stability, the major reason why women and men remarry in older age is a desire for companionship and support. In "Happiness in Cornwall," Raymond Carver depicts the development of a relationship between a widower and his housekeeper as a progression to companionship. From what we know about why women and men remarry after widowhood, it is fitting that his new companion was hired initially to take care of his daily cleaning and cooking needs.

In Carver's poem, it is unclear whether the new couple is married. We do know that others around them are accepting of this new relationship. Increasingly today, more older women and men cohabit with nonmarital partners. Remarriage of adults in early old age is complex, particularly because older adults bring a long history of prior family relationships into their new marriages. In some cases, women and men choose not to remarry at this age to preserve economic or inheritance patterns. Some older adults, especially women, may not want to remarry for a number of other reasons. Unhappiness in a previous marriage, the desire to be independent, and the fear of future caregiving responsibilities for a husband may motivate some women to reject remarriage as an option altogether (McDonald, 1987). Because they may want to avoid disapproval from children, widows may also decide not to remarry (Lopata, 1996).

When in need, family members turn to those with whom they feel the most intimate and close. Losing a spouse often mobilizes needed support from adult children. Adult daughters are key in providing both care and support to parents, especially mothers. Sons, also, help parents but primarily give instrumental help such as making household repairs or providing money. The type of care received by recently widowed mothers and fathers is greatly influenced by the gender of the adult child. For instance, when an older parent dies, daughters provide less care to and receive less help from their fathers than their mothers. Simply, the strongest lines of support between widowed parents and their adult children occur along gendered lines (Aquilino, 1994).

The group identities and support systems created within the constraints of a person's race and social status will continue to shape the experiences of women and men who lose partners. For example, widows of color are less likely than White widows to live alone. Women of color may feel a duty to maintain family cohesiveness. This duty overrides feelings of privacy and independence for them (Choi, 1991).

The size of families also may influence the type and amount of aid widows receive from their children. Hispanic and Asian widows have more of their needs met through informal family sources than through formal community services (Pelham & Clark, 1987). Kin relationships are central in families of color in which an older family member has lost a spouse. The economic vulnerability of many women (and men) in these situations may be a factor in forming multigenerational households.

In "The Unexpected Community," Arlie Russell Hochschild describes the importance of family relationships in the lives of a group of White widows living in senior housing. Although the relationships the widows formed with each other were rich and involved, almost all the women reported an emotionally closer relationship with their adult children. When peer activities and kin ties were in conflict (i.e., how will I spend my evening?), time spent with family members always took priority. The widows, however, did establish strong peer relationships based clearly on reciprocity. Ties with adult children, especially daughters, and other family members were based on economic dependence and a history of connection. The women of Merrill Court illustrate the importance of peer relationships for a woman who loses her husband. More important, these women show us the importance of kin relationships to personal identity and emotional well-being.

25

Retirement and Marital Satisfaction

Robert C. Atchley

Most people retire as members of a couple; therefore, the effect of the retirement of one or both spouses on the couple is an important potential determinant of individual perceptions of retirement and retirement adjustment. In addition, each spouse's retirement adjustment has potential effects on the marital relationship, as measured by individual marital satisfaction. The relative impact of retirement on marital satisfaction compared with the impact on marital satisfaction of other life changes, such as health problems, disability, and declining income adequacy, is of particular interest. We do not merely wish to know whether retirement has an effect, but rather how the magnitude of retirement's effect, if any, compares with other life changes that could be expected to affect marital satisfaction.

Effects of Retirement on Marital Satisfaction

Conventional wisdom holds that retirement is a stressful life transition that could be expected to have a negative impact on the quality of marital relationships. However, three decades of gerontological research on retirement por-

trays retirement as a rather mild change in most people's lives and, therefore, little threat to marital quality. To sort out these competing perspectives, we first need to explore ideas about what produces marital satisfaction, what diminishes marital satisfaction, and what happens to marital satisfaction over the life course of the couple.

Marital satisfaction is generally conceived of as an individual's *perception* of the quality of her or his marriage. Such perceptions can exist on a continuum ranging from extremely satisfied through neutral (neither satisfied nor dissatisfied) to extremely dissatisfied. The dynamics of how individuals come to hold a particular perception of marital quality and the stability of that perception in the face of change are not well understood.

Marital satisfaction is presumed to be promoted, probably indirectly, by good health and adequate income in much the same way that these enabling factors have been found to be associated with overall life satisfaction (Okun, 1987).

On the other hand, there are factors connected with retirement that might diminish marital quality. Probably the most common belief in this regard is that retirement of the husband impinges on the wife's domain (the household), limits her privacy, and disrupts her routines (Keating & Cole, 1980; Lipman, 1961). But overly high expectations of marriage (Thurnher, 1975), lack of clarity about household routines (Dorfman & Heckert, 1988), marital complaints (Vinick & Ekerdt, 1989), and marital conflict and abuse (Bachman & Pillemer, unpublished manuscript) are other factors that (a) potentially could have negative results for marital satisfaction and (b) may stem from or be exacerbated by retirement. Finally, if retirement causes poor health or involves loss of income adequacy, it could be expected to have negative effects on marital satisfaction by diminishing these important factors enabling social participation.

Life-Course Patterns of Marital Satisfaction

The literature on the effect of retirement on marital satisfaction tends to compare retired people with people who are still working or to look at marital satisfaction in retirement with little reference to previous levels of marital satisfaction. It is important to view what happens to marital satisfaction in retirement in the context of what happens to marital satisfaction over the life course.

In general, the marital satisfaction of people who marry in young adulthood, have children, and stay married into later life follows a U-shaped pattern (Bengtson, Rosenthal, & Burton, 1990). Marital satisfaction tends to be high in the early years of marriage, falls significantly in the early child-rearing years, and then rises steadily after that (Troll, Miller, & Atchley, 1979).

Research Findings

Results of research on the effects of retirement on marital satisfaction have been mixed. Some investigators have found negative effects of retirement, others have found no effect, and still others have found positive effects. Nearly all of the studies to date have suffered from major methodological difficulties, particularly problems with measurement of marital satisfaction and lack of longitudinal data.

Lee and Shehan (1989) looked at marital satisfaction in a large representative sample of older people from the state of Washington and generally found that marital satisfaction was quite high and that retirement was only slightly correlated with marital satisfaction.

Vinick and Ekerdt (1989) found that 60% of the husbands and wives in their study said their quality of life was better following the husband's retirement. Only 10% said it was worse. Half of the couples reported an increase in companionate activities—activities done by the couple together without the presence of others. There was little change after retirement in social activities or personal leisure activities. Among wives, 40% said that they had modified their activities to accommodate their husbands' retirement, but few wives resented this change. Vinick and Ekerdt (1991) found that, although many wives mentioned problems connected with impingement of the husband into the household, most reported that these were short-term problems and that they had quickly become accustomed to the new situation without any need for confrontations. They had simply adjusted unilaterally.

Dorfman and Hill (1986) looked at wives' perceptions of positive and negative aspects of their husbands' retirement. Only 19% thought that their husbands had too much free time and only 11% felt that they were spending too much time with their spouses. On the other hand, 88% reported that their husbands now had more time for them and the family, 85% said that the husbands had more time to do what their wives wanted, and 57% reported that husbands had increased the time they spent on household chores.

Data from a longitudinal study of people aged 50 and over (Atchley & Miller, 1983) were used to look at the distribution of marital satisfaction, the influence of retirement on marital satisfaction, and the relative impact of retirement on marital satisfaction compared to effects of illness, disability, or income decline.

Dissatisfaction with marriage was rare in this study, with only seven people (1.8%) saying they were dissatisfied and none saying they were extremely dissatisfied. Overall, 68.1% of respondents said they were extremely satisfied with their marriages. The only significant difference in marital satisfaction occurred between employed and retired husbands, with retired husbands being significantly more likely to say that they were extremely satisfied with their marriages. This finding is in the opposite direction of the conventional wisdom. For wives, there were no significant differences in marital satisfaction by employment status. There were no significant gender differences.

Each married person who was retired was asked the open-ended question: "What changes did retirement make in the quality of your relationship with your spouse?" A large majority (87%) reported no changes. Of those who reported changes, most had only good things to say. Here are some examples:

> We have more time together, more pursuing of mutual interests, more *loving*. (woman, age 64)

> Now that we are retired, we have better appreciation for one another—more understanding, empathy, and sympathy. This has led to a warmer, closer relationship. (man, age 61)

> I did not believe it was possible, but retirement has enhanced our marriage. We spend much more time together, have more time to share, more time to *do* for each other. (man, age 63)

There were a few negative comments about the effects of retirement:

> Since I retired, what I expect of my wife is sometimes unrealistic. I do not communicate with her like I should. When she comes home from work, I expect her to go places with me—places I want to go. (man, age 68)

> I found it to be more confusing, being with my husband 24 hours a day and giving up much of my privacy and quiet times. There are more meals to cook and more housework. (woman, age 66)

> I thought we would have more time for mutual recreation, but he works as hard as ever, so I've become more self-sufficient than I expected to be. (woman, age 67)

Several women mentioned increased housework as a negative factor in retirement. Interestingly, all but one of the 12 people who made negative comments about the effect of retirement on marital quality were still satisfied or very satisfied with their marriage. These findings are consistent with those of Vinick and Ekerdt (1989, 1991) who also found that adjustment problems connected with retirement were not seen as major.

Future Research

In future research, it is important to think about retirement for couples as occurring in a complex situational environment made up of (a) society's macrosocial retirement institution with its multiplicity of retirement age policies, funding arrangements, incentives and disincentives, and sensitivity to the business cycle; (b) the marriage with its history, structure and functions, and interaction style; and (c) the individuals with their differing personalities, coping styles, and degrees of adult development. These multiple dimensions can intersect to form a huge variety of combinations, which may make the study of retirement's effect on couples difficult.

Research on couples' retirement must also take into account the varying routes that lead people to retirement. Most people appear to retire because they want to, but labor market dislocations, age discrimination, and poor health and disability all can lead to retirement too. The type of retirement may have a significant effect on whether retirement stresses couples or not. And what may appear to be stresses may actually improve marital satisfaction by bringing the couple together to cope with the stress.

The effect of the joint timing of retirement is unclear. Lee and Shehan (1989) suggested that when husbands retire before their wives do wives' marital satisfaction may suffer. Future studies need to explore this issue in more depth, based on strong theoretical ideas about why this pattern may be problematic.

It is also vital to place retirement in the context of the pattern of marital satisfaction for the couple prior to retirement. Based on the present study and earlier results, it appears that retirement occurs in a context of rising marital satisfaction. Longitudinal data can help us identify whether retirement affects this gradient.

References

Atchley, R. C., & Miller, S. J. (1983). Types of elderly couples. In T. H. Brubaker (Ed.), *Family relationships in later life.* Beverly Hills, CA: Sage.

Bachman, R., & Pillemer, K. (no date). *Retirement: Does it affect marital conflict and violence?* Unpublished manuscript.

Bengtson, V. L., Rosenthal, C., & Burton, L. (1990). Families and aging: Diversity and heterogeneity. In R. H. Binstock & L. K. George (Eds.), *Handbook of aging and the social sciences* (3rd ed.). New York: Academic Press.

Dorfman, L. T., & Heckert, D. A. (1988). Egalitarianism in retired rural couples: Household tasks, decision-making, and leisure activities. *Family Relations, 37,* 73-78.

Dorfman, L. T., & Hill, E. A. (1986). Rural housewives and retirement: Joint decision-making matters. *Family Relations, 35,* 507-514.

Keating, N., & Cole, P. (1980). What do I do with him 24 hours a day? Changes in the housewife role after retirement. *The Gerontologist, 20,* 84-89.

Lee, G. R., & Shehan, C. L. (1989). Retirement and marital satisfaction. *Journal of Gerontology: Social Sciences, 44,* S226-S230.

Lipman, A. (1961). Role conceptions and morale of couples in retirement. *Journal of Gerontology, 16,* 267-271.

Okun, M. A. (1987). Life satisfaction. In G. Maddox et al. (Eds.), *Encyclopedia of aging.* New York: Springer.

Thurnher, M. (1975). Midlife marriage: Sex differences in evaluation and perspectives. *International Journal of Aging and Human Development, 7,* 129-135.

Troll, L., Miller, S. J., & Atchley, R. C. (1979). *Families in later life.* Belmont, CA: Wadsworth.

Vinick, B. H., & Ekerdt, D. J. (1989). Retirement and the family. *Generations, 13,* 53-56.

Vinick, B. H., & Ekerdt, D. J. (1991). The transition to retirement: Responses of husbands and wives. In B. B. Hess & E. Markson (Eds.), *Growing old in America* (4th ed.). New Brunswick, NJ: Transaction Books.

26

U.S. Old-Age Policy and the Family

Madonna Harrington Meyer
Marcia L. Bellas

The U.S. Old-Age Welfare State

The U.S. welfare state is generally regarded as fragmented and incomplete. A vehement adherence to the liberal work ethic prevents us from developing the sorts of comprehensive social welfare programs enjoyed by other Western democracies (Myles, 1984; Quadagno, 1988a; Acker, 1988; Esping-Andersen, 1989). U.S. policymakers and voters alike maintain what Katz (1986) referred to as the convenient fiction that poverty is not an economic misfortune but a moral failure. Requests for assistance are regarded as symptomatic of individual rather than societal shortcomings. One notable exception is the U.S. old-age welfare state. Historically regarded as the deserving poor, the aged have shrinking incomes and expanding needs, particularly health care, through no fault of their own (Marmor, 1970; Katz, 1986; Quadagno, 1988a, 1990). In response to a variety of historical and social factors, the U.S. government has implemented numerous public policies to address the needs of elderly persons that are not available to other age groups.

Social provision is generally based on one of two opposing principles: (1) social assistance or (2) social insurance. Social assistance programs target only those with the greatest financial need. Early social assistance programs placed the burden of caring for the aged, disabled, and otherwise unemployed squarely on the shoulders of families. Benefits provided temporary subsistence only when families failed (Katz, 1986; Myles, 1988). The reigning principle of less eligibility meant that treatment of the poor should be less desirable than treatment of the lowest wage earners in order to discourage reliance on social assistance (Myles, 1988). Therefore, gate-keeping was, and continues to be, an important element of social assistance programs (Katz, 1986). Over time, yesterday's poor laws have given way to today's "means-tested" programs, which provide basic services only to those who dem-

Excerpts from "U.S. Old-Age Policy and the Family," by Madonna Harrington Meyer and Marcia L. Bellas, in *Handbook of Aging and the Family* (pp. 263-283), edited by R. Blieszner and V. H. Bedford. Westport, CT: Greenwood. Copyright © 1994, 1996 by Rosemary Blieszner and Victoria Hilkevitch Bedford. Used by permission.

onstrate that they have no other means of support (Beeghley, 1989). Reliance on social assistance is associated with degradation, humiliation, and persistent poverty (Adams, Meiners, & Burwell, 1992; Harrington Meyer, 1994; Katz, 1986; Esping-Andersen, 1989).

Contemporary social welfare programs are increasingly designed to provide a form of social insurance. In contrast to social assistance programs, social insurance programs distribute benefits to citizens regardless of financial need. The goal of programs that provide universal benefits is not subsistence, but wage replacement and continuity of living standards over the life course (Myles, 1988). Unlike social assistance programs, social insurance programs distribute the burden of caring for the aged, disabled, and otherwise unemployed across all citizens rather than concentrating responsibility on individual families. Whereas social assistance programs are politically divisive, pitting tax-paying contributors against welfare recipients, social insurance programs enjoy broad-based political support because all who contribute benefit from the program (Esping-Andersen, 1989; Quadagno 1988a).

Social insurance and social assistance programs now exist side by side in the U.S. old-age welfare state. Social insurance programs, namely Social Security and Medicare, provide monthly income and limited health care to nearly all elderly persons. Social assistance programs, such as Supplemental Security Income (SSI) and Medicaid, provide monthly income and health care only to the poorest of the aged.

Social Security

When Congress passed the Social Security Act of 1935, providing monthly public pensions to the aged, the permanently blind, and the disabled, the elderly were disproportionately poor. Now, to a great extent *because* of Social Security, the poverty rate among persons aged 65 and over has dropped below the national average (Beeghley, 1989). Social Security initially excluded workers in many occupations, including agriculture and domestic service, as well as the self-employed and those employed by religious, charitable, and educational organizations (Quadagno, 1984; Abramovitz, 1988). These exclusions eliminated from coverage nearly one-half of all workers and nearly all women and blacks. Over time, Social Security incorporated most of these categories of workers and, in 1992, provided monthly benefits to more than 82% of the aged (Social Security Administration, 1992). Although originally designed as an income supplement, Social Security is the primary source of income for many older Americans, particularly those who are poor (Quadagno, 1988b; Harrington Meyer, 1990). Among all elderly persons, Social Security provides 40% of total income. For those with incomes below the federal poverty line, Social Security provides 70% of total income (Harrington Meyer, 1990).

Social Security is a universal program in the sense that coverage is extensive, and benefits are based on contributions or family relationships rather than financial need. Eligibility for Social Security is generally determined by one's relationship to the labor force (Olson, 1982; Harrington Meyer, 1990; Esping-Andersen, 1990). Maximum benefits, $1,147 per month in 1994, are available only to those with lengthy and continuous labor force participation in higher-paying jobs. Those with interrupted participation and lower-paying jobs are penalized substantially. Blacks, plagued by significantly higher unemployment rates and segregation into lower-paying jobs, receive smaller benefits than whites on average (Davis, 1978; Hochschild, 1988; Quadagno, 1987). Women of all races, burdened by the conflicting demands of waged and unwaged labor, persistent sex segregation in the labor force, and wages averaging only two-thirds those of men, receive the lowest benefits of all (O'Rand & Henretta, 1982; Reskin & Hartmann, 1986). Thus eligibility rules maximally benefit white men (Olson, 1982; Quadagno, 1988a).

Social Security benefits are funded through a regressive income tax system. In 1994, workers paid 6.2% of their earnings to Social Security on any income below $60,600 (Social Security Administration, 1994). Because earnings above the $60,600 ceiling are not subject to Social Security taxes, lower-income earners contribute a larger proportion of their total earnings to Social Security than higher-income earners, while ultimately receiving the smallest benefits. Racial differences in median income suggest that blacks are hardest hit by the regressive tax structure. Davis (1978) demonstrated that 100% of the median annual income for black families, compared with 70% of the median annual income for white families, is subject to Social Security taxes.

Although reduced Social Security benefits are now available at age 62 and full benefits at age 65, by the year 2027 full benefits will not be available until age 67. This policy change is based on increased longevity and is intended to delay retirement. The degree to which it will do so is unclear, however, given the increasing trend toward early retirement (Hess, 1991). Delaying eligibility for full Social Security benefits will most certainly increase economic hardship for those who are forced out of the labor force by layoffs or poor health (Harrington Meyer & Quadagno, 1990). Delaying benefits also magnifies one source of racial bias already built into the system. Because older blacks and Hispanics have lower life expectancies than whites (black male life expectancy at birth is just under 66 years), their chances of ever drawing benefits are considerably fewer (Harrington Meyer, 1990; Hess, 1991).

Worker Benefits

To qualify for Social Security, a worker must have contributed to Social Security for at least 40 quarters or 10 years (Greenberg, 1978).

The quarters need not be consecutive, so eligibility is not compromised when women interrupt waged labor to rear children or to perform other unpaid domestic work (Harrington Meyer, 1990). Such disruptions do, however, affect benefit size, which is based on earnings averaged over 35 years—the number of years between age 21 and 62, minus the five lowest earning years (Greenberg, 1978; Burkhauser & Holden, 1982). Because women's average earnings are lower than men's and because women are more likely than men to interrupt waged labor, women's Social Security benefits average just 76% of men's (Reskin & Hartmann, 1986; Social Security Administration, 1992). Thus, women are penalized for conforming to a role that they are strongly encouraged to assume—unpaid household worker—and their disadvantaged economic position carries into old age (Arendell & Estes, 1991).

Spousal Benefits

Initially, only those who contributed to Social Security were eligible to receive benefits. In 1939, Congress extended coverage to spouses and widows, as well as to the blind and permanently disabled. Women married for at least 20 years to a qualified retired worker could receive a spousal "allowance" equal to one-half their husbands' benefit. In 1950, Congress extended spousal benefits to the husbands of retired women workers and in 1972 reduced the length of a qualifying marriage to 10 years. Nonetheless, of all spousal beneficiaries, 99% are women (Social Security Administration, 1992). Married women's spousal benefits are equal to one-half of their current husband's benefits. Divorced women qualify for one-half the amount of their ex-husband's benefits, provided the marriage lasted at least 10 years.

The establishment of spousal benefits created a dual eligibility structure based on either beneficiaries' own or their spouses' earnings record, whichever provides the greater benefit

(Harrington Meyer, 1990; Social Security Administration, 1992). Because husbands typically earn substantially more than their wives, most men receive benefits based on their work records, whereas the majority of women receive spousal benefits. Consequently, despite the apparent gender neutrality of spousal benefits, women are vulnerable to changes in family status in a way that men typically are not (Harrington Meyer, 1990). Women married fewer than 10 years receive no compensation, regardless of any direct or indirect contributions they made to their husbands' earnings. In addition, divorced women who qualify for spousal benefits forfeit previous claims if they are remarried when they apply for benefits. Moreover, if married men choose not to apply for Social Security benefits, their wives will not receive spousal benefits. Ostensibly created to protect women with limited histories of paid labor, the structure of spousal benefits highlights and reinforces women's dependence on men's earnings across the life course.

Dual Entitlement

As women's labor force participation increases, more women are dually entitled for Social Security benefits. In other words, they qualify on the basis of both their own and their husbands' work records. The proportion of women who are dually entitled has more than doubled since 1970 (Social Security Administration, 1992). Nonetheless, women who are dually entitled often receive larger benefits through spousal, rather than through worker, entitlement. For example, of new women beneficiaries in 1982, 60% received spousal, rather than worker, benefits (Social Security Administration, 1985). Holden (1982) reported that 84% of dually entitled women who had any zero-earnings quarters were eligible for spousal benefits greater than their worker benefits.

Dual entitlement is increasingly under fire precisely because so many women receive the spousal benefit—a benefit to which they would have been entitled even if they had never contributed to Social Security. Thus the contributions married women make as workers appear unnecessary and unfair. Aware of the rising controversy, the Social Security Administration describes dually entitled women who draw spousal benefits as receiving a "combined benefit" (Social Security Administration, 1985). This is misleading because, in fact, these women would be entitled to the same benefit amount had they never participated in the labor force. Although the spousal benefit provides essential economic security to women with low lifetime earnings, some suggest that it also acts as a working wife's penalty (Burkhauser & Holden, 1982). By implementing payment policies that optimally benefit those with traditional family arrangements, U.S. old-age policies encourage and reward women's economic dependence (Pascall, 1986; Acker, 1988; Harrington Meyer, 1990; Miller, 1990).

Widow/Widower Benefits

In 1939, Congress added widow's benefits to the Social Security Act. Policymakers recognized that widowhood is often accompanied by a pronounced decline in income and marked by poverty, particularly for women (Lopata & Brehm, 1986). Congress first created surviving spouse benefits for women, then extended coverage to men in 1950. However, because men's worker benefits are typically higher than their wives', few men actually receive this benefit. In 1990, 99% of all nondisabled widow/widower beneficiaries were women (Social Security Administration, 1992). Initially, beneficiaries received 75% of their deceased spouses' Social Security benefit (Social Security Administration, 1992). In 1972, the benefit was raised to 100%. Divorced persons may also receive widow/widower benefits following the death of a former spouse provided the marriage lasted at least 10 years. Because women are more likely to be widowed and because divorcées are among the poorest of the elderly, increased benefits provide welcome economic relief for many older women (Harrington Meyer, 1990).

Supplemental Security Income

In 1972, Congress eliminated the Social Security minimum benefit, as well as a series of federal-state programs, and created the federally administered Supplemental Security Income program (SSI). In 1991, nearly 1.5 million aged persons received SSI. One-half of SSI recipients are ineligible for Social Security benefits; the remainder receive Social Security benefits below the SSI income limit. Because women live longer than men on average and because they are more likely to be poor, three-fourths of elderly SSI recipients are women (Social Security Administration, 1992).

In contrast to Social Security, a universal program, the strict income and asset limits of SSI characterize poverty-based social assistance programs. Although SSI benefits are indexed to inflation and have risen steadily since the program began, neither the asset limit nor the income disregard is adjusted for inflation. In fact both amounts have increased only slightly since the program began (Social Security Administration, 1992). Thus, by failing to adjust for 20 years of inflation, eligibility requirements have become more stringent by default rather than through explicit policy changes.

Of particular concern to the families of elderly recipients is the requirement that SSI be discontinued upon institutionalization (Olson, 1982). Nursing home residents are generally ineligible for SSI unless Medicaid pays at least 50% of their care. Prior to 1986, SSI recipients lost benefits entirely during nursing home stays of even one month. Since 1987, institutionalized recipients may receive SSI for up to three months if benefits are needed to maintain a home (Social Security Administration, 1992).

Once the three-month grace period has elapsed, SSI benefits to nursing home residents receiving Medicaid are limited to $30 per individual, the equivalent of the personal needs allowance permitted all Medicaid recipients (Harrington Meyer, 1991). Those who remain in nursing homes for more than three months often risk losing their place of residence and might be forced into permanent institutionalization (Olson, 1982).

Medicare

Medicare has provided universal health care benefits to the aged, blind, and permanently disabled since 1965. Medicare is funded, in part, through payroll taxes of 1.45% on all earnings (the 1993 ceiling, $135,000 per year, was eliminated in 1994) (Social Security Administration, 1994). Before the program began, just 56% of the aged had hospital insurance. In 1992, at least 97% of all older persons in the United States had coverage because all who qualify for Social Security are eligible for Medicare. Medicare Part A coverage is compulsory insurance for hospital inpatient services. For an additional premium, deducted directly from the Social Security check, Medicare Part B provides supplemental coverage for physician and related services.

Although Medicare is nearly universal in terms of eligibility, it is hardly comprehensive in its coverage. Recent estimates indicate that Medicare pays for just 44% of all old-age health care costs (Brown, 1984; Holden & Smeeding, 1990). Gaps in Medicare coverage include long-term care, preventive care, Medicare Part B premiums, deductibles, copayments, and any fees that surpass allowable charges. As a result, three-fourths of older people obtain at least one supplemental private health insurance, or Medigap, package (Iglehart, 1992). Despite Medicare and Medigap policies, older people pay higher out-of-pocket health care expenses than any other age group (Davis, 1986). In 1965, elderly people spent 15% of their annual incomes on health care expenses. This percentage declined following implementation of Medicare, but by 1990 expenses approached 19%. Each year, one-third of the near-poor elderly population is reduced to the federal poverty line by out-of-pocket health care expenses alone (Commonwealth Fund, 1987). Moon (1987) contended that the increase in Medicare's cost-sharing provisions is substantial enough to deter some from seeking care. Out-of-pocket health care costs continue to rise for the elderly despite Medicare's soaring budget, which topped $100 billion in 1990. The majority of Medicare expenditures go to a small fraction of beneficiaries (Iglehart, 1992). Average benefits in 1990 were $4,000, yet 20% of Medicare enrollees received no benefits at all while another 20% accounted for 80% of program expenditures.

Prospective Payment System (DRGs)

Between 1965 and 1983, Medicare reimbursed hospital and doctors retrospectively on a cost-plus-profit basis. Health care costs skyrocketed, quadrupling in one 10-year period alone (Iglehart, 1992; Brown, 1984). Physicians and hospitals enjoyed unparalleled profits while the elderly received unprecedented, and often unwarranted, medical care (Brown, 1984). In the early 1980s, as medical care costs continued to rise faster than inflation, the Health Care Financing Administration (HCFA) implemented cost-containment measures such as Medicare's prospective payment system (PPS). Under this system, physicians categorize patients into diagnostic related groupings (DRGs) based on their condition. Medicare then reimburses hospitals the average cost of care for patients in these diagnostic categories (Fischer & Eustis, 1989).

DRGs have forced hospitals to contain costs and curb unnecessary treatments somewhat. Early fears that the quality of inpatient care would decline are so far unsubstantiated (Iglehart, 1992). Evidence suggests, however, that hospitals have sustained their profits by releasing older patients "quicker and sicker," with profound implications for family members (U.S. House Select Committee on Aging, 1986; Estes, 1989; Fischer & Eustis, 1989). For example, average hospital stays declined by 18% between 1981 and 1991. Shorter stays are generally interpreted as a positive outcome, but in the 20-month period following implementation of DRGs, HCFA reported 4,724 cases of premature discharge and inappropriate transfers (U.S. House Select Committee on Aging, 1986).

Medicaid

In 1965, Congress created the Medicaid program in conjunction with Medicare. Although intended to provide health care to poor persons of all ages, Medicaid dollars are disproportionately directed toward aged and institutionalized individuals. Persons aged 65 and older constitute 12% of the total U.S. population but account for at least 50% of Medicaid expenditures (Eustis, Greenberg, & Patten, 1985). Three-fourths of this amount goes to nursing home care alone, although only 5% of the elderly reside in nursing homes at any given time. After elderly persons themselves, Medicaid is the principal payer of nursing home care. This nation spent roughly $54 billion on nursing home care in 1990, and Medicaid paid 42% of the cost (Harrington, 1991; U.S. Senate Select Committee on Aging, 1988). Despite these staggering figures, only one-third of the poor elderly actually receive Medicaid (Neuschler, 1987; Margolis, 1990).

Like other social assistance programs, eligibility for Medicaid is based on family assets and income. Assets include savings and checking accounts, stocks, bonds, mutual funds, and any form of property that can be converted to cash. Under specified conditions, certain assets are excluded, including a home, a car, some life insurance policies, burial space, and funds up to $1,500 per person. Remaining assets must total less than $2,000 for a single person and $3,000 per elderly couple (Social Security Administration, 1992). Income restrictions are more varied and complex than asset guidelines. Generally, states must provide Medicaid coverage to the *categorically needy*—those who qualify for SSI and whose incomes fall below 7% of the federal poverty line (Neuschler, 1987; Tilly & Brunner, 1987). In addition, states may provide coverage to the *medically needy*—those who can demonstrate for a period of one to six months that income minus medical expenses leaves a monthly income near or below the SSI limit.

Reliance on poverty-based welfare programs is generally regarded as stigmatizing and degrading, a humiliation to be avoided if possible (Katz, 1986; Branch, Friedman, Cohen, Smith, & Socholitzky, 1988; U.S. Senate Select Committee on Aging, 1988; Adams et al., 1992). Although Medicaid provides medical care to those with few resources, eligibility is often accompanied by discrimination, restricted access to medical care, and lower-quality care (Brown, 1984; Katz, 1986; Wallace, 1990; Margolis, 1990). The government reimburses health care providers at a lower rate and often at a slower pace than private insurers or payers. Consequently, many providers refuse Medicaid recipients altogether. Brown (1984) reported that one-fifth of all physicians refuse to see Medicaid patients, and just 6% of physicians care for one-third of Medicaid patients. Nursing homes often discriminate against applicants with Medicaid coverage. When Medicaid recipients are admitted, they often find that their accommodations are more cramped and barren and their treatment is less comprehensive than private payers experience (Margolis, 1990). Moreover, because Medicaid recipients living in nursing homes are wards of the state, recipients' entire monthly incomes, save a small personal needs allowance, go toward paying monthly nursing home bills (Harrington Meyer, 1991). Left with only $30 to $70 (depending on the state), many nursing home residents cannot afford basic necessities such as clothing, haircuts, transportation, and even some medical expenses. If family members cannot pay for these items, the elderly person must do without them.

Spenddown

Spenddown has received considerable attention in the gerontological literature and in public policy debates because it is so troublesome for families. Spenddown represents the loss of economic and social status in old age (Harrington Meyer, 1994). When individuals are ineligible for Medicaid because of excess income or assets, they might deplete those resources to become eligible. In the process of spending down, many older people go without needed medical care and home improvements before ultimately relying on Medicaid to meet their health care needs. Although spenddown can occur among those living in the community, it is most common in nursing homes. Adams et al. (1992) concluded that between 20% and 25% of those who enter nursing homes as private payers convert to Medicaid before discharge, that most who spend down do so within one year of nursing home admission, and that women are at somewhat greater risk than men of spending down in nursing homes (Liu & Manton, 1989; Liu, Doty, & Manton, 1990; Spence & Weiner, 1990).

The Medicaid Gap

When Medicaid applicants do not qualify for coverage because of excess assets, they can deplete them by paying additional medical bills. When applicants are ineligible because their monthly income exceeds Medicaid's limit, in many instances they can never qualify for Medicaid (Quadagno, Harrington Meyer, &

Turner, 1991). Only 30 states provide coverage to the medically needy in nursing homes whose incomes—after medical expenses—fall below an established threshold (Neuschler, 1987). The remaining 20 states do not provide coverage to the medically needy. In these states, older people whose incomes exceed the income test never qualify for Medicaid regardless of how high their health care costs soar. These families are caught in the Medicaid gap. One study of Florida residents caught in the Medicaid gap revealed how devastating this can be for the elderly and their families (Quadagno et al., 1991). Some families were able to contribute enough money to cover the Medicaid gap, enabling the older relative to remain in a nursing home. However, lower-income families were generally unable to sustain financial support and removed the older person from the nursing home to provide round-the-clock informal care.

Spousal Impoverishment

Many older people unwittingly impoverish their spouses in the process of spending down to become eligible for Medicaid coverage, particularly when one spouse enters a nursing home and the other remains in the community (Harrington Meyer, 1994). Spousal impoverishment is most likely to affect women for several reasons. First, 32% of men in nursing homes are married, compared with 11% of women. Thus older men are three times more likely than older women to have a spouse in the community who may become impoverished (Commonwealth Fund, 1988). Second, whereas younger couples may increasingly stress joint ownership of marital properties, older couples were more likely to place much of their property in the husband's name only. Historically, when determining Medicaid eligibility for nursing home residents, states used federal "name on the instrument" rules, through which ownership was assigned only to the spouse whose name was on the check, account,

or title. Over time, some states began to apply community property guidelines, while others deemed all joint properties the sole property of the institutionalized spouse. In 1988, the Medicare Catastrophic Coverage Act eliminated state variation in the division of spousal income and assets. Congress later repealed the bill but kept the provision stipulating that all assets be available to the institutionalized spouse. A noninstitutionalized spouse may, however, retain a "monthly allowance" of at least 150% of the federal poverty line, and one-half or $12,000 of the couple's assets, whichever is greater (Carpenter, 1988). Thus the provision is aimed at easing impoverishment without eliminating spousal responsibility. However, in a simulated analysis, Holden and Smeeding (1990) found little reduction in the risk of impoverishment. Additionally, they found that the real beneficiaries of the legislative change were middle- and upper-class women, who are more likely than lower-class women to be married in old age and to have income and assets approaching the new ceilings. This demonstrates that tinkering with a poverty-based program might produce little real benefit, as well as unforeseen consequences (Harrington Meyer, 1994).

Conclusions

Unlike other Western democracies, the United States restricts its social insurance programs to elderly persons. Social Security and Medicare boast near-universal participation rates and are widely praised for improving the social and economic status of the aged (Marmor, 1970; Brown, 1984; Quadagno, 1988b; Minkler, 1991). Yet these programs provide incomplete coverage. For those with tenuous relationships to the labor force or substantial long-term care needs, benefits are far from comprehensive. Women, blacks, Hispanics, and the poor are particularly vulnerable under current guidelines. Two need-based programs—SSI and

Medicaid—provide safety nets of sorts. The poorest of the poor may qualify for SSI benefits to bring their incomes up to 77% of the federal poverty line. One-third of the aged poor receive health care benefits through Medicaid. However, the majority of poor elderly persons do not receive assistance via these poverty-based programs, and those who do must wrestle with gaps in coverage, discrimination, and the stigma that accompanies reliance on welfare. A fragmented old-age welfare state places much of the responsibility for the care of older people on the shoulders of family members, mainly women, with profound consequences.

References

Abramovitz, M. (1988). *Regulating the lives of women: Social welfare policy from colonial times to the present.* Boston: South End Press.

Acker, J. (1988). Class, gender, and the relations of distributions. *Signs, 13,* 473-497.

Adams, K., Meiners, M., & Burwell, B. (1992). *A synthesis and critique of studies on Medicaid asset spenddown.* Report by the Office of Family, Community and Long Term Care Policy. Office of the Assistant Secretary for Planning and Evaluation. Washington, DC: Department of Health and Human Services.

Arendell, T., & Estes, C. (1991). Older women in the post-Reagan era. In M. Minkler & C. Estes (Eds.), *Critical perspectives on aging: The political and moral economy of growing old* (pp. 209-226). New York: Baywood.

Beeghley, L. (1989). *The structure of social stratification in the United States.* Needham Heights, MA: Allyn & Bacon.

Branch, L., Friedman, D., Cohen, M., Smith, N., & Socholitzky, E. (1988). Impoverishing the elderly: A case study of the financial risk of spenddown among Massachusetts elderly people. *Gerontologist, 28,* 648-652.

Brown, R. (1984). Medicare and Medicaid: The process, value and limits of health care reform. In M. Minkler & C. Estes (Eds.), *Readings in the political economy of aging* (pp. 117-143). New York: Baywood.

Burkhauser, R., & Holden, K. (1982). *A challenge to Social Security: The changing roles of women and men in American society.* New York: Academic Press.

Carpenter, L. (1988). Medicaid eligibility for persons in nursing homes. *Health Care Financing Review, 10,* 67-77.

Commonwealth Fund. (1987). *Medicare's poor.* Washington, DC: Commission on Elderly People Living Alone.

Commonwealth Fund. (1988). *Aging alone: Profiles and projections.* Washington, DC: Commission on Elderly People Living Alone.

Davis, F. (1978). *The black community's Social Security.* Washington, DC: University Press of America.

Davis, K. (1986). Paying the health care bills of an aging population. In A. Pifer & L. Bronte (Eds.), *Our aging society* (pp. 299-318). New York: Norton.

Esping-Andersen, G. (1989). The three political economies of the welfare state. *Canadian Review of Sociology and Anthropology, 26,* 10-36.

Esping-Andersen, G. (1990). *The three worlds of welfare capitalism.* Cambridge: Polity.

Estes, C. (1989). Aging, health and social policy: Crises and crossroads. *Journal of Aging and Social Policy, 1,* 17-32.

Eustis, N., Greenberg, J., & Patten, S. (1985). *Long term care for older persons: A policy perspective.* Monterey, CA: Brooks, Cole.

Fischer, L., & Eustis, N. (1989). Quicker and sicker: How changes in Medicare affect the elderly and their families. *Journal of Geriatric Psychiatry, 22,* 163-191.

Greenberg, J. (1978). *The old age survivors and disability insurance (OASDI) system: A general overview of the social problem* (HS 7094 U.S. Report No. 78-200 EPW). Washington, DC: U.S. Government Printing Office.

Harrington, C. (1991). The nursing home industry: A structural analysis. In M. Minkler & C. Estes (Eds.), *Critical perspectives on aging: The political and moral economy of growing old* (pp. 153-164). New York: Baywood.

Harrington Meyer, M. (1990). Family status and poverty among older women: The gendered distribution of retirement income in the United States. *Social Problems, 37,* 551-563.

Harrington Meyer, M. (1991). Political organization of the frail elderly. In B. Hess & E. Markson (Eds.), *Growing old in America* (pp. 363-376). Brunswick, NJ: Transaction.

Harrington Meyer, M. (1994). Gender, race and the distribution of social resources: Medicaid use among the frail elderly. *Gender & Society, 8,* 8-28.

Harrington Meyer, M., & Quadagno, J. (1990). Ending a career in a declining industry: The retirement experience of male autoworkers. *Sociological Perspectives, 33,* 51-62.

Hess, B. (1991). Growing old in America in the 1990s. In B. Hess & E. Markson (Eds.), *Growing old in America* (pp. 5-22). New Brunswick, NJ: Transaction.

Hochschild, J. (1988). Race, class, power, and the American welfare state. In A. Gutmann (Ed.), *Democracy and the welfare state* (pp. 157-184). Princeton, NJ: Princeton University Press.

Holden, K. (1982). Supplemental OASI benefits to homemakers through current spouse benefits, a homemaker credit, and child-care drop-out years. In R. Burkhauser & K. Holden (Eds.), *A challenge to Social Security: The changing roles of women and men in American society* (pp. 41-72). New York: Academic Press.

Holden, K., & Smeeding, T. (1990). The poor, the rich and the insecure elderly caught in between. *Millbank Quarterly, 68,* 191-219.

Iglehart, J. (1992). Health policy report: The American health care system—Medicare. *New England Journal of Medicine, 327,* 1467-1472.

Katz, M. (1986). *In the shadow of the poorhouse: A social history of welfare in America.* New York: Basic Books.

Liu, K., Doty, P., & Manton, K. (1990). Medicaid spenddown in nursing homes. *Gerontologist, 30,* 7-15.

Liu, K., & Manton, K. G. (1989). The effect of nursing home use on Medicaid eligibility. *Gerontologist, 29,* 59-66.

Lopata, H., & Brehm, H. (1986). *Widows and dependent wives: From social problem to federal program.* New York: Praeger.

Margolis, R. (1990). *Risking old age in America.* Boulder, CO: Westview.

Marmor, T. (1970). *The politics of Medicare.* New York: Aldine.

Miller, D. (1990). *Women and social welfare: A feminist analysis.* New York: Praeger.

Minkler, M. (1991). Generational equity and the new victim blaming. In M. Minkler & C. Estes (Eds.), *Critical perspectives on aging: The political and moral economy of growing old* (pp. 67-80). New York: Baywood.

Moon, M. (1987). The elderly's access to health care services: The crude and subtle impacts of Medicare changes. *Social Justice Research, 1,* 361-375.

Myles, J. (1984). Conflict, crisis and the future of old age security. In M. Minkler & C. Estes (Eds.), *Readings in the political economy of aging* (pp. 168-176). New York: Baywood.

Myles, J. (1988). Decline or impasse? The current state of the welfare state. *Studies in Political Economy, 26,* 73-107. Boston: Little, Brown.

Neuschler, E. (1987). *Medicaid eligibility for the elderly in need of long term care.* (Contract No. 86-26). Washington, DC: National Governor's Association, Congressional Research Service.

Olson, L. K. (1982). *The political economy of aging.* New York: Columbia University Press.

O'Rand, A., & Henretta, J. (1982). Delayed career entry, industrial pension structure and early retirement in a cohort of unmarried women. *American Sociological Review, 47,* 365-373.

Pascall, G. (1986). *Social policy: A feminist critique.* London: Tavistock.

Quadagno, J. (1984). Welfare capitalism and the Social Security Act of 1935. *American Sociological Review, 49,* 632-647.

Quadagno, J. (1987). Theories of the welfare state. *Annual Review of Sociology, 13,* 109-128.

Quadagno, J. (1988a). *The transformation of old age security.* Chicago: University of Chicago Press.

Quadagno, J. (1988b). Women's access to pensions and the structure of eligibility rules: Systems of production and reproduction. *Sociological Quarterly, 29,* 541-558.

Quadagno, J. (1990). Race, class and gender in the U.S. welfare state: Nixon's failed family assistance plan. *American Sociological Review, 55,* 11-28.

Quadagno, J., Harrington Meyer, M., & Turner, B. (1991). Falling into the Medicaid gap: The hidden long term care dilemma. *Gerontologist, 31,* 521-526.

Reskin, B., & Hartmann, H. (1986). *Women's work and men's work: Sex segregation on the job.* Washington, DC: National Academy of Sciences Press.

Social Security Administration. (1985). *1982 new beneficiary survey: Women and Social Security, 48,* 17-26. Washington DC: U.S. Department of Health and Human Services.

Social Security Administration. (1992). *Social Security bulletin annual statistical supplement.* Washington, DC: Health Care Financing Administration.

Social Security Administration. (1994). *Social Security bulletin annual statistical supplement.* Washington, DC: Health Care Financing Administration.

Spence, D., & Weiner, J. (1990). Estimating the extent of Medicaid spenddown in nursing homes. *Journal of Health Politics, Policy and Law, 15,* 607-626.

Tilly, J., & Brunner, D. (1987). *Medicaid eligibility and its effect on the elderly* (Publication #8605). Washington, DC: American Association of Retired Persons.

U.S. House Select Committee on Aging. (1986). *Out sooner and sicker: Myth or Medicare crisis?* (Publication No. 99-591). Washington, DC: U.S. Government Printing Office.

U.S. Senate Select Committee on Aging. (1988). *Developments in aging, 1987: Vol. 3, The long term care challenge.* Washington, DC: U.S. Government Printing Office.

Wallace, S. (1990). Race versus class in the health care of African American elderly. *Social Problems, 37,* 517-534.

27

Elderly Mexican American Men:
Work and Family Patterns

Norma Williams

Who Are the Mexican Americans?

Most official government reports use the terms "Hispanic" or "Latino." However, these administrative categories fail to distinguish among distinct cultural groups. The term "Hispanic" encompasses Mexican American, Puerto Ricans, Cubans, Central and South Americans, and Other Hispanics.

As Aponte (1991) documents, the concept of Hispanic glosses over significant social, cultural, and historical differences that exist among the subgroups noted above. Although Mexican Americans can be distinguished from other major Hispanic groups as well as Anglos, there are also important regional and class differences within the Mexican American population. In general, however, Mexican Americans are an economically disadvantaged group within the United States (cf. Maril, 1989), and unfortunately, many of the Mexican American elderly live in impoverished conditions.

Sources of Data

This chapter is a by-product of a larger study on elderly Mexican Americans in Dallas, Texas.

I have data on 23 males, all 60 years of age or older, most over 65. In conducting the in-depth interviews, I used an interview guide and asked one set of questions regarding demographic characteristics of each respondent. Another set of questions was intended to elicit information regarding the personal and social issues that the elderly defined as of primary importance to them. Throughout the interviews, I probed for the respondents' definitions of the situation (Snow, Zurcher, & Sjoberg, 1982).

The Restructuring of the Extended Family

To understand some of the problems confronting elderly Mexican American men, particularly their isolation from family and social environment, we need to understand ongoing changes in the Mexican American family. On the basis of past research by anthropologists such as Rubel (1966) and Madsen (1964) as well as the work of Sena-Rivera (1979) and Keefe and Padilla (1987), many social scientists still assume that the extended family continues to be an integral part of the Mexican American community. For example, Queen, Habenstein, and Quadagno (1985) accept this premise without qualification (Vega, 1991).

The extended family does not play a significant role in the lives of the elderly Mexican American men and women I interviewed. This research lends support to Trevino's (1988) contention that "a common misconception about the Hispanic elderly is that they are taken care of by their extended family" (p. 67). The elderly men in Dallas had little, if any, social interaction with their brothers and sisters (cf. Townsend, 1967) and almost no ties with their nieces or nephews. None of the elderly men (and only one elderly woman) mentioned the role of nephews and nieces in providing them with support in daily life.

Educational and Work Histories

The elderly I studied in Dallas were poor and often very poor. Markides and Mindel (1987) argue that the minority elderly have always had a lower standard of living than the white aged. Only 1 of the 23 men I interviewed might be classified as having been a white-collar worker.

Data on Mexican Americans living in Texas show that the elderly are likely to have low educational levels and to live in poverty.

My respondents not only had limited educational opportunities, but also had to go to work at an early age in order to help their parents provide food and shelter for the family. The majority of the respondents spoke Spanish only. This pattern is in keeping with data on the poor Hispanic elderly (Andrews, 1989). Given their limited education and English skills these Mexican American men generally worked as unskilled or, at best, semiskilled laborers. They worked extremely hard at jobs that the middle class considers "dirty work."

Tuve muchos trabajos. Hago todo. Y todavía hago todo. Yo aprendí solo. Carpentería, electricidad, limpiar pisos, todo. Ni quiero acordarme. Mi vida ha sido muy triste.
(I had a lot of jobs. I do everything. And I still do everything. I learned alone. Carpentry, electricity, cleaning floors, everything. I don't want to remember. My life has been very sad.)

In light of these kinds of life histories, it is not surprising that most of these men had worked in unstable jobs that paid low wages and provided little job security. These jobs also provided inadequate old-age and disability benefits (Santos, 1981).

Even among the minority of respondents who had held stable jobs, some could rely only on Social Security benefits. These job and income patterns, in turn, have direct relevance for present-day family relationships.

My data are in keeping with the findings of a report by the National Council of La Raza (1991) regarding the lack of the Hispanic elderly's financial resources during retirement. According to this report,

Hispanic elderly are also less likely than Whites to receive private pensions or to have incomes from interest and other assets, and less likely than either Blacks or Whites to receive Social Security. As of 1988, only 77% of Hispanic elderly received Social Security, compared to 93% of White elderly and 89% of Black elderly. (p. ii)

Present Social Circumstances

My data indicate that elderly men's living conditions, lack of knowledge about the organizational structure of social service agencies, and especially their family relationships make old age a difficult period of life for Mexican Americans.

These men, for the most part, live in substandard housing in the poorer sections of the city. Their apartments or homes are in very poor condition, and many do not have adequate heating and cooling.

The social backgrounds of the elderly men in Dallas affected them in still other ways. Because they had not acquired basic knowledge of the programs and benefits available to the elderly, they had difficulty securing services to which they were entitled.

Limited knowledge reduces access to social service agencies and further undermines the quality of life among the elderly. For example, some elderly men are unable to take advantage of the Food Stamps program. The public transportation facilities in Dallas are inadequate for the elderly, and thus a number of these men suffered from health impairments that made it difficult for them to ride buses to various agencies if multiple transfers were required. The cost of taxi fare to the welfare agency to get food stamps often exceeded the value of any stamps they could get.

If these elderly men had not been so isolated from family, they might have known more about and had better access to social services. However, the restructuring (or breakdown) of the extended family has limited the respondents' relationships with their family. These men could not rely on their nephews or nieces, who because they are likely to have somewhat more formal education, could have provided them with much-needed assistance (Korte, 1981), and other social support from extended family members was not available. More important, the tenuous nature of social bonds between the men and their own children and grandchildren made it impossible for them to rely on the latter for knowledge or assistance in acquiring social services. In one instance, a stepdaughter helped her elderly father fill out the proper forms because he did not know the names or locations of the social service agencies. A number of these men did not read and write English, and without support from their children or grandchildren they were totally dependent on English-speaking agency personnel for assistance. Therefore the lack of either a strong family support system or English-speaking personal advocates further undermined the quality of life for many elderly men.

Relationships With Family Members

On the basis of this exploratory study, I delineate two main types of family patterns. In one type the elderly man is neglected and isolated from his own family. In another type the elderly man plays a provider role. After describing these types and their variations, I discuss some exceptions to these patterns.

Only a minority of elderly men have close interpersonal relationships with their children (cf. U.S. Senate, 1991). In some instances in my sample, the children did not live within the Dallas metropolitan area. In other cases, there was tension between the men and their children. For example, one respondent whose daughter married an Anglo believed that the daughter had distanced herself from the family, and this belief limited his interaction with his grandchildren. In a number of other cases, the children of the elderly had married and had families, but because the children also were poor and struggling to survive, they were unable to assist their father and seemed to have little time to spend with him.

The Neglected-and-Isolated Role

One indicator of the social distance from their children is the fact that the men could not identify where their children lived. Even when their children lived in Dallas, they did not know the exact location of their residences. Although some respondents could identify their children's residences with a particular section of Dallas such as Oak Cliff, it was apparent that typically the men had not visited their children's homes on any regular basis.

Again, poverty was a contributing factor. These men either did not own cars or were unable to drive, and the public transportation system is highly inadequate. Their social isolation was heightened because many suffered from health problems that limited their mobility. Further, their children often had limited transportation because they either did not own cars or had automobiles in poor working condition. For example, one respondent was deeply troubled because his son had recently asked him to co-sign for a car. He reported:

> Mi hijo quería que le firmara para un carro. No podemos. El no tiene trabajo seguro, y nosotros no tenemos dinero. Nosotros no podemos hacer los pagos. Es mucha responsibilidad para nosotros.
>
> (My son wanted me to co-sign for a car. We can't. He does not have a secure job, and we do not have any money. We cannot make the payments. It's too much responsibility for us.)

In this case, in addition to contributing to his physical isolation from his children, poverty has caused special stress and tension in the father's relationship with his son.

Another respondent described his efforts to assist his daughter despite the fact that his actions created special difficulties for him. His daughter asked to borrow his car because her car was being repaired and her son needed transportation to the university. The father lent the daughter the car. But the respondent had forgotten that he had a doctor's appointment 2 days later. He called a social service agency for a ride to the doctor's office. After he explained why he did not have a car a volunteer agreed to take him to the doctor. Yet technically the personnel of the agency were not supposed to provide transportation for their clients.

The respondent experienced considerable personal tension and stress because his own responsibilities conflicted with his efforts to reduce the social distance between himself and his daughter. Because she lived in a suburb on the other side of town, he saw her very infrequently. As a father he felt obligated to assist his daughter because she was without an automobile and was experiencing family problems of her own. However, the daughter provided little social support for him.

The next two cases illustrate the pattern of social isolation. One man in his 70s had been a widower for over two decades. His five children lived in the Dallas metropolitan area; however, they seldom visited him. One son came to see him periodically, but stayed only for a short time. This Mexican American man did not know his children's occupations. When I probed regarding his ties to his children, he stated:

> Están ocupados con sus familias. No les importa de mí, no los necesito.
>
> (They are busy with their families. They don't care about me; I don't need them.)

Although this man had rationalized his children's neglect of him, his comments and my observations revealed that because of his physical disabilities, he required financial and other kinds of social support. He depended on the Senior Citizen's Center to pick him up for lunch twice a week, which appeared to be his sole contact with the "outside world."

Another man was married, had heart problems, and did not drive because he was afraid of wrecking the car. He did not have a good relationship with his only son, who had been divorced and remarried. The son on occasion helped with grocery shopping, but the father was estranged from his son's ex-wife as well as his daughter-in-law. The grandchildren are adults, and one granddaughter has twin daughters. In speaking about his grandchildren he observed:

> Yo les doy consejos pero no quieren escucharme. Les digo que se eduquen. Que trabajen y alcen dinero. El tiempo se va poner muy duro. Yo tengo experiencia pero ellos no quieren aprender.

(I give them advice but they don't want to listen to me. I tell them to get educated. To work and save money. Times are going to get hard. I am experienced but they don't want to learn.)

The Provider Role

Although the neglect and isolation of elderly Mexican American men is a dominant pattern, one important subpattern also exists. Some men were providers for at least some of their children (and grandchildren). In one instance, a divorced daughter had moved back in with her father and mother. In another instance, the man was a widower. In these cases the respondents found themselves helping to rear their grandchildren, and they worried about what would happen to their daughters and the grandchildren after their death. They defined themselves as "providers" rather than as "grandparents." Another case points to the complexities that arise among some of the elderly in coping with the provider role. An elderly couple was at one time living in a house provided by their son when a daughter divorced and moved back with her parents. Although the divorce settlement awarded her house to her ex-husband, the ex-husband could not keep up with the maintenance of the home, and after a short time, gave it to his ex-wife and children. The elderly parents then moved out of their residence (over the objections of their son) to join their single-parent daughter because she needed their assistance and support. The grandparents took care of the grandchildren while the daughter worked. But now the grandchildren were teenagers and tensions existed in the family. The grandfather wanted to move out but was unable to return to the son's house because his son's feelings were hurt.

In another case, the divorced daughter and her children moved in with her elderly father after the divorce. The grandfather took care of the children while their mother worked 5 hours a day. He was very concerned about his daughter's present economic situation because she did not earn sufficient money to support herself and the children and could not afford to pay for day care services. He feared that she would be unable to care for her family if something should happen to him. He, too, felt that he was still in the provider rather than the grandfather role.

Another elderly man (and his wife) reported that they had taken care of their grandchildren at times when their son had experienced financial problems. However, the son had recently found a steady job, and his wife had hired a baby-sitter for the children. When the respondents called their son to ask if they could continue to take care of the grandchildren, they were shocked by his response. He informed them that he did not want them to take care of the children because their car did not have an infant's seat and was in poor condition and thus not reliable in case of an emergency. In addition, the children could not communicate with their grandparents because the former did not understand Spanish. The respondents' feelings were hurt because the son had sought their assistance only in times of family crises and need.

Conclusions

In this exploratory study, which is based on field research carried out in Dallas, Texas, I have shown how the work and educational histories of elderly Mexican American men are interwoven with their family patterns.

The work histories of the elderly men I interviewed have led to limited resources in their old age. With rare exceptions, because they have worked in low-paying unstable jobs, they must rely solely on minimum or near-minimum Social Security benefits.

Typically these elderly Mexican American men live in poverty. Their quality of life is undermined because of their lack of knowledge of, as well as access to, the social service organizations in the community.

The men's two main family patterns—isolated and neglected versus struggling provider—are a result of these men's life histories. They have worked very hard, but had limited education and had to work in low-status jobs that provided limited retirement benefits. In addition to their poverty, the processes of urbanization, industrialization, and bureaucratization have fostered the isolation and neglect by members of their immediate family or have placed these men in a position to help care for some of their adult children (and grandchildren) with meager resources. Further, the decisions by the privileged sector of society restrict the resources or other support systems that might otherwise alleviate the suffering and difficulties these men experience in old age.

References

Andrews, J. (1989, September). *Poverty and poor health among elderly Hispanic Americans.* Baltimore, MD: Commonwealth Fund Commission on Elderly People Living Alone.

Aponte, R. (1991). Urban Hispanic poverty: Disaggregations and explanations. *Social Problems, 38,* 516-528.

Keefe, S., & Padilla, A. (1987). *Chicano ethnicity.* Albuquerque: University of New Mexico Press.

Korte, A. O. (1981). Theoretical perspectives in mental health and the Mexicano elders. In M. Miranda & R. Ruiz (Eds.), *Chicano aging and mental health* (pp. 156-184). San Francisco: Human Resources Corporation. (U.S. Department of Health and Human Services, DDH Adm. 81-952)

Madsen, R. (1964). *The Mexican-Americans of south Texas.* New York: Holt, Rinehart & Winston.

Maril, R. L. (1989). *Poorest of Americans.* Notre Dame, IN: University of Notre Dame Press.

Markides, K. S., & Mindel, C. H. (1987). *Aging and ethnicity.* Newbury Park, CA: Sage.

National Council of La Raza. (1991, February). *Becoming involved in the aging network: A planning and resource guide for Hispanic community-based organizations* (Prepared by C. Lopez with E. Aguilera). Washington, DC: Policy Analysis Center and Office of Institutional Development.

Queen, S. A., Habenstein, R. W., & Quadagno, J. S. (1985). *The family in various cultures.* New York: Harper & Row.

Rubel, A. (1966). *Across the tracks: Mexican-Americans in a Texas city.* Austin: University of Texas Press.

Santos, R. (1981). Aging and Chicano mental health: An economic perspective. In M. Miranda & R. Ruiz (Eds.), *Chicano aging and mental health* (pp. 156-184). San Francisco: Human Resources Corporation. (U.S. Department of Health and Human Services, DDH Adm. 81-952)

Sena-Rivera, J. (1979). Extended kinship in the United States: Competing models and the case of la familia Chicana. *Journal of Marriage and the Family, 41,* 121-129.

Snow, D., Zurcher, L. A., & Sjoberg, G. (1982). Interviewing by comment: An adjunct to the direct question. *Qualitative Sociology, 5,* 385-411.

Townsend, P. (1967). *The family life of old people.* London: Routledge & Kegan Paul.

Trevino, M. C. (1988). A comparative analysis of need, access, and utilization of health and human services. In S. R. Applewhite (Ed.), *Hispanic elderly in transition* (pp. 61-71). New York: Greenwood.

U.S. Senate. (1991). *An advocate's guide to laws and programs addressing elder abuse* (Special Committee on Aging, Serial No. 102-1). Washington, DC: U.S. Government Printing Office.

Vega, W. A. (1991). Hispanic families in the 1980s: A decade of research. In A. Booth (Ed.), *Contemporary families: Looking forward, looking back* (pp. 297-306). Minneapolis, MN: National Council on Family Relations.

28

Family Ties and Motherly Love

Arlie Russell Hochschild

Women have traditionally bound the generations together, and in Merrill Court it is the daughters who most often visit and call. There was a saying there: "If you have a daughter, you have her for life. If you have a son, you lose him to a wife."[4] A visit to a daughter typically involved sitting out on the lawn at the daughter's home, over a cup of coffee, inspecting the new home appliances, or interior decorating, or boat-building projects. It might also mean a shopping visit or giving or getting a home permanent wave. If the "daughter for life" happened to work, as many did, the grandmothers often saw more of a daughter-in-law who did not. In two cases, a daughter who worked outside the home gave the grandmother work outside her home. These two grandchildren were often taken on outings and bowling with the grandmothers, and they were collective property inside the Recreation Room.

Most grandmothers approved of their daughters' working: "You can't manage these days on just the one salary." But one woman who had worked on the farm most of her life commented:

These women today go out and work. They could get along without it, so their kids would be reared up right. They could grow cabbages and carrots in their backyards and make do. . . . I've worked all my life but I had an eye on ma young.

The grandmothers liked to visit their children, but as they often put it, they "wouldn't want to live there." All but four strongly opposed the idea of living with their children, including ten who had tried it within the last ten years. One woman who moved in with her daughter's family after her husband died had this to say:

Most of the people here feel like I do. I don't want to be living with my kids. I love them. I don't want to have, you know, any misunderstandings. Why, if I were to live there, I couldn't have friends in so easy or cook on my stove. They have their friends and the kids have their friends. It's better all 'round, just visiting and being close.

Physical separation did not mean emotional distance. On the contrary, most had not only close but what they called "good," emotionally rewarding relations with their children. I know of only five exceptions, two of whom had close but "bad" relations. The adoptive daughter of one grandmother had turned to drink and become more and more isolated. The other regularly called her daughter and son but resented them bitterly. But the bitterness had two sides and a history. After her husband died, Ada left her farm in Wisconsin—and eight small children—to come to California and work as a tank cleaner in the shipyards. She was the only resident who fit Edward Albee's description, in *The American Dream*, of the plight of the old. As she put it,

> I have three children nearby and they don't have time for Grandma. Grandma don't count. My daughter-in-law, she calls me every night, they call all right but they don't visit and they don't ask me to visit them. They go fishing on the weekends and either it's too hot for me to come or it's too cold for me to come or the fish ain't bitin'. Well, I can sit and wait for those fish to bite as well as they can. I don't like it. I sit by the phone on Saturday and they say, "We tried to call you." I've had enough of that stuff. Grandma don't count. I'm gonna take a trip to Wisconsin and I'm not going to tell them. Let them worry for once.

Although most of the widows sympathized with Ada, she was not in their eyes quite a "poor dear," for, as they remarked offhandedly in her absence, "You reap what you sow."

But is it true that those with weak family ties made up for it with peer ties? The question is not so simple as it sounds, as a look at the interactional surface of the two bonds shows. Bonds with kin were most of the time managed separately from bonds with peers. By keeping the two contexts separate, loyalties were kept separate too. In this way the grandmothers resembled the widows in Charlotte Armstrong's novel *The Seventeen Widows of Sans Souci*:

> The division was understood. Whenever one of them had visitors—relatives or old friends

from back home—the other widows of Sans Souci by a never mentioned convention would keep away. Not many of those being visited attempted to bring the two lives together. It was not that the relatives . . . could not have met the new "friends" in the building and been mutually polite. It was as if the widows were each two women and the mixing of the two selves was what might be confusing.[5]

In Merrill Court, too, relatives brought out "another self." Nevertheless the two selves, the two lives, were in some ways integrated. For example, when a daughter came to Merrill Court to take her mother shopping, to the hairdresser, or to drop off groceries, she was often told the latest activities in the community. Again, after one woman was elected President of the Service Club, she remarked, "I can't wait to tell my kids about this." Thus, the status earned in the peer community carried over into family life. Among themselves the old often discussed their kin, and, as suggested earlier, the more children, the higher their status in the old age community. Residents showed off and shared their visiting relatives.

Kin came in mainly on special occasions—at the installation of officers, birthday parties, potlucks, and Christmas. Sometimes the grandmothers rounded up their grandchildren to serve at the table, but only on important occasions when they thought it unseemly for club members to be getting up and around during the meal. On most club trips to shows and movies there was a sprinkling of grandchildren.

Kin also provided services to the grandmothers. One daughter worked in a beauty parlor and, disobeying union rules, gave home permanents for a moderate price to her mother's friends at Merrill Court. Another son-in-law worked in an upholstery company and supplied scraps of cloth to be worked into rag dolls for the bazaar. Another son was a plumber and occasionally fixed dripping faucets. Two granddaughters cleaned their grandmothers' apartments every week, and were paid for it.

Thus, not only were kin drawn into Merrill Court, kin pulled the residents outside it. "Visiting" or "seeing mine" was a legitimate excuse for getting out of doing something. When one commitment conflicted with another, kin ties usually won over peer ties—but not always without a struggle. On one occasion Delia and Rosie were playing their weekly game of marbles with a married couple on the same floor. As Delia recounted:

Iffy's daughter is very demanding. We were there, as guests. We were playing marbles and Barbara [Iffy's daughter] called on the phone to invite them [the couple] over for some watermelon. Iffy told her, she said, "We have guests just now. We'll be along over later." But Barbara called up ten minutes later and asked when they were coming. Barbara knows how long a game takes. We didn't think that was nice, insisting like that when we were visiting.

In eleven other similar instances reported in my field notes, kin ties won and peer ties lost. A child's leisure is hemmed in by work but a marbles game with age peers can always be arranged for another night.

In a few cases kin ties won out altogether. For example, Laura, who played the washtub bass in the band but complained bitterly about the $3 yearly dues, planned to move out of Merrill Court to live in a trailer on her son's farm:

I don't like it here much. I can't do my canning and fishing and you can't raise chickens here . . . can't even have a dog. I lived in the trailer once before I came here. Reckon I can do it again. I visit them [her children] a lot. They want me to stay.

Although relations with kin and with peers were sometimes brought together, on the whole they were kept separate. When they were brought together they usually did not conflict. But when they did conflict, kin ties usually won. This pattern held true for women with both strong ties to family *and* to peers—and that included almost everyone. The few whose family ties were feebly held together by Christmas cards and graduation notices did not "make up for it" by plunging themselves into Merrill Court affairs. They remained aloof from the subculture as well. Moreover, those who had especially strong and rewarding family ties were—like Delia, whose granddaughters courted in her living room—always on the phone or downstairs arranging for the bazaar or the Bowling Club banquet. In fact, with the ambiguous exception of Laura, those closest to their families were among the most active in Merrill Court society.[6]

In a deep sense and over the long run, the two kinds of relationships did not really compete; one could not replace the other even in the "time filling" sense. To the widows, children are a socio-emotional insurance policy that peers can never be. Kin ties run deeper and have a longer history than peer ties. When a grandmother is in deep trouble, she turns to blood ties first. When a widow needs a lot of money, she turns to kin; when she needs "something to tide her over till payday," she turns to a neighbor. When there was an accident or death in the building, peers were the first to find out, but kin were the first to be called.

Whereas relationships between peers had a "tit for tat" exchange of goods and services, relations with kin were not, in the strictly economic sense, reciprocal.[7] Children usually gave their parents—through money for a doctor's bill, part of the rent, a new sofa or rug—slightly more than they got back. The grandmothers, in partial return, knitted Christmas socks, baked cakes, or bought a prom dress or class ring for a grandchild.

Parallel to the economic dependence that distinguished the grandmothers' relations with children from those with peers was an emotional dependence of a very special identity-branding kind. The widow's identity at this point in her life seemed to be like this: "I am my children's mother, my grandchildren's grandmother, my peers' friend, my late husband's wife, my doctor's patient, the club's officer, my welfare worker's client, my deceased friend's friend, and my ex co-worker's buddy." Both within Merrill Court and outside it, "my daughter's mother" was a most important source of identity.

Notes

[Only the notes that are included in the excerpted material appear here.]

4. Komarovsky, 1950; Townsend, 1957, pp. 58, 87-88, 200.

5. Armstrong, 1959, p. 55.

6. Clark and Anderson, 1967, p. 303; Cumming and Henry, 1961; Messer, 1966, p. 57.

7. Streib, 1958, p. 57; also see Shanas, 1966; Riley and Foner, 1968, p. 552; Robins, 1962; Streib and Thompson, 1960.

References

Armstrong, Charlotte (1959). *The Seventeen Widows of San Souci.* New York: Coward McCann Inc.

Clark, Margaret, and Barbara Gallatin Anderson (1967). *Culture and Aging.* Springfield, Illinois: Thomas Publishing Co.

Cumming, Elaine, and W. Henry (1961). *Growing Old: The Process of Disengagement.* New York: Basic Books.

Komarovsky, Mirra (1950). "Functional Analysis of Sex Roles," *American Sociological Review,* Vol. 15, No. 4, pp. 508-516.

Messer, Mark (1966). "The Effects of Age Groupings on Organizational and Normative Systems of the Elderly," Proceedings, Seventh International Congress of Gerontology, Vol. 6. Vienna: Wiener Medizinischen Akademie, pp. 253-258. Also Ph.D. Dissertation, Northwestern University.

Riley, Matilda W., and Anne Foner (1968). *Aging and Society,* Vol. 1. New York: Russell Sage Foundation.

Robins, Arthur (1962). "Family Relations of the Aging in Three Generation Households," in Clark Tibbitts and Wilma Donahue (eds.), *Social and Psychological Aspects of Aging.* New York: Columbia University Press, pp. 464-473.

Shanas, Ethel (1966). "Family Help Patterns and Social Class in Three Countries." Presented at the Meetings of the American Sociological Association, Miami.

Streib, Gordon F. (1958). "Family Patterns in Retirement," *Journal of Social Issues,* Vol. 24, No. 2, pp. 46-60.

Streib, Gordon F., and Wayne Thompson (1960). "The Older Person in a Family Context," in Clark Tibbitts (ed.), *Handbook of Social Gerontology,* Chapter 13. Chicago: University of Chicago Press.

Townsend, Peter (1957). *The Family Life of Old People.* London: Routledge and Kegan Paul.

29

Predictors and Outcomes of the End of Co-Resident Caregiving in Aging Families of Adults With Mental Retardation or Mental Illness

Marsha Mailick Seltzer
Jan S. Greenberg
Marty Wyngaarden Krauss
Jinkuk Hong

Research on parental caregiving for adults with disabilities has revealed that there are both frustrations and gratifications associated with this role (Pruchno, Patrick, & Burant, 1995). The balance of positive and negative adaptations depends in large part on the specific disability of the adult child, the level of societal acceptance or stigma, and the formal and informal support systems available to or created by parents. We have found that aging mothers of adults with mental retardation report more gratifications, less subjective burden, more social support, and more effective coping strategies than aging mothers of adults with mental illness (Greenberg, Seltzer, & Greenley, 1993; Seltzer, Greenberg, & Krauss, 1995). To continue this line of comparative research, in this paper we contrast the predictors and consequences of the end of co-resident caregiving in two contexts: aging mothers caring for an adult son or daughter with mental

retardation and aging mothers caring for an adult child with severe mental illness.

We selected mental retardation and mental illness because older parents whose child has one of these two types of disabilities face overlapping yet distinct sets of stressors. Their experiences are similar with respect to their feelings of loss and grief associated with the realization that their child will not experience a normal life. Both mental retardation and serious mental illness are chronic conditions that limit one's capacity to function independently in the community without support. In response to these limitations, there are commonalities in the caregiving tasks these parents must perform for their adult child in areas such as personal hygiene, transportation, and money and medication management. In addition, a common history of deinstitutionalization in the 1960s and 1970s has increased the importance of the caregiving role of family in the lives of adults with mental retardation and mental illness. Finally, parents of both groups experience similar concerns and worries about their child's future when they, the parents, are no longer able to provide the needed care or supervision.

There are also distinct differences between each group and the parents' caregiving experiences. First, whereas mental retardation is ordinarily diagnosed at birth or within the first few years of the child's life, the onset of mental illness generally occurs during adolescence or young adulthood. Second, the course of mental illness is less stable than the course of mental retardation. The cyclical nature of mental illness creates a situation in which parents experience considerable uncertainty regarding how their child will react in everyday interactions. In contrast, most adults with mental retardation show stability in their functional and cognitive abilities (Eyman & Widaman, 1987) and their parents experience more predictable caregiving demands (Wikler, 1986). Third, there are many differences in the mental retardation and mental health service delivery systems. In particular, community-based services for adults with mental illness historically have been less well-developed than such services for persons with mental retardation, putting a greater burden on the family. In addition, especially in the generation we are studying, mental health professionals in the past have blamed families for the son or daughter's condition, and have been less likely to form a supportive alliance with families (Hatfield, 1988; Holden & Lewine, 1982); this has created additional challenges in the caregiving context.

In this investigation, we posed three research questions. First, what factors predict the end of co-resident caregiving in these two types of aging caregiving families? Second, what are the circumstances of the adult's life after he or she moves away from the parental home and what is the pattern of continued contact with the parents? Third, what are the consequences of this transition for the mother's feelings of subjective burden and depressive symptoms?

Methods

Our studies of aging mothers of adults with mental illness and aging mothers of adults with mental retardation share many common features. In both, families met two criteria when initially recruited: the mother was age 55 or older and the adult with disabilities lived at home with her. Both studies are longitudinal. Although the schedule of data collection is different in the two studies, for these analyses the first point of data collection (called Time 1) preceded the second point (Time 2) by 36 months in both studies. However, this was actually the second and the fourth waves of data collection from the sample of mothers of adults with mental retardation.

Sample

The sample members were recruited via three strategies. For the majority, recruitment was accomplished with the assistance of the state agency on aging and state or county agencies responsible for providing services to persons with either mental retardation or mental illness. Others were referred by service providers, and still others were nominated by participating sample members. All sample members volunteered to participate. The recruitment procedures for the two groups were identical.

All adults with mental illness had been diagnosed by a psychiatrist as having a serious mental illness, including schizophrenia (70%), bipolar disorder (19%), major depression (7%), or other psychiatric diagnosis (4%). The adults with mental retardation had primarily mild (35%) or moderate (45%) retardation, while the remaining 20% had severe or profound retardation. More than one-third (41%) had Down syndrome.

The initial samples in these studies included 461 mothers of adults with mental retardation (half of whom lived in Wisconsin and half in Massachusetts) and 107 mothers of adults with mental illness (all of whom lived in Wisconsin).

The two groups of mothers were similar in several respects. Both were about 65 years of age, on average, and about two-thirds were married at the time of the study. They were also similar in health status, as most (70.8% of the mothers of the adults with mental retardation and 80.8% of the mothers of adults with mental illness) were in excellent or good health. Mothers of adults with mental retardation had somewhat larger social support networks than mothers of adults with mental illness (8.2 versus 6.9 persons).

The samples were different in the sources of caregiving stress. Mothers of adults with mental illness had to contend with a greater number of behavior problems in their adult child than mothers of adults with mental retardation (3.0 versus 1.9, respectively), while mothers of adults with mental retardation provided more help to their adult child than mothers of adults with mental illness did (helping with 6.8 versus 3.3 tasks, respectively). Mothers of adults with mental illness were more likely to focus on and vent their emotions than mothers of adults with mental retardation. Although not an explicit source of caregiving stress, the sample of adults with mental illness included more sons (72.6%) than the sample of adults with mental retardation (53.9%).

Prior to the Time 2 data collection, 30.1% of the adults with mental retardation were on a waiting list for residential services, and 34.2% of the adults with mental illness experienced a psychiatric crisis (defined as hospitalization or involvement with the criminal justice system). At Time 2, 10.2% ($n = 31$) of the adults with mental retardation and 31.5% ($n = 23$) of the adults with mental illness had moved away from the parental home. Of these adults, the majority had lived away from the parental home for at least one year prior to the Time 2 point of data collection (25 of the adults with mental retardation and 18 of the adults with

mental illness), and all had established what the mothers hoped would be permanent homes elsewhere.

Discussion

Mothers of adults with mental retardation who relinquish their co-resident caregiving role are older and in poorer health than mothers who continue to have their son or daughter live at home with them. Thus, declining caregiving capacity of the mother seems to be driving the transition to post-parental care for adults with mental retardation. The transition to post-parental care is hastened by the use of a waiting list for formal residential services, which serves as the gatekeeper between the informal and the formal support system for adults with mental retardation.

A different set of factors is operative for aging mothers of adults with mental illness. For this group, the end of co-residence is more likely when the mother focuses on and vents her emotions and when the adult has higher levels of behavior problems. Thus, for these families, stress in the caregiving context is predictive of the transition to post-parental care. This pattern is consistent with a stress process model of caregiving, which predicts the end of caregiving when the level of stress becomes too great for the caregiver to manage (Aneshensel, Pearlin, Mullan, Zarit, & Whitlatch, 1995). Also, the end of co-residence is more likely when the adult experiences a psychiatric crisis resulting in hospitalization or problems with the law. The crisis may serve to mobilize the efforts of the service system to find alternative housing in an effort to reduce family stress and to promote independence for the adult.

It is noteworthy that these indicators of stress in the caregiving context were not predictive of the end of co-residence for mothers of adults with mental retardation, and conversely that the indicators of declining maternal caregiving capacity were not predictive of this transition for mothers of adults with mental illness. Thus, as we hypothesized, there were different paths to the end of co-residence depending on the nature of the adult son or daughter's disability.

Additionally, we found that having a son with mental illness rather than a daughter was predictive of the end of co-residence. To explain this finding, we note that past research has shown that there is often more interpersonal stress between elderly mothers and their adult sons than their adult daughters (Rossi & Rossi, 1990), making long-range co-residence less likely in this subgroup.

Although the paths to the end of co-residence were distinct for mothers of adults with mental retardation and mothers of adults with mental illness, the consequences of relinquishing the caregiving role were similar for the two groups. For both, we found that feelings of subjective burden are sensitive to the daily demands of caregiving, as mothers experienced a reduction in feelings of burden following the end of co-residence, even when prior levels of subjective burden were controlled. This finding was consistent with our hypotheses for both mothers of adults with mental retardation and mothers of adults with mental illness.

In contrast, we found that depressive symptoms are less easily modified, as there was no change in depressive symptoms associated with relinquishing the co-resident caregiving role for either mothers of adults with mental retardation or mental illness. We had predicted that mothers of adults with mental retardation would remain constant with respect to level of depressive symptoms, as they had levels of depression comparable to other women their age while still living with their son or daughter. For mothers of adults with mental illness, however, we had hypothesized that there would be a reduction in level of depression after the adult son or daughter moved away from home, based on their higher level of depressive symptoms during co-residence and

their more normative expectations for their son or daughter's potential for independence than mothers of adults with mental retardation. However, no such reduction was found. It is possible that the elevation in depressive symptoms in mothers of adults with mental illness is slow to change, having been the response to years of distress. For these mothers, the caregiving experience may result in a fundamental transformation of psychological well-being, altering how the individual functions and ultimately changing her life course. In support of this interpretation, we note that mothers who tend to focus on and vent their emotions at Time 1 show increased depressive symptoms 36 months later, regardless of the residential status of their adult child.

For both groups of families, we were impressed by the frequency of contact between these aging mothers and their son or daughter after the period of co-residence ended. Also, the size of the sub-group of mothers who continued to provide some care was unanticipated. These data speak to the continuity of the caregiving career even after the residential arrangements change.

Recently, Pruchno et al. (1995) argued that there are generalized effects of the caregiving process, common to different types of caregivers—family caregivers for the elderly, aging mothers of adults with developmental disabilities, and aging mothers of adults with mental illness. Their data showed a pattern of similarity of response to the caregiving challenge across different types of caregiving situations. In contrast, other studies, including our own past research (Greenberg et al., 1993; Seltzer et al., 1995), have shown how differences in the caregiving context are associated with unique rather than common profiles of caregiver coping and well-being (Biegel, Sales, & Schulz, 1991). The present analysis of aging mothers of adults with two different types of disabilities—mental retardation and mental illness—provided support for both generalized and specific effects. Evidence of the specific effects of the caregiving context was found with respect to the distinct constellation of factors that *predict* the end of co-resident caregiving for mothers of adults with mental retardation and mothers of adults with mental illness (i.e., declining caregiving capacity versus stress effects, respectively). Evidence of the generalized effects across caregiving contexts was found with respect to the *effect* of the end of co-residence, as this transition brought both groups of mothers relief from subjective caregiving burden but no diminution in depressive symptoms. We view this pattern of both specific and generalized effects to be indicative of the complex nature of the caregiving career, which is shaped by multiple factors, including the stage of the family life course (i.e., the aging of the parental caregiver), the persistent obligations of family life (i.e., the continuing nurturance of adult children by their aging parents), and the unique demands of different types of disabilities (i.e., stable need for care versus fluctuating levels of independence and dependence).

Practice Implications

This study offers a number of implications for service delivery to aging families with an adult son or daughter with a disability. For parents of adults with mental illness, there is a need for service providers to attend to high levels of interpersonal distress, as signaled by behavior problems in the adult or by maternal focusing on and venting of emotions.

The findings of this study also support the need for psychoeducational programs for families of persons with mental illness. A major goal of such programs is to teach families effective strategies for managing behavior problems and alternate ways to respond to the stressors associated with mental illness.

For parents of adults with mental retardation, a signal to the service system that the period of parental care is nearing an end is declining health in the mother. It is evident that most of these mothers will continue in their caregiving role as long as possible. However, abrupt downturns in health will result in the need for emergency placements unless the necessary arrangements have been made in advance.

Aging parents of adults with disabilities should be recognized as a tremendous resource to the service system, having provided decades of unpaid labor as caregivers to their adult son or daughter. Their tenure as caregivers is time-limited, either because of the natural aging process which brings declines in caregiving capacity, or because of interpersonal strains among family members which make continued co-residence untenable. In either case, the partnership between the family and the service system eventually will undergo a dramatic shift. Prior to the transition away from the parental home, the parents provide virtually all of the care that the son or daughter receives. After the transition, the parents generally have continued contact with their adult child, although their level of caregiving decreases dramatically. One factor that distinguishes the two groups of mothers after their adult child has moved away from the parental home is that mothers of adults with mental retardation can rely on the service system to provide supervision and support to their adult son or daughter while they negotiate this transition, as the adult is likely to move to a fully supervised setting. In contrast, mothers of adults with mental illness have a more tenuous partnership with the service system, as in most cases their adult child has only limited supervision.

In conclusion, caregiving by aging mothers of adults with disabilities is a career that transcends co-residence and persists even after the adult moves to a new living arrangement. In this sense, parental caregiving is a lifelong role rather than a career from which one exits, defined not by objective living arrangements or patterns of assistance but instead by ongoing commitment to sustaining one's adult child as he or she traverses life's challenges.

References

Aneshensel, C. S., Pearlin, L. I., Mullan, J. T., Zarit, S. H., & Whitlatch, C. J. (1995). *Profiles in caregiving: The unexpected career.* San Diego: Academic Press.

Biegel, D. E., Sales, E., & Schulz, R. (1991). *Family caregiving in chronic illness.* Newbury Park, CA: Sage.

Eyman, R. K., & Widaman, K. F. (1987). Life-span development of institutionalized and community based mentally retarded persons, revisited. *American Journal of Mental Deficiency, 91,* 559-569.

Greenberg, J. S., Seltzer, M. M., & Greenley, J. R. (1993). Aging parents of adults with disabilities: The gratifications and frustrations of later life caregiving. *The Gerontologist, 33,* 542-550.

Hatfield, A. (1988). Issues in the psychoeducation for families of the mentally ill. *International Journal of Mental Health, 1,* 48-64.

Holden, D., & Lewine, R. R. J. (1982). How families evaluate professionals, resources, and effects of illness. *Schizophrenia Bulletin, 8,* 626-633.

Pruchno, R. A., Patrick, J. H., & Burant, C. J. (1995). *Mental health of aging women with children who are chronically disabled: Examination of a two-factor model.* Paper presented at the 48th Scientific Meeting of the Gerontological Society of America, Los Angeles, CA.

Rossi, A. S., & Rossi, P. H. (1990). *Of human bonding: Parent-child relations across the life course.* New York: Aldine de Gruyter.

Seltzer, M. M., Greenberg, J. S., & Krauss, M. W. (1995). A comparison of coping strategies of aging mothers of adults with mental illness or mental retardations. *Psychology and Aging, 10,* 64-75.

Wikler, L. (1986). Periodic stresses in families of children with mental retardation. *American Journal of Mental Deficiency, 90,* 703-706.

30

Gender and Control Among Spouses of the Cognitively Impaired: A Research Note

Baila Miller

The dementias, such as Alzheimer's disease and related disorders, have complex symptomatology with variation in rate and pattern of decline in functioning. An impaired spouse's behavior can vary on a moment-to-moment basis so that a caregiver can rarely anticipate exactly what response will be to an interaction. Thus, caregivers are faced with the task of trying to maintain control over segments of their spouse's behavior and over their own lives in such a way as to reduce their feelings of uncertainty. Examined was whether men and women taking care of a cognitively-impaired spouse emphasized different dimensions of control in four areas: interpretations of the disease process, assumption of authority, control over the environment, and use of social support.

The Sample

Fifteen caregivers (6 husbands and 9 wives) of cognitively impaired spouses were interviewed as part of an evaluation of a small respite program for persons with memory loss located in an upper middle-class white suburban community. The nature of the respondents' relationship with the respite program varied and a random sample at each level of participation was selected for the study. The final sample consisted of 5 spouses who attended the center's bi-monthly family support group only, 8 who had mates who attended the day care program only; and 2 who were involved with both.

The 9 wives were in their mid 60s and 70s with a median age of 72. All were in general good health with no disabling conditions reported, except for occasional periods of depression. The male spouses were older than the female spouses, with 3 husbands aged 88 or 89, 2 in their 70s, and one 60 years old. Except for the 60 year-old, all the men were retired businessmen or professionals with some physical deterioration, typically a form of arthritic condition. With two exceptions of recent diagnoses, all caregivers had been aware of their spouses' cognitive impairments for at least 3 years. Of the 15 impaired spouses, 10 had diagnoses of Alzheimer's disease; the rest had related diagnoses of brain dysfunction such as Parkinson's disease, multi-infarct dementia, and severe depression.

Interpreting the Disease Process

None of the women explained their husbands' behavior in terms of a disease process, although many said they read whatever they could about brain dysfunctioning. Instead, they described the results of the dysfunction in terms of its impact on changes in their relationship with their husbands, using the analogy of taking care of children as the way to express their struggles with a changing relationship. For Mrs. F., the differences between child and adult were most important. "It's a difficult life—it's worse than a child because he's stronger and yet he has emotional senses . . . he talks about being lonesome and knows when people are laughing at him." For some others, the analogy with child care best conveyed the quality of the care needed. "When we go out socially, it's like having a child that you have to wait on." The analogy was used also to express the range of control over behavior. As Mrs. P. commented: "When he was taking medication, he was easier to manage in the sense that an infant would be easier to manage than a child."

Most of the husbands referred to "mind problems" or "problems getting through to the brain" to explain the changes in their wives. They attributed their spouses' dependency and confusion specifically to the disease process, focusing on specific incidents. For example, Mr. T. described how he asked his wife to get a glass from the dining room table, noting, "You have to take into consideration the failure of the mind all the time . . ." The older men especially had little interest in learning more about Alzheimer's disease, as they were convinced nothing could be done for it. Instead they tried to accept their wives' behavior as inevitable correlates of illness. It was not clear how they defined their own role in responding to these mind problems, although some appeared to assume the role of teacher when they described how they made their instructions very specific. Mr. M. (whose wife suffered from multi-infarct dementia, not Alzheimer's) devised assignments for his wife, telling her what she should do in order to "get her mind working so she can think of these things herself."

Assuming Authority

Both husbands and wives expressed the need to manage and take control over most details of their impaired spouses' lives. The males described how they took charge of their wives' behavior and activities in all spheres. In a typical comment, Mr. J. noted that if he's strong about what he wants done, his wife is too weak to cross him. The males' assumption of authority over their wives was presented as a natural extension of their authoritative role in the family. A few husbands, however, expressed discomfort about having to dress their wives and monitor their bathroom behavior.

For the wives, assuming an authority position over another adult, especially a man who had probably been the authority figure in the marriage, was one of the hardest aspects of the caregiving role. Many talked about how difficult it was to tell their husbands what to do in financial areas and every day decisions, such as use of the car. Two women found it difficult because of fear of violent reactions from their spouses. But most saw the shift in authority relationships as a burden with heavy personal costs. This was especially true for Mrs. B, a woman who had only been married to her husband for 6 years: "Since this is a second marriage for me, I feel uncomfortable making many of the decisions . . . like selling his car, or taking him to an unusual medical treatment. It's not my nature to raise my voice, but I do it more now. That's the hardest thing."

The most devastating effect of assuming authority for many of the women seemed to be their feelings of anger and harshness as they told their husbands what to do. This awareness of parts of their personality that they had never acknowledged affected not only their emotional balance, but their self image as well. For example, Mrs. T. became frightened by how angry she could become, as she had always seen herself as a quiet woman.

Many of the wives showed great sensitivity to their spouse's feelings as they assumed these new authority roles, especially in business areas. They tried to stage their involvement, maintaining the fictions of their husband's previous roles in innovative ways. Thus Mrs. R. rented a post office box to divert the bills from the house, so her husband, a retired accountant who eagerly collected the daily mail, would not be faced with his inability to manage them. Mrs. J. wrote out the checks, but then gave them to her husband to sign, so he maintained his sense of control over his money. In this way, the wives sought to define a balance between previous marital role relationships and the new realities, drawing on a previous repertoire of support-oriented behaviors.

The husbands were less likely to comment on changes in their wives' roles, mentioning instead their own ease in assuming household responsibilities. None of the men showed any concern that these activities were not appropriate to their self-definitions. Many, however, did try to involve their wives in kitchen-related activities such as cutting vegetables or clearing the table.

Controlling Time and Space

All 9 female caregivers had been full-time homemakers and talked about their loss of control over their home environment. Their impaired husbands were constantly present and perceived as intruding into all their personal time. "For a while, I found it unbearable to live with him in the house . . . he breaks things, changes things around . . . he gets bored and loves the kitchen . . . puts things in different places, likes to work at the sink scrubbing silverware" (Mrs. F.).

Like the females, most of the male spouses described caregiving responsibilities as time consuming and fatiguing. But they were more likely to present a greater sense of control by focusing on caregiving tasks and projects rather than on their changed relationship with their wives. Unlike the females, many of the males described their routines on a weekly basis with events planned for each day of the week. For example, Mr. T. told me he went marketing on Monday, took his wife to the day care center on Tuesday while he attended senior center activities, went shopping while his wife had her hair done on Wednesday, did errands on Thursday, and repeated the day care and senior center on Friday.

Surprisingly, most of the men continued to carve out their own territory in the home. They described with enthusiasm their household projects, such as gardening or painting. In stark contrast to the female spouses, they assumed that their wives wouldn't interfere too much in their projects. For example, Mr. U. said: "[Joan] spends a lot of time sleeping here . . . she's not interested in television . . . if nobody is coming in to do something that I have to show around and take care of—I try to get in some gardening which is my favorite occupation . . . Joan doesn't ask any questions . . . just watches me work." The male spouses were also more willing to leave their wives home alone despite awareness of potential dangers. Perceiving their wives as primarily passive and nondemanding seemed to reinforce their illusion of safety.

Most female spouse caregivers were interested in finding supplementary help to act as companions or babysitters, although few had regular plans for respite. Living on a day to day basis, some women noted that when they had a last minute offer from someone to stay with their husbands, they couldn't take advantage of it, because most of their friends were not available on short notice. Uncertainty about what kind of household help would be appropriate was strong. Should they seek a housekeeper who would do cleaning, or seek a companion for their spouse?

Complicating the distinction between looking for a sitter and a helper was concern about their husband's acceptance of this person. The wives took complaints about "why is so and so coming" seriously and struggled (usually unsuccessfully) with ways to explain the role of this new person to their husbands. Most believed that their husbands felt demeaned by the babysitting connotation of not being able to stay alone. For the male spouses, this belief was not as salient an issue because they rarely defined the situation as requiring a companion for their wives.

Using Social Support

Adult children provided emotional support in many instances for both male and female spouses, but little concrete help. It was suggested by the overall tone of most respondents' references to children that current relationships mirrored the quality of relationships before the spouse became impaired.

Relationships with friends, however, were seen as quite different as the impairments of the spouse increased. For all spouses, social life was curtailed drastically by their caregiving responsibilities. The reasons for curtailment ranged from self-withdrawal because of lack of time or available in-house help, to a decrease in invitations from friends, to problematic public behavior of their spouses. Both men and women were upset that friends did not pay enough attention to their impaired spouses on visits. They continued to present themselves as a couple, but others saw them now as individuals, one healthy and one impaired.

Yet the women and men focused on different solutions to this problem. Many of the women seemed to devote more effort, with some success, to finding social activities such as ballroom dancing, in which their husbands could still participate. They also participated more actively in the support group, thus rein-

forcing their role as caregiver and their tie to their husbands. The men, on the other hand, were more successful in locating activities for themselves as individuals because their weekly planning perspective often included regular participation in activities outside the home. Most of the husbands did not attend the family support group, claiming it was upsetting to hear of other difficulties associated with Alzheimer's disease. For example, Mr. T. thought "they overdo the medical talks at the center anyhow." The husbands generally believed it was more helpful to use free time for interests unrelated to their family situation.

Case Examples

Case A: Mrs. F.

After 2 years of sporadic evaluation, Mr. F. was diagnosed with Alzheimer's disease by the Mayo Clinic in 1980. Although varying in intensity over the years, Mr. F.'s behavioral symptomatology has included suspiciousness, occasional hallucinations, wandering, and most recently, bladder incontinence. Mrs. F. experienced a long period of grief after hearing the diagnosis. "I think I've gone through every emotion there is—anger, frustration, disbelief at first, trying to get him to do things. . . . He looks so sad, it's very difficult to see him and know that there's nothing you can do for him. It scares me." She continues to feel very close to her husband. "We had a beautiful marriage. . . I'm very sympathetic and I love him dearly. For a while, I didn't. For a while, I hated him. I felt trapped by it."

Over the past 5 years, Mrs. F. reported a sense of accommodation to her caregiving role, but still had periods of high stress and doubt about her accomplishments. "Well, I've been told that I do very well. Sometimes I think that I do very badly. I think I'm kind of proud of the fact that I do keep him busy and active. It takes two to tango, and when I can understand and go along with it, he is fine; but as soon as I get upset—and I do . . . I just can't really believe how I react to it sometimes. It scares me, really, but it's happening less. Going away for one week did help a lot." She believes that frustration, both by her husband and herself, has caused most of her management problems, holding herself to a standard that they have no problems and he is easy to manage when she is calm and collected and understanding.

Mrs. F. expressed much concern that her husband has nothing to do because there's nothing he can do. He breaks things, shifts everything around in the kitchen, and often breaks doors. Mrs. F. finds she will do anything to amuse him, even encouraging his tearing up magazines and emptying out the kitchen drawers. At the same time, she resents not being able to keep her house neat and has resisted moving her breakable knick-knacks.

Mrs. F.'s previously active social life has now been drastically curtailed, as much by her pulling back from others, as by her friends dropping her. "I don't want to push myself on anyone. I would rather have people ask me to join them." She can not entertain at home because her husband's behavior is unpredictable, but because vestiges of some of his social skills remain, she does go out to dinner with him and close friends. Managing her husband's incontinence in public places, however, is a major problem, limiting her efforts to take him out more. Although friends provide respite on a regular basis, making it possible for Mrs. F. to volunteer at a local hospital, sporadic respite offered by friends has been a mixed blessing. She is often too tired to go out or has no place to go on short notice and becomes upset when she realizes how constrained her life has become. On the whole, however, Mrs. F. is grateful for the emotional support she receives from her children and friends. Mrs. F. admits, however, that she cannot think about the future and has no contingency plans if her husband becomes too much for her to manage.

Case B: Mr. G.

About 4 years ago, his wife, Maria, had a series of small strokes, resulting in a diagnosis of multi-infarct dementia.

After her strokes, Mrs. G. changed from a lively person to one who is now fairly quiet with occasional periods of suspiciousness. These personality changes no longer bother Mr. G. very much as he reported he has accepted them. Mr. G., however, is quite disappointed by his wife's inability to carry out any of the activities he was so proud of, such as her avid reading and doing crossword puzzles. He remains quite proud and pleased whenever she is able to remember things.

Mr. G. doesn't mind the additional household responsibilities, but does mind that these take up so much time. He had anticipated having much more time to do what he wanted during his retirement. The most difficult times for him occur when his wife becomes belligerent and accusatory. She says things that go under his skin, but he tries hard to overlook them. Although a psychiatrist told him his wife wouldn't get any better, Mr. G. has not yet given up on his wife's ability to regain some memory and judgment. "One has to do everything that needs to be done, otherwise you slack off and your work is going to pot on you." He has been quite creative in devising mechanisms to aid his wife's memory and self-care abilities. For example, he has set up a cabinet and labelled shelves by type of clothing to prevent her constantly misplacing her things. Although Mr. G. keeps in close contact with both children, he is more apt to share his concerns and situation with his daughter. Because she has moved out of town, he worries about who will care for his wife if he becomes sick.

Mr. G. has not cut back on his social life and has a weekly routine of golfing, fishing, and visits to the senior center. In addition, he plans major tasks at home, such as painting the trim and building storm windows. When he is working at home, he takes his wife out and sits her in a chair where she sits and watches him work or dozes. She rarely gets in his way. Mr. G.'s only use of social services is taking his wife to the adult day care center 2 days a week. He uses the respite time for fishing and golfing. He doesn't attend the family support group meetings because he would rather spend his time golfing with friends. Mr. G. does not anticipate ever needing nursing home care for his wife.

Summary and Conclusions

Issues of control of the caregiving relationship were more problematic for the wives, affecting their previously established self and role definitions to a greater degree than for the male caregivers. Suggested by this study is that for the males, being in charge of another person was an extension of the role as authority figure in the home and at work. Although nurturing activities may be new experiences for men, taking charge of a situation is not. For the women, this is not the case. The control associated with raising children provides little preparation or anticipatory socialization for assumption of authority and responsibility over an adult, especially a male adult.

The greater attention to interpersonal relationships by the females also was an indication of continued congruence with past role behaviors. Males assumed a longer range view in part because they were not as caught up in the daily vagaries of their relationship with their wives. The females, however, wanted to see their husbands content, or at least busy and out of their way at home. By focusing at this level of interaction, the variability of behavior was a dominant concern for the wives, leading to an emphasis on living for the moment, rather than planning on a longer-term basis. The men stressed the continuity in the environment for those aspects of it under their control, such as their involvement in household projects and non-attendance at support group meetings. In this way they selectively ignored some of the uncertainty they experienced as caregivers.

31

Two-Part Invention: The Story of a Marriage

Madeleine L'Engle

Now I am setting out into the unknown. It will take me a long while to work through the grief. There are no shortcuts; it has to be gone through.

Slowly the house empties. Maria and John must go back to their babies. Josephine and Alan and their three leave. My friend Pat comes from Florida to be with me for a week, that same Pat with whom I have shared life and death and love and sorrow and tears and laughter since we were both gawky teenagers. The evening after she arrives she gets a phone call from her youngest son, and his wife has just had a baby boy. They had come from Fairfield to be at Hugh's funeral just three days before the baby was born. The next Sunday Pat and I drive over for a visit. I am ultimately given the baby to hold, and since it is in my arms that this charming five-day-old creature falls asleep, I hold him longest, slowly rocking, holding new life.

The phone continues to ring, many of our beloved godchildren who live too far away to have come to us, sobbing into the phone. One of my love-children wails, "But what happened to our prayers? Didn't they do any good? Were they all wasted?"

"No, no," I reassure, "never wasted. Of course they did good. Hugh never had intractable pain. His last weeks were a beautiful witness of sweetness and courage and humor."

"But they didn't work!"

"Of course they worked. Not the way you wanted them to, but your godfather died a good and holy death."

A friend calls, reaching out via the phone, and tells me that she has just come from running an Elderhostel weekend. She had this group of older men and women go outdoors to try to find a symbol in nature that would be meaningful for them. One woman came to her with an empty nutshell, saying, "My husband died a year ago, and I am like this nutshell, empty."

I know that my nutshell is not empty. It is full of memory, memory of all my life, memory of the forty years of Hugh's and my marriage. It is the foundation of this memory which helps me keep on with my work, and that is what Hugh would want me to do. I go to a university campus to give a lecture, and it is hard, because the last two times I was there I was with Hugh, giving readings with him. But this year's students do not know the past. The lecture goes well. I am exhausted, but the step has been taken.

Someone tells me a story of a bishop who lost his wife and child in a tragic accident. And he said to his people, "I have been all the way to the bottom. And it is solid."

Yes.

A couple of years ago a friend called me from her hospital bed, demanding, "Madeleine, do you believe everything that you have written in your books?"

I said *yes* then. It is still *yes* today.

But grief still has to be worked through. It is like walking through water. Sometimes there are little waves lapping about my feet. Sometimes there is an enormous breaker that knocks me down. Sometimes there is a sudden and fierce squall. But I know that many waters cannot quench love, neither can the floods drown it.

We are not good about admitting grief, we Americans. It is embarrassing. We turn away, afraid that it might happen to us. But it is part of life, and it has to be gone through.

I think of the character Mado (modeled after my great-grandmother Madeleine L'Engle) in *The Other Side of the Sun.* She lost home, husband, children, and she made the journey through the burning flames of the sun. It cannot be gone around; it has to be gone through. But my grief is a clean grief. I loved my husband for forty years. That love has not and does not end, and that is good.

I think again of that evening after I had come home from a speaking trip and said to Hugh, "Wherever I go, you are with me." Surely that is still true.

Does a marriage end with the death of one of the partners? In a way, yes. I made my promises to Hugh "till death us do part," and that has happened. But the marriage contract is not the love that builds up over many years, and which never ends, as the circle of our wedding band never ends. Hugh will always be part of me, go with me wherever I go, and that is good because, despite our faults and flaws and fail-

ures, what we gave each other was good. I am who I am because of our years together, freed by his acceptance and love of me.

One evening I sit in my quiet place in my room, to read evening prayer, write in my journal, have some quiet *being* time. The sky over the Hudson is heavy with snow. Léna and Charlotte are downtown at a Chelsea coffeehouse with friends; they will have to take the subway home. I write in my journal that the more people I love, the more vulnerable I am.

Vulnerable—the moment we are born we are vulnerable, and a human infant is the most vulnerable of all creatures. The very nature of our being leads us to risk.

When I married I opened myself to the possibility of great joy and great pain and I have known both. Hugh's death is like an amputation. But would I be willing to protect myself by having rejected marriage? By having rejected love? No. I wouldn't have missed a minute of it, not any of it.

The girls and I have acquired two kittens. They are vying for my attention. One of them starts diligently grooming me. The other bats at my pen. This is less an invitation to play than an announcement that it is time for bed. Even with the kittens I am vulnerable as they curl up trustingly beside me and hum their contented purrs.

I get to Crosswicks whenever I can, to relax in the deep rhythm of the house, filled with the living of over two centuries. That richness of experience permeates the rooms, life lived to the utmost, birth and death, joy and grief, laughter and tears.

It is good to be part of the laughter as we sit around the table by candlelight. A wood fire both lightens and warms the room. None of the fullness of life in this old house is lost. The forty years of Hugh's and my marriage is part of the rhythm.

Music I heard with you was more than music, and bread I broke with you was more than bread.

Yes. And always will be.

32

Happiness in Cornwall

Raymond Carver

His wife died, and he grew old
between the graveyard and his
front door. Walked with a gait.
Shoulders bent. He let his clothes
go, and his long hair turned white.
His children found him somebody.
A big middle-aged woman with
heavy shoes who knew how to
mop, wax, dust, shop, and carry in
firewood. Who could live
in a room at the back of the house.
Prepare meals. And slowly,
slowly bring the old man around
to listening to her read poetry
in the evenings in front of
the fire. Tennyson, Browning,
Shakespeare, Drinkwater. Men
whose names take up space
on the page. She was the butler,
cook, housekeeper. And after
a time, oh, no one knows or cares
when, they began to dress up
on Sundays and stroll through town.
She with her arm through his.
Smiling. He proud and happy
and with his hand on hers.

No one denied them
or tried to diminish this
in any way. Happiness is
a rare thing! Evenings he
listened to poetry, poetry, poetry
in front of the fire.
Couldn't get enough of that life.

1   Traditional models of retirement, such as the case of the retirement of a company man with a pension after 30 years of service, reflect the work lives of middle-class White men better than those of others. How would you describe other retirement experiences of women and people of color?

2   Madonna Harrington Meyer and Marcia Bellas describe women's economic vulnerability as they age. What would you include in a letter to lawmakers as they consider government programs that provide financial security to older family members?

3   How have older members of your family experienced retirement? Do you see your path as similar to or different from those of your parents or grandparents? Why?

4   Caregiving for a child with a disability often translates into lifelong responsibility for mothers. What support programs might you implement to support older women on whom adult children are dependent for care?

5   Mothers in young, heterosexual couples often lower their investment in the paid labor force to balance their extra responsibilities at home. How might this pattern influence their transition into old age?

6   Do you think people should marry in their 70s, 80s, or even 90s? Describe how you would feel if your grandmother entered a new relationship and chose to live with, rather than marry, her new partner. Would you feel the same way if it was your grandfather? Why or why not?

7   Many older adults prefer age-segregated housing. What are the implications of such residential arrangements for younger people in society? For older people?

8   What are some specific ways to support wives or husbands when they lose a partner? Would you provide similar or different programs to widows versus widowers? Why or why not?

1   Oliver, M. L., & Shapiro, T. M. (1995). *Black wealth/White wealth: A new perspective on racial inequality.* New York: Routledge.

Oliver and Shapiro analyze the different experiences of Black and White families with regard to wealth. Even when African Americans earn income similar to that of Whites, their limited access to other forms of capital hinders their ability to create better lives for themselves and their families.

2   Holden, K. C., & Kuo, H. D. (1996). Complex marital histories and economic well-being: The continuing legacy of divorce and widowhood as the HRS cohort approaches retirement. *The Gerontologist, 36,* 383-390.

The authors analyze the influence of marital history on retirement. Individuals in a second marriage typically have lower income and assets relative to continuously married persons. Given the high rates of divorce in the 1970s and 1980s, economic vulnerability will become more prevalent for retirees in the future.

3   Glazer, N. Y. (1990). The home as workshop: Women as amateur nurses and medical care providers. *Gender & Society, 4,* 479-499.

Changes in health care have required women, who care for ill family members, to function as lay health care providers. At a structural level, women's unpaid caregiving labor contributes to the profits of the health care industry and puts the lowest-level health service workers, also mostly women, at risk for losing their paid positions.

4   Cook, J. (1988). Who mothers the chronically mentally ill? *Family Relations, 37,* 42-49.

Mothers of adult children with mental illness are their primary caregivers, reporting feelings of anxiety, grief, hopelessness, and emotional drain as a result.

5   Lopata, H. Z. (1996). *Current widowhood: Myths and realities.* Thousand Oaks, CA: Sage.

Lopata provides a foundation for understanding how the loss of a partner influences a woman's identity and family relationships. A widow's social location and access to resources shape her experience of widowhood.

6 Caine, L. (1974). *Widow.* New York: William Morrow.

Although no longer in print, Caine's book is a startling account of adjustment to unexpected widowhood. Her cautionary tale illustrates the potential problems of making major decisions during a time of crisis. This book is used as a resource by many organizations that provide support for recent widows and is available in most public libraries.

7 Rylant, C. (1992). *Missing May.* New York: Orchard Books.

In this children's book, Rylant describes the life of an orphaned girl who comes to live with her older aunt and uncle in West Virginia. The widowed uncle and his niece share their memories of Aunt May as they support each other through their grief after her death.

8 Myerhoff, B. (1978). *Number our days.* New York: Simon & Schuster.

This book describes the strength and spirit of elderly Jews who participate in a senior center in Southern California. Myerhoff uses the voices of these older adults to describe the rich variety of relationships that develop among the participants. A film based on her research received an Academy Award for best short documentary.

SUGGESTIONS FOR BROWSING THE WEB

1 *www.alz.org*

The Alzheimer's Association provides a variety of resources for female and male caregivers of persons with dementia. This site includes details about the disease itself, resources for coping with the illness, and other pertinent information for caregivers.

2 *www.cpr4womenandfamilies.org*

The National Center for Policy and Research for Women and Families provides information about Social Security and its outcomes for women. The site is updated regularly on Social Security changes and their implications.

3 *www.aarp.org/griefandloss*

AARP provides information for widows and widowers on common reactions to loss of a partner and types of resources and services that are available.

4 *www.aarp.org/indexes/money.html*

AARP also provides extensive information on the transition to retirement for older adults.

SUGGESTIONS FOR VIDEOS TO RENT FROM YOUR LOCAL VIDEO STORE OR BORROW FROM YOUR PUBLIC LIBRARY

---

1 *Eat Drink Man Woman* (1994)

Set in Taipei, this family story depicts a widowed chef and the ritual preparation of family meals for his three adult daughters. As each daughter faces challenges in adulthood, the father's table provides a bridge to personal meaning and family connection.

2 *My Left Foot* (1989)

This film depicts the life of Irish writer and artist Christy Brown, who struggles with cerebral palsy. It shows how obstacles in Brown's youth helped shape his adult life. The support and care provided by his mother are especially critical to his later professional success.

3 *Strangers in Good Company* (1991)

On a tour through the Canadian wilderness, eight older women learn about each other's pasts and develop new friendships when their bus breaks down in a remote area. This film effectively portrays the ways in which older women create relationships and connections with each other.

4 *To Dance With the White Dog* (1994)

A moving depiction of widowhood in later life, this film focuses on an older husband who experiences the enduring love of his deceased wife when she inhabits the body of a stray dog. It provides insight into the initial grief and later adjustment of older family members who lose longtime partners.

PART V

Challenges and Possibilities in Later Life

What is life like for persons aged 85 or older? Some say that this stage of the life span is one of depression because of the deaths of family members and friends. Others say that it is problematic because physical declines are inevitable for oldest old adults. Together, these experiences with loss and physical decline are expected to build to a state of despair.

Most oldest old adults, however, are survivors. Colleen Johnson and Barbara Barer (1997) studied individuals aged 85 and beyond and found that most experience enhanced well-being despite social and physical losses. They are survivors because they act with agency in interpreting their life experiences as beneficial. Instead of falling into depression, oldest old persons come to think of themselves in ways appropriate to their circumstances. In other words, they adapt to the realities of their lives. They narrow the focus and range of their activities, and they carefully schedule their time to maximize their energy and capabilities. Those who need to rethink ideas of autonomy and independence welcome the help from others on which they depend.

Johnson and Barer's (1997) study fills a crucial niche in our understanding of development in adulthood. Only in the last several decades have large numbers of persons been living well into their 80s and 90s. Although long-lived persons have always been present, their numbers today are growing dramatically. The oldest old group is one of the fastest growing age groups in the United States and around the world (Kinsella, 1995).

Key Issues

The key issues we address in Part V will illustrate the following:

1. The rate of widowhood is high in later life. Only a small number of individuals in their 80s and 90s live out their lives with spouses. Because men usually die at younger ages than do women, women are particularly likely to live out their last years as widows.

2. Across all ages, including later life, individuals continue to desire and need connections with others. Relationships that are emotionally close assume greater prominence among oldest old adults.

3. Feelings of mastery and psychological well-being are as important to people in their 80s and 90s as they are to young, middle-aged, and young-old adults. This is evident in oldest old persons, who maximize the benefits of their social connections by exercising choice in how and with whom to spend their time.

4. Individuals who experienced hardship and poverty earlier in their lives are likely to have a reduced quality of life in old age, should they live that long. Older women and people of color seem to be particularly vulnerable to the effects of an accumulation of a lifetime of disadvantages. This vulnerability is evident both in their poorer health status and in their shorter life spans.

5. Persons who emigrated to the United States during their adult years face unique challenges in this country. These challenges are exacerbated by difficulties with the English language and when their adult children see their "old ways" as not fitting into U.S. society.

6. For some oldest old persons, their last years are characterized by dependence on others to carry out the essential activities of daily living. A number of those who are care receivers are subject to abuse and neglect from caregivers.

7. Paid work can continue to be important in later life. This is especially true for the poor and working classes, for whom there is no alternative. For others in their 80s and 90s, well-being is enhanced by productive activity in unpaid work and in the pursuit of leisure.

What Is the Importance of Connection to Others During the Latest Stages of Adulthood?

What do we know about the emotional ties of oldest old persons? If we see old age as a time of inevitable disability and decline, it would be hard to think of old people as engaged actively in social connections. Across the life span, however, people are motivated to interact with others, and doing so is an important influence on their well-being. This is as true for oldest old persons as it is for younger adults.

The Importance of Intimate Partnerships

As we have already noted, close relationships, at all stages of the life span, are a key vehicle for personal well-being and satisfaction (Rook, 1997). Laura L. Carstensen has given considerable thought to the importance of social ties among oldest old persons. For a time, gerontologists described older adults as individuals who were disengaging from their social connections at the same time that society was withdrawing from them. As you will see in her chapter, "Selectivity Theory: Social Activity in Life-Span Context," Carstensen formulated a theoretical perspective that explains the smaller social world of old-old adults in a way that acknowledges their sense of personal agency. Her framework demonstrates that older people make choices to maximize their use of time and energy.

Carstensen provides convincing evidence that regardless of age, adults choose to restrict their social interaction when faced with major limitations on their time. Partners, if still living, and children are within the circle of people who are closest to them. Grandchildren and great-grandchildren are more peripheral and less important at this stage of life. The social connections of old-old persons, then, even if they are fewer in number than at earlier life stages, continue to be of primary importance. One particular way in which they matter is that they provide potential sources of support during periods of need.

Those who are fortunate enough to have a partner with whom to live out their later years are in the minority, no more than 20% at the age of 85 (Johnson & Barer, 1997). As already noted, most heterosexual persons in the oldest age groups are widowed. In general, remarriage after widowhood is not common, particularly among older adults

(Kinsella, 1995). Men are more likely than women to remarry, and Blacks are more likely than Whites, but remarriage does not occur for the majority. Wallace and Juanita Nelson, in the excerpt from Studs Terkel's book, *Coming of Age,* are two of the lucky ones, whose marriage has survived into their old age. On the one hand, we expect that they would still be together because Juanita is only 70, within the life span parameters for African American women. On the other hand, Wallace is 85 and has lived well beyond expectations. Wallace, then, is a survivor (Johnson & Barer, 1997).

Juanita and Wallace illustrate well the typical pattern for couples in long-term partnerships. Few such relationships are characterized by frequent and intense conflicts. The most problematic marriages have long since been dissolved through divorce, and older couples have had many years to work out patterns of interaction with which both partners can be comfortable. Furthermore, they continue to value the physical and emotional closeness that they have established and nurtured through many years.

Less is known about the intimate partnerships of lesbians and gay men. Older partnered lesbians may be particularly advantaged in later life because they are more likely than heterosexual women to live out their years with a companion (Huyck, 1995). The evidence for gay and lesbian partnerships in later life is scant, however; today's oldest old lesbians and gay men would have come of age in an era when homosexuality was more hidden and more punished than it is currently. We will have to wait several decades to accumulate a body of knowledge about older nonheterosexual women and men.

As we have seen earlier in this volume, our connection to others, particularly those who are closest to us, is central to our identity. This is as true in our 90s as it is in our 20s, our 40s, or our 70s. Older persons without living partners may seek to establish new intimate partnerships. In the last decades of the 20th century, the number of persons aged 65 and older who were cohabiting with a heterosexual partner grew from below 10,000 to more than a half million (Chevan, 1996). Although a half million persons represent a relatively small proportion of the population, this change in the rate of cohabitation is quite dramatic.

Why do people cohabit in old age? One obvious reason for cohabitation is the desire for connection, companionship, and physical contact. These desires are more easily met when a person lives with a spouse or partner. In the readings for Part V, Martha Elizabeth demonstrates these desires through her poem, "Manon Reassures Her Lover." Further, in excerpts from *Final Rounds: A Father, a Son, the Golf Journey of a Lifetime,* James Dodson describes his dying father's wish "to crawl in bed with" James's mother.

Another reason for the increasing rates of cohabitation by older heterosexual adults is poverty: Lower-income older adults are more likely to cohabit than are those with higher incomes (Chevan, 1996).

Cohabitation is a way for two persons to share expenses, which can be particularly helpful when they are on fixed incomes. Whatever the reason, men are more likely than women to cohabit in later life. Because most old-old persons are women, men have many more opportunities to find partners than women do.

Widowhood in Later Life

For the majority of older adults, the latest stage of life is widowhood. Only 14% of those age 90 and older are married (Johnson & Troll, 1996). We acknowledge the high rate of widowhood among oldest old adults in the readings for Part V by including three entries involving widows or widowers. A fourth describes a woman who is about to become widowed. In the final paragraph of our excerpt from James Dodson's book, *Final Rounds*, we see his mother right before his father's death. In Elissa Goldberg's "Starboys," we meet two widowers: Jack Manasky, who has been widowed for six years, and Joel "Flash" Weinstein, who lost his wife four months earlier. In "Obasan in Suburbia," we are not told how long Susan Ito's grandmother has been widowed, but we imagine that it has been at least several years.

In many ways, these readings portray what we learned about the adjustment to widowhood in Part IV. The period closest to becoming widowed is perhaps the most difficult. During this time, tears may come often, as they do for Joel Weinstein in "Starboys." One also might experience a loss of one's bearings, which James Dodson's mother seems to do in *Final Rounds*. Although Jack Manasky, in "Starboys," has been a widower for six years, he still remembers "that pain. It is like a dagger, every time you take a breath." He grieves the loss of his wife intensely, but the grief no longer interferes with his ability to function, as it does for Joel Weinstein and James Dodson's mother. With time, behavior is less disrupted, but the loss remains present. Jack Manasky writes letters to his wife, for example, because she continues to be central to him (Troll, 1995).

With widowhood, in addition to any loss of emotional support and companionship, which happens for both women and men, men lose the person who helped them meet their daily needs for meals, clean clothes, and a clean house. Women often lose a major source of financial support and the person who negotiated arrangements with the world outside the home, such as the bank, the social security office, and, in Sadao Kitayama's case, an apartment manager. One way in which the readings in Part V do not reflect the typical patterns of widowhood is that men are overrepresented. Here, we read about two widowers (Manasky and Weinstein) and two (soon-to-be) widows (Dodson and Kitayama). For the most part, the end of a marriage through widowhood is a change of status that affects women (Johnson & Troll, 1996).

The experience of widowhood influences relationships with adult children. With a parent's widowhood, adult children also experience the loss of a parent. As a result, they may feel compelled to reach out more to the parent who is left behind (Rossi & Rossi, 1990). Not surprisingly, however, adult children worry more about how their widowed fathers will get along than about how their widowed mothers will fare after the other parent's death. Jack's daughter, Marilyn, checks in on him routinely. She even does his grocery shopping. Sadao Kitayama, the widowed grandmother, does her own shopping, navigates public transportation, maintains a wage-earning job, and, by the end of the story, lives on her own, although she is 80 years old. Her family members do not seem to worry about her ability to do these things. Her older son and his wife do help her find an apartment, however, and they move her and her belongings to the new place.

The Loss of Others Who Are Emotionally Close

By the time people reach their late 80s or 90s, they have experienced multiple losses (Moss & Moss, 1995). Most are widowed, and, in addition, they have lost most if not all their siblings and closest friends. Although these losses are important ones, leaving feelings of great sadness, Johnson and Barer (1997) discovered that oldest old adults experience such losses as inevitable at their stage of life. These on-time losses, then, do not have as extensive an impact as we might think when we look at them from the frame of our own developmental stage.

Notably, one third of the older adults in Johnson and Barer's (1997) study had experienced the death of an adult child. This is a serious off-time loss, in part because children are important sources of emotional and instrumental support to parents, especially in old age. Although friends have a greater influence on one's well-being earlier in adulthood, children are increasingly important to one's well-being in later life. Johnson and Barer suggest several reasons for this. One is that fewer friends are available. If they are not available, they can hardly be counted on as sources of emotional and instrumental support. Another reason is that as Carstensen demonstrates, old-old adults have narrowed their social connections and involvements to include only those who are the most central and important to them. Together, these changes increase the importance of children to the well-being of older adults.

In What Ways Might Older Persons Be Uniquely Vulnerable?

Throughout this volume, we have drawn attention to variability across individuals and families. At no stage in the life span are individuals more different from each other than in later life, as differences among people continue to increase throughout adulthood. In part, these differences have been shaped by the experiences people have had, the choices they have made, and the constraints they have faced throughout their lives. You can imagine how much variability is created by 80, 90, or even 100 years of experiences, choices, and constraints. As we have noted before, one of the major influences on people comes from their position in the social structure. Gender, race and ethnicity, social class, and ability can work together to enhance the well-being of some and diminish the well-being of others.

Gender and Vulnerability

Among oldest old adults, older women generally have more difficult lives than do older men (Gibson, 1996). For one thing, they tend to be poorer. Although they live longer than men do, on average, they have higher rates of morbidity. That is, they have more illness and disease than men have. They have less access to adequate housing and private transportation. They also are more likely to be institutionalized.

Older women do have some important advantages, however. Older women have had a lifetime of building social networks and social support such as strong kin ties. In Diane Gibson's (1996) view, women's history of experience and strong networks position them to be better able than men to deal with the losses and health challenges associated with a long life.

Changes in Kin Relationships

We have already shown how women have more contact and exchange more aid with their family members within and across generations than men do. For the most part, these kin relations continue to be an important source of support for older adults. Changing demographic patterns, however, have led to speculation about potential problems for older adults in the future, when they may not be able to count on kin for help.

In "Divorce and Reconstituted Families: Effects on the Older Generation," Colleen L. Johnson speculates on how changes in the rate of marriage, the rate of divorce, and the rate of remarriage may influence the kin connections of older adults. Because younger generations are marrying at lower rates and divorcing and remarrying at higher rates than older generations, the imbalance of resources between the young and the old has grown. Although aid normally flows from older to younger generations, when adult children divorce, they often require even more assistance from their parents than is true of their continuously married or their continuously single siblings. Furthermore, this additional aid might be needed for a sustained period.

Johnson suggests that a child's remarriage may again change the network of obligations among kin. That is, younger family members may not be as reliable in helping older family members as is true in less complex family circumstances. This is because family relationships are more numerous and ties somewhat more tenuous following marital disruption and remarriage. When parents bring a child from a previous marriage to a later marriage, for example, family members have an expanded number of roles and relationships. There may now be step-grandmothers and step-grandfathers, and perhaps even step-aunts and step-uncles.

Typically, parents and their adult children relate to each other in ways that are consistent with social norms or expectations (Rossi & Rossi, 1990). There seems to be an extensive amount of agreement about these norms when considering the obligations of mothers and fathers to their children and of daughters and sons to their parents. Remarriage has the potential to disrupt these social norms. Andrew Cherlin (1978) describes remarriage as an "incomplete institution." By this, he means that there are no clear expectations about the behaviors of family members when a remarriage is involved.

What is the proper way for a stepdaughter to address the parents of her stepmother? Are they grandparents? Biological grandparents, especially maternal grandmothers, often are encouraged to play a role in disciplining their grandchildren. Is the same expected of step-grandmothers? As you saw earlier, grandparents are important sources of aid for their grandchildren. Are step-grandparents expected to provide the same level of assistance? There is no agreement among people on the answers to these questions. In this way, then, the institution of remarriage is incomplete. Cherlin argues that this incompleteness or the nature of these relationships creates the potential for greater disagreement within and across generations. It also makes it more likely that extended kin will not feel as obligated to respond in times of an older person's need.

Another group of especially vulnerable older people includes those who have no surviving family members. This group includes individuals who never married, those who are widowed but did not have children, and those whose children have not outlived them (Johnson & Barer, 1997). Johnson and Barer suggest that these older adults live in "attenuated families" (p. 91). Attenuated families place individuals at risk of being without the family supports that may be needed later in life. Individuals in attenuated families may overcome the problems inherent in this abbreviated family structure if they have the social and economic resources that enable them to cultivate new ties that function as kin do. This is a more difficult task to do in one's 80s and 90s than in one's younger years, but there is some evidence that older adults without children have some capacity to build new relationships (Rubinstein, Alexander, Goodman, & Luborsky, 1991).

The Role of Health Problems and Functional Ability

Two ways in which old-old adults may be uniquely vulnerable result from changes in their health and functional status. Declines in health and the development of chronic health problems are increasingly likely with age. This is not to say that all old people are in poor health. It is true, however, that health problems are more common among those who are very old than among younger adults. Health problems have important effects on the quality of life for older adults because they sometimes interfere with the ability to function independently.

Functional impairment, such as the inability to walk, problems getting in and out of bed, and being unable to perform the other activities of daily living, is a primary risk factor for depression (Zeiss, Lewinsohn, Rohde, & Selley, 1996). It also increases the risk of abuse (Godkin, Wolf, & Pillemer, 1995). Functional impairment is far more important to well-being than is health status. For example, in "Letters From a Father," we witness how health problems and chronic health conditions may have a limited influence on the well-being of active, engaged older adults.

Health problems are particularly likely among individuals who had poor health care throughout their lives. This means that people in poverty, those in the working classes, and people of color, who often faced insufficient or substandard health care and poor working conditions, are more vulnerable to health problems than are middle- and upper-class Whites. Latinos, for example, develop disabilities at earlier ages and have a greater number of disabilities than Whites do (Aranda & Knight, 1997). Mexican Americans and Puerto Rican Americans are more likely than Whites to develop diabetes, and when they do develop it, the onset occurs 10 years earlier on average than it does in Whites. Their generally lower access to health care also means that diabetes usually is diagnosed later in Latinos, which has consequences both for the severity of the disease and for long-term survival.

Because Latinos rely on family members more than Whites do for support in a health crisis, as you saw in Part IV, they are particularly vulnerable when family support is not available (Aranda & Knight, 1997). African Americans, with broader definitions of family than those of Whites and Latinos, rely more on nonkin to help in times of need. But increasingly, it is evident that poor families of color have less access to support from kin and fictive kin than had been thought previously (Roschelle, 1997). Many in the social networks of these families simply lack the resources that are necessary to be able to help others.

The absence of supportive social connections means that individuals lose this form of insurance that can help people with health problems. Despite myths that older people spend much of the later parts of their lives in institutions, most of those who need assistance generally receive it from family members. Much of that aid, as seen in Part II, comes from a spouse or life partner, if still living. If not, adult children—usually daughters when they are available—are a key source of support in times of need.

Recall Jack Manasky from "Starboys," a healthy widowed father whose daughter, Marilyn, checks up on him and does his grocery shopping. Jack gets around well on his own, as many older people do. Nevertheless, older people are at greater risk than younger people for events such as heart attacks, falls, and so on, that may require quick intervention. They also are at risk of decline resulting from chronic health problems. One major way in which older people receive assistance is that family members may check on them from time to time, acting as monitors and making sure that things are okay.

In "Starboys," Marilyn checks up on her father in this way, but she also intervenes. Jack ignores some of her help and makes his own choices. This is not unusual, particularly in cross-generational aid. Although family members help each other in times of need, they maintain the right of persons in each adult generation to be autonomous and to make their own decisions (Johnson, 1995). Too much monitoring may put older people at risk for losing their autonomy. Not enough monitoring may leave them vulnerable in the event of an acute health crisis, a fall, or a similar emergency.

Mostly, the people who do the monitoring of older family members are women. Because we as a society hold women responsible for the well-being of family members (see Emily Abel's historical analysis of caregiving in Part II), there is some evidence that daughters may sometimes provide more care than is actually needed (Matthews & Heidorn, 1998). Sons, however, are more likely than daughters to assume that everything is okay, sometimes providing less care than required. From Jack's point of view, Marilyn stepped in when her help was not required. Although she remains concerned about her father's health and wishes that he would do as she suggests, she says, "okay," when Jack says he will do it his own way. Caregivers, then, mostly adhere to this norm of noninterference.

High rates of chronic health problems and functional disability among today's old-old adults do not mean that these rates will continue in the future. The health of older adults seems to be improving in recent cohorts (Crimmins, Saito, & Reynolds, 1997; Kinsella, 1995). In part, this may be due to changes in the quality of life during the 20th century. Consider that those who are currently in the oldest age group lived a significant portion of their childhood years during the Great Depression of the 1930s. The widespread poverty and the limited social resources during this time have had long-term consequences for individual health. Presumably, as the majority of the nonpoor had better health care and nutrition during their early years, the benefits of these advantages to them are now evident in the later stages of their lives. Similarly, the disadvantages of poor circumstances early in life are now evident as well.

Old-Old Immigrants to the United States

Florentius Chan (1988) has described the special vulnerability of old-old adults who are immigrants to the United States. Many of the oldest Asian and Pacific Islanders in this country were born elsewhere. In 1990, for example, two thirds of Asians in the United States were foreign born (Espiritu, 1997). Older Asian Americans who were born in this country are similar to older Whites. They tend to live near and have regular contact with their children (Chan, 1988).

Those who were foreign born, however, face different lives. Beyond middle-aged when they emigrated, they came to the United States primarily with or following their children. They left significant social networks behind in their home countries, and they have much smaller networks here. Many came from countries where older adults are revered to a country where older adults are not so highly valued. Those who do not speak English may end up sitting at home with little to occupy their time. They are dependent on children, grandchildren, or others to mediate or interpret for them. Negotiating public transportation is virtually impossible without English language skills, and few have a driver's license. They use the expression "no legs" to describe their inability to get around (Chan, 1988).

In their own countries, older women and men are believed to have a wealth of knowledge and much to teach younger people. Here, however, what they know may be seen as outdated or irrelevant to the lives of their Americanized family members. As Susan Ito describes her in "Obasan in Suburbia," Sadao Kitayama is in just this situation. Her son and daughter-in-law do not let her speak to their daughter for fear that Jenney will be unable to learn English or that she will speak English with a Japanese accent. Sadao is seen as living in the old world, instead of being part of the new.

Challenges From the Environment

Although Sadao Kitayama has no problem living on her own, many of the oldest adults are unable to carry out all the essential activities of daily living. With declines in functional ability, the environment becomes increasingly challenging to them. Navigating a few stairs is nothing to a child or a young adult, but for someone with chronic arthritis, a heart condition, or a breathing disorder, a few stairs can seem like 10 stories.

Many of the oldest old adults live in residences that present such insurmountable obstacles (Lawton, 1982). These difficulties may force older people to move to more accommodating housing. The majority, however, continue to live in the same residence (Johnson & Barer, 1997), although this may put them at risk for injury from falls. Others relocate to senior housing for low-income older adults or, for those with more economic resources, to retirement settings. Among those who make this move, most do so because chronic health problems or functional disabilities limit their ability to navigate in their own homes (Johnson & Barer). Senior and retirement housing is designed to minimize some of the environmental challenges facing older people. The move to an institution, such as a nursing home, occurs for only a minority and usually in response to an acute health crisis or a decline in cognitive ability (Johnson & Barer). As noted earlier, for Whites, such moves are more likely when older adults live alone and when no adult daughter lives nearby. People of color, who often have more extensive kin and fictive kin networks, are even less likely to be institutionalized (Choi, 1991).

Regardless of where they live, older adults may continue to require assistance from others in meeting their needs. Even nursing home care may depend on intervention from family members. The role of others in helping older people who are at risk cannot be overstated. Dependence on others, however, can also put older people at risk.

Interpersonal Violence: Abuse and Neglect

In the fifth reading in Part V, "Understanding Elder Abuse and Neglect," Rosalie S. Wolf describes various types of abuse. Such abuse ranges in frequency and severity. We see how difficult it is to identify abuse in Susan Ito's story, "Obasan." In applying the definitions that Wolf provides, we can find evidence that the grandmother has been psychologically and financially abused by her son and daughter-in-law. That Sadao Kitayama does not seem to have any of the risk factors Wolf identifies demonstrates that elder abuse and neglect continue to be poorly understood.

In research conducted with colleagues (Godkin et al., 1995), Wolf showed that having functional limitations compromising one's ability to care for oneself, walk around, prepare meals, and manage the household; having poor cognitive functioning; and being dependent on a caregiver make one vulnerable to abuse and neglect. A *recent* decline in functioning also seems to make abuse more likely, perhaps because there is a period of adjustment for caregivers when the dependence level of the care receiver increases. Furthermore, that the decline in functioning is recent may contribute to the unrealistic expectations that characterize abusive caregivers. When care receivers are socially isolated, they also are far more vulnerable to abuse. Such isolation decreases the likelihood of intervention and removes some of the threat to abusive caregivers that they will be caught.

Abusive caregivers tend to be dependent financially on the care receiver. Furthermore, the relationship between the caregiver and care receiver seems to have been characterized by a history of conflict. Coresidence also contributes to interpersonal violence in that caregivers who live with care receivers have more opportunities to be abusive or neglectful. Finally, although we talk generally about family members who abuse older people, Wolf's (Godkin et al., 1995) research has shown that men are far more likely to be abusers, and women far more likely to be abuse victims. Because women are more likely than men to be caregivers, and men are more likely than women to be abusive, there may be a greater need for monitoring and intervention programs for caregiving men.

What Role Does Work, Paid and Unpaid, Play in One's Identity and Relationships in Old Age?

Throughout this volume, we have identified work, paid and unpaid, as a vehicle through which individuals may experience a sense of mastery. Despite myths about oldest old adults, work, in all its forms, continues to be just such a vehicle in the last decades of life. Paid work is less likely than other avenues to be a source of mastery for old-old persons, however. In part, this is because the opportunities for paid work are limited for very old adults. This is especially so because most old-old adults are women, many of whom have had limited involvement in waged labor. Furthermore, women, even the oldest among them, continue to be drawn into the unpaid work of caregiving for family members and the routine household work that others rely on women to do. In addition, many oldest old persons are no longer able to maintain paid work schedules. Surely a major reason is that oldest old adults are choosing to spend their limited time and energy engaged in other pursuits.

Leisure and volunteer activities are two avenues that enable oldest old persons to experience a sense of well-being. You may know very old people who are generative and productive through their leisure activities. For example, you may have a grandmother who loves baking for her family and friends or who teaches her grandchildren and great-grandchildren about local wildflowers. Your grandfather might be a great storyteller or an outstanding volunteer leader in a local civic organization. In some racial and ethnic groups, older adults serve in a revered and crucial role as sources of wisdom and as conservators of the culture.

Some older adults, however, have little choice but to earn a living. Wallace and Juanita Nelson sell vegetables from their garden as a way to support themselves. Together, they earn around $5,000 annually (mid-1990s dollars). "If we don't work," Wallace says, "we don't eat," Juanita finishes. Neither Wallace nor Juanita participates in the Social Security system. Although their primary motivation for work is survival, both gain a sense of mastery and accomplishment from the work that they do. Each has a special task, and both are essential to their joint success. One additional source of satisfaction for them is that they do this work together.

Not all elderly poor persons have choices about their waged labor. As noted earlier, those who are foreign born and who do not speak English are particularly limited in their paid work options (Chan, 1988). Yet these are the very individuals who are at the lowest poverty levels with the highest need for financial support. Those with limited speaking ability who seek employment are confined to low-wage segments of the economy. For women, a common outlet is the poorly paying garment industry (Espiritu, 1997). This industry is a typical work site for Asian immigrant women, as we see in Susan Ito's story. Others are self-employed as part of a family member's business. You may have seen older Korean Americans selling groceries or working in a dry cleaning business, Chinese Americans in gift shops or restaurants, South Asians in hotels and motels, and Cambodians in doughnut shops. Through their unpaid or minimally paid labor, these older adults help the family business survive. Rather than in storefronts, however, many older Asian immigrant grandmothers may spend their time watching young children so that the parents and older children can work in the family shop.

Paid work, however, is not an outlet for the majority of oldest old adults. For many, old age is a time characterized by everyday routines that help them maintain their strength and vitality (Johnson & Barer, 1997). For others, it is a period that facilitates reflection on a lifetime of experiences and accomplishments. For still others, it is an opportunity for enjoyment.

The parents in Mona Van Duyn's "Letters From a Father" become interested in feeding, watching, and learning about birds. Soon, they are a source of information for others. This story and the lives of many older adults demonstrate that even with chronic health problems, it is fully possible for older people to remain active, vibrant, contributing members of society who enjoy life and the living of it.

33

Final Rounds:
A Father, a Son, the Golf Journey of a Lifetime

James Dodson

The next day I drove out of town to do a bit of work. It had been three weeks since I last worked on anything, and I was relieved to steer Old Blue four hours to the east to Wilmington, where I sat down with Ike Grainger, the famous USGA rules official. Grainger had just turned one hundred years old and my piece on him—a man who had made some of the most critical rulings in many of the biggest matches in the history of the game—was for the centennial edition program of the U.S. Open, which was to be held at Shinnecock Hills in June.

Later that night, as Dad and I sat watching the conference semifinals of a basketball tournament from some arena out West, I told him some of what Grainger and I had discussed— how the rule of equity is the heart and soul of golf, how whenever there's no formal rule to cover a situation or dispute, you must try and do what's most *fair*—and said how much Grainger's love of the game had reminded me of his. I also told my father I wished he could accompany me to Shinnecock.

"Maybe I'll get out of this contraption and we'll go," he said quietly, thumping the arm of the wheelchair. I said I'd be pleased to arrange the passes.

"I'm sorry for so much trouble," he added, coughing dryly, shifting uneasily in his chair.

"It's no trouble, Dad."

"You'll just never know how much I loved you all."

"We love you, too." My mother had quietly appeared in the kitchen doorway, dressed in her quilted bathrobe, the overhead light shining behind her, fingers to her throat. She was helpless to do anything but wait. My father didn't see her. She was crying. She turned and went back to bed.

A little while later, Dad said, "You know what I'd really like, Jim? I'd like to crawl in bed with your mother."

"You got it."

I woke up my mother and carried my father to their bed. Switching off the light, I heard my mother planting soft kisses on her husband's face. Her voice had a girlish cant. "You scoot over here, hon, and let's snuggle, just you and me. *There* now. Warm enough?" His reply possessed more strength than I had heard or seen for days. "Yes. Thanks. Delighted to be in bed with you."

"My goodness, sweetie, you need a shave."

The next day, he asked me to give him a shave.

I shaved my father with his own safety razor, slipping glances at his eyes. His pale gray eyes were even paler, farther away. They made me think of Gorky's description of the dying Tolstoy: *He listens attentively as though recalling something which he has forgotten, or as though for something new and unknown.*

Afterward, while he slept, I went out to see a man who gave hot-air balloon rides for weddings, anniversaries, and other "special occasions," it turned out, except dying. He couldn't believe I wanted to take my dying father up in a hot-air balloon. There were insurance considerations.

"I'll pay you twice your normal fee, sign a waiver, whatever's necessary," I pressed him. "Just a few minutes up in the air. You, my father, my mother, and a little bottle of good French wine." *Something new and unknown.*

He thought about it, chewing his lip. Then he consulted a schedule log, shrugged, and said he was booked until April. He smiled apologetically. He said he might be able to do something for me in April.

Buddhists and Native American people believe the way a person dies tells the story of how he lived. To them, dying is a living art, the beginning of further passage to something new and unknown.

For a change, I tried not to think too much about the future, what was going to happen to my mother after my father was gone, how our lives would change, how I would feel. As a child, my greatest unspoken fear was that my father would somehow just *disappear.* I don't know where this illogical terror came from. He never gave me the slightest reason to believe it might happen. As I grew from boy to man and then to middle-aged man with children of his own, he was always *there.*

Now, as my father slipped away, I simply could not imagine a world without him in it. As long as your father is alive, someone said, you will always be a son.

My father's younger brothers arrived. First Jim, then Bob, then Ben. They sat with my aging aunts on the den couch and talked about the trials of their own grown families while my mother, alternately smiling and hiding out in the kitchen, went slowly out of her mind.

34

Manon Reassures Her Lover

Martha Elizabeth

When I cannot sleep, I stroke you,
and like a napping cat that purrs
and stretches when touched, you linger
with pleasure on the edge of waking,
curling far into slumber. You know
that I am watching, you are safe.
Your skin is soft, smells fresh.

I love how your face is sculpted,
the drapes and furrows, how your cheek
laps over your forearm as you sleep.
I love how your skin moves under my hand,
the way it sags on the muscle and bone,
as the skin of a ripe peach
slips loose almost without the knife.

I have no hunger for young flesh,
unripe, firm but tasteless by comparison.
You are still at the very peak
of ripeness, sweet, with the tang
that quenches thirst. I would like
to take a gentle bite from your shoulder,
golden in the faint light from the window.

35

Starboys

Elissa Goldberg

Dear Anna,

I am writing this from a coffee shop. My seat is by the window. Why, you are thinking, am I sitting in a coffee shop when I have a perfectly good house to sit in? Okay, I will tell you.

Marilyn, our dear daughter, may she have a long and wonderful life, this dear child of ours who is no longer a child, decided last month to cure me. Cure me of what, I do not know. I did not ask. One day she came in. A day no different from any other, I was sitting in the living room watching the television news.

Marilyn went into the kitchen to empty her grocery bags. "Dad," she said. "I bought you new coffee. It's decaffeinated."

"What does this mean, decaffeinated?" I asked. This I said from my chair, why should I walk into the kitchen?

"Unleaded, Dad. You shouldn't be drinking regular coffee. It's a diuretic."

"Tell me, Marilyn," I said. "And what does this mean, diuretic?"

By this time she was standing in the doorway of the kitchen, folding her paper bag.

"It means it takes too much water out of you. You're too old for that."

Nu? Decaffeinated. Diuretic. Too much water. Let her do what she wants. What did I care?

I forgot about it. The next day, I got up, I fed the birds, read the newspaper, and drank my coffee. No big deal. But that afternoon, a headache. And what a headache, loud, pounding, I could not think. This was not so new to me. Headaches. They come, they go. But this one, it was different. The next day, it was still with me. And the next day also. Like a black cloud, it filled my head with thunder, everywhere I went.

When Marilyn came on the third day, I remembered. "Marilyn," I said, "this decaffeinated coffee, however you call it, it is killing me."

"Ha, ha," she laughed. "It's not killing you, Dad. It's good for you."

"It is murdering me. Go, buy me some coffee. Or tomorrow you will be pouring this decaffeinated coffee on my grave."

"Dad," she said. "You have a headache? You'll get over it. It's not the decaf that's giving it to you. It's from no caffeine. It'll stop soon." She laughed again, and then she was gone.

This is what she does. Comes into my house, checks things off her list, and then disappears.

I sat down. "Okay," I said to the floor. "I will buy my own coffee."

It was a cold day. No rain, clear sky, but a wind that shook the tree against the houses. I walked to the Fred Meyers grocery store. But before I got there, a few blocks away, I saw Joel Weinstein. Dr. Weinstein. Flash, we used to call him, do you remember, for the way he was always dressed. Always the most dapper fellow, black hat, grey coat, wing tips when we were still wearing loafers. A snappy dresser.

He was getting out of his car. How did I recognize him? I don't know. I had not seen him in years. He moved in different circles than ours after a while. We were not, you remember, as well-to-do as he. Still, I knew it was him.

"Flash," I said, "Dr. Weinstein." And I held out my hand.

He looked at my hand. Then he stared into my face with his runny grey eyes.

"Jack Manasky," I said.

"Yes," he said. "Of course." And then, Anna, he began to cry. Water dripped through the creases by his eyes, and his breath broke like teacups from his mouth. I looked down, I should not see another man cry.

"I'm sorry. Excuse me," he said. He did not have a handkerchief. And I did not offer him mine.

"You want to talk?" I asked.

He shook his head. "It's life." Then he told me that he lost his Rebecca four months earlier. A stroke, one leg and one arm useless, her speech hitting a wall in her head before ever reaching her lips. A prisoner in her own body until the blood in her brain broke another time, with mercy.

"I am a dead man," he said, his arms stretched out. Spittle dropped from his chin.

"Do you have time now?" I said. "You want to have a bite to eat, a cup of coffee?"

"No," he said. "Another time." He shook my hand, and then walked away. Not even a hat on his head.

I watched him walk, Anna. A lost man. His coat stained. His figure bent like the head of a cane.

I turned to go on my way, when what did I see? A coffee store. A store selling nothing but coffee, they have such things these days. Nu, Dr. Joel Weinstein, he saved my life.

I went inside this store. Starbins, it is called. Or Starboys.

"I want a cup of coffee," I said to the young man.

"Short or tall," he said.

"I am short," I said, and he laughed. He told me his name was Tim.

"Tim, I am Jack," I said. "Give me a cup of coffee." And in a minute, Anna, magic. My headache was gone.

Nu, so the next day, I did the same thing. And the next day, again. By now it is my routine. Wake up, feed the birds, read up on Mr. President Clinton's new ideas. Then I walk to Starbuds, buy myself a nice cup of coffee from Tim.

"Tim." I say, "You don't know, but you and Dr. Weinstein saved my life."

Still, this whole time, Anna, I was thinking about him, Flash. I remember that pain. It is like a dagger, every time you take a breath. Sometimes even now, six years after you have left me, may you rest in peace, I feel it. The memories, they choke me.

I remember your last two weeks in the hospital. I walked like a machine. I would sit you up in bed, your skin white like the moon. Four pillows it took, do you remember? Two behind your back, and one on either side so your thin body could be straight. And then you let me comb your hair. Such thin hair that you would not let them cut. You watched the trees out your window. Sometimes our eyes met. We had no words.

When you died, I sat by your bed for a long time. No one came, not a nurse, nobody from the family. Maybe they all thought things were fine, seeing me in that chair. They did not know I could not move. I didn't know that I could.

Remembering these things, I thought, who better than myself to talk to Dr. Weinstein? Someone else who has gone through what he is going through. So I called him up on the telephone. I said, "Dr. Weinstein, this is Jack Manasky."

He is a bit deaf, this man. "Who?" he said.

"Jack Manasky. I saw you the other day," I said.

"Frank?" he said.

I was ready to hang up. But he caught on. As soon as he knew who I was, he was silent.

I asked him, "Listen, you want to meet me for lunch? Maybe we could meet at the Jewish Center?"

He was still silent. So I repeated myself. I should have known to say everything twice.

"No," he said. His voice, Anna, was like a buzz saw.

"No?" I said. "You do not want to?"

"I will not go out with you," he said, and then he hung up the phone. What could I do? It is not often that I feel like a teenager, but I felt like one then. He does not like me, I thought. He has never liked me. We were never really friends. Maybe his family has taken up all his time. He is too busy.

Then I told myself other things. Who needs him? Like a hole in my head, I need him. I, too, am busy. I was not even thinking of him for twenty years before I saw him that day.

Still, I tried again. One night I could not sleep. At about two o'clock in the morning, I had an idea to call Flash Weinstein to invite him to the movies. Perfect, I thought. He doesn't want to talk, he won't have to talk. We'll be two old friendly faces watching a screen together. But I was smart. I waited until eight o'clock to call him.

"Hello, Flash," I said. "This is Jack Manasky. You want to see a movie with me?"

"Do I want to be a what?" he said.

"A movie. A movie. You want to go see a movie with me?"

"*Oi, got,*" he said, and I could tell he was crying. Eight o'clock in the morning and this man was crying. "No," he said. "Let me call you."

I put down the telephone and stared at it. Then I walked slowly to buy my cup of coffee.

That morning, Marilyn came over.

"Dad," she said. "You are not drinking coffee at all anymore? You can drink this stuff. This stuff isn't bad for you."

"Marilyn, it's bad for me."

"Dad," she said. Her face looked torn, crumpled like a piece of paper. "Dad, I got you this. It's special coffee. It's not bad for you like that other stuff you were drinking."

"Marilyn," I said. "I like my coffee. When I want you to buy me different coffee I will let you know."

Marilyn didn't look at me after that. She reached for her purse. "Okay," she said, but I saw her hand shake. And, as she walked to her car, twice she blew her nose.

I sat down in my chair. I felt heavy as an elephant. Sometimes, Anna, since you have gone, I do not know what to do.

Until we meet again,
Jack

36

Divorced and Reconstituted Families: Effects on the Older Generation

Colleen L. Johnson

Marriage, divorce, and remarriage are part of a reorganization process that entails a series of major changes in the family. The cleavages created in the nuclear family during this dynamic period have ramifications that affect the kinship system and ultimately the status of the older generation. While most research findings to date have focused on the impact these marital changes have had on parents and children, the effects on the flow of benefits between them and grandparents are beginning to attract interest among gerontologists.

Recent Trends in Divorce and Remarriage

Survey and census data, most of which report only on women, indicate that the divorce rate has peaked but remains at a high level of frequency. In fact, 56 percent of the early baby boomers have already divorced or are likely to do so in the future (Norton and Moorman, 1987). Divorce is generally a problem for young adults; the divorce rate declines continuously over the adult years. Consequently, by

age 50, the rate is only one-quarter as large as that at age 20. In fact, 74 percent of all divorces occur before age 40, and very few, only 1.3 percent, occur after age 65. Virtually nothing is known about the adjustment of this very small minority who divorce in later life. It has been suggested that elderly women have more problems after a divorce than do younger ones (Berardo, 1982; Cooney, 1989; Hagestad and Smyer, 1982). Since divorce is so rare in old age, women with marital breakups may have few age peers of similar status with whom to share their problems. It is also likely that divorced women receive fewer supports from family and friends than do the widowed. In any case, intergenerational helping patterns are disturbed. A recently divorced grandparent is less likely than her married counterpart to be available to her children and grandchildren, some of whom are also likely to be divorced. Likewise, divorced children may be too distracted to provide supports to an elderly parent (Johnson, 1988b).

Demographers also predict that there will be a later age of marriage and increased numbers of women who will never marry; both trends, in combination with a high divorce rate, will affect the future family and the numbers of children in future generations who will be available to assist the elderly. Given the current rates of divorce, Norton and Moorman (1987) point out, there will be a marked decline in the numbers of women in old age who are married or widowed, while the numbers who are divorced will increase. Moreover, women in the future will spend more years as divorcees than they will as wives or widows.

The increased interest in the impact the divorces of children are having on older people focuses mainly on the reallocation of family resources. Divorce is a period of upheaval for individuals at any age, and it involves a process of profound and often stressful changes in families. On one hand, such changes could lead to parental distractions and declines in resources and competencies that ordinarily would have been directed toward intergenerational helping patterns. On the other hand, a divorce might bring the divorced into closer contact with parents as they turn to them for help.

Grandparenting in Divorced Families

Sociologically, divorce and the grandparent role converge at two ambiguous points in our social structure. On one hand, divorce and remarriage are events that are incompletely institutionalized. Their occurrence comes without clear guidelines as to how to behave or without ritual markers that indicate a socially regulated passage from one status to another (Johnson, 1988c). Likewise, our norms do not specify how grandparents should function in satisfying the basic needs of grandchildren, those needs that in normal times are delegated to the parents. Given the fact that a divorced child, particularly a daughter, is fulfilling functions formerly performed by two parents, the need for help is generally high.

On the other hand, researchers on grandparenting conclude that the role of grandparent

is without clear normative guidelines on the allocation of responsibilities. The role has been described as sentimentalized and having a ritualized quality (Neugarten and Weinstein, 1964; Kahana and Kahana, 1970; Robertson, 1977). While the guidelines for grandparents are unclear and grandparents can voluntarily choose their course of action, they do so within the boundaries mediated by the parents (Bengtson and Robertson, 1985; Johnson, 1988a). In other words, grandparents are not free agents; they tend to consider their role as personally negotiated and situationally defined. Likewise, grandparents are generally at a stage in life where they welcome a decrease in family responsibilities; they can thus be ambivalent about substituting for parents in meeting the needs of grandchildren. Given these ambiguities, major dilemmas arise when their grandchildren need help. As one of my respondents commented, "If I do too much for my grandchildren, I might have to do it all. If I do too little, I might lose them."

In my study, the actions of grandparents varied according to their age and the ages of their grandchildren. Like most researchers, I found that younger grandparents provided economic help and practical assistance after a divorce more than did older grandparents. Consequently, grandparenting tends to be a middle-aged role and one that entails relationships with younger grandchildren.

The grandparent role also varies by kinship relationship. Maternal grandparents are more actively involved than are paternal, so the mediator is a daughter who is more likely than a son to have custody of dependent children. Evidence indicates that the father's link to his child progressively weakens over the years, so he may no longer be able to provide his parents with access to his children of a divorce. Not surprisingly then, there is usually a decline in involvement of paternal grandparents with the passage of time after a divorce. In some cases, where a divorced son is unable to provide his parents access to his children, the parents may bypass him and personally establish an independent relationship with their former daughter-in-law.

Parents and Their Divorced Children

In my study, parents played a significant role in easing the strains created by their son's or daughter's divorce (Johnson, 1988b). Almost two-thirds were in weekly or more-frequent contact, 89 percent were assisting with baby-sitting and other services, and 75 percent were providing economic assistance. Other divorced individuals went to their parents for advice and solace. In all, we estimated that 59 percent were dependent upon their parents in the sense that their lives would be negatively affected without such help.

After a divorce, the relationships between parents and their divorcing children are commonly renegotiated (Johnson, 1988b). In my study, three types of solidarities were observed to result from the reorganization process. First, increased emphasis on the solidarity of the generational bond occurred in 38 percent of the families. It entailed strengthening the blood relationship between parents, the adult child, and the grandchildren. In this case, the divorce resulted in some return to dependency upon parents and an increased flow of aid from them. Such a transition (or some would say, regression)—returning to the parents—is incongruent with our culture's most treasured norms, the norm of noninterference on the parents' part and the norm of independence on the part of the child. Where these norms are endorsed, there is a conflict between the need to depend upon a parent for some help and the desire to be independent. In the process, expectations regarding roles and relationships may be revised, and patterns of reciprocity may change.

If the parents come to the assistance of a divorcing child, the shield of privacy around the child's life is generally lowered. In the course of helping their child, parents have the opportunity to observe their child's activities and comment on her or his child-rearing practices and household management. Parents can also infer other aspects of their child's lifestyle, such as dating and sexual practices. In keeping with the norm of noninterference, however, most parents are indirect about their comments and advice to their child if they want to preserve a cordial relationship. Over time, most of the divorced children who had strengthened their generational tie had stabilized their lives. In doing so, they were eventually able to establish more independence from their parents. Over the four years, they generally drew away from their parents and reasserted the primacy of their own nuclear family.

In the second pattern of reorganization, 27 percent of the divorced children struck out alone and retained the private, bounded, but abbreviated nuclear family. After a divorce, their parents respected the privacy of the adult child's household and rarely intruded in his or her life. Consequently, the intergenerational bond was characterized by "intimacy at a distance." In these families, the parent-child relationship was likely to be distant and sometimes conflictual. Contacts were infrequent, and "we bend over backwards not to intrude in each other's lives" was the prevailing attitude. Also, this group was financially better off than the rest of the sample, so they could afford to seek help outside their family of origin. They were also likely to have more close friends in whom they confided. Not surprisingly, more individuals in this category either remarried or had a lover over the course of the study than did those who had a strong generational tie.

Third, loose-knit social networks resulting from a divorce occurred in 35 percent of the cases. With these permissive and flexible individuals, conventional family units were sometimes difficult to identify, because there was a blurring between relatives by blood, marriage, divorce, and remarriage. Relationships with relatives of divorce continued as new relationships were formed with remarriage. These patterns will be described in more detail below, but here the parent-child relationship becomes flexible and diffused. As one man commented, "My mother and I have a mellow relationship." These relationships were sustained on the basis of "liking" and personal preferences rather than norms of responsibility.

Reconstituted Families

Over the years, these families experienced frequent marital changes, and during the process, the older generation commonly retained some relatives of divorce at the same time that they accumulated new in-laws with their child's remarriage. Dependent children generally are the connecting link facilitating contacts between relatives of divorce and remarriage. These relatives occupy positions along divorce and remarriage chains that are three generations deep, and new linkages, disconnections, and relinkages are continually being made.

Forty-eight percent or almost one-half of the sample of grandmothers had expanded kinship networks after a child's divorce (Johnson and Barer, 1987). The expanding networks were more common among paternal grandparents, who were far more likely than maternal grandparents to retain a relationship with their child's former spouse. The oldest generation potentially can have expanding kin networks from three sources.

1. *In-law coalitions.* A grandparent's kinship system expands when relationships with their child's former in-laws are retained, and new relatives are added with their child's remarriage. In this case, members of the grandparent generation affirm the bond with their former child-in-law by emphasizing their shared biological linkage to the grandchildren.

2. *Divorces and remarriages of multiple children.* With the divorces and remarriages of several children, new subsets of in-laws accumulate. Some older people have busy lives managing a complex kinship system created by frequent marital changes of more than one child. If mothers of sons intend to stay in contact with their grandchildren, that is their only alternative.

3. *Two-generation divorce and remarriage chains.* With widowhood or divorce, grandparents too are likely to remarry. In doing so, they potentially add another set of step and in-law-relations to their networks. In these cases, the kinship network is the most expansive.

Conclusions

Divorce is a stressful life event for the parties involved. As this article attempts to demonstrate, in many cases it changes the status and roles of the older generation. In some families, there are positive outcomes. The grandparents in divorcing families intervene to assist their child and their grandchildren to the extent that some harmful effects of divorce are ameliorated, and in the process, grandparents restore more content to their roles. Mostly these grandparents are younger and healthier; they are also maternal grandparents who have easy access to their grandchildren. Since the grandparent role is mediated by the parents, it is easier to deal with their own blood relative. The situation for parents of sons is more complicated, for the person through whom they receive access to their grandchildren is a former in-law. If the divorce has been a stormy one, a son might not be able to renegotiate his parents' status and role with his children.

On the negative side, in some situations, divorce deprives grandparents of their relationship with grandchildren. Divorce may also deprive older and sicker grandparents of their child's support. If that child has been recently divorced, he or she may be too distracted to come to a parent's assistance. Given the fact also that many older people disapprove of divorce in general, its occurrence in their family is a source of conflict between generations.

An examination of remarriage and reconstituted families reveals a situation with even greater possibilities for grandparents. From the point of view of the older generation, children's remarriages enlarge their kinship network with the addition of new in-laws of remarriage and the retention of in-laws of divorce. It is here that the flexibility of our kinship system and the elasticity of its boundaries result in positive benefits to older people.

Such results may not be found in more traditional families, which have more clear-cut distinctions between relatives by blood and by marriage. However, these results are consistent with the changes in the past few decades, with their relaxation of sexual and gender constraints. In some subcultures, moreover, such flexible kinship systems are common. For instance, older African Americans benefit in regard to their social supports from just such networks in which they have freedom to mold their relationships to suit their needs (Burton and Dilworth-Anderson, 1991; Johnson and Barer, 1990). Our contemporary family and kinship system is perhaps moving in such a direction—a latent web of relationships can be activated when needed (Riley, 1983).

References

Bengtson, V. and Robertson, J., eds., 1985. *Grandparenthood.* Beverly Hills, Calif.: Sage.

Berardo, D. J., 1982. "Divorce and Remarriage at Middle Age and Beyond." *The Annals of the American Academy of Political and Social Science* 464:132-39.

Burton, L. M. and Dilworth-Anderson, P., 1991. "Intergenerational Family Roles of Aged Black Americans." *Marriage and Family Review* 16:311-22.

Cooney, T. M., 1989. "Co-Residence with Adult Children: A Comparison of Divorced and Widowed Women." *Gerontologist* 29:779-84.

Hagestad, G. O. and Smyer, M. A., 1982. "Dissolving Long-Term Relationships: Patterns of Divorcing in Middle Age." In S. Duck, ed., *Personal Relationships.* New York: Academic Press.

Johnson, C. L., 1988a. "Active and Latent Functions of Grandparenting during the Divorce Process." *Gerontologist* 28:185-91.

Johnson, C. L., 1988b. "Post-Divorce Reorganization of the Relationship between Divorcing Individuals and Their Parents." *Journal of Marriage and the Family* 50:221-31.

Johnson, C. L., 1988c. "Socially-Controlled Civility: Family and Kinship Relations during the Divorce Process." *American Behavioral Scientist* 31(6): 684-701.

Johnson, C. L. and Barer, B., 1987. "American Kinship Relationships with Divorce and Remarriage." *Gerontologist* 27(3):330-35.

Johnson, C. L. and Barer, B., 1990. "Families and Social Networks among Older Inner-City Blacks." *Gerontologist* 30:726-33.

Kahana, E. and Kahana, B., 1970. "Grandparenthood from the Perspective of the Developing Child." *Journal of Aging and Human Development* 2:261-68.

Neugarten, B. and Weinstein, M. S., 1964. "The Changing American Grandparent." *Journal of Marriage and the Family* 26:199-204.

Norton, A. J. and Moorman, J. E., 1987. "Current Trends in American Marriage and Divorce." *Journal of Marriage and the Family* 49:3-14.

Riley, M., 1983. "The Family in an Aging Society." *Journal of Family Issues* 4:439-54.

Robertson, J. F., 1977. "Grandmotherhood: A Study of Role Conceptions." *Journal of Marriage and the Family* 39:165-74.

37

Understanding Elder Abuse And Neglect

Rosalie S. Wolf

In spite of the headway that has been made in explaining how and why elder abuse occurs, it still remains a poorly understood problem. No simple definition can encompass its many aspects. Elder mistreatment may be an act of commission (abuse) or omission (neglect). It may be an intentional act, that is, a conscious attempt to inflict suffering, or it may be unintentional because of inadequate knowledge, infirmity, or laziness on the part of the person responsible. The manifestations of elder mistreatment are numerous but are generally grouped under four headings:

Physical abuse, the infliction of physical pain or injury, e.g., slapping, bruising, sexually molesting, restraining;

Psychological abuse, the infliction of mental anguish, e.g., humiliating, intimidating, threatening;

Financial abuse, the illegal or improper exploitation and/or use of funds; and

Neglect, refusal or failure to fulfill a caretaking obligation, e.g., abandonment, denial of food or health related services.

Whether behavior is labelled as abusive or neglectful may depend on how frequently the mistreatment occurs, its duration, intensity, severity, and consequences. Adding to the complexity of identification and reporting of cases is the fact that each state operates under its own set of definitions. An act may be considered abuse in one state but not in another. Some states do not even use the word "abuse." Neglect may refer either to the condition of the victim or the intent of the person responsible. Inconsistent definitions have hindered efforts to obtain prevalence and incidence data and have prevented useful comparisons among research findings. Without an agreed upon meaning, the criteria and principles needed for clinical practice or policymaking cannot be standardized. Most recently, some researchers have questioned the legal and professional definitions of elder mistreatment, suggesting that the older person's perception of a particular behavior may be the salient factor in identification and intervention.

Variations in definitions have not been the only barrier to progress in the field. When elder abuse first received national attention, there was an over-reliance on the child abuse model in dealing with the problem. Victims were viewed by agency staff and researchers as very dependent older women mistreated by well-meaning, but overburdened, adult daughters. Within a relatively short time, most states had passed mandatory reporting legislation patterned after child abuse statutes. But many situations did not fit that model. Later findings suggested that spouse abuse might offer a more useful framework for study and intervention since the individuals involved were legally independent adults. To some health researchers, however, the family violence paradigm was also not suitable in the majority of cases. They recommended that elder abuse be considered from the perspective of "inadequate care," since it is easier to measure unmet needs than inappropriate behavior. It is now very clear that no one interpretation can cover all aspects of the problem. Agreement on clear principles to guide collection of data and clinical practice is further complicated by other sets of issues relating to institutional abuse and self-neglect, two problems which are not covered in this discussion.

Risk Factors and Characteristics

A multitude of risk factors for elder abuse has been proposed from "violence as a way of life in America" to "ageism in society." Based on the limited research on abuse and neglect, the explanations that seem to be the most likely at this time are the unhealthy dependency of the perpetrator on the victim and vice versa, the disturbed psychological state of the perpetrator, the frailty, disability or impairment of the victim, and the social isolation of the family. According to the studies so far, stress factors, such as poverty, job status, loss of family support, etc. do not seem to be important. The cycle of violence theory, which predicts that victims become perpetrators, and is closely associated with child and spouse abuse, has not been substantiated in elder abuse cases. One constant, however, is that as with other forms of domestic violence, alcohol is present in a large proportion of elder abuse cases.

The need to understand how familial and individual circumstances relate to elder abuse has led researchers to compare cases by type of mistreatment, victim-perpetrator relationship, gender, and most recently, race. When 328 physical, psychological, and financial abuse and neglect cases, reported to elder abuse projects in three states, were analyzed, three distinct profiles emerged. In the case of *physical and psychological abuse,* the perpetrators were more likely to have a history of psychopathology and to be dependent on the victim for financial resources. The elderly victims were apt to be in poor emotional health but relatively independent in their activities of daily living. Since this type of abuse involved family members who were most intimately related and emotionally connected (perpetrators were spouses and adult children), the violence may be attributed to unhealthy interpersonal relationships that become more highly charged because of illness or financial need.

In *neglect* cases, the victim was more likely to be widowed, very old, cognitively and physically impaired, with few social contacts. In sharp contrast to the cases of physical/psychological abuse, those involving neglect appeared to be very much related to the frailty and disability and dependency needs of the victim. Neither psychological problems nor financial dependency were significant factors in the lives of the persons responsible. For them, the victim was a source of stress.

In cases of *financial abuse,* the physical and mental state of the victims seemed to be relatively unimportant. However, the victims were generally unmarried and had few social contacts. Rather than interpersonal pathology or victim dependency, the risk factors appeared to be financial needs or "greed" of the perpetrator and loneliness of the victim.

While a specific case may not exactly conform to a profile, knowledge of these distinctive patterns have been helpful in identifying risk factors and in designing intervention strategies.

A comparison of parent abuse cases (abuse perpetrated by adult children on their parents) and spouse abuse showed that older mistreated spouses were more likely to be physically abused, to be in poorer emotional health, and to be more dependent on their abusers for companionship. Adult children were more likely to neglect their elderly parents or to abuse them psychologically. These children tended to have money problems, to be financially dependent on their elderly parents, and to have a history of mental illness and alcoholism. The abusing spouses were more apt to have medical complaints and to have experienced a recent decline in physical health. For some couples, the stresses of later life, particularly physical illness, exacerbate an already tension-filled and unhappy marriage.

Prevalence and Incidence

Although estimates of the prevalence of elder abuse in the United States have ranged from about 4 to 10 percent of the population 65 years and older, there has been only one community-based study. Using a methodology that was validated previously in two national family violence surveys, a research team surveyed over 2,000 non-institutionalized elders living in the metropolitan Boston area and found that 3.2 percent had experienced physical abuse, verbal aggression, and/or neglect since they had reached 65 years of age. Spouse abuse (58 percent) was more prevalent than abuse by adult children (24 percent), the proportion of victims was roughly equally divided between males and females, and economic status and age were not related to the risk of abuse.

This survey, to which the category of financial abuse was added, was repeated in Canada with a nationally representative sample. Four percent of Canadian elders able to respond on the telephone were found to have recently experienced one or more forms of mistreatment. Again, the rates for men and women were about equal, but financial abuse was more prevalent than physical abuse, verbal aggression, or neglect. Two other studies have been reported in the literature. One used written questionnaires and clinical evaluations to determine the rate of abuse and neglect in a small semi-industrialized town in Finland. The results indicated a 2.5 percent elder mistreatment prevalence rate for men and 7.0 percent for women, or 5.4 percent for both sexes.

The second study, conducted in Britain, added several questions from the Boston and Canadian forms to a national representative survey. It found that 5 percent of individuals aged 65 years and over reported having been recently verbally abused by a close family member or relative, 2 percent physically abused, and 2 percent financially abused. Since all these surveys are based on self-reporting, it is safe to say that the percentages represent an underestimate of the problem rather than an exaggeration.

Knowing whether cases are on the increase or not cannot be determined without good national prevalence data collected over a span of years. However, state reports of abuse and neglect cases have shown a steady rise since first summarized in 1987, from an estimated 117,000 nationwide to 227,000 in 1991. It appears that a substantial part of this increase is due in great part to heightened awareness of elder abuse by the public and professionals and more highly developed systems for reporting. Of the estimated 227,000 reports, slightly more than half were substantiated cases, and were about equally divided among abuse, neglect, and exploitation by others, and self-neglect. However, cases that come to the attention of adult protective services are believed to represent only a small fraction of the estimated one and one-half million to two million cases of elder abuse and neglect in the elderly living in the community.

Service Delivery

All of the 50 states have some form of legislation (e.g., elder abuse, adult protective services, domestic violence laws, mental health commitment laws) that authorizes the state to protect and provide services to vulnerable, incapacitated, or disabled adults. In more than three-quarters of the states, the services are provided through the state social service department (adult protective services); in the remaining states, the State Units on Aging have the major responsibility. Calls are received on special phone lines (in some states operating 24 hours a day, 7 days a week) and are screened for potential seriousness. If mistreatment is suspected, an investigation is conducted. If the case is deemed an emergency, the investigation must be completed within a few hours of the receipt of the call. On the basis of a comprehensive assessment, a care plan is developed which might involve, for example, obtaining emergency shelter for the victim, admitting the victim to the hospital, arranging for home care, calling the police, or referring the case to the state prosecuting attorney. In most states, once the immediate situation has been addressed, the case is turned over to other community agencies for ongoing case management and service delivery.

When elder abuse was thought to be mainly a result of caregiving stress, helping the caregiver was the treatment of choice: bringing into the home skilled nursing, homemaker assistance, personal care, meals-on-wheels, chore services, and respite care, or placing the victim in adult day care, or enhancing the ability of the caregiver to cope through counseling, training, and skill building. Although these services are still very much a part of care plans, the strong association between dependency of the abuser (adult children) and physical abuse has suggested another approach: overcoming the financial and emotional dependency of the perpetrator through vocational counseling, job placement, housing assistance, alcohol and drug treatment, mental health services, and financial support, and providing counseling for the victim. Because physical abuse as well as financial abuse often involves criminal or civil offenses, law enforcement personnel and officials of the criminal justice system are increasingly being called upon to assist. Many communities have found multidisciplinary teams with representation from various professions to be extremely useful in dealing with these very complicated cases.

38

Obasan in Suburbia

Susan Ito

When my grandmother was eighty years old, she got kicked out of her house for leaving her nighttime *kimono* in the bathroom one time too many. I remember the day she moved; I was ten. I sat in the backseat of my parents' station wagon while my father loaded her things— they fit easily into three or four cartons. He wrapped her little black and white television in a white chenille bedspread and laid it on the floor by my feet. She sat next to me, looking out the window, with a Kleenex in her fist.

She was living with my uncle Taro, her youngest son, his wife and my little cousin Jenney, in the big pink house she and my grandfather had bought after the war. When Uncle Taro brought his bride, Michiko, down from Canada, my grandparents invited them to stay until their savings grew. They never got any savings. They bought a car, a big one with automatic windows. They bought a fur coat. They bought television sets for every room in the pink house, and when my grandfather died ten years later, it was clear that Uncle Taro and his family weren't going anywhere.

That was all right. Nana would have been sad if they'd left her alone in all that space. But by that time the house had filled up with their things, pushing my grandmother to the outer perimeters of the house. She slept in the attic, in a small room with a slanted ceiling. Even though she was tiny, not even five feet tall, she could only stand up in the center of the room. She took her meals in the basement, back behind the laundry room where my grandfather had built a small, second kitchen, a one-burner stove next to an industrial size freezer. Sometimes she rested her plate on the ping-pong table and watched the Lawrence Welk Show while she ate.

The rest of them ate above her, Jenney spilling her Spaghetti-O's on the linoleum floor. It was like a split screen television, America above, and Japan below. Upstairs, they called themselves Ray and Lillian. Lil. I think Michiko chose that name intentionally, knowing that my grandmother would never be able to pronounce it. "Lil-lian," she tried to say, but it always came out sounding like "Re-run." Changing their names never seemed right, anyway. Once, my mother told me that Aunt Michi's mother up in Canada never knew she was calling herself Lil. To me, they were always Uncle Taro and Aunt Michi. Ray and Lil sounded like something out of I Love Lucy. But there they were, upstairs, trying to fit that suburban life around them. He joined the volunteer fire department. She gave Tupperware parties.

In the downstairs kitchen, my grandmother shuffled on the cement floor in her rubber-soled *zoris*. She washed the rice in the sink where Lil's nylons hung, dripping. There was a pantry down there, next to the enormous refrigerator. One shelf was designated for her food, the cans she carried in a canvas bag on the subway from Manhattan. *Kamaboko,* and the stinky yellow *daikon.* White fish cakes with the hot pink coating. I stacked the cans and cellophane packages, neatly, on her shelf, playing Japanese grocer with my play money. *"Ikura?"* I asked my grandmother. "How much?" "Two hundred dollar, please," she laughed. Her teeth clicked in her mouth, and she covered her face with the back of her hand.

After a while they stopped letting her talk to Jenney. "She won't be able to learn English," said Aunt Michi. "When she goes to school, people will think she talks funny."

Ray and Lil gave barbecues in the backyard, my uncle wearing a red butcher's apron. They couldn't keep Nana locked in the attic, not on weekends with everyone around, so she sat in the cool basement, rolling logs of *sushi* on little bamboo mats. I helped her with the *nori,* thin sheets of green-black seaweed. You had to toast it first, holding it carefully over a gas flame or a candle. Nana didn't mind when I burned holes in it. "Don't worry. It's a window for the *gohan* to look out." We arranged the sushi pieces on a big round platter, and brought them out to the picnic table. Nana put it down right next to whatever Aunt Michi had made, green Jell-O or fruit cocktail with little marshmallows in it. Michi would make a face when she saw the *sushi,* like it was something strange and disgusting, so none of her friends would eat it either. She didn't tell them it was the same thing she loved to eat when she was a little girl. But sometimes I'd see her, after everyone went home, and she'd be standing next to the refrigerator, popping the little *norimaki* in her mouth when she thought no one was looking.

One of the problems with the house was that it only had one bathroom. Aunt Michi made it clear that it was *her* bathroom, and that other people, namely my uncle and cousin and Nana, were allowed to use it, but only because of her generosity. There were rules. The shampoo had to stay under the sink, not on the bathroom ledge. All her knick-knacks had to be arranged just so: the pink yarn sweater with the dog's head that covered the extra toilet tissue; the porcelain mermaid whose tail spread into a soap dish. Wet towels had to be taken directly down to the laundry room, and put in the dryer, set to high so that they'd fluff up. Wet towels were ugly.

One day, I was sitting in Nana's room, and the window was open. Michiko was out on the back patio with Kit. Kit was their next-door neighbor with red hair, who smoked, inhaling and exhaling like an accordion.

Aunt Michi said, "Tell me, Kit, what's it like to have your own house?" They were sitting in matching white Adirondack chairs, balancing glasses of iced tea on the armrests.

"Lil, believe me, it's no picnic. I've gotta clean up after the kids, after Mister Air-Conditioner King, with no help. At least you get a hand around here!" Kit took another long puff, and then let it out. "I don't think Ray's mother is so bad. What's the matter, she pick on you?"

I leaned against the window screen, not breathing.

After a pause, I heard Aunt Michi say, in her low gravelly voice, "She drives me nuts. She won't speak English. She won't eat anything that comes in an aluminum package. She shuffles around in those damn zoris like she's Mrs. Buddha. Kit, that woman has been here more than fifty years, and she acts like she just popped up out of a rice paddy!"

Kit laughed. "So she hasn't learned to say the Pledge of Allegiance yet. I think she's cute, Lil."

Aunt Michi snorted. "Cute. She's a pain in the *oshiri.*"

"What?"

"You know what I mean."

Nana, at eighty years old, was still making a daily commute over the Hudson River to Manhattan, where she worked in a curtain factory. More than once, I watched her wrap Band-Aids around her fingers, which sometimes got caught under the machine's running needle. Her nails were purple and scarred, and each finger pad was a callous, but she liked her job. The sweatshop where she earned less than minimum wage was a place to feel busy, useful, a place to gossip with her Chinese lady friends.

My grandmother signed her paychecks, "Sadao Kitayama" in a long, snaky scrawl, the only English characters she knew. Then she turned them over to Uncle Taro for the mortgage payment. He went to the bank for her and deposited them in their joint account, keeping the little leather passbook in the locked drawer of his mahogany desk. It wasn't the money that mattered to her though, it was the work. Crossing the Hudson each morning on the big silver commuter bus gave her a sense of confidence, knowing that she could maneuver through places that Michi was afraid to go. She wandered by herself through the alleys of Chinatown, picking up unusual vegetables, carrying them in a bag made of plastic fishnet. Every night she came home, prepared dinner quietly by herself in the basement, and retired to her room in the attic. There was no sound to indicate her presence except the soft lilt of Lawrence Welk through the floor.

The crime that committed her to solitude though, the final insult, was the kimono, indigo and white in a bamboo pattern. She kept hanging it on the bathroom hook and forgetting to remove it in the morning. It riled my aunt; she didn't want to touch the thing, so she would leave it there and seethe all day. By the time Nana came home from work, Michi's face was set in steel. Two words only: "Kimono, Obasan."

No one ever told me the details of how it happened, how the family split that summer, like a tree struck by lightning. I imagined my aunt and uncle saying something to her about how there wasn't enough space for all of them. My parents offered up our spare room, told her she could move in with us right away. But Nana was too sad, and too proud to accept. She insisted that they help her find an apartment, something small enough to be rented on her paycheck. It was an old brick building, in the same complex where my parents had lived as newlyweds. There was talk of a legal battle, of my grandmother winning her house back, but she refused to do it. "Taro my smallest baby," she said, wiping her runny eyes. "No fight him with lawyer." She turned away from the pink house without a struggle.

After she moved, my parents and I drove to Nana's place every Wednesday night and took her out to dinner. It made me sad to see her whole life in such a tiny box, her studio apartment. One room held a miniature kitchen, a folding metal table which she used for meals, and to iron on. Underneath the window was her single bed, a plastic cube-shaped nightstand and a phonograph on a rolling tea cart. The bed was covered with the white chenille spread and two plain yellow throw pillows she had taken from my uncle's couch.

My father tried once, a few years later, to build a bridge to the other side, but it was already too late. He went to Uncle Taro's house and stood on the front step, shaking the quarters and pennies in his pockets. Taro talked to him from behind the screen door, repeating, "There's nothing to say." My father's effort collapsed like a thing made of old, hollow bones, and when he came back to our house that night, we knew there wouldn't be another try. He stood in the driveway and opened the door to the station wagon, and my mother and I got in. It was a Wednesday, fried chicken night at Howard Johnson's, and my grandmother was waiting for us.

39

Selectivity Theory:
Social Activity in Life-Span Context

Laura L. Carstensen

Toward the end of the life span, people interact with others less frequently. There is no argument among gerontologists that this occurs, but there is great disagreement about the psychological precursors and ramifications of the reduction. A substantial literature has addressed social interaction in late life. Historically, this literature has emphasized social problems and isolation in old age. This clinical bent—both in the generation of hypotheses and in the selection of study samples—effectively steered us to think of old age as a time of social pathology. However, in recent years, empirical studies have revealed that older people are happy (Ryff, 1989), less depressed (Blazer, 1989; Meyers et al., 1984), and less lonely (Revenson, 1984) than their younger counterparts, despite the fact that they are less socially active.

The time has come to reconsider reduced social activity in old age as it relates to successful aging. In this chapter, I review evidence about social activity and integrate it within the framework of *selectivity theory*. Selectivity theory is a life-span model of socioemotional aging that views reductions in social activity in old age as reflective of the culmination of selec-

tion processes that begin early in life and have substantial adaptive value (Carstensen, 1987).

Social Interaction Across the Life Span

Changes in Social Activity With Age

The observation that social interaction declines in old age has been supported by both large-scale cross-sectional (Cumming & Henry, 1961; Gordon & Gaitz, 1976) and longitudinal research (Palmore, 1981). Despite indisputable declines in the overall rates of interaction, a closer look at the data shows that certain types of social contact remain relatively unaffected by age, whereas others decline more sharply (Palmore, 1981). Reductions in contact with co-workers occur reliably after retirement, for example, but contacts with family and friends do not decline until roughly age 80. Similarly, declines in memberships in voluntary organizations do not appear until about 80. Contact with grandchildren diminishes with advanced age, but contact with children remains stable (Field & Minkler, 1988).

Insights into when and how age-related reductions occur have been elucidated by longitudinal studies. We know from the Duke Longitudinal Study that there is a slow but steady decline in social activity from middle age on, intensifying in very old age. And we know that individual differences in levels of social activity show strong continuity into old age (Palmore, 1981).

Still, much of what we know about social contacts across the life span is based on people's self-reports about activity at a fairly gross level (e.g., number of club memberships, overall frequency of contact with others). Less is known about qualitative aspects of people's relationships, including whether and how they change and how people subjectively experience changes when they do occur. Field and Minkler (1988) recently reported an analysis of intensive interviews that spanned a 14-year period based on the Berkeley Intergenerational Studies Samples. They examined contact with and commitment to relationships from early to late old age. Essentially, they found evidence for considerable continuity in interaction patterns in old age. Contact with adult children was highly stable, and satisfaction with these relationships increased over time. Contact with friends was somewhat reduced, more so for men than women. And contact with grandchildren declined in very old age even though satisfaction with grandchild relationships remained stable.

Contact with siblings often declines during the middle years, when resources are directed more locally to children and work, but the renewal of sibling ties is common in old age (Troll, 1971). Eighty percent of older Americans have at least one living sibling. With age, the percentage declines, but even in advanced old age most people include siblings in their social networks. Cicirelli (1989) argues that siblings represent important attachment figures in advanced age and are viewed as secondary helpers when primary caregivers are unavailable; siblings commonly provide psychological support, assistance with transportation, and temporary aid during illness. There is some evidence that sibling ties are closer among lower socioeconomic groups, very likely because fewer alternative resources are available (Gold, Woodbury, & George, 1990). Gender too is highly significant in sibling relationships: the absence of a close bond with a sister predicts depression and reduced well-being for men and women in old age, whereas closeness to a brother does not (Cicirelli, 1989).

In old age, most friends are old friends. Seventy-two percent of Field and Minkler's (1988) respondents said that most of their friends were people they had known for many years. Likewise, in the Duke sample, 70% of older people said that most of their friends were old friends (Palmore, 1981). The significance of friendship in people's lives varies along with several factors. Not surprisingly, widows and widowers report greater contact with friends than do married people (Field & Minkler, 1988). Throughout life, women have relatively more close friends and see them more often than men see theirs (Candy, Troll, & Levy, 1981; Field & Minkler, 1988).

Individual Differences

Any discussion of social activity demands consideration of individual differences. There is, of course, substantial variability in the degree of sociability people display, and these differences seem to persist throughout the life span (Costa & McCrae, 1984). Other individual differences pertinent to social relationships include gender, ethnicity, and health. Each is discussed briefly below.

Gender

The social contexts for aging are quite different for women and men. These contexts have important implications for the maintenance of social relationships and social contact. First, for reasons as yet unknown, women outlive men by about 7 years, so the elderly population comprises many more women than men. Second, because most women in our culture marry men who are approximately 7 years their senior, women live, on average, 15 years as widows. Among men 65 years and older, 76% are married; among women in the same age group, only 37% are married (Serow & Sly, 1988). Moreover, men widowed in late life are much more likely to remarry than are women. Thus, it appears that men can and do rely on women for emotional support throughout their lives, but women cannot count on same-age or older men in the same way. In old age, women are likely to live alone and, subsequently, compared to men, are at increased risk for institutionalization.

Second, an alarming number of older women are poor and subsequently experience limited access to social resources. Many come to old age poor, but another group becomes poor for the first time, a fact that often reflects outliving a spouse who suffered a lengthy and costly illness before death. Twenty percent of Caucasian elderly women are poor, and percentages among American people of color are much higher. Forecasts suggest that the feminization of poverty will be even greater in the future: an estimated 25% of young women today will live in poverty in old age.

Third, for the health and longevity reasons mentioned above, as well as socialization processes present throughout life, women are more likely than men to be caregivers in old age. Caregiving for an infirm relative takes a profound toll on the social lives of older people. Caregivers are at extremely high risk for social isolation and depression. Not surprisingly, the likelihood of spouses assuming a caregiving role is much greater among the poor, reflecting reduced access to formal support services.

In short, with age, social networks shrink for both women and men but exert differential effects. Women are more likely than men to experience the death of their primary intimate, usually a spouse, and they are more likely to be poor and live alone. Men face a shorter life span and the related increased risk of morbidity at a younger age. Thus, there is a certain paradox in the life course of gender differences. As we age beyond the child-rearing years, men and women grow increasingly similar in many ways, but by this time in life, circumstances place us in very different situations. Old age places us at risk for a number of deleterious outcomes—illness, institutionalization, loss, and death—and sex ensures the inequality of the risk.

Ethnicity

When considering attitudes toward aging, Americans tend to overidealize and at the same time homogenize ethnic minorities, although they are, of course, highly diverse. The prevailing myth is that minority families uniformly respect and care for their elderly relatives and that Caucasian families abandon theirs (Shanas, 1979). Yet such images do not reflect the reality. American families do not abandon their relatives. On the contrary, most maintain close family ties. Indeed, 80% of the assistance community elderly receive is provided by family members as opposed to professional workers (Brody, 1980).

And, although Hispanic, black, and Asian Americans are more likely than Caucasian Americans to live in extended family households, living arrangements are often determined more by economic need than by desire. Older people are frequently dissatisfied with their circumstances. Weeks and Cuellar (1981) found, for example, that although Hispanic-American elderly were much more likely than their Caucasian counterparts to live with relatives, they were less likely to view families as emotional resources. They also found that among Asians living with adult children, loneliness and dissatisfaction were common. Assumptions about harmonious coexistence may become increasingly inaccurate.

Sokolovsky (1985) attributes some of the dissatisfaction to a growing schism between the values of minority group cultures and the *ability* of minority families to care for their aging relatives.

The confound between social class and minority status can lead to misattributions about ethnicity. When socioeconomic status is controlled, interactional patterns among different ethnic groups are much more similar than different. For example, some studies show that among blacks, older women are more likely to live with younger relatives (Tate, 1983). However, when social class is controlled, interaction patterns of blacks and whites appear highly similar (Cantor, 1979).

To the extent that minority status compounds the negative effects of age—referred to as double jeopardy or, when referring to females, triple jeopardy—it influences income, health care, housing quality, and social opportunities. These corollaries of minority status demand serious practical considerations for social policy. However, in theoretical discussions it is important to acknowledge that although cultural norms about interaction and filial responsibility may vary by ethnicity, the extent to which members of a given culture adhere to these norms may represent a different reality (Rosenthal, 1986). It is essential, however, that we do not misattribute to ethnic *preferences* outcomes that are, in fact, driven by economic demands.

Health

Health relates to activity level and life satisfaction at any age. People in poor health are inevitably affected psychologically. Given the relatively high incidence of disease among older people, it is essential to consider the relationship of health status to any social or psychological dimension of interest. In many cases, healthy older people do not show the supposed patterns of social aging. Indeed, a number of otherwise compelling psychological theories have been reduced to corollaries of health. For example, retirement was long thought to exert a deleterious effect on health, but now it appears that retirement relates to health because sick people retire early, not because retirement causes illness (Ekerdt, 1987).

Healthy people at any age tend to be more active than unhealthy people. It is quite clear that levels of social activity predict psychological well-being *when health status is not controlled.* When health status *is* controlled, activity levels do not predict well-being (Lee & Markides, 1990).

Social Support

Supportive social relationships play a pivotal role in the well-being of the elderly (Antonucci & Jackson, 1987). Indeed, close ties with family and friends may be even more meaningful in late life than in younger years. The passage of time frequently can strengthen and refine supportive relationships. Interpersonal conflicts have often been resolved, or at least have subsided, and time has provided the opportunities to fulfill and change role assignments, leading to richer social lives.

It should be noted, however, that social *contact* is not equivalent to social *support*, in spite of the fact that contact is widely used as a proxy for support in the literature (Carstensen, 1987). Social support refers to the perceptions and expectations one holds about members in one's social network. Declining rates of contact do not necessarily lead to reductions in perceived social support; indeed, in some cases, lowered rates of contact may be associated with increased feelings of support (Carstensen, 1989).

In an investigation of life-course changes in the function and structure of social support networks, Antonucci and Akiyama (1987) found that the support networks of older people were as large as those of younger people, but older people were in contact with network members less often. Older and younger people received comparable amounts of support from their networks, although older people *provided* less support than did younger people.

More attention has been paid to the amount and type of assistance younger people provide to older people than vice versa. This focus results in an unfortunate misrepresentation of asymmetries that exist across generations. In fact, older people provide a great deal of instrumental assistance to younger relatives in the form of child care and financial aid (Johnson, 1988). In addition to these more tangible functions, older people frequently function as central sources for information about other network members (e.g., siblings often remain apprised of one another's status via parents).

Psychological Concomitants of Reduced Social Activity

Fredrickson and Carstensen (1990) argue that older people think about prospective social partners differently than younger people do. In an examination of age-related differences in the social cognitions surrounding social interaction, they asked young and old people to make cognitive distinctions about prospective social partners. Respondents were asked to sort cards into piles based on how similarly they would feel interacting with the people described on them. In other words, if they would feel similarly interacting with a sibling or a close friend, they would place those cards in the same pile. If the experience would be quite different, they would place the cards in separate piles. Using multidimensional scaling, three dimensions emerged as the principal cognitive dimensions along which people made their categorical decisions: anticipated affect, future contact, and information seeking.

Interesting age differences were apparent in the salience of these three dimensions to different age groups. Older people placed greater emphasis than did middle-aged or young people on the anticipated affect in an interaction, whereas younger people placed greater emphasis on future contact and information seeking. The tendency for affect to be the most salient sorting dimensions among older respondents was strongest among those who were also infirm. Older people told us, sometimes quite explicitly, that their days were numbered and that they made careful choices about their expenditure of time and energy. When asked about their preferences for interaction with the described social partners, older people voiced strong preferences for familiar over novel social partners, in some cases adding that they did not have time for people they did not know well.

In a second study, Fredrickson and Carstensen (1990) explored what it is about being old and infirm that might alter people's interactional goals. They proposed that social behavior prior to upcoming social endings might resemble that of old age, and they tested this idea by manipulating anticipated endings and querying people about their social preferences. Specifically, they asked 380 people, aged 11 to 92, which of three partners they would choose to spend social time with (1) "a member of your immediate family," (2) "a recent acquaintance with whom you seem to have much in common," and (3) "the author of a book you've just read." Under unspecified conditions, younger people were more likely to choose a novel social partner; older people were more likely to choose the familiar person. Next, subjects answered the question again, only this time were asked to imagine that soon they would be moving across the country by themselves. Under this condition, which made endings salient for young and old, young people responded just as older people did, showing strong preferences for familiar social partners. Thus, older people preferred familiar over novel social partners under both conditions, but younger people's preferences changed depending on the condition.

Together, these studies suggest that not only do older people prefer familiar social partners over novel partners but that younger people respond similarly to older people under conditions that force them also to view their time as limited.

Social Interaction in Nursing Homes

Nursing homes are interesting from a social standpoint because they are settings where potential social partners are abundant but interaction rates are strikingly low (Carstensen & Fremouw, 1988). Indeed, much of the work of applied gerontologists has been to increase rates of contact among the institutionalized aged. The gerontology literature is replete with studies designed to enhance the social environments of elderly nursing home residents by increasing social contact. Approaches range from visitation programs to socialization programs to operant reinforcement procedures aimed at increasing rates of social contacts.

Yet a close examination of the data shows that although rates of interaction can be manipulated this does not result in an improvement in subjective well-being. In fact, interventions aimed at increasing rates of interaction are notorious for their failure to maintain social activity after external contingencies for interaction cease; that is, as soon as prompting and / or tangible rewards for interaction are removed, social interaction returns to originally low levels (Carstensen, 1986; Carstensen & Erickson, 1986).

An alternative explanation for the very low rates of interaction in nursing homes is that withdrawal represents an adaptive response to overcrowded and unpredictable social environments. Carstensen and Fremouw (1988) found that very low rates of interaction in nursing homes were not associated with depression. Rather, socially withdrawn people said that they actively avoided social contact with other residents, an observation also made by Fredrickson and Carstensen (1990).

Summary

As a whole, the literature on social interaction in old age provides compelling evidence for the argument that perceived social connectedness influences both physical and mental health, yet just as persuasive is evidence that social contact declines. Health status and mobility clearly play a role in the reduction in social activity, but these factors do not account for all of the variance; even healthy older people report reductions in social activity. The fact that social interaction declines even when the opportunities for interaction are available demands questions about the function of social interaction in late life, questions about both the costs and the benefits, and, more important, about the interactive link between the two.

Theoretical Views of Social Activity in Old Age

Selectivity Theory

The fundamental premises of selectivity theory are that place in the life cycle influences (1) the salience of the goals of interaction and (2) the effectiveness of social interaction as a means to obtain desired goals.

Previous models of social aging have viewed lowered rates of contact as uniquely late-life phenomena. A basic assumption of selectivity theory is that rates of interaction do not begin to decline suddenly in old age, rather the changes identified in old age reflect gradual lifelong selection processes. A recent reanalysis of the Berkeley longitudinal data supports this contention. Contact with acquaintances begins to decline very early in adulthood and continues to show reductions throughout middle age. During the same period, contact with close friends and relatives increases (Carstensen, 1989). Thus, when we enlarge the window of time, the picture better resembles social selection than social withdrawal.

Three central functions of social interaction—information acquisition, the development and maintenance of identity, and emotional regulation—are discussed below:

Information Acquisition

For young people, the world is so novel that interaction with virtually any social partner will likely result in information gain. Even interactions with social partners who do not articulate new information provide important lessons about individual differences, interactions with peers, and one's own place in the world out there. But with age, fewer people have the information we need. Much of what we hear and experience we have heard before (Schulz, 1985).

Thus, interaction for the sake of obtaining information is less *effective* as we age for two basic reasons: First, as our own stores of information increase, novel information is harder to come by. Second, as we begin to seek more technical and ephemeral information, social interaction is a less effective means to obtain it. To illustrate, a young child can obtain most information he or she desires from virtually any adult caretaker. When he or she grows up and becomes an accomplished scientist, there are fewer, if any, people to turn to for answers to the questions she pursues. Rather, nonsocial means are necessary to obtain new information.

Another aspect of information acquisition that changes with age is related to the idea of "banking" for the future. When we are young, even information that is not immediately pertinent holds value because it may be useful in the future. An adolescent boy talks to his uncle, who has just become a father, about parenting. It may be years before he becomes a parent himself, but at a young age the future holds many possibilities, and much information gained through interaction will become relevant at some point in the future. The limited future imposed by old age, however, changes the value of futuristic banking.

The Development and Maintenance of Identity

Swann (1987) argues that we invest much social energy in maintaining a stable self-concept, tacitly negotiating our identities with those around us and seeking confirmatory evidence for our self-conceptions. According to Swann, central self-verification processes are strategically selecting social partners and adopting interaction strategies that lead to self-confirmatory responses.

In old age, fewer people can help preserve our self-concepts, and careful discriminations among potential social partners becomes necessary to minimize interactions that actively erode self-concept. Many social partners will not share sufficient history to verify identity; other social partners will behave in stereotypical and demeaning ways in response to the stimulus of old age. In other words, even people who come to old age with identities firmly established risk self-concept with indiscriminant social contact.

Role theorists have eloquently portrayed the significance of losing important role functions in late life, leaving only ambiguous prescriptions in place of unambiguous rules that previously guided interaction (Rosow, 1974). And deaths of longtime friends and family represent the loss of irreplaceable social partners, who no longer affirm our self-conceptions. In addition to role loss, the aging process alters some of the identity cues we relied on in self-verification processes. Physical aging conspires with changing social mores to project a very different identity than old people intend. Younger people, for example, may see an old woman who dresses in high fashion as defensively clinging to her youth, even if she has always dressed the same way.

The Regulation of Emotion

The cultivation of the social environment to maximize the potential for the experience of positive emotions and minimize the potential for negative ones is one of the principal ways we regulate affect (Thompson, 1990). From infancy on, we become increasingly adept at understanding characteristics of emotions, perceiving the emotion states of others and understanding causal relationships between events and emotions (Masters & Carlson, 1984). There is no reason to think that we lose this adeptness with age. On the contrary, evidence is beginning to accrue that suggests old age brings an improved understanding of emotional contexts and meanings (Labouvie-Vief, DeVoe, & Bulka, 1989). One central premise of selectivity theory is that the regulation of emotion assumes greater centrality among the functions of social interaction in advanced years.

As noted earlier, older people greatly emphasize the affective potential in making discriminations among potential social partners (Fredrickson & Carstensen, 1990). Interactions likely to be devoid of positive affect are the least compelling to older people. Far from being emotionally flattened, older people appear to be emotionally conscious, making judicious decisions about activities and giving thoughtful consideration to their function as affect regulators.

The Costs of Interaction

One key to understanding reduced social interaction in the elderly is the *cost* of interaction (Carstensen, 1987). Psychologists have paid a great deal of attention to the benefits of interaction but little attention to the potential costs. For a number of reasons, including heightened physiological arousability, reduced physical energy, and ageist beliefs evidenced in the behavior of some social partners, the costs of interaction increase in old age.

Two studies have demonstrated that well-being among the aged is better predicted by *aversive* aspects of support systems than by positive aspects. In a study of the social networks of elderly women, Rook (1984) found that problematic, not positive, aspects of social relationships predicted poor adjustment. More recently, in a prospective study of adult caregivers of dementia patients, Pagel, Erdly, and Becker (1987) found similar results. Problematic elements of social relationships predicted depression and dissatisfaction; helpful aspects were only indirectly related to well-being.

Moreover, the risk of interacting with new people increases with age due to the potentially ageist behavior displayed by the social partner. The odds of initiating a conversation with a stranger and finding the response condescending, hostile, or simply indifferent increases with age, contributing further to escalating risks. Even in interactions in which a social partner emits no overt derogatory behavior, when age is more salient than individual characteristics, self-concept is placed in jeopardy.

Selectivity theory assumes that the basic psychological functions of social contact do not change over the life span, but social and physical influences may operate differentially on the choices people make. It may make sense to invest time in an information-rich relationship tinged with negative affect when we are young because the information we acquire may be sufficiently valuable to compensate for negative affect. Presented with identical circumstances in late life, the gains may be fewer and the costs greater. This is not to say that the acquisition of information is unimportant to older adults or that affect regulation fails to drive interaction in youth. On the contrary, general functions of social interaction probably remain consistent throughout life. However, across the life span, as we are becoming increasingly effective at using emotion regulation strategies, other functions of social interaction diminish in importance due either to decreased likelihood (e.g., information acquisition) or to the resolution of earlier life goals (e.g., mate selection). And increased physical fragility with age requires that we work to maintain emotional homeostasis.

It follows, then, that interaction frequency with long-term friends and relatives would not change much over the life cycle because these contacts typically serve to generate positive emotional experience and increase subjective feelings of security and self-worth. But interaction with acquaintances and novel social partners would change because they are less likely to generate positive emotional outcomes. Limiting social interactions in old age to those with predictable, supportive, social partners represents a mechanism for maximizing the probability of positive outcomes of social contact (e.g., a sense of companionship, maintenance of self-concept, assistance) and minimizing negative outcomes (e.g., negative affect and depletion of physical energy).

Summary and Conclusions

A life-span examination of the literature reveals three consistent themes. First, the reduction in social interaction in late life is evinced *only* within specific classes of relationships (e.g., less intimate relationships; Palmore, 1981; Carstensen, 1989). Second, an examination of the social cognitions surrounding declining rates of interaction suggests that older people play an active role in limiting social contacts (Fredrickson & Carstensen, 1990). And third, a perusal of the literature provides no evidence for *emotional* withdrawal from significant relationships (Field & Minkler, 1988). The process of limiting interaction with some classes of social partners may be best conceptualized as *selectivity*, that is, increased discrimination about the people with whom one interacts.

Previous models of socioemotional aging tacitly view changes in social behavior as portentive of decline. I argue that these models stem from a decremental view of the aging process in which differences between old and young lead inevitably to conclusions about deterioration in the old. Viewed instead within a life-span developmental framework, observed changes can be interpreted as highly adaptive and contributing to successful, vital aging.

The view that older people are more selective in their choices of social partners helps to make sense of the limited effects of interventions aimed at increasing interactions. In virtually all of these applications, older people are encouraged to interact with people they do not know. If, indeed, older people are even less likely than younger people to find such interactions rewarding, it may explain why they resist.

Selectivity also helps to explain the extremely limited interactions so frequently observed in nursing homes. Initiating a conversation with another nursing home resident may reveal that the prospective social partner is demented. He or she may believe that you are a long-lost relative. Or alternatively, the person may not hear you and subsequently fail to respond at all. The picture I am painting may be excessively pessimistic. My point is merely that when you are a nursing home resident, the pursuit of interaction with other residents is undertaken with substantial risk. For an infirm older person, the cost may not be worth the potential gains.

In short, selectivity in one's choice of social partners—investing in the most important social partners and disregarding less satisfying ones—may work in the service of optimizing the social world in old age.

References

Antonucci, T. C., & Akiyama, H. (1987). An examination of sex differences in social support in mid and late life. *Sex Roles, 17,* 737-749.

Antonucci, T. C., & Jackson, J. (1987). Social support, interpersonal efficacy, and health: A life course perspective. In L. L. Carstensen & B. A. Edelstein (Eds.), *Handbook of clinical gerontology* (pp. 291-311). New York: Pergamon.

Blazer, D. (1989). Depression in late life: An update. In M. P. Lawton (Ed.), *Annual review of geriatrics and gerontology* (Vol. 9, pp. 197-215). New York: Springer Publishing Co.

Brody, E. (1980). Women's changing roles and care of the aging family. In J. P. Hubbard (Ed.), *Aging: Agenda for the eighties* (pp. 11-16). Washington, DC: Government Research Corp.

Candy, S. E., Troll, L. W., & Levy, S. O. (1981). A developmental exploration of friendship functions in women. *Psychology of Women Quarterly, 5,* 456-472.

Cantor, M. (1979). The informal support system of New York's inner city elderly: Is ethnicity a factor? In D. Gelfand & A. Kutzik (Eds.), *Ethnicity and aging* (pp. 153-174). New York: Springer Publishing Co.

Carstensen, L. L. (1986). Social support among the elderly: Limitations of behavioral interventions. *Behavior Therapist, 6,* 111-113.

Carstensen, L. L. (1987). Age-related changes in social activity. In L. L. Carstensen & B. A. Edelstein (Eds.), *Handbook of clinical gerontology* (pp. 222-237). New York: Pergamon Press.

Carstensen, L. L. (1989, November). *A longitudinal analysis of social and emotional dimensions of interpersonal relationships.* Paper presented at the annual meeting of the Gerontological Society of America, Minneapolis, MN.

Carstensen, L. L., & Erickson, R. E. (1986). Enhancing the social environment of elderly nursing home residents: Are high rates of interaction enough? *Journal of Applied Behavior Analysis, 19,* 349-355.

Carstensen, L. L., & Fremouw, W. J. (1988). The influence of anxiety and mental status on social isolation among the elderly in nursing homes. *Behavioral Residential Treatment, 3,* 63-80.

Cicirelli, V. (1989). Feelings of attachment to siblings and well-being in later life. *Psychology and Aging, 4,* 211-216.

Costa, P. T., & McRae, R. R. (1984). *Emerging lives, enduring dispositions: Personality in adulthood.* New York: Little, Brown.

Cumming, E., & Henry, W. E. (1961). *Growing old: The process of disengagement.* New York: Basic Books.

Ekerdt, D. J. (1987). Why the notion persists that retirement harms health. *Gerontologist, 27,* 454-457.

Field, D., & Minkler, M. (1988). Continuity and change in social support between young-old, old-old, and very-old adults. *Journal of Gerontology, 43,* P100-P106.

Fredrickson, B. L., & Carstensen, L. L. (1990). Choosing social partners: How old age and anticipated endings make people more selective. *Psychology and Aging, 5,* 163-171.

Gold, D. T., Woodbury, M. A., & George, L. K. (1990). Relationship classification using grade of membership analysis: A typology of sibling relationships in later life. *Journals of Gerontology: Social Sciences, 45,* S43-S51.

Gordon, C., & Gaitz, C. (1976). Leisure and lives. In R. Binstock & E. Shanas (Eds.), *Handbook of aging and the social sciences* (pp. 310-341). New York: Van Nostrand Reinhold.

Johnson, C. L. (1988). *Ex familia.* New Brunswick, NJ: Rutgers University Press.

Labouvie-Vief, G., DeVoe, M., & Bulka, D. (1989). Speaking about feelings: Conceptions of emotion across the life-span. *Psychology and Aging, 4,* 425-437.

Lee, D. J., & Markides, K. S. (1990). Activity and mortality among aged persons over an eight-year period. *Journals of Gerontology: Social Sciences, 45,* S39-S42.

Masters, J. C., & Carlson, C. R. (1984). Children's and adult's understanding of the causes and consequences of emotion states. In C. Izard, J. Kagan, & R. B. Zajonc (Eds.), *Emotions, cognitions and behavior* (pp. 438-463). Cambridge: Cambridge University Press.

Meyers, J. K., Weissman, M. M., Tisckhler, G. L., Holzer, C., Leaf, P. J., Orvaschel, H., Anthony, J. E., Boyd, J. H., Burke, J. D., Kramer, M., & Stoltzman, R. (1984). Six-month prevalence of psychiatric disorders in three communities. *Archives of General Psychiatry, 41,* 959-967.

Pagel, M., Erdly, W., & Becker, J. (1987). Social networks: We get by with (and in spite of) a little help from our friends. *Journal of Personality and Social Psychology, 53,* 793-804.

Palmore, E. (1981). *Social patterns in normal aging: Findings from the Duke Longitudinal Study.* Durham, NC: Duke University Press.

Revenson, T. A. (1984). Social and demographic correlates of loneliness in late life. *American Journal of Community Psychology, 12,* 338-342.

Rook, K. S. (1984). The negative side of social interaction: Impact on psychological well-being. *Journal of Personality and Social Psychology, 46,* 1097-1108.

Rosenthal, C. J. (1986). Family supports in later life: Does ethnicity make a difference? *Gerontologist, 26,* 19-24.

Rosow, I. (1974). *Socialization to old age.* Berkeley, CA: University of California Press.

Ryff, C. (1989). In the eye of the beholder: Views of psychological well-being among middle-aged and older adults. *Psychology and Aging, 4,* 195-210.

Schulz, R. (1985). Emotion and affect. In J. E. Birren & K. W. Schaie (Eds.), *Handbook of the psychology of aging* (2nd ed., pp. 531-543). New York: Van Nostrand Reinhold.

Serow, W. J., & Sly, D. F. (1988). The demography of current and future aging cohorts. In Committee on an Aging Society (Ed.), *America's aging: The social and built environment in an older society* (pp. 42-102). Washington, DC: National Academy Press.

Shanas, E. (1979). Social myth as hypothesis: The case of the family relations of old people. *Gerontologist, 19,* 3-9.

Sokolovsky, J. (1985). Ethnicity, culture and aging: Do differences really make a difference? *Journal of Applied Gerontology, 4,* 6-17.

Swann, W. B. (1987). Identity negotiation: Where two roads meet. *Journal of Personality and Social Psychology, 53,* 1038-1051.

Tate, N. (1983). The black aging experience. In R. McNeely & J. Colen (Eds.), *Aging in minority groups* (pp. 95-106). Beverly Hills, CA: Sage.

Thompson, R. A. (1990). Emotion and self-regulation. In R. A. Thompson (Ed.), *Socioemotional development: Nebraska symposium on motivation* (Vol. 39, pp. 367-467). Lincoln: University of Nebraska Press.

Troll, L. (1971). The family of later life: A decade of review. *Journal of Marriage and the Family, 44,* 263-290.

Weeks, J., & Cuellar, J. (1981). The role of family members in the helping networks of older people. *Gerontologist, 21,* 338-394.

40

Wallace Nelson, 85, and Juanita Nelson, 70: Deerfield, Massachusetts

Studs Terkel

Wally: Juanita and I do live on very little. Our income is something like five thousand dollars between us. If people in the so-called Third World could live the way we're living, they would think they were rich. But I know we're rich. Look around you. We go out here and we work. We don't worry about getting ill. We do get ill. I do more than Juanita. She's the strong one. We have a vegetable garden. That's how we make our living, selling to the farmer's market. And it provides most of our own food. We own a little truck that we need for our vegetables, and it helps us raise that five thousand.

We're not deprived. We are accepting a marvelous opportunity of trying to live a life that measures up to our talk. We do a lot of talking. We say a lot of things. Talking is easy, but how are we living?

We began this whole process when we moved out of Philadelphia to New Mexico, from an eight-room house to a small adobe house. It's been a growing, exciting experience. It's not deprivation.

When we first moved out of Philadelphia and went to New Mexico, we were often asked whether we were a retired couple. We laughed. It means you've retired from some job you've been doing for a million years and you've got a pension from that and an old-age

pension. So you do nothing but live around, go from one senior citizen center to another, take trips. We laughed because, if we don't work—

Juanita: —We don't eat. [*They laugh joyfully.*] We got nothing. As far as social security is concerned, I don't even use my number. I guess we'd get the lowest. We made a wee bit when I was on the paper.

Wally: You may not even have made the minimum.

Juanita: That settles it, that's nice. We used to say we don't want to take social security, but we've never made an absolute about it. If we were disabled, we said maybe we would. But now that's all clear. [*Laughs, a pause.*] I think we've slowed.

Wally: Not at the same pace. Do we have the same energy as when we left Philadelphia? The answer is no. Not too long ago, we were observing that we don't go as fast as we used to.

Juanita: On Saturday, we get up at five o'clock in the morning, because that's market day and we have to get ready to go. We sell at a farmer's market in Greenfield. Wally has to be there around seven. The market opens at eight and he has to get set up. I stay behind and keep working in the garden. The market is over at

12:30. He has to pack up, and if anything is left, he has to peddle that, and maybe gets home in the middle of the afternoon. We count our money and see if we've made one hundred dollars that day. [*Laughs.*] It's hard to describe a typical day for us. From March on, it's garden, garden, garden.

Wally: There's a book I've come across about the Mondragos Cooperative in Spain: *We Make the Road as We Travel*. You see, I don't think there is any blueprint. It's a constant. You're never going to get there, you're always on the way.

If there is a what's next, it's moving this foot before the other one and not letting it stay behind. I won't move if I don't put this foot before the other—I'm gonna stand still. Therefore, the hope is to continue to put one foot before the other and without knowing where that's leading you to. I think we're wrong to have to know. It's good to know where I'd like to go. It's good to feel that I'm headed the way I want to go. But the important thing is that you go. You may find yourself there or you may not. You turn around and you take another course. But just don't stop putting that foot before the other.

41

Letters From a Father

Mona Van Duyn

I

Ulcerated tooth keeps me awake, there is
such pain, would have to go to the hospital to have
it pulled or would bleed to death from the blood thinners,
but can't leave Mother, she falls and forgets her salve
and her tranquilizers, her ankles swell so and her bowels
are so bad, she almost had a stoppage and sometimes
what she passes is green as grass. There are big holes
in my thigh where my leg brace buckles the size of dimes.
My head pounds from the high pressure. It is awful
not to be able to get out, and I fell in the bathroom
and the girl could hardly get me up at all.
Sure thought my back was broken, it will be next time.
Prostate is bad and heart has given out,
feel bloated after supper. Have made my peace
because am just plain done for and have no doubt
that the Lord will come any day with my release.
You say you enjoy your feeder, I don't see why
you want to spend good money on grain for birds
and you say you have a hundred sparrows, I'd buy
poison and get rid of their diseases and turds.

I I

We enjoyed your visit, it was nice of you to bring
the feeder but a terrible waste of your money
for that big bag of feed since we won't be living
more than a few weeks longer. We can see

them good from where we sit, big ones and little ones
but you know when I farmed I used to like to hunt
and we had many a good meal from pigeons
and quail and pheasant but these birds won't
be good for nothing and are dirty to have so near
the house. Mother likes the redbirds though.
My bad knee is so sore and I can't hardly hear
and Mother says she is hoarse from yelling but I know
it's too late for a hearing aid. I belch up all the time
and have a sour mouth and of course with my heart
it's no use to go to a doctor. Mother is the same.
Has a scab she thinks is going to turn to a wart.

III

The birds are eating and fighting, Ha! Ha! All shapes
and colors and sizes coming out of our woods
but we don't know what they are. Your Mother hopes
you can send us a kind of book that tells about birds.
There is one the folks called snowbirds, they eat on the
     ground,
we had the girl sprinkle extra there, but say,
they eat something awful. I sent the girl to town
to buy some more feed, she had to go anyway.

IV

Almost called you on the telephone
but it costs so much to call thought better write.
Say, the funniest thing is happening, one
day we had so many birds and they fight
and get excited at their feed you know
and it's really something to watch and two or three
flew right at us and crashed into our window
and bang, poor little things knocked themselves silly.
They come to after while on the ground and flew away.
And they been doing that. We felt awful
and didn't know what to do but the other day
a lady from our Church drove out to call
and a little bird knocked itself out while she sat
and she brought it in her hands right into the house,
it looked like dead. It had a kind of hat
of feathers sticking up on its head, kind of rose
or pinky color, don't know what it was,
and I petted it and it come to life right there
in her hands and she took it out and it flew. She says

they think the window is the sky on a fair
day, she feeds birds too but hasn't got
so many. She says to hang strips of aluminum foil
in the window so we'll do that. She raved about
our birds. P. S. The book just come in the mail.

V

Say, that book is sure good, I study
in it every day and enjoy our birds.
Some of them I can't identify
for sure, I guess they're females, the Latin words
I just skip over. Bet you'd never guess
the sparrows I've got here, House Sparrows you wrote,
but I have Fox Sparrows, Song Sparrows, Vesper Sparrows,
Pine Woods and Tree and Chipping and White Throat
and White Crowned Sparrows. I have six Cardinals,
three pairs, they come at early morning and night,
the males at the feeder and on the ground the females.
Juncos, maybe 25, they fight
for the ground, that's what they used to call snowbirds. I miss
the Bluebirds since the weather warmed. Their breast
is the color of a good ripe muskmelon. Tufted Titmouse
is sort of blue with a little tiny crest.
And I have Flicker and Red-Bellied and Red-
Headed Woodpeckers, you would die laughing
to see Red-Bellied, he hangs on with his head
flat on the board, his tail braced up under,
wing out. And Dickcissel and Ruby Crowned Kinglet
and Nuthatch stands on his head and Veery on top
the color of a bird dog and Hermit Thrush with spot
on breast, Blue Jay so funny, he will hop
right on the backs of the other birds to get the grain.
We bought some sunflower seeds just for him.
And Purple Finch I bet you never seen,
color of a watermelon, sits on the rim
of the feeder with his streaky wife, and the squirrels,
you know, they are cute too, they sit tall
and eat with their little hands, they eat bucketfuls.
I pulled my own tooth, it didn't bleed at all.

V I

It's sure a surprise how well Mother is doing,
she forgets her laxative but bowels move fine.
Now that windows are open she says our birds sing

all day. The girl took a Book of Knowledge on loan
from the library and I am reading up
on the habits of birds, did you know some males have three
wives, some migrate some don't. I am going to keep
feeding all spring, maybe summer, you can see
they expect it. Will need thistle seed for Goldfinch and Pine
Siskin next winter. Some folks are going to come see us
from Church, some bird watchers, pretty soon.
They have birds in town but nothing to equal this.

So the world woos its children back for an evening kiss.

1   People tend to make assumptions about others, regardless of age, and about their relationships. As you read Martha Elizabeth's poem, "Manon Reassures Her Lover," did you think that her lover was a man or a woman? Any assumptions about the relationships of others create the potential for problems. How might assumptions about the relationships of older persons complicate the provision of services to them?

2   In Goldberg's story, "Starboys," Jack Manasky makes several overtures to try to help Joel "Flash" Weinstein deal with the loss of his wife. Weinstein rejects these overtures. Jack indicates several reasons why his attempts are thwarted. What might be some other reasons that Jack does not see?

3   Martha, an 80-year-old widowed grandmother, recently married Frank, an 88-year-old widowed grandfather, three years after her first husband's death. This first husband died of complications related to Parkinson's disease. Martha had been his caregiver for his entire illness—more than eight years. Frank had been in excellent health, but he suddenly has a stroke that leaves him paralyzed on one side and unable to speak. His prognosis for a full recovery is bleak, but his vital signs are excellent. His doctor says that he possibly could live for a number of years with continuing functional impairment. Martha struggles with the idea of spending yet another long period as a caregiver. How might you react in her situation? What should be expected of a spouse? If Frank needs institutional care and his own savings are inadequate to support it, should Martha use her savings to pay the high cost of institutionalization, knowing that she is in excellent health and comes from a long-lived family?

4   Poor and working-class women and men and people of color are at risk for higher rates of morbidity and mortality than are those who have had advantages throughout life. Their family members, who are also likely to be challenged economically and in other ways, may not be able to help them in times of need or to the degree that might be required. What types of social programs (i.e., programs to assist older people directly and programs designed for caregivers) could help families provide assistance to these disadvantaged older persons? How important is it for these programs to be sensitive to the cultural backgrounds of those they are intended to serve? What sorts of needs (e.g., health-related, environmental needs) would be the most important to address first? Why?

5 Rosalie Wolf cites greed as one factor in the financial abuse of older people. To what extent do you think greed played a role in the financial abuse of Sadao Kitayama evident in Susan Ito's story, "Obasan"? Why do you think this case of abuse never came to the attention of adult protective services?

6 Because people are living longer and in better health, it is possible that older adults will be out of the paid labor force for 25, 30, even 35 or more years. Paid work is a primary way through which adults of all ages experience a sense of mastery. In what ways might business, industry, education, and social services make use of the abilities and knowledge of older adults without compromising their interest in controlling how they spend their time and energy?

SUGGESTIONS FOR FURTHER READING

---

1 Chan, F. (1988). To be old and Asian: An unsettling life in America. *Aging, 358,* 14-15.

Chan describes the experiences of older Asian and Pacific Islanders in the United States, most of whom live in major metropolitan areas. The difficulties many Asian immigrants face in their relationships with their adult children and children-in-law are discussed as well.

2 Johnson, C. L., & Barer, B. M. (1997). *Life beyond 85 years: The aura of survivorship.* New York: Springer.

The authors describe the ways in which individuals aged 85 and older adapt to the challenges they encounter. They also identify the capabilities these older adults need to continue to remain in their communities.

3 Rowe, J. W., & Kahn, R. L. (1997). Successful aging. *The Gerontologist, 37,* 433-440.

The authors define successful aging as avoiding disease and disability, maintaining high physical and cognitive function, and remaining engaged in social and productive activities. They identify the factors that predict success in each of these areas, emphasizing the role of lifestyle choices in maintaining health; the effectiveness of education, strenuous physical activity, and belief in one's ability in maintaining functioning; and the importance of social ties and social support in sustaining productive activity.

4   Lustbader, W., & Arellano, S. (Eds.). (1994). *Counting on kindness: The dilemmas of dependency.* New York: Free Press.

This collection of stories describes caregiving from the view of the care receiver and identifies the small acts that provide joy and contentment to a person dependent on others. It is a compelling source of help for caregivers looking for insight into their experience.

5   Cooney, B. (1982). *Miss Rumphius.* New York: Viking.

This children's story about legacy is told from the perspective of a great niece. Miss Rumphius follows her grandfather's advice to leave the world a more beautiful place and has the courage to follow a life of her dreams.

6   Terkel, S. (1996). *Coming of age: The story of our century by those who've lived it.* New York: St. Martin's.

Studs Terkel interviews older adults who were active in the most important social movements of the 20th century. Most continue to be involved in ways that reflect their values and that enhance their sense of well-being.

7   Pillemer, K., Hegeman, C. R., Albright, B., & Henderson, C. (1998). Building bridges between families and nursing home staff: The Partners in Caregiving program. *The Gerontologist, 38,* 499-503.

The authors describe a successful program designed to address communication problems and conflict between the family members of residents and the staff of a nursing home.

8   Kidder, T. (1994). *Old friends.* Boston: Houghton Mifflin.

Two old men, roommates in a nursing home, develop a caring friendship, despite their many differences. This book recognizes and honors the continuing capacity for love, close relationships, and integrity in later life.

9   Flagg, F. (1987). *Fried green tomatoes at the Whistle-Stop Café* (1st ed.). New York: Random House.

An older woman energizes a middle-aged woman by telling the story of two women who devoted their lives to each other.

1 *www.aoa.gov/aoa/pages/state.html*

This site provides an index of state agencies on aging, with hyperlinks when available. Agencies on aging provide information and resources for older people and their families.

2 *www.cdc.gov/nchs/products/pubs/pubd/series/sr3/30-21/30-21.htm*

The National Center for Health Statistics site includes links to information on trends in the health of older adults in the United States.

3 *www.4woman.org/minority/causes.htm*

This site of the Health Information for Minority Women provides information on the leading causes of death for women of color in the United States.

4 *www.gwjapan.com/NCEA/*

This site of the National Center on Elder Abuse contains links to resources with information on the incidence of elder abuse as well as links to related publications.

SUGGESTIONS FOR VIDEOS TO RENT FROM YOUR LOCAL VIDEO STORE OR BORROW FROM YOUR PUBLIC LIBRARY

1 *Antonia's Line* (1995)

A moving story of continuity and change during the last 40 years in the life of an unconventional Dutch woman and the diverse group of individuals who comprise her extended family, this charming, offbeat movie won the Academy Award for best foreign film.

2 *The Autobiography of Miss Jane Pittman* (1973)

An African American woman looks back over her 110 years, which serves as a history of African Americans from slavery to the present.

3 *On Golden Pond* (1981)

An alienated, middle-aged daughter, her boyfriend, and his son visit the daughter's parents. The developing connection between the young boy and her bristly, 80-year-old father, Norman, provides the backdrop against which the daughter, her mother, and her father come to terms with each other. This film won three Academy Awards.

4 *A Woman's Tale* (1991)

This moving film depicts the last days of a 78-year-old, independent, energetic woman who is dying from lung cancer. Notably, the star was terminally ill herself throughout the making of this movie.

Sources and Permissions

INTRODUCTION

Reading 1: "The Gathering," by Lois Tschetter Hjelmstad, in *Grow Old Along With Me: The Best Is Yet to Be* (p. 89), edited by S. H. Martz. Watsonville, CA: Papier-Mache Press. Copyright © 1996. Reprinted by permission.

PART I

Reading 2: Excerpts from "Four Models of Adolescent Mother-Grandmother Relationships in Black Inner-City Families," by Nancy H. Apfel and Victoria Seitz. *Family Relations, 40*, 421-429, October 1991. Copyright © 1991 by the National Council on Family Relations, 3989 Central Ave. NE, Suite 550, Minneapolis, MN 55421. Reprinted by permission.

Reading 3: Excerpts from "One Week Until College," by Sandi Kahn Shelton, in *Mothers Who Think: Tales of Real-Life Parenthood* (pp. 76-82), edited by C. Peri and K. Moses. New York: Villard Books/Random House. Copyright © 1999 by *Salon* Magazine. Used by permission of Salon.com

Reading 4: "The Good Daughter," by Caroline Hwang, from *Newsweek, 132*(12), p. 16, September 21, 1998. Copyright © 1998. All rights reserved. Reprinted by permission.

Reading 5: Excerpts from "Forgotten Streams in the Family Life Course: Utilization of Qualitative Retrospective Interviews in the Analysis of Lifelong Single Women's Family Careers," by Katherine R. Allen and Robert S. Pickett. *Journal of Marriage and the Family, 49*, 517-526, August 1987. Copyright © 1987 by the National Council on Family Relations, 3989 Central Ave. NE, Suite 550, Minneapolis, MN 55421. Reprinted by permission.

Reading 6: Excerpts from "Social Demography of Contemporary Families and Aging," by Christine L. Himes, in *Generations, 17*(3), 13-16, Summer 1992. Copyright © 1992 by the American Society on Aging, San Francisco, California. Reprinted with permission from *Generations.*

Reading 7: "The Last Diamond of Summer," by B. K. Loren. Excerpted from *For She Is the Tree of Life: Grandmothers Through the Eyes of Women Writers* (pp. 15-18) edited by Valerie Kack-Brice. Copyright © 1995 by Valerie Kack-Brice. Used by permission of Conari Press.

Reading 8: Excerpts from "Intergenerational Solidarity and the Structure of Adult Child-Parent Relationships in American Families," by Merril Silverstein and Vern L. Bengtson, in *American Journal of Sociology, 103*(2), 429-460, September 1997. Copyright © 1997 by The University of Chicago. Used by permission.

PART II

Reading 9: Excerpts from "Dancing With Death," by Camille Peri, in *Mothers Who Think: Tales of Real-Life Parenthood* (pp. 255-272), edited by C. Peri and K. Moses. New York: Villard Books/Random House. Copyright © 1999 by *Salon* Magazine. Used by permission of Salon.com

Reading 10: Excerpts from "Historical Perspectives on Caregiving: Documenting Women's Experiences," by Emily K. Abel, in *Qualitative Methods in Aging Research* (pp. 227-240), edited by J. F. Gubrium and A. Sankar. Thousand Oaks, CA: Sage Publications. Copyright © 1994 by Sage Publications, Inc. Used with permission of Sage Publications, Inc.

Reading 11: "Only Daughter," by Sandra Cisneros, 1990, reprinted in *The Beacon Book of Essays by Contemporary American Women,* (pp. 10-13), edited by Wendy Martin. Boston, MA: Beacon Press. Copyright © 1990 by Sandra Cisneros. First published in *Glamour,* November 1990. Reprinted by permission of the Susan Bergholz Literary Service, New York City. All rights reserved.

Reading 12: Excerpts from "The Experience of Grandfatherhood," by Sarah Cunningham-Burley, in *Reassessing Fatherhood: New Observations on Fathers and the Modern Family* (pp. 91-105), edited by C. Lewis and M. O'Brien. London: Sage Publications Ltd. Copyright © 1987 by Charlie Lewis and Margaret O'Brien. Used by permission.

Reading 13: Excerpts from "Father's Sorrow, Father's Joy," by Darrell G. H. Schramm, in *A Member of the Family: Gay Men Write About Their Families* (pp. 85-94), edited by J. Preston. New York: Dutton/Penguin. Copyright © 1992 by John Preston. Used by permission of David G. H. Schramm.

Reading 14: Excerpts from "Last Christmas Gift From a Mother," by Lois F. Lyles, in *Double Stitch: Black Women Write About Mothers and Daughters* (pp. 241-251), edited by P. Bell-Scott, B. Guy-Sheftall, J. J. Royster, J. Sims-Wood, M. DeCosta-Willis, & L. Fultz. Boston: Beacon Press. Copyright © 1991 by Patricia Bell-Scott, Beverly Guy Sheftall, and The SAGE Women's Educational Press, Inc. Used by permission.

Reading 15: Excerpts from "Extended Kin Networks in Black Families," by Peggye Dilworth-Anderson. Reprinted with permission from *Generations, 17*(3), 29-32, Summer 1992. Copyright © 1992 by the American Society on Aging, San Francisco, California.

Reading 16: Excerpts from *Looking After: A Son's Memoir*, by John Daniel. Copyright © 1996 by John Daniel. Reprinted by permission of Counterpoint Press, a member of Perseus Books, L.L.C.

PART III

Reading 17: Excerpts from "Marriage and Family Life of Blue-Collar Men," by David Halle, in *Families and Work* (pp. 316-337), edited by N. Gerstel and H. E. Gross. Philadelphia: Temple University Press. Copyright © 1987 by Temple University. Previously adapted from *America's Working Man: Work, Home, and Politics Among Blue-Collar Property Owners*, by David Halle, by permission of The University of Chicago Press. Copyright © 1984 by The University of Chicago.

Reading 18: Excerpts from *Breathing Lessons*, by Anne Tyler, pp. 120-126. New York: Berkley/Alfred A. Knopf. Copyright © 1988 by ATM, Inc. Used by permission of Alfred A. Knopf, a division of Random House.

Reading 19: Excerpts from "Grandparenting Styles: Native American Perspectives," by Joan Weibel-Orlando, in *The Cultural Context of Aging: Worldwide Perspectives* (pp. 109-125), edited by J. Sokolovsky. Copyright © 1990 by Jay Sokolovsky. Used by permission of Greenwood Publishing Group, Inc., Westport, CT.

Reading 20: Excerpts from *Silent Dancing: A Partial Remembrance of a Puerto Rican Childhood* (pp. 23-29), by Judith Ortiz Cofer. Copyright © 1990 by Judith Ortiz Cofer. Used by permission of the publisher, Arte Público Press, University of Houston.

Reading 21: Excerpts from "Closeness, Confiding, and Contact Among Siblings in Middle and Late Adulthood," by Ingrid Arnet Connidis and Lori D. Campbell. *Journal of Family Issues, 16*(6), 722-745, November 1995. Copyright © 1995. Used by permission of Sage Publications, Inc.

Reading 22: Excerpts from "Shared Filial Responsibility: The Family as the Primary Caregiver," by Sarah H. Matthews and Tena Tarler Rosner. *Journal of Marriage and the Family, 50,* 185-195, February 1988. Copyright © 1988 by the National Council on Family Relations, 3989 Central Ave. NE, Suite 550, Minneapolis, MN 55421. Reprinted by permission of Alfred A. Knopf, a division of Random House, Inc.

Reading 23: "What remains," from *My Mother's Body* (pp. 24-25), by Marge Piercy. Copyright © 1985 by Marge Piercy. Reprinted by permission of Alfred A. Knopf, a division of Random House, Inc.

Reading 24: Excerpts from "Marriage as Support or Strain? Marital Quality Following the Death of a Parent," by Debra Umberson. *Journal of Marriage and the Family, 57,* 709-723, August 1995. Copyright © 1995 by the National Council on Family Relations, 3989 Central Ave. NE, Suite 550, Minneapolis, MN 55421. Reprinted by permission.

PART IV

Reading 25: Excerpts from "Retirement and Marital Satisfaction," by Robert C. Atchley, in *Families and Retirement* (pp. 145-158), edited by M. Szinovacz, D. J. Ekerdt, and B. H. Vinick. Newbury Park, CA: Sage. Copyright © 1992 by Sage Publications, Inc. Used by permission.

Reading 26: Excerpts from "U.S. Old-Age Policy and the Family," by Madonna Harrington Meyer and Marcia L. Bellas, in *Handbook of Aging and the Family* (pp. 263-283), edited by R. Blieszner and V. H. Bedford. Westport, CT: Greenwood. Copyright © 1994, 1996 by Rosemary Blieszner and Victoria Hilkevitch Bedford. Used by permission.

Reading 27: Excerpts from "Elderly Mexican American Men: Work and Family Patterns," by Norma Williams, in *Men, Work, and Family* (pp. 68-85), edited by J. C. Hood. Newbury Park, CA: Sage. Copyright © 1993 by Sage Publications, Inc. Used by permission.

Reading 28: Excerpts from *The Unexpected Community: Portrait of an Old-Age Subculture* (pp. 90-97), by Arlie Russell Hochschild. Copyright © 1973 by Prentice-Hall, Inc., Englewood Cliffs, New Jersey. Used by permission.

Reading 29: Excerpts from "Predictors and Outcomes of the End of Co-Resident Caregiving in Aging Families of Adults With Mental Retardation or Mental Illness," by Marsha Mailick Seltzer, Jan S. Greenberg, Marty Wyngaarden Krauss, and Jinkuk Hong. *Family Relations*, 46(1), 13-22, 1997. Copyright © 1997 by the National Council on Family Relations, 3989 Central Ave. NE, Suite 550, Minneapolis, MN 55421. Reprinted by permission.

Reading 30: Excerpts from "Gender and Control Among Spouses of the Cognitively Impaired: A Research Note," by Baila Miller. Republished with permission of The Gerontological Society of America, from *The Gerontologist, 27*, pp. 447-453, by B. Miller. Copyright © 1987. Permission conveyed through Copyright Clearance Center, Inc.

Reading 31: Excerpts from *Two-Part Invention: The Story of a Marriage* (pp. 228-232), by Madeleine L'Engle. San Francisco: HarperSan Francisco. Copyright © 1988 by Crosswicks Ltd. Reprinted by permission of Farrar, Straus and Giroux, LLC.

Reading 32: "Happiness in Cornwall," by Raymond Carver, from *Songs of Experience: An Anthology of Literature on Growing Old* (pp. 220-221), edited by M. Fowler and P. McCutcheon, 1991. New York: Ballantine Books. Copyright by Raymond Carver, 1991. Used by permission of International Creative Management, Inc.

PART V

Reading 33: Excerpts from *Final Rounds: A Father, a Son, the Golf Journey of a Lifetime*, by James Dodson. New York: Bantam. Copyright © 1996 by James Dodson. Used by permission of Bantam Books, a division of Random House, Inc.

Reading 34: "Manon Reassures Her Lover," by Martha Elizabeth, in *Growing Old Along With Me: The Best Is Yet to Be*, edited by S. H. Martz. Copyright © 1996 by Papier-Mache Press, Watsonville, CA. Previously published 1991 in *The Macguffin, 8*(1). Used by permission.

Reading 35: "Starboys," by Elissa Goldberg, in *Generation to Generation: Reflections on Friendships Between Young and Old* (pp. 135-140), edited by S. Martz and S. Coe. Watsonville, CA: Papier-Mache Press. Copyright © 1998. Used by permission.

Reading 36: Excerpts from "Divorced and Reconstituted Families: Effects on the Older Generation," by Colleen L. Johnson.

Generations, 17(3), 17-20, Summer 1992. Copyright © 1992 by the American Society on Aging, San Francisco, California. Used by permission.

Reading 37: Excerpts from "Understanding Elder Abuse and Neglect," by Rosalie S. Wolf. *Aging,* No. 367, 1996. Washington, DC: U.S. Department of Health and Human Services, Administration on Aging.

Reading 38: "Obasan in Suburbia," by Susan Ito. Excerpted from *For She Is the Tree of Life: Grandmothers Through the Eyes of Women Writers* (pp. 77-81) edited by Valerie Kack-Brice. Copyright © 1995 by Valerie Kack-Brice. Used by permission of Conari Press.

Reading 39: Excerpts from "Selectivity Theory: Social Activity in Life-Span Context," by Laura L. Carstensen, in *Annual Review of Gerontology and Geriatrics,* Vol. 11, 1991 (pp. 195-217), edited by K. Warner Schaie. Copyright © 1992 by Springer Publishing Company, New York 10012. Used by permission.

Reading 40: Excerpts from "Wallace Nelson, 85, and Juanita Nelson, 70: Deerfield, Massachusetts," in *Coming of Age: The Story of Our Century by Those Who've Lived It* (pp. 240-247), by Studs Terkel. New York: St. Martin's Griffin, 1996. Copyright © 1995 by Studs Terkel. Used by permission.

Reading 41: "Letters From a Father," from *If It Be Not I,* by Mona Van Duyn. Copyright © 1982 by Mona Van Duyn. Reprinted by permission of Alfred A. Knopf, a division of Random House, Inc.

References

AARP. (1998). *A profile of older Americans: 1998.* (Available from the Resource Services Group, American Association of Retired Persons, 601 E Street, NW, Washington, DC 20049)

Alford-Cooper, F. (1998). *For keeps: Marriages that last a lifetime.* New York: M. E. Sharpe.

Allen, K. R., & Demo, D. H. (1995). The families of lesbians and gay men: A new frontier in family research. *Journal of Marriage and the Family, 57,* 111-127.

Andersen, M. L., & Collins, P. H. (1995). *Race, class, and gender: An anthology* (2nd ed.). New York: Wadsworth.

Antonucci, T. C., & Akiyama, H. (1995). Convoys of social relations: Family and friendships within a life span context. In R. Blieszner & V. H. Bedford (Eds.), *Handbook of aging and the family* (pp. 355-371). Westport, CT: Greenwood.

Aquilino, W. S. (1994). Later life parental divorce and widowhood: Impact on young adults' assessment of parent-child relations. *Journal of Marriage and the Family, 56,* 908-922.

Aquilino, W. S. (1997). From adolescent to young adult: A prospective study of parent-child relations during the transition to adulthood. *Journal of Marriage and the Family, 59,* 670-686.

Aranda, M., & Knight, B. G. (1997). The influence of ethnicity and culture on the caregiver stress and coping process: A sociocultural review and analysis. *The Gerontologist, 37,* 342-354.

Archbold, P. G., Stewart, B. J., Greenlick, M. R., & Harvath, T. (1990). Mutuality and preparedness as predictors of caregiver role strain. *Research in Nursing & Health, 13,* 375-384.

Atchley, R. C. (1993). Continuity theory and the evolution of activity in later life. In J. R. Kelly (Ed.), *Activity and aging: Staying involved in later life* (pp. 5-16). Newbury Park, CA: Sage.

Bakan, D. (1966). *The duality of human existence: An essay on psychology and religion.* Chicago: Rand McNally.

Barrett, M., & McIntosh, M. (1982). *The anti-social family.* London: Verso.

Bedford, V. H. (1995). Sibling relationships in middle and old age. In R. Blieszner & V. H. Bedford (Eds.), *Handbook of aging and the family* (pp. 201-222). Westport, CT: Greenwood.

Belgrave, L. L. (1988). The effects of race differences in work history, work attitudes, economic resources, and health on women's retirement. *Research on Aging, 10,* 383-398.

Bengtson, V., & Allen, K. R. (1993). The life course perspective applied to families over time. In P. G. Boss, W. J. Doherty, R. LaRossa, W. R. Schumm, & S. K. Steinmetz (Eds.), *Sourcebook of family theories and methods: A contextual approach* (pp. 469-499). New York: Plenum.

Bengtson, V., Rosenthal, C., & Burton, L. (1990). Families and aging: Diversity and heterogeneity. In R. H. Binstock & L. K. George (Eds.), *Handbook of aging and the social sciences* (3rd ed., pp. 263-287). San Diego, CA: Academic Press.

Benin, M., & Keith, V. M. (1995). The social support of employed African American and Anglo mothers. *Journal of Family Issues, 16,* 275-297.

Bern-Klug, M., & Chapin, R. (1999). The changing demography of death in the United States: Implications for human service workers. In B. de Vries (Ed.), *End of life issues: Interdisciplinary and multidimensional perspectives* (pp. 265-280). New York: Springer.

Blieszner, R. (1994). Feminist perspectives on friendship: Intricate tapestries. In D. L. Sollie & L. A. Leslie (Eds.), *Gender, families, and close relationships: Feminist research journeys* (pp. 120-144). Thousand Oaks, CA: Sage.

Bould, S. (1993). Familial caretaking: A middle-range definition of family in the context of social policy. *Journal of Family Issues, 14,* 133-151.

Brubaker, T. H. (1991). Families in later life: A burgeoning research area. In A. Booth (Ed.), *Contemporary families: Looking forward, looking back* (pp. 226-248). Minneapolis, MN: National Council on Family Relations.

Calasanti, T. M. (1996). Gender and life satisfaction in retirement: An assessment of the male model. *Journal of Gerontology: Social Sciences, 51B,* S18-S29.

Chan, F. (1988). To be old and Asian: An unsettling life in America. *Aging, 358,* 14-15.

Cherlin, A. J. (1978). Remarriage as an incomplete institution. *American Journal of Sociology, 84,* 634-650.

Cherlin, A. J., & Furstenberg, F. F. (1986). *The new American grandparent: A place in the family, a life apart.* New York: Basic Books.

Chevan, A. (1996). As cheaply as one: Cohabitation in the older population. *Journal of Marriage and the Family, 58,* 656-667.

Choi, N. G. (1991). Racial differences in determinants of living arrangements of widowed and divorced elderly women. *The Gerontologist, 31,* 496-504.

Collins, P. H. (1991). The meaning of motherhood in Black culture and Black mother-daughter relationships. In P. Bell-Scott, B. Guy-Sheftall, J. J. Royster, J. Sims-Wood, M. DeCosta-Willis, & L. Fultz (Eds.), *Double stitch: Black women write about mothers and daughters* (pp. 42-60). Boston: Beacon.

Connidis, I. A., & Campbell, L. D. (1995). Closeness, confiding, and contact among siblings in middle and late adulthood. *Journal of Family Issues, 16,* 722-745.

Coontz, S. (1992). *The way we never were: American families and the nostalgia trap.* New York: Basic Books.

Crimmins, E. M., Saito, Y., & Reynolds, S. L. (1997). Further evidence on recent trends in the prevalence and incidence of disability among older Americans from two sources: The LSOA and the NHIS. *Journal of Gerontology: Social Sciences, 52B,* S59-S71.

DeGenova, M. K. (Ed.). (1997). *Families in cultural context: Strengths and challenges in diversity.* Mountain View, CA: Mayfield.

DeVault, M. L. (1991). *Feeding the family: The social organization of caring as gendered work.* Chicago: University of Chicago Press.

DiLeonardo, M. (1987). The female world of cards and holidays: Women, families, and the life work of kinship. *Signs, 12,* 440-453.

Dressel, P. L., & Clark, A. (1990). A critical look at family care. *Journal of Marriage and the Family, 52,* 769-782.

Elder, G. H., Jr. (1974). *Children of the Great Depression.* Chicago: University of Chicago Press.

Espiritu, Y. L. (1997). *Asian American women and men: Labor, laws, and love.* Thousand Oaks, CA: Sage.

Ferree, M. M. (1991). Feminism and family research. In A. Booth (Ed.), *Contemporary families: Looking forward, looking back* (pp. 103-121). Minneapolis, MN: National Council on Family Relations.

Ford, D. Y. (1994). An exploration of perceptions of alternative family structures among university students. *Family Relations, 43,* 68-73.

Gallagher, S. (1994). Doing their share: Comparing patterns of help given by older and younger adults. *Journal of Marriage and the Family, 56,* 567-578.

Gerstel, N., & Gallagher, S. (1994). Caring for kith and kin: Gender, employment and the privatization of care. *Social Problems, 41,* 519-539.

Gibson, D. (1996). Broken down by age and gender: "The problem of old women" redefined. *Gender & Society, 10,* 433-448.

Glenn, E. N. (1983). Split household, small producer and dual wage earner: An analysis of Chinese-American family strategies. *Journal of Marriage and the Family, 45,* 35-46.

Godkin, M. A., Wolf, R. S., & Pillemer, K. A. (1995). A case-comparison analysis of elder abuse and neglect. In J. Hendricks (Ed.), *The ties of later life* (pp. 113-131). Amityville, NY: Baywood.

Goetting, A. (1986). The developmental tasks of siblingship over the life cycle. *Journal of Marriage and the Family, 48,* 703-714.

Gottman, J. (1999). *Why marriages succeed or fail: And how you can make yours last.* New York: Fireside.

Hagestad, G. O. (1985). Continuity and connectedness. In V. L. Bengtson & J. F. Robertson (Eds.), *Grandparenthood* (pp. 31-48). Beverly Hills, CA: Sage.

Hatch, L. R., & Thompson, A. (1992). Family responsibilities and women's retirement. In M. Szinovacz, D. J. Ekerdt, & B. H. Vinick (Eds.), *Families and retirement* (pp. 99-113). Newbury Park, CA: Sage.

Heaton, T. B., & Albrecht, S. L. (1991). Stable unhappy marriages. *Journal of Marriage and the Family, 53,* 747-758.

Heaton, T. B., Jacobson, C. K., & Holland, K. (1999). Persistence and change in decisions to remain childless. *Journal of Marriage and the Family, 61,* 531-539.

Herzog, A. R., Kahn, R. L., Morgan, J. N., Jackson, J. S., & Antonucci, T. C. (1989). Age differences in productive activities. *Journal of Gerontology, 44,* 129-138.

Hirshorn, B. A., & Piering, P. (1998-1999). Older people at risk: Issues and intergenerational responses. *Generations, 22*(4), 49-53.

Holden, K. C., & Kuo, H. D. (1996). Complex marital histories and economic well-being: The continuing legacy of divorce and widowhood as the HRS cohort approaches retirement. *The Gerontologist, 36,* 383-390.

Hooyman, N. R., & Gonyea, J. (1995). *Feminist perspectives on family care: Policies for gender justice.* Thousand Oaks, CA: Sage.

Horowitz, R. (1983). *Honor and the American dream: Culture and identity in a Chicano community.* New Brunswick, NJ: Rutgers University Press.

Huyck, M. H. (1995). Marriage and close relationships of the marital kind. In R. Blieszner & V. H. Bedford (Eds.), *Handbook of aging and the family* (pp. 181-200). Westport, CT: Greenwood.

Hynde, C. (1998, November 1). Celebs: Interview with Paul McCartney. *USA Weekend*, pp. 4-6.

Johnson, C. L. (1995). Cultural diversity in the late-life family. In R. Blieszner & V. H. Bedford (Eds.), *Handbook of aging and the family* (pp. 307-331). Westport, CT: Greenwood.

Johnson, C. L., & Barer, B. M. (1997). *Life beyond 85 years: The aura of survivorship.* New York: Springer.

Johnson, C. L., & Troll, L. (1996). Family structure and the timing of transitions from 70 to 103 years of age. *Journal of Marriage and the Family, 58,* 178-187.

Kahn, R. L., & Antonucci, T. C. (1980). Convoys over the life course: Attachment, roles, and social support. In P. B. Baltes & O. G. Brim (Eds.), *Life-span development and behavior* (Vol. 3, pp. 253-286). New York: Academic Press.

Kamo, Y. (1998). Asian grandparents. In M. E. Szinovacz (Ed.), *Handbook on grandparenthood* (pp. 97-112). Westport, CT: Greenwood.

Kaufman, G., & Uhlenberg, P. (1998). Effects of life course transitions on the quality of relationships between adult children and their parents. *Journal of Marriage and the Family, 60,* 924-938.

Keith, C. (1995). Family caregiving systems: Models, resources, and values. *Journal of Marriage and the Family, 57,* 179-189.

Keith, P. M. (1985). Work, retirement, and well-being among unmarried men and women. *The Gerontologist, 25,* 410-416.

Kimmel, D. C. (1992). The families of older gay men and lesbians. *Generations, 17*(3), 37-38.

Kinsella, K. (1995). Aging and the family: Present and future demographic issues. In R. Blieszner & V. H. Bedford (Eds.), *Handbook of aging and the family* (pp. 32-56). Westport, CT: Greenwood.

Klagsbrun, F. (1985). *Married people: Staying together in the age of divorce.* New York: Bantam.

Kunde, D. (2000, January 24). Retirees easing into golden years by going back to work. *Corvallis Gazette-Times,* p. C1.

Laird, J. (1993). Lesbian and gay families. In F. Walsh (Ed.), *Normal family processes* (2nd ed., pp. 282-328). New York: Guilford.

Laird, J. (1998). Invisible ties: Lesbians and their families of origin. In C. J. Patterson & A. R. D'Augelli (Eds.), *Lesbian, gay, and bisexual identities in families: Psychological perspectives* (pp. 197-228). New York: Oxford University Press.

Lawton, M. P. (1982). Competence, environmental press, and the adaptation of older people. In M. P. Lawton, P. G. Windley, & T. O. Byerts (Eds.), *Aging and the environment: Theoretical approaches.* New York: Springer.

Lee, G. R., Peek, C. W., & Coward, R. T. (1998). Race differences in filial responsibility expectations among older parents. *Journal of Marriage and the Family, 60,* 404-412.

Lesher, E. L., & Bergey, K. J. (1988). Bereaved elderly mothers: Changes in health, functional activities, family cohesion, and psychological well-being. *International Journal of Aging and Human Development, 26,* 81-90.

Levenson, R. W., Carstensen, L. L., & Gottman, J. M. (1993). Long-term marriages: Age, gender, and satisfaction. *Psychology and Aging, 8,* 301-313.

Logan, J. R., & Spitze, G. D. (1996). *Family ties: Enduring relations between parents and their grown children.* Philadelphia: Temple University Press.

Lopata, H. Z. (1996). *Current widowhood: Myths and realities.* Thousand Oaks, CA: Sage.

Lund, D. (1993). Conclusions about bereavement in later life and implications for interventions and future research. In D. A. Lund (Ed.), *Older bereaved spouses: Research with practical applications* (pp. 217-231). New York: Hemisphere.

Lund, D. A. (1996). Bereavement and loss. In *Encyclopedia of gerontology* (Vol. 1, pp. 173-183). New York: Academic Press.

Lynott, P. P., & Roberts, R. E. L. (1997). The developmental stake hypothesis and changing perceptions of intergenerational relations, 1971-1985. *The Gerontologist, 37,* 394-405.

Marks, N. (1996). Caregiving across the lifespan: National prevalence and predictors. *Family Relations, 45,* 27-36.

Marks, S. R. (1986). *Three corners: Exploring marriage and the self.* Lexington, MA: Lexington Books.

Martin, P., Hagestad, G., & Diedrick, P. (1988). Family stories: Events (temporarily) remembered. *Journal of Marriage and the Family, 50,* 533-541.

Matthews, S. H. (1995). Gender and the division of filial responsibility between lone sisters and their brothers. *Journal of Gerontology: Social Sciences, 50,* S312-S320.

Matthews, S. H., & Heidorn, J. (1998). Meeting filial responsibilities in brothers-only sibling groups. *Journal of Gerontology: Social Sciences, 53B,* S278-S286.

McAdams, D. P., Ruetzel, K., & Foley, J. M. (1986). Complexity and generativity at mid-life: Relations among social motives, ego development, and adults' plans for the future. *Journal of Personality and Social Psychology, 50,* 800-807.

McDonald, J. M. (1987). Support systems for American Black wives and widows. In H. Z. Lopata (Ed.), *Widows* (Vol. 2, pp. 139-157). Durham, NC: Duke University Press.

McIntosh, P. (1998). White privilege and male privilege: A personal account of coming to see correspondences through work in women's studies. In M. L. Andersen & P. H. Collins (Eds.), *Race, class, and gender: An anthology* (3rd ed., pp. 76-87). Belmont, CA: Wadsworth.

Mezy, M., Miller, L. L., & Nelson, L. L. (1999). Caring for caregivers of frail elders at the end of life. *Generations, 23*(1), 44-51.

Miner, S., & Uhlenberg, P. (1997). Intragenerational proximity and the social role of sibling neighbors after midlife. *Family Relations, 46,* 145-153.

Moen, P. (1998). Recasting careers: Changing reference groups, risks, and realities. *Generations, 22,* 40-45.

Moen, P., Robison, J., & Fields, V. (1994). Women's work and caregiving roles: A life course approach. *Journal of Gerontology: Social Sciences, 49,* S176-S186.

Moss, M. S., & Moss, S. Z. (1989). The death of a parent. In R. A. Kalish (Ed.), *Midlife loss: Coping strategies* (pp. 89-114). Newbury Park, CA: Sage.

Moss, M. S., & Moss, S. Z. (1995). Death and bereavement. In R. Blieszner & V. H. Bedford (Eds.), *Handbook of aging and the family* (pp. 422-439). Westport, CT: Greenwood.

Myerhoff, B. (1978). *Number our days.* New York: Simon & Schuster.

Neal, M. B., Hammer, L. B., Rickard, A., Isgrigg, J., & Brockwood, K. (1999, November). *Dual-earner couples in the sandwiched generation: Who they are, what they do, how they manage.* Paper presented at the annual meeting of the Gerontological Association of America, San Francisco.

Neal, M. B., Ingersoll-Dayton, B., & Starrels, M. E. (1997). Gender and relationship differences in caregiving patterns and consequences among employed caregivers. *The Gerontologist, 37,* 804-816.

Neugarten, B. L. (1972). *Middle age and aging.* Chicago: University of Chicago Press.

Neugarten, B. L., & Weinstein, K. K. (1964). The changing American grandparent. *Journal of Marriage and the Family, 26,* 199-204.

Nussbaum, J. E., & Bettini, L. M. (1994). Shared stories of grandparent-grandchild relationship. *International Journal of Aging and Human Development, 39,* 67-80.

O'Rand, A. M., Henretta, J. C., & Krecker, M. L. (1992). Family pathways to retirement. In M. Szinovacz, D. J. Ekerdt, & B. H. Vinick (Eds.), *Families and retirement* (pp. 81-98). Newbury Park, CA: Sage.

Osmont, K. (1988). Please see me through my tears. *What can I say? How to help someone who is grieving: A guide.* Portland, OR: Nobility Press.

Ozawa, M. N. (1995). The economic status of vulnerable older women. *Social Work, 40,* 323-331.

Palmore, E. B., Burchett, B. M., Fillenbaum, G. G., George, L. K., & Wallman, L. M. (1985). *Retirement: Causes and consequences.* New York: Springer.

Pavalko, E. K., & Artis, J. E. (1997). Women's caregiving and paid work: Causal relationships in late midlife. *Journal of Gerontology: Social Sciences, 52B,* S170-S179.

Paz, J. J. (1993). Support of Hispanic elderly. In H. P. McAdoo (Ed.), *Ethnicity: Strength in diversity* (pp. 177-183). Newbury Park, CA: Sage.

Pebley, A. R., & Rudkin, L. (1999). Grandparents caring for grandchildren: What do we know? *Journal of Family Issues, 20,* 218-242.

Pelham, A. O., & Clark, W. F. (1987). Widowhood among low-income racial and ethnic groups in California. In H. Z. Lopata (Ed.), *Widows* (Vol. 2, pp. 191-222). Durham, NC: Duke University Press.

Peplau, L. A. (1991). Lesbian and gay relationships. In J. C. Gonsiorek & J. D. Weinrich (Eds.), *Homosexuality: Research implications for public policy* (pp. 177-196). Newbury Park, CA: Sage.

Quadagno, J., & McClellan, S. (1989). The other functions of retirement. *Generations, 13,* 7-12.

Reitzes, D. C., Mutran, E. J., & Fernandez, M. (1998). The decision to retire: A career perspective. *Social Science Quarterly, 79,* 607-619.

Riley, M. W. (1983). The family in an aging society: A matrix of latent relationships. *Journal of Family Issues, 4,* 439-454.

Rook, K. S. (1997). Positive and negative social exchanges: Weighing their effects in later life. *Journal of Gerontology: Social Sciences, 52B,* S167-S169.

Roschelle, A. R. (1997). *No more kin: Exploring race, class, and gender in family networks.* Thousand Oaks, CA: Sage.

Rosenthal, C. J. (1985). Kinkeeping in the familial division of labor. *Journal of Marriage and the Family, 47,* 965-974.

Rossi, A. S., & Rossi, P. H. (1990). *Of human bonding: Parent-child relations across the life course.* New York: Aldine de Gruyter.

Rubinstein, R. L., Alexander, B. B., Goodman, M., & Luborsky, M. (1991). Key relationships of never married, childless older women: A cultural analysis. *Journal of Gerontology: Social Sciences, 46,* 270-277.

Siegel, J. M. (1995). Looking for Mr. Right? Older single women who become mothers. *Journal of Family Issues, 16,* 194-211.

Skolnick, A. (1991). *Embattled paradise.* New York: Basic Books.

Stacey, J. (1993). Good riddance to "the family": A response to David Popenoe. *Journal of Marriage and the Family, 55,* 541-547.

Suitor, J. J., Pillemer, K., Keeton, S., & Robison, J. (1995). Aged parents and aging children: Determinants of relationship quality. In R. Blieszner & V. H. Bedford (Eds.), *Handbook of aging and the family* (pp. 223-242). Westport, CT: Greenwood.

Szinovacz, M. E. (1998). Grandparents today: A demographic profile. *The Gerontologist, 38,* 37-52.

Tatum, B. D. (1987). *Assimilation blues: Black families in a white community.* Northampton, MA: Hazel-Maxwell.

Thorne, B. (1982). Feminist rethinking of the family: An overview. In B. Thorne & M. Yalom (Eds.), *Rethinking the family* (pp. 1-24). New York: Longman.

Thorne, B. (1992). Feminism and the family: Two decades of thought. In B. Thorne & M. Yalom (Eds.), *Rethinking the family: Some feminist questions* (2nd ed., pp. 3-30). Boston: Northeastern University Press.

Troll, L. E. (1995). Foreword. In R. Blieszner & V. H. Bedford (Eds.), *Handbook of aging and the family* (pp. xi-xx). Westport, CT: Greenwood.

Troll, L. E., Miller, S., & Atchley, R. (1979). *Families in later life.* Belmont, CA: Wadsworth.

Uhlenberg, P., & Kirby, J. B. (1998). Grandparenthood over time: Historical and demographic trends. In M. E. Szinovacz (Ed.), *Handbook on grandparenthood* (pp. 23-39). Westport, CT: Greenwood.

U.S. Bureau of the Census. (1993). *Statistical abstract of the United States: 1993* (113th ed.). Washington, DC: Government Printing Office.

U.S. Senate Special Committee on Aging. (1992). *Aging America: Trends and projections, 1990-1991.* Washington, DC: U.S. Department of Health & Human Services.

Waite, L. J., & Harrison, S. C. (1992). Keeping in touch: How women in mid-life allocate social contacts among kith and kin. *Social Forces, 70,* 637-655.

Walker, A. J., & Allen, K. R. (1991). Relationships between caregiving daughters and their elderly mothers. *The Gerontologist, 31,* 389-396.

Ward, R., & Spitze, G. (1996). Will the children ever leave? Parent-child coresidence history and plans. *Journal of Family Issues, 17,* 514-539.

West, C., & Zimmerman, D. H. (1991). Doing gender. In J. Lorber & S. Farrell (Eds.), *The social construction of gender.* Newbury Park, CA: Sage.

Weston, K. (1991). *Families we choose.* New York: Columbia University Press.

Whitbeck, L., Hoyt, D., & Huck, S. (1993). Family relationship history, contemporary parent-grandparent relationship quality, and the grandparent-grandchild relationship. *Journal of Marriage and the Family, 55,* 1025-1035.

White, L. K., & Rogers, S. J. (1997). Strong support but uneasy relationships: Coresidence and adult children's relationships with their parents. *Journal of Marriage and the Family, 59,* 62-76.

Williams, N., & Torrez, D. J. (1998). Grandparenthood among Hispanics. In M. E. Szinovacz (Ed.), *Handbook on grandparenthood* (pp. 87-96). Westport, CT: Greenwood.

Zeiss, A. M., Lewinsohn, P. M., Rohde, P., & Selley, J. R. (1996). Relationship of physical disease and functional impairment to depression in older people. *Psychology and Aging, 11,* 572-581.

Author Index

Elder, G. H., 5, 41, 42, 43, 58
Elizabeth, M., 236, 249
Elster, A., 29
Erdly, W., 272
Erikson, E. H., 43
Esping-Andersen, G., 191, 192
Espiritu, Y. L., 243, 246
Estes, C., 193, 196
Eustis, N., 196
Eyman, R. K., 213

Farley, R., 105
Farrell, J. J., 87
Fee, E., 84
Fernandez, M., 180
Ferraro, K. F., 58, 165
Ferree, M. M., 7
Field, D., 265, 266, 273
Fields, V., 70
Fillenbaum, G. G., 180
Finch, J., 149, 150, 154
Fischer, L., 196
Fitzgerald, N. E., 29
Flagg, F., 284
Foley, J. M., 8
Foner, A., 210, 211n7
Foster, H. J., 105
Fox, B., 84, 150
Franklin, J. H., 104
Frazier, E. F., 104
Fredrickson, B. L., 269, 272
Fremouw, W. J., 270
Friedman, D., 197
Fuller, C., 69
Furstenberg, F., 3, 4, 48, 58, 75, 111, 121, 122

Gaitz, C., 265
Gallagher, S., 70, 71
Gans, H., 128, 134n
George, L. K., 180, 266
Gerstel, N., 71
Gibson, D., 239
Gillespie, Sarah, 86
Glazer, N. Y., 229
Glenn, E. N., 16, 164
Glick, P. C., 42
Godkin, M. A., 241, 244, 245

Goetting, A., 123, 149, 151, 153
Goffman, E., 165
Gold, D. T., 153, 266
Goldberg, E., 237, 250
Goldscheider, F. K., 58
Gonyea, J., 182
Goodman, M., 240
Gordon, C., 265
Gottman, J., 116, 117
Gove, W. R., 164
Greenberg, J., 182, 193, 196, 212, 215
Greenley, J. R., 212, 215
Greenlick, M. R., 72
Grob, G. N., 83
Gutman, H., 104

Habenstein, R. W., 203
Hagestad, G., 58, 75, 120, 253
Halle, D., 117, 127, 134n
Halle, David, 117
Hammer, L. B., 71
Hansen, D. A., 54
Hao, L.-X., 105
Hareven, T. K., 41, 42, 43
Harrington Meyer, M., 192, 193, 194, 195, 197-198
Harrison, S. C., 120
Hartmann, H., 192, 193
Harvath, T., 72
Hatch, L. R., 180
Hatfield, A., 213
Hearth, A. H., 173
Heaton, T. B., 23, 116
Hechter, M., 54
Heckert, D. A., 188
Hegeman, C. R., 284
Heider, F., 54
Heidorn, J., 242
Henderson, C., 284
Henretta, J., 180, 192
Henry, W., 210, 211n6, 265
Herkovits, M., 104
Hess, B., 193
Hill, E. A., 42, 54, 188
Himes, C., 17, 23, 24, 47
Hjelmstad, L. T., 11, 12
Hochschild, A., 186, 192, 208
Hofferth, S., 29
Hogan, D., 105

Holden, D., 194, 195, 198, 213
Holden, K. C., 182, 229
Holland, K., 23
Holmes, L. D., 144
Holzer, C., 265
Hong, J., 182, 212
Hooyman, N. R., 182
Horowitz, J., 112
Horowitz, R., 16, 63
Horton, C. P., 105
Hoyt, D., 122
Huck, S., 122
Hughes, M., 164
Huyck, M. H., 236
Hwang, C., 20, 74
Hynde, C., 184

Iglehart, J., 195, 196
Ihinger-Tallman, M., 153
Ingegneri, D., 48
Ingersoll-Dayton, B., 71
Irish, D. P., 112
Isgrigg, J., 71
Ito, S., 262

Jackson, J., 9, 268
Jackson, Nannie, 87
Jacobson, C. K., 23
Jansen, L. T., 54
Jaynes, D. J., 105
Jick, T. D., 154
Johnson, C. L., 16, 19, 118, 119, 233, 234, 235, 236, 237, 238, 239, 240, 242, 244, 246, 253, 254, 255, 256, 269, 283

Kahana, B., 254
Kahana, E., 254
Kahn, R. L., 9, 283
Kamo, Y., 123
Katz, M., 43, 84, 191, 197
Katz, M. B., 42
Kaufman, G., 21, 22, 24
Keating, N., 188
Keefe, S., 202
Keeton, S., 20, 23, 24
Keith, C., 18, 125, 182
Kendig, H. L., 151

Kessler, R. C., 58, 165, 169
Kidder, T., 284
Kimmel, D. C., 16
Kincaid, Gwendoline, 86
Kinsella, K., 236, 242
Kirby, J. B., 73
Klagsbrun, F., 116
Knight, B. G., 241
Komarovsky, M., 128, 134n, 208, 211n4
Korte, A. O., 204
Kramer, M., 265
Krauss, M. W., 182, 212, 215
Krecker, M. L., 180
Kulis, S. S., 56
Kunde, D., 180
Kuo, H. D., 183, 229

Labouvie-Vief, G., 272
Laird, J., 69, 110, 117
Lamb, M., 29
Land, S., 127, 134n
LaRossa, M. M., 157
LaRossa, R., 157
Lasch, C., 53
Lawton, M. P., 244
Leaf, P. J., 265
Lee, D. J., 153, 188, 268
Lee, G. R., 72, 153
Lee, T. R., 151
Lehman, D. R., 165
Leigh, G. K., 150
L'Engle, M., 111, 184, 224
Lesher, E. L., 77
Levenson, R. W., 117
Lever, J., 154
Levy, S. O., 266
Lewine, R. R. J., 213
Lewinsohn, P. M., 241
Lipman, A., 151, 188
Litwak, E., 55
Liu, K., 197
Lively, E., 128, 134n
Logan, J. R., 120
Longino, C. F., 151
Lopata, H., 184, 185, 194, 229
Loren, B. K., 25, 26, 51
Luborsky, M., 240
Lund, D., 78, 184
Lundquist, K. F., 112

Lustbader, W., 284
Lyles, L., 72, 75, 76, 100
Lynott, P. P., 18, 23, 25

Madsen, R., 202
Mancini, J. A., 151, 153
Manton, K., 197
Margolis, R., 196, 197
Maril, R. L., 202
Markides, K. S., 203, 268
Marks, N., 70
Marks, N. F., 164
Marks, S. R., 7
Marmor, T., 191, 198
Martin, E. P., 105, 120
Martin, J. M., 105
Martin, P., 120
Martinez, D., 63
Mason, J., 150
Masters, J. C., 272
Matthews, S. H., 125, 150, 151, 152,
    153, 156
Maxwell, J. W., 151, 153
McAdoo, H. P., 56
McAnarney, E., 29
McCartney, P., 184
McClellan, S., 179
McDonald, J. M., 185
McIntosh, M., 15
McIntosh, P., 5
McLeod, J. D., 170
Meiners, M., 192
Menken, J. A., 47-48
Menon, G., 106
Messer, M., 210, 211n6
Meyer, M. H., 182, 191
Meyers, J. K., 265
Mezy, M., 70, 71
Mieners, M., 197
Miller, B., 183, 188, 189, 194, 218
Miller, D., 71, 116
Miller, L. L., 70
Mindel, C. H., 203
Miner, S., 123, 124
Minkler, M., 173, 198, 265, 266, 273
Mitchell, L. S., 85
Moen, P., 70, 180
Moon, M., 196
Moorman, J. E., 253, 254

Morgan, J. N., 9, 48, 58
Moss, M. M., 76, 165, 238
Moss, M. S., 164
Moss, S. Z., 76, 164, 165, 238
Motz, M. F., 83
Mugford, S., 151
Mullan, J. T., 214
Mutran, E., 105, 165, 180
Myerhoff, B., 144, 179, 230
Myerson, J., 85
Myles, J., 191, 192

Naylor, G., 173
Neal, M. B., 71
Nelsen, V. J., 112
Nelson, L. L., 70, 71
Nelson, Wallace and Juanita, 276-277
Neugarten, B. L., 7, 121, 254
Neuschler, E., 196, 197
Nord, C. W., 58
Norton, A. J., 253, 254
Nussbaum, J. E., 75

O'Bryant, S. L., 56
Okun, M. A., 187
Oliver, M. L., 229
Olson, L. K., 193, 195
Oppenheimer, V., 130, 134n
O'Rand, A., 58, 180, 192
Orvaschel, H., 265
Osmont, K., 79
Ozawa, M. N., 181, 182

Padilla, A., 202
Pagel, M., 272
Palmore, E., 165, 180, 265, 266, 273
Parish, W., 105
Parsons, T., 130, 134n
Pascall, G., 194
Patrick, J. H., 212, 215
Patten, S., 196
Pavalko, E. K., 71
Pearlin, L. I., 214
Pebley, A. R., 122
Peek, C. W., 72
Pelham, A. O., 186
Peplau, L. A., 117
Peri, C., 77, 78, 80

Peri, Camille, 78
Perkins, H. W., 164
Pickett, R. S., 17, 22, 26, 41, 42
Piercy, M., 125-126, 163
Piering, P., 71
Pillemer, K., 20, 23, 24, 165, 169, 188, 241, 244, 245, 284
Popenoe, D., 53
Pruchno, R. A., 212, 215

Quadagno, J., 179, 191, 192, 193, 197-198, 203
Quindlen, A., 111

Reid, A. J., 86
Reitzes, D. C., 180
Reskin, B., 192, 193
Revenson, T. A., 265
Reynolds, S. L., 242
Rezac, S. J., 58
Richards, L. N., 54
Rickard, A., 71
Riedmann, A., 153
Riley, J. W., 4, 53, 210, 211n7, 256
Roberts, R. E. L., 18, 23, 54
Robertson, J., 254
Robins, A., 210, 211n7
Robison, J., 20, 23, 24, 70
Rodgers, R. H., 42
Roe, K. M., 173
Rogers, E. M., 20, 54
Rohde, P., 241
Rook, K. S., 235, 272
Room, R., 131, 134n
Roos, P., 127, 134n
Roosa, M. W., 29
Roschelle, A. R., 241
Rosenbaum, L., 27
Rosenberg, C. E., 83, 85
Rosenmayer, L., 55
Rosenthal, C., 8, 120, 124, 188, 268
Rosner, T., 125, 156
Rosow, I., 271
Rossi, A. S., 4, 18, 21, 22, 24-25, 26, 58, 59, 64, 118, 120, 122, 123, 127, 134n, 150, 215, 238, 240
Rossi, P. H., 4, 18, 21, 22, 24-25, 26, 64, 118, 120, 122, 123, 150, 215, 238, 240

Rothman, D. J., 84
Rowe, J. W., 283
Rubel, A., 202
Rubinstein, R. L., 240
Rudkin, L., 122
Ruetzel, K., 8
Ryan, M., 83
Ryder, N. B., 42
Ryff, C., 265
Rylant, C., 230

Sager, C., 132, 134n
Saito, Y., 48, 242
Sales, E., 215
Sangl, J., 48
Santos, R., 203
Saum, L. O., 85
Say, A., 173
Schrader, S. S., 54
Schramm, D. G. H., 69, 76, 97
Schulz, R., 215, 271
Schweibert, P., 112
Scott, J. P., 152, 153
Sebald, H., 54
Seitz, V., 16, 19, 27, 73, 119
Selley, J. R., 241
Seltzer, M. M., 182, 212, 215
Sena-Rivera, J., 202
Serow, W. J., 267
Shanas, E., 149, 210, 211n7, 267
Shapiro, T. M., 229
Shehan, C. L., 188
Shelton, S., 20, 25
Siegel, J. M., 22, 84
Silverstein, M., 19, 21, 25, 26, 53, 122
Simic, A., 144
Simon, B. L., 150
Sjoberg, G., 202
Sly, D. F., 267
Smeeding, T., 195, 198
Smith, J. C., 105, 197
Smyer, M. A., 253
Snow, D., 202
Socholitzky, E., 197
Sokolovsky, J., 268
Spence, D., 197
Spencer, M. B., 104
Spilerman, S., 127, 134n
Spitze, G. D., 19, 120

Subject Index

AARP (American Association of Retired Persons), 2, 3, 54
Abuse of elders, 241, 244-245, 258-264
Acquisition of information, 271
Acts of commission/omission in elder abuse, 258
Adjustment to retirement, 180-181, 188-189
Adolescent parenthood. *See* Teen mothers
Adult children:
    and parents' widowhood, 237
    becoming parents, 22-23
    caregiving by, 70
    contact with, by older adults, 266
    death of, 238
    dependent, 19, 26
    divorce of, 254
    imposing wish for grandchildren on, 93
    perceptions of family by, 13
    relationships with parents, 14, 53-59, 278-281
    role of gender of in family relationships, 58
    social support from, 184
    tension between parents and young, 20
    understanding of parents by, 69
    with disabilities, 183, 212-216

Adulthood, transitions to, 18-25
Adult siblings, as caregivers of parents, 156-162
Advantaged people, access to resources by, 6
Affect, regulation of, 272
Affect among family members, 54
Affectional closeness between siblings, 150
African Americans. *See also* Black families
    cultural norms and caregiving, 72
    divorced, 257
    divorce rates among, 49
    fictive kin patterns in, 119
    health problems in, 241
    impact of parental death on, 167
    kinship patterns, 118
    life expectancy of women, 236
    marriage patterns of men/women, 48-49
    mother/daughter bonds, 100-103
    parent/child relationships in, 19
    poor health care treatment for, 76
    proportion of childless women, 48
    sibling relationships among, 124
    work histories/retirement issues, women's, 181-182
Age as predictor of paternal relationship ties, 57
Ageism, 259, 272

Environmental challenges for old-old adults, 243-244
Ethnicity:
    and attitudes toward aging, 267-268
    influence of on retirement, 181-182
    lifelong single women by, 42-46
    sibling relationship variations by, 124
Ethnic Variations in Dying, Death, and Grief: Diversity in Universality (Irish, Lundquist, Nelsen), 112
Excuses, legitimate, 150, 152
Expectations of spouses, 169-170
Experience of grandfatherhood, 95-96
Exploitation of elders. *See* Abuse of elders
Extended families, 104-106, 146-148, 202-203
Extrafamilial ties, 160-162
Extramarital affairs, 129
    social support, 168

Familial bonds, 51-52
"Familial caretaking: A middle-range definition of family in the context of social policy" (Bould), 62
Familial relationships, ranking of, 150
Familial support, in mother-grandmother relationships models, 34
Families:
    attenuated, 240
    beliefs about versus reality, 14
    characteristic of 21st century, 24-25
    classes of contemporary, 55
    concepts of, 1
    definitions of, 15-16, 17, 104
    experiences of members of, 17
    extended, 146-148
    female-female relationships in, 26
    kinship patterns in, 118-120
    perceptions of, 13
    with gay/lesbian child, 69
    with persons with mental illness, 216
Families (Tax), 63
Families We Choose (Weston), 63
Family allegiances, dual, 58

Family conflict, 159-160
Family connections, kinkeeping, 120-121
Family gerontology, definition, 1
Family history issues, 160
Family life:
    among blue-collar men, 127-134
    and work, connection between, 9
    for older people, 3-5
    shaping of by social context, 5-7
    transitions, 68
Family patterns of Mexican American men, 202-207
Family relationships:
    generational ties, types of, 8
    grandparenthood in context of, 96
    influences on, 14
    typology of, 57-59
Family structure:
    changes in, 47-48
    complex, due to divorce/remarriage, 8
    intergenerational solidarity study, 53-59
    sibling groups and caregiving, effects of on, 158-159
    variations in, 13
Family support, for older women, 181
Family systems, 149
Family ties versus peer ties, 209, 210
Family unit, Census definition of, 47
Family violence paradigm, 259
Fathering and grandfathering, differences between, 93-94
Fathers, death of, 166, 167
Fathers, relations with, 57
Father/son bond, 97-99, 247-248
"Female world of cards and holidays, The: Women, families, and the work of kinship" (DiLeonardo), 173
Feminization of poverty, 267
Fertility rates, 48
Fictive grandparenting style, 139, 142
Fictive kin. *See also* Kinship
    and caregiving, 72
    definition, 119
    in Black families, 104
    othermothers, 16
Final Rounds (Dodson), 236, 237

Health problems:
  cancer, 80-82
  caregiving by adult children, 70
  cognitively impaired spouses, 216-
    223, 272
  diabetes, 241
  effects of on marriage, 131-132
  functional ability and, 241-243
  increases due to longer life expec-
    tancy, 48
  multi-infarct dementia, 218, 222-223
  19th-century caregiving, 83-87
  parental caregiving to adult chil-
    dren with disabilities, 212-216
  Parkinson's disease, 70, 218
  social aging and, 268
Hierarchy, social, positioning of individuals in families, 6-7
Hierarchy of familial obligations, 150
Hispanic Americans:
  family support received by wid-
    ows, 185-186
  grandparenting styles in, 122
  never-married elderly, 49
  regard for elderly in, 267-268
  relationships with parents
    among, 19
  vulnerability of women, 198-199
  work/retirement issues for
    women, 182
"Hispanic," definition of term, 202
Historical context, kinship patterns
  in, 118
Historical perspectives on caregiving,
  83-87
"Home as workshop, The: Women as
  amateur nurses and medical
  care providers" (Glazer), 229
Homeownership and maternal/
  paternal relations, 56, 57
Honor and the American Dream: Culture
  and Identity in a Chicano Community (Horowitz), 63
Horizontal kinship ties, 118, 124
Hostile-detached partners, 117
Hostile-engaged couples, 117
Husbands:
  as caregivers to cognitively
    impaired wives, 216-223

loss of, 224-225
loss of control as caregivers of
  cognitively impaired wives,
  220-221
spousal loss, 226
support for parental caregiving by,
  160-162

Identity. See also Cultural identity
  as widow/widower, 184
  challenges of in middle age, 7-8
  children of immigrants', 39-40
  connection between adult and as
    family member, 68-69
  connection to others as central
    to, 236
  developmental themes of, 7-8
  development/maintenance of, 271
  importance of grandparenthood
    in, 121
  in old-old age, 233
  Mexican American, 89-91
  of parent after child loss, 77
  of young-old adults, role of work
    transitions, 178-181
  role of death of family member on,
    75-79
  role of death on, 75-79
  role of paid/unpaid work in old
    age, 245-246
  widows', 211
  young adults', 20
Immigrants:
  Asian Americans, 262-264
  children of, 39-40
  family associations, 16
  kinship patterns among, 118-119
  old-old to U.S., 243
Impaired spouses, 218-223
Inadequate care of elders, 259.
  See also Abuse of elders
Income, 56, 167
Indirect services to parents-in-law, 161
Individuals, within families, social
  position of, 6-7
Individual well-being, 164
Inequity, system of, 5
Information acquisition, 271

Life expectancy. *See also* Demographics
  African American women, 236
  by ethnic/racial background, 2-3, 179
  health problem increases due to longer, 48
  in industrialized countries, 179
  White/nonwhite population, 47-48
Lifelong single women, 17, 41-46, 49
Life-span social activity, 265-273
Lifestyles, of blue-collar employees versus white-collar employees, 133
Limiting social interactions in old age, 273
Longevity, 2-4
Long-term committed partnerships, 117
Looking After: A Son's Memoir (Daniel), 111
Loss. *See also* Death; Grief
  coping with of relationship partner, older adults, 183-186
  early experiences of, 43
  nonnormative, 77, 238
  normative, 75-77, 238
  of control by wives of cognitively impaired husbands, 220
  of emotional support/companionship in later life, 237
  of family support in old age, 240
  of role functions, 271
  symbolic parental, 165
Loss of the Ground-Note: Women Writing About the Loss of Their Mothers (Vozenilek), 174

Marital contentment/discontentment:
  after death of a parent, 164-171
  effects of retirement on, 187-190
  of blue-collar men, 128-131
  retirement and, 187-190
Marital status:
  effects of on sibling relationships, 152
  importance of to couples, 17
  of parents, 21-22

of women, retirement experience based on, 182
  parental/child, 56
Marital strain, 126
Marriage:
  after children leave home, 131-133
  among blue-collar men, 127-134
  as transitional stage, 21
  experience of in midlife, 116-117
  happiness as goal of, 134n7
  happy, 116
  Marks's description of, 7
  perception of quality of, 187
  struggles over leisure time in, 134n8
  types of, 117
Marriage rates, 48-49
Married women, Social Security benefits for, 193-194
Maternal bonds, 51-52, 56
Maternal grandparents, 254-255
Matrix, latent kin, 53
Maturity, description of, 1
McCartney, Paul and Linda, 184
Medicaid, 192, 196-198
Medically needy, Medicaid benefits for, 197, 198
Medicare, 195-196
Medicare Catastrophic Coverage Act, 198
Men:
  abuse by, 245
  childless, 97-99
  friendships among, 129
  grief experience for, 78
  impact of death of parent on, 166-167
  marriage/family life of blue-collar, 127-134
  Mexican American, 202-207
  remarriage rates, 49
  ties with siblings, 151, 152
  views of on remarriage, 185
Mental illness/retardation, co-resident caregiving for adult children with, 212-216
Mexican Americans:
  family patterns of, 89-91

Responsibility, generalized sense of, 54-55
Retirement:
    changes in understanding of, 179-180
    definition, 177-178
    effects of on marriage, 132, 187-190
    reasons for, 190
    reductions in contact with coworkers after, 265
    shaping of by earlier life conditions/choices, 181-182
    traditional, 179
    working after, 276-277
Risk factors for elder abuse, 259
Rituals, family, connecting to past, 78
Role commitments after death of parent, 165
Role functions, loss of, 271
Roles:
    in caregiving to cognitively impaired spouses, 219, 220-221
    of adult women, lifelong, 41
    of fathers, changing, 94
    of grandfathers, 92, 95
    of grandparents, 73
    of grandparents in divorced families, 254-255
Routine style of parental caregiving, 157, 159

Same-gender partnerships, 21, 117
Same-generation ties, 8
"Sandwiched generation," 71
Schramm, D. G. H., 69
Selection processes, lifelong, 270
Selectivity theory, 265-273
Self-image in old-old age, 233
Self-verification processes, 271
Separation, affect of on intergenerational relations, 58
Service programs, 216, 261
Seventeen Widows of Sans Souci, The (Armstrong), 209
Sexual friendships with other women among blue-collar men, 129
Shall We Dance (video), 175
Shirley Valentine (video), 175

Sibling relationships:
    caregiving to siblings, 125
    childless siblings, 125
    closeness/contact in, 149-154
    decline of contact in middle years, 266
    importance of in later life, 123-125
    number of siblings, 153
    parent-care systems, 156-162
Single older adults, 49, 153. See also Lifelong single women; Never-married persons
Single women. See Lifelong single women
Sisters. See Sibling relationships
Sociable family classification, 55
Social activity:
    changes in with age, 265-266
    individual differences in, 266
    psychological concomitants of, 269
Social change, 22, 94-95
Social circumstances of Mexican American men, 203-204
Social contact versus social support, 268
Social context, family life shaping by, 5
"Social convoy," 8
Social hierarchies, 6
Social interaction in nursing homes, 270
Social isolation, 205, 267
Social markers, 7
Social networks after divorce, 255-256
Social policies, U.S., 179
Social provision principles, 191
Social relationships, changes to, 165
Social Security Act of 1935, 192-193
Social Security Administration, 192, 193, 194, 195, 197
Social Security benefits, for men versus women, 182
Social Security system, 48
Social status of blue-collar men, 130
Social support:
    failed, 167
    for elderly, 268-269
    from adult children/family members, 184

mid-20th century patterns of, 19
role of paid/unpaid in identity/
relationships in old age, 245-246
transitions, role of, 178-181
unpaid, 182-183
Worker benefits for Social Security,
193
Workers:
blue-collar men, 127-134
Mexican American men, patterns
of, 202-207

psychological well-being of, 134n7
workaholism among blue-collar
men, 129
working-class women, 4, 42-46
Working-class families, 23-24, 153

Yellow Raft in Blue Water (Dorris), 173
Young adulthood, 19-26
Younger families, demographics of, 50
Younger grandparents, 254-255

DATE DUE

OCT 0 4 '05			

#47-0108 Peel Off Pressure Sensitive